Daily Grace for the Daily Grind

by

Larry Briney

Daily Devotional Readings With Scripture and Topic Indexes

Daily Grace for the Daily Grind
by Larry Briney

Printed in the United States of America

ISBN 1-594679-39-8

Certain names have been changed in accounts used as illustrations.

www.xulonpress.com

Acknowledgements:

Daily Grace for the Daily Grind is a collection of articles originally titled *Up Close and Practical.* They were written for the congregation of Valley Christian Center in Fresno, California. In 1986 my wife Beth and I joined the staff at the invitation of Senior Pastor, Dr. Roger Whitlow. That was over 18 years and more than 950 articles ago.

I've been honored by the trust that Pastor Roger placed in me, and have received constant encouragement from him, and from the congregation to continue. The leadership of the church has released me to compile this work.

I'm grateful to Noriko Warnes, Shannon Davis, and Tessa Eubanks for help in the proofing process. My wife has been most helpful and patient, and has inspired much of what I write.

Preface

Daily Grace for the Daily Grind is intended to be a daily resource for Christians to deepen their devotional walk with the Lord. It contains a Scripture Index and a Topic Index for those who wish to use it for Bible study; it is also a useful resource for pastors and speakers.

The common theme of the book is a sense of wonder: the wonder of God's nature, the wonder of His grace, the wonder of His creation, the wonder of words, and the amazing wonder of daily life itself. God is doing something in each one of our days.

I've taken Habakkuk 1:5 quite literally. It says, *Look among the nations! Observe! Be astonished! Wonder! Because I am doing something in your days - you would not believe if you were told.*

Daily Grace for the Daily Grind follows the calendar with respect to holidays, special days, and seasons. It is submitted with the prayer that it will bring glory and honor to Jesus Christ and give helpful insight into the daily wonder of God's marvelous grace.

LB

January 1 – 1/1 **An Open Door**

And to the angel of the church in Philadelphia write, "These things says He who is holy, He who is true, He who has the key of David, He who opens and no one shuts, and shuts and no one opens: I know your works. See, I have set before you an open door, and no one can shut it..." (Revelation 3:7, 8)

If January First is anything, it's an open door. Through it we enter the unknown world of a new year. I like doors. They're fascinating gateways from one place to another – from one reality to another.

Some doors are automatic. All you have to do to open them is move toward them, and somehow your presence is acknowledged. With others, you must knock and request entry. Still others require a key and not everyone has one.

The door to the New Year is one of those automatic ones. It opened as we approached it at midnight last night without anyone knocking or even asking permission to enter. But it is Jesus Who has the key in His nail-scarred hand to all that God has for us in the New Year. It's said of Him, *He is holy, He is true, and He opens and no one shuts and shuts and no one opens.*

The One who opens the door to God's provision for us this year can be trusted. While the territory inside is unknown to us, it's not unknown to Him. As a matter of fact, He's already been there. *And when he brings out his own sheep, he goes before them; and the sheep follow him, for they know his voice.* (John 10:4)

Another thing about the door to this year; I didn't have a choice about it. I did go through it. The only choice I have is how I will go through it. I can enter fearfully or faithfully; sadly or gladly; pouting or praising, but enter I must!

I took some baggage with me when I went through this door. Some of it I will need, like memories of God's goodness and the love of friends and family. Other things I should leave behind, like bad habits and sins unforgiven. I didn't have a choice about passing through this door, but I do have a choice in what I will take with me.

We walked through this door together, you and I, and all those whom God has graciously placed in our lives. God has plans for each of us individually which He will unfold as we walk into the expanse on the other side of the door. But He also has some marvelous designs for us together. Our lives are irreversibly intertwined, since we became part of His forever family.

What does the old song say? "I don't know what the future holds, but I know who holds the future." That's good news. Behind the door are many things unknown to me, but not to Him.

One of the things I'm sure of – there will be opportunity to share His grace and see His good hand at work. It will not be boring. So, ready or not, here we go, through the door to a brand new year.

Annual Introspection *1/2 – January 2*

Let a man examine himself, and so let him eat of the bread and drink of the cup. So says Paul in his first letter to the Corinthians in 11:28. Many people are obsessed with introspection. They live in a constant state of self-absorption that makes their lives miserable. Scripture doesn't advocate such an unhealthy preoccupation with one's self but rather a holy preoccupation with Jesus.

However, the Lord does ask us to periodically examine our hearts as in the regular observance of communion. The point is that if we have regular times of introspection we need not be obsessed with it every day and can get on with the business of loving Jesus and touching the world in His name. That's what communion is about – let's check our hearts and get on with it.

As it happens we're also at the beginning of the New Year. For me, this is an annual inspection, the kind that catches some things a monthly exam may miss. It's also a time to measure vital signs that may not register in the short term but can be important indicators in the long term.

This is a good time to measure spiritual growth, for instance. I may not be able to tell from week to week or month to month if I've grown in the Lord or not, but I should be able to measure it year by year. Do I stand a little taller today than I did this time last year? I've been fed lots of good food and given lots of occasion to exercise by serving so chances are I've grown, even if I don't feel a much bigger.

It's also a time to measure spiritual depth, which is different than spiritual growth. I grow spiritually when I keep feeding on the Word of God and doing what it says. Spiritual depth, however, comes through crisis. For many, last year was difficult, and they're glad it's behind them. But if the trial of our faith takes us deeper into the knowledge of the Holy One, then we can "count it all joy," as the scripture says. Spiritual depth is like our roots growing down into Him. Spiritual growth is like the branches growing upward to bear fruit. A healthy tree will have both.

Another vital sign worth checking out is one's spiritual "blood pressure." Blood pressure is related to the flow of life through the body for "the life of the flesh is in the blood." This speaks to me of worship, the life-flow of my spirit. I'm not satisfied with the reading I get when I check myself at this point. I want to worship better than I do because He is worthy of better worship than I give Him.

It's time for an annual inspection. May I borrow the words of the psalmist and pray, *Search me, O God, and know my heart; try me and know my thoughts; and see if there be any hurtful way in me...* (Psalm 139:23, 24)

January 3 – 1/3 **_What's New?_**

What's so new about the New Year? That's a good question. There isn't even much new about the news these days. It's the same old story of man's inhumanity to man and the consequences of unrighteousness.

We've been so bombarded by this word "new" that it hardly has meaning anymore. New is a pitchman's favorite word. It's used to sell everything from soap to missiles.

We speak of a new car, but there's still an awful lot about a new car that's old stuff. There've been lots of improvements but it still has four wheels, an internal combustion engine, a steering wheel, two head lights, and hundreds of parts that are basically the same as they were last year and the year before that, and so on, back to the Model T.

What's so new about a new car? Not much except that it hasn't been driven by its owner yet. That's about all we can say about the New Year. There is very little that is new about it – except that it hasn't been lived in yet.

If we expected everything to be different after the New Year's celebrations we've set ourselves up for great disappointment. Nothing really changes except a man-made device for marking the passage of time. Life goes on basically unchanged.

I'm beginning to sound like old Solomon who said, *there is nothing new under the sun.* (Ecclesiastes 1:9) In a sense he was right. Nothing new, or essentially different, can spring from under the sun, the realm of man's influence.

Man's ingenuity brings change in form but not change in substance. That's what science is about – changing the form of things. Newness in substance, the awesome power to create, is the specialty of the One whose throne is far above all principalities and powers. He can and does make all things new.

If anything new is to appear it will be the work of His hand and not man's. In Isaiah 43:19 He says, *Behold, I will do a new thing, now it shall spring forthl*

He said in Ezekiel 11:19, *I will but a new spirit within you.* The newness that God brings is inside of me and, I am made new – under the Son, Jesus!

The best news: as He watches over my year, from beginning to end – *His faithfulness is great - His mercies are new every morning.* (Lamentations 3:22,23)

What's new about the New Year? His mercy every day – that's what's New?

The Name of the Lord in the Scriptures: *Who walks in darkness and has no light? Let him trust in the Name of the Lord his God.* (Isaiah 50:10) His name is:

Alpha • Adonai • Almighty • Altogether Lovely • Amen • Ancient of Days • Advocate • Author and Finisher of Our Faith • Beloved • Branch • Bread of Life • Bright Morning Star

Captain of the Lord's Hosts • Captain of Our Salvation • Chief Shepherd • Christ • Consolation of Israel • Chief Cornerstone • Commander • Counselor • Day Spring • Day Star • Deliverer • Desire of Nations • Door

El Elyon • Elohim • El Shaddai • Emmanuel • Eternal Life • Everlasting Father • Faithful Witness • First and Last • First Begotten of the Dead • First-born of Every Creature • Friend of Sinners • God

Good Shepherd • Great High Priest • Governor • Head of the Church • Heir of All Things • High Tower • Holy One • Holy One of Israel • Hope of Israel • Horn of Salvation • I Am • Jehovah

Jehovah-Jireh, Lord my Provider • Jehovah-M'Kaddesh, Lord my Sanctifier •Jehovah-Nissi, Lord my Banner • Jehovah-Rapha, Lord my Healer • Jehovah-Roi, Lord my Shepherd • Jehovah-Sabaoth, Lord of Hosts • Jehovah-Shalom, Lord my Peace • Jehovah-Shammah, Lord is Present • Jehovah-Tsidkenu, the Lord our Righteousness

Jesus • Judge of the Living and the Dead • Just One • King • King of the Jews • King of Kings • King of Saints • Law-Giver • Lamb • Lamb of God • Leader • Life • Lifter of My Head • Light of the World

Lily of the Valley • Lion of Judah • Lord • Lord of All • Lord of Glory • Lord God Omnipotent • Lord Jesus Christ • Man of Sorrow • Mediator • Messenger of the Covenant

Messiah • Mighty God • My Song • My Strength • Offspring of David • Omega • Only-Begotten • Passover • Physician • Prince of Life • Prince of Peace • Prince of the Kings of the Earth • Prophet • Ransom • Redeemer

Resting Place • Resurrection and the Life • Rock • Rock of Ages • Rock of My Salvation • Root of David • Root of Jesse • Rose of Sharon • Ruler of Israel • Savior • Servant • Shepherd and Bishop of Our Souls

Shiloh • Son of God • Son of the Highest • Son of David • Son of Man • Sun of Righteousness • Sure Foundation • Surety • True God • True Vine • Truth

Way • Wisdom • Witness • Wonderful • Word • Word of God • Word of Life •

Blessed be the Name of the Lord!

January 5 – 1/5 *Take Care of Yourself*

The stewardess stood in the front of the coach section of the 747 giving the preflight safety message. She talked about the oxygen masks dropping down in case of loss of cabin pressure, and she addressed parents with children.

She said, "You must first put your oxygen mask over your own face. Then, secure the mask over the face of the child." The message I heard was clear. Before I can take care of my children, or any one else for that matter, I must take care of myself.

This goes against some of the instincts that rage within the heart and mind of those of us who are caregivers. We consider it a virtue to always put others first. But the truth is that by seeing to our own health and safety, we can see to the needs of others more effectively and for a longer period of time.

That's been a hard lesson for me to learn. I come from a spiritual discipline characterized by a statement from a man I deeply admired in my young ministry days. He said, "I'd rather wear out than rust out!" And he did. I was a pallbearer at his funeral in 1965. He was a man in his early fifties who didn't take care of himself. He was my pastor, my mentor, and my role model.

I'll not forget the day the Lord spoke to me about my attachment to this man. We were serving on the North Coast and had started a Bible study in the town of Ferndale. I looked forward to sharing life with these dear people each week.

I was running late one day for the study, and when I came to the bridge over the Eel River I had a problem. The bridge was narrow and long and just ahead of me was a truck full of dairy cattle. I couldn't get around the truck so, in my impatience, I got as close as I could to the rear of the truck so I could pull out quickly and pass when the opportunity presented itself.

That was a big mistake. In the back of the cattle truck one of the cows had a "gastro-intestinal problem," if you know what I mean. The windshield of my car was covered with an ugly, smelly substance that made me gag. I was forced to stop because I couldn't see a thing.

While I was cleaning the windshield, God spoke to me in the way I've learned to recognize. He said, "You're following too close." I knew instantly that He wasn't talking about the obvious.

He was talking about my mentor, who had died just a few weeks earlier. I knew that He was telling me that I must not follow him or any one else so closely. And I was not to emulate his lifestyle. I must take care of myself.

My only hero now is Jesus. He didn't wear out; He didn't rust out; He was poured out for you and me. I love Him for that!

The Waterline *1/6 – January 6*

No temptation has overtaken you but such as is common to man; and God is faithful, Who will not allow you to be tempted beyond what you are able to bear, but with the temptation will provide the way of escape, that you may be able to endure it. (I Corinthians 10:13)

For nearly half of my life I lived by the sea. I learned a lot from watching people and birds and waves and ships. One of my favorite activities was to slip out of my office and drive five minutes to a place from which I could see ships coming and going on Humboldt Bay.

One thing that I learned is that you could tell by looking at a ship how full it was even though you couldn't see its cargo. There's a thing called a water line on the side of the ship. If the ship's water line is above the surface of the water, the ship is nearly empty. If the ship's water line is at or below the surface of the water, the ship is loaded and can't take on any more.

The placement of the water line on the ship is determined by very specific criteria that are determined when the ship is built. For the life of that ship the water line will remain the same. It represents the load limit of that ship.

When the Bible speaks of temptation, it's synonymous with testing or trial. The passage above says that God will not put on us more than we are able to bear. Well, who determines what I'm able to bear? I've been at my limit many times according to my observations – but I made it through.

God established a "water line" for me when He made me. In my mother's womb He knew me and fashioned me to bear a certain load. I have a water line – a load limit, and He promised never to put so much on me that I would sink under the load of it. It is God, my Creator, Who says where the water line is for me – not me.

That can be a bit of a problem if I think I'm about to go under. But since God said what my limit is, He is bound by His own Word to provide a way for me to escape the disaster of over-load.

I've often had to bear more than I think I can – but I've never had to bear more than Jesus says I can. And underneath me – always – are His everlasting arms.

January 7 – 1/7 — *Walls*

The Great Wall of China, the walls of Jericho, the Berlin Wall, the Wailing Wall; all of these walls divide somebody from somebody else. That's what walls do best. That's why they were built. Make the wall tall enough and thick enough and you could be safe – until somebody found a way to get over, under, around or through it.

Walls are not much good these days as a means of national defense. They never were what they were cracked up to be. But now a nation can be threatened from the sky, and how do you build a wall to deal with that? The thing about walls is that when you build one to defend against threat from any possible direction you've just made yourself a prisoner.

One of my favorite walls is the ancient wall around the city of Jerusalem. Nehemiah was busy minding the king's business in Susa when he became distressed that the wall protecting his beloved city was in shambles. He spent a good share of the rest of his life supervising the rebuilding of that wall so that the Temple and the city folk could be secure. It was a good wall. Part of that wall exists today and has become a rallying point for the hopes of Jews that Messiah will come and build another temple, and that God Himself will once again dwell there.

A wall I've heard a lot about in recent years is the Berlin Wall. It was built by East Germany to "protect" East Berliners from the ravages of Western values. Many people were killed trying to escape such "protection" and now the wall has come tumbling down. There's freedom of sorts in Eastern Europe now but the dissolving of bitterness and the healing of a generation's wounds will take more than the shattering of a physical barrier.

Ephesians 2:13,14 talks about a wall that divided people from each other and people from God. *Now in Christ Jesus you, who formerly were far off, have been brought near by the blood of Christ. For He Himself is our peace, who made both into one, and broke down the barrier of the dividing wall...* Jesus brings people together with each other and with God. That's what He does best.

There's another wall that's breaking all the rules about walls; the Vietnam Wall, as it's called. Its real name is the Vietnam Veteran's Memorial in Washington D.C. This wall has had an astonishing effect upon those who spend time reading the names of thousands of men and women who gave their lives in defense of freedom.

Our nation was divided about the war in Vietnam but "The Wall" is changing some things. Walls are built to keep people apart; this one brings people together. Walls are designed to protect people from threat – this one is disarming with its stark simplicity. Walls are supposed to be barriers – this one has become a bridge!

The Duration *1/8 – January 8*

I was six years old when World War II began. I don't remember very much about the war but I can recall how it affected our family. My uncle was in the Army so his family came to live with us. My grandparents also came to live with us. We were one big happy family – we really were!

It was then that I learned the word "duration." The government issued special stamps so people could buy limited quantities of gasoline and tires. Food and clothing were rationed and one of my favorite things – professional baseball – was suspended in our area. Even copper pennies were no longer produced because they needed copper for the war. Zinc alloy pennies replaced them. The government said it would be that way for the duration, which I understood to mean, until the end of the war.

World War II was a time of great sacrifice for all Americans. I remember asking how long we would all be together in one house, and how long until we could get enough gas to take a trip to the zoo in St. Louis, and when would the air raid drills be over? My father said we were in this for the duration.

There was something strangely comforting about having a timeframe for our sacrifice, such as it was. It was useless to complain. I wouldn't get a new tire for my bike; I'd have to do with what I had for the duration. We made do, and we were happy enough. We simply limited our desires, prayed and waited patiently for the end of the war.

And it came! I remember it well. Bells rang all day long on VE Day (Victory in Europe) and everybody laughed and sang and danced in the streets. The war was over, the boys would be coming home, the sacrifice of a nation had paid off – we won! We had endured the duration! Now we could go to St. Louis.

I'm hearing the phrase again these days in reference to terrorism in our world. Restrictions are placed on travel to certain countries, security is an issue in airports, and good people are dying in defense of freedom. How long will these conditions exist? For the duration – and that may be a while.

The duration mind-set is not a bad thing for the people of God. Jesus spoke of these very days in Matthew 24:6-13. *You will be hearing of wars and rumors of wars... for nation will rise against nation, and kingdom against kingdom... and because lawlessness is increased, most people's love will grow cold. But the one who endures to the end will be saved.*

There are lots of things that I wish were different. It's good to have faith that God will change our circumstances, but it's also true that patient endurance in unchanging circumstances is an expression of faith. Longsuffering means to suffer for a long time. But when the war is over, our joy will know no bounds.

Our celebration at the end is in proportion to our endurance until the end. The longer the duration, the greater our joy when He comes!

A ceremony in ancient times is pictured in the language of Scripture. When a slave was adopted into a family, the adopting father would declare before witnesses, "You are my son, this day have I begotten you!" The traditional response from the slave was the cry, "Abba father!"

Adoption today is also a means by which an outsider may become a family member by a means other than birth, but this is not so in the family of God. In fact, there is no way to enter God's family except by birth – new birth. *You must be born again.* (John 3:7) We are not adopted into God's family in lieu of birth – we become His sons and daughters by being born from above.

We have an adopted daughter and she is precious to us. A choice made her ours – our choice, and hers. She was eighteen, old enough to choose, when we both signed the adoption papers. What beautiful word – chosen.

This is a beautiful picture of our relationship with our Heavenly Father. We are His by choice; His choice first – then ours. And in that mutual choosing, we are born again into His forever family. He says, *But you are a chosen people, a royal priesthood, a holy nation, a people belonging to God, that you may declare the praises of him who called you out of darkness into his wonderful light.* (I Peter 2:9)

The word adoption means, "to place as a son." The term "son" is contrasted with the term "child" in Galatians 4:1-7, which indicates that a child is not to be trusted with an inheritance, but a son, suggesting responsibility and maturity, is given his inheritance. Adoption, then, is also the act of the Father making a child into a son, a minor into an adult. After becoming a child of God by new birth, I am immediately advanced to the mature position of son, in the eyes of God if not in my own sight.

An adopted child in God's family is a responsible, mature son with all of the benefits. And to help us live responsibly, the Word says: *Because you are sons, God sent the Spirit of His Son into our hearts crying out, 'Abba Father'. Therefore you are no longer a slave but a son, and if a son, then an heir of God through Christ.* (Galatians 4:6, 7)

From the beginning of our new birth into His family, Jesus has been living inside of us to help us live, not as babies but as mature sons and daughters of God, and responsible heirs of all that God has promised.

Love and Marriage *1/10 – January 10*

Today is my wife's birthday so I dedicate these words to her. As of January 1, 2005, we've been married for fifty years. Happy birthday, honey.

"Love and marriage, love and marriage; they go together like a horse and carriage;" so says the old song. But which comes first? Which is the horse and which is the carriage? In the case of the life-long commitment of two people to each other, is love the horse that pulls the marriage carriage, or is marriage the horse that draws love?

Can two people really love each other enough, in the beginning, to carry them all the way, for better or worse, for richer or poorer, in sickness and in health, 'til death us do part? Or does love grow as a result of facing fears and tears and years together in marriage? If we expect that first love is sufficient to carry us through to the end, we may be like the man who said, "I have enough money to last me the rest of my life – if I die next Tuesday!"

In our case, we could not carry enough love into our marriage to last a lifetime. We had to pick some up along the way. Young people often come to the marriage altar with fairy-tale idealism, believing that once a person falls in love, he lives happily ever after. Marriages may be made in heaven but they must be lived on earth.

In Psalm 4:1, David expresses the key to an enlarged capacity to love. He said, *O God... You have enlarged me when I was in distress.* The word "distress" means "to be pressed out of shape." The stress is relieved, not by eliminating stress, but by enlarging capacity. In other words, David says: "When I get pushed out of shape, my capacity to contain stress is enlarged and I am relieved."

We can react rigidly to stressful situations, refuse to be enlarged, and break under the pressure, or we can be flexible and forgiving and find that we are growing in our capacity to love. There are ample stresses in marriage to break us or to allow for love to grow, but there is no enlarging without pressure to go beyond our limits, and pressure is pain.

My wife and I have grown in our capacity to love each other, and Jesus, because we have learned to be enlarged by our stresses, and we've had some whopper size challenges. To embrace, rather than simply tolerate, the inevitable flaws we all bring to marriage is to be enlarged to love more. To insist on perfection and a flawless union is to become hard and rigid and bitter, ready to crack at the appearance of stress.

Trees and people break because they will not bend. Thanks for bending with my flaws, dear one.

January 11 – 1/11 *Integrity*

Honesty is a missing element in much of our society because of a missing element in our character – integrity. Honesty is the effect – integrity is the cause. Honesty is the fruit – integrity is the tree. Integrity is the character trait – honesty is the action that proceeds from it.

To understand this vital quality let's look at the word "integrity." Its origins are revealing. The root of it is the noun "integer," meaning the whole of anything. An integer is a whole number. From there we go to the adjective "integral;" "constituting an essential part of the whole." Then to the verb "integrate," meaning to make entire, or whole. Finally we come to our noun "integrity." Literally, integrity is "the state of being whole or entire."

The U. S. Navy uses this word to describe the reliability of its submarines. They speak of the integrity of a vessel; is it whole, are there flaws or cracks that will cause failure under the tremendous pressure of deep-sea dives? If flaws are found, the integrity of the vessel is compromised, and it's not sea worthy. It can't sail until repairs are made.

A few years ago, our nation was shocked and grieved by the loss of seven people aboard the space shuttle Challenger. We watched in horror as the vehicle that carried them exploded and fell to earth in thousands of pieces. In fact, the space shuttle failed because it did not have integrity. It had flaws in its "character" that caused it to fail under pressure.

We fail under the pressure of temptation because we are not whole, we do not have integrity. Wholeness is God's answer to the allurements of the world. If I am whole, I need nothing else to complete me. But if I'm not whole, the empty spaces in me attract whatever is there.

Integrity is much more than mere honesty. It's the result of wholeness that God is working in me to fill up the empty places.

The Scripture says a lot about integrity. *The integrity of the upright will guard them.* (Proverbs 11:3) *Let integrity and uprightness preserve me.* (Psalm 25:21)

But the best description of integrity comes from Deuteronomy 6:5 and it doesn't even use the word. It says, *And you shall love the Lord your God with all your heart and with all your soul and with all your might.*

That is wholeness – that is integrity.

Abounding Grace *1/12 – January 12*

Let us come boldly before the throne of grace that we may obtain mercy and find grace to help in the time of need. (Hebrews 4:16)

I'm reluctant to speak of grace in a few words because it's so central to all of God's dealings with us. It deserves more consideration than one page allows.

One of my favorite expressions about the subject is "Grace is not a blue-eyed blond." In other words, grace isn't a synonym for beauty or poise, like a ballerina or an Olympic skater. We say Michelle Kwan is very graceful on the ice, a picture of smoothness and beauty of movement. But the grace of God is entirely something else; it transcends all else in its beauty.

When God took on human flesh, John 1:14 says He was *full of grace and truth.* Jesus is grace-full – full of grace. Jesus is truth-full – full of truth.

On the cross His body was penetrated by thorns and nails, and then a spear, but out of Him flowed grace and truth. *Father, forgive them, they know not what they do,* He said. Under pressure, whatever one is full of comes out like toothpaste from its tube. Every crisis in Jesus' life was an occasion for grace and truth to pour forth from within Him.

I want to be like that. I'd like to be so full of grace that when I'm squeezed by circumstances, out of me pours grace. What are you full of? You can tell what you're full of by what comes out of you when the pressure's on.

God intends that grace be the central core of my relationship with Him. In fact, He intends that grace be as dominant now, as sin was in my life. *Where sin abounded, grace did much more abound; that as sin has reigned unto death, even so might grace reign unto eternal life by Jesus Christ our Lord.* (Romans 5:20-21)

There it is! Grace is to reign, dominate, control, and abound in my life now just as sin reigned, dominated, controlled, and abounded in my life before Jesus came to free me from the law of sin and death.

Grace is God giving Himself to us. It took something more powerful than sin to save us and keep us from falling flat on our faces in utter defeat. Grace is that power, greater than all our sin, and we all know the power of sin.

God says, "My grace is sufficient (enough) for you." By the way, this isn't a promise; it's a fact – a present reality.

I need not ask Him to make what is!

January 13 – 1/13 **God Sets The Table**

The LORD is my shepherd, I shall not want. He makes me lie down in green pastures; He leads me beside quiet waters. He restores my soul; He guides me in the paths of righteousness for His name's sake. Even though I walk through the valley of the shadow of death, I fear no evil; for Thou art with me; Thy rod and Thy staff, they comfort me. Thou dost prepare a table before me in the presence of my enemies; Thou hast anointed my head with oil; my cup overflows. Surely goodness and lovingkindness will follow me all the days of my life, and I will dwell in the house of the LORD forever. (Psalm 23)

In this well-known psalm the Lord says that, in the Valley of the Shadow of Death, His rod and His staff (His rule and protection) would comfort us. He says further that He has prepared a table for us in the presence of our enemies and He invites us to come and partake of His gracious provision.

I've been pondering these beautiful words. They mean a lot to me because of a valley that I've recently gone through, and there was indeed, a table of provision for me in that dark place.

One question I had was, "Why did you prepare a table for me right in the middle of conflict with my enemies surrounding me. Wouldn't it have been better to put it in a peaceful place?" He said, in a way that I've come to know His voice, "That's the only place I could put it."

This statement implies one of three things. First, that God was powerless to place the table anywhere but in the presence of my enemies. This would mean that there were forces greater than He that determined where He would set the table. Unthinkable! Jehovah, Almighty God, the Maker of heaven and earth, at the mercy of greater powers that limit His options? Incredible!

Second, God could be saying that I have so many enemies that it's impossible to set it anywhere without it being in their presence. On the other hand, the real enemies are not flesh and blood, and not even the devil, but they are sin, fear, guilt, bitterness and death. These are always lurking in the shadows. Perhaps this is what He meant.

Third, and this is what it meant to me, God said that His plan for my life required that the table be spread in the presence of my enemies. To set it anyplace else would be less than the best for me. It wasn't that God was powerless to control its placement. It wasn't that it was impossible to set it where there wasn't an enemy. It is that He is committed to His purpose and that conflict and confrontation with my enemies is part of the development of character and the fulfillment of His plan for my life.

So, to assure that I am sustained in the heat of battle, He spreads a feast for me on the field of conflict and invites me to dine as His special guest.

Incidentally, He also gives firm notice to my enemies that I am His!

Satisfying Rain **1/14 – *January 14***

There's a place in Scripture that relates to a most essential element for life on planet earth – rain. It's Deuteronomy 11:10-15. Here's what it says:

For the land, into which you are entering to possess it, is not like the land of Egypt from which you came, where you used to sow your seed and water it with your foot like a vegetable garden. But the land into which you are about to cross to possess it, a land of hills and valleys, drinks water from the rain of heaven, a land for which the Lord your God cares; the eyes of the Lord your God are always on it, from the beginning even to the end of the year.

And it shall come about, if you listen obediently to my commandments which I am commanding you today, to love the Lord your God and to serve Him with all your heart and all your soul, that He will give the rain for your land in its season, the early and late rain, that you may gather in your grain and your new wine and your oil. And He will give grass in your fields for your cattle, and you shall eat and be satisfied.

Israel had been in Egypt for 400 years, and now they were on their way to the Promised Land. Egypt wasn't a bad place; it was the intellectual, scientific, cultural, and financial center of the world at that time. But it was bondage for God's people. That's a pretty good picture of life in these United States in the Twentieth-first Century; all the affluence, culture, technology, and education the world can amass is here – but many of God's chosen are in the grip of its influence and don't realize that a better land awaits.

According to this passage, there was one big difference between Egypt and the Land of Promise – rain. There's not much of it in Egypt. Life is huddled close to the banks of the river Nile, and a few miles east or west of the river no vegetable or animal life can be sustained without some unusual provision of water. It says in verse ten of the account that in Egypt you had to sow your seed and "water it with your foot..."

That's a strange statement. But when I was in Egypt I saw a device called a shaduf, which is a kind of multiple bucket arrangement on a wheel powered by foot pedals. As the worker pedaled, the buckets were lowered into the river, brought up full and dumped into channels, which carried the water to the crops. It was an ingenious system, necessary because there was no rain.

When God's people came into their land – a land of hills and valleys (ups and downs) – the labor needed to water the crops was unnecessary. The land, which lay before them drank *water from the rain of heaven* – a picture of the blessing of the Lord for those who walk in His ways.

I will give you rain in its season... and you shall eat and be satisfied!

It's beginning to rain – Yes!

January 15 – 1/15 **Putting Jesus First**

He is before all things, and in Him all things hold together. He is also head of the body, the church; and He is the beginning, the first-born from the dead; so that He Himself might come to have first place in everything. For it was the Father's good pleasure for all the fullness to dwell in Him... (Colossians 1:17-19)

One of the most profound pieces of advice I've received is this: "Never forget that the main thing is to keep the main thing the main thing." The challenge is to decide what the main thing really is.

Actually, the main thing is no thing at all – it's Jesus, the Head of the church, and the Preeminent One in the entire universe. He is the Center around which everything moves, the Foundation upon which everything rests, and, according to Colossians 1:17, *By Him all things are held together.* In God's order of things Jesus is definitely Number One.

But, in practical terms, how do I keep Him in His place of preeminence in my life? There is only so much time in a day, so many hours in a week, and so many heartbeats in a lifetime. With the demands of job, family, school, and church how can I keep the main thing the main thing?

So, if the main thing is to keep the main thing the main thing, how can I be sure that Jesus is the main thing – "Numero Uno" – in my life? What does it mean for Him to have first place in my life. It boils down to this:

I choose to give Him –

- The first moments of my day.
- The first portion of my income.
- The first day of my week – Sunday.
- And first consideration in all my decisions.

If I can do these things consistently, I'm assured that Jesus is in the driver's seat; He is seated on the throne of my heart... He is indeed, Numero Uno!

What's It To You? ***1/16 – January 16***

One of my favorite stories came from Whittier, Ca. in 1983. Hoodlums broke into a department store there one night. They didn't steal or destroy anything; they just had a wonderful time – switching price tags. The next morning customers were puzzled and delighted to find fur coats selling for $5. Face cream was priced at $150; a silver service for $1.75; a pair of ladies hose for $390; umbrellas for $1000. Diamond rings were tagged at $2 each.

Is this what has actually happened in our society? Has someone, or something, crept into our hearts and switched price tags so that our values are confused?

I've been pondering the value of the church to my family. While it may be difficult, it may be helpful to try to give an actual dollar value to the things I'm about to list.

For instance, what's it worth that the church is a respected voice for righteousness in this community? What's it worth to have a well-kept, pleasant place to gather to worship the Lord our God?

What is the value of a year-round Christian education ministry, encouraging principles in our kids that will enrich their lives for time and eternity?

What's it worth that there is well planned, spiritually sound ministry to pre-teens, teenagers, and young adults being carried on continuously by gifted people who care? What's it worth to have fellowship with people worth knowing, who are going in the same direction you are?

What's it worth that, in the church a life-style, free from harmful addictions, is encouraged and modeled which results in many added years of active life for all who choose to so walk? What's it worth to have consistent, gifted teaching by godly men and women that leads us into the treasures of the knowledge our Lord and His ways?

What is the value of music; music that lifts the spirit, heals the emotions and expresses the deepest longings of the heart; music that effectively cancels the noise of the world; music that you hear and learn and sing here in this place?

What's it worth to have people with whom to celebrate the passages of life; the birth and dedication of babies, the marriage of sons and daughters, the baptism of new believers, and the joyous home going of loved ones?

All of these things and more have great value, and they come with a price tag. Even the redemption we freely enjoy was not without great price.

Do you have your price tags on the right things?

Lately, I've been pondering the wonder of language. The ability to credibly communicate an idea is an awesome thing. I have great admiration for anyone who can put words together in meaningful sentences. Such skill is a holy thing and gift from God, in whose image we are made.

It's a sign of our times that movies, books, songs, and conversations are filled, not with carefully thought out dialogue, but with expressions of vulgarity, filth and blasphemy known as "expletives." Conversation, a movie, book, or song spiced with expletives is offensive not only because the expressions vainly invoke the Name I love, but the chosen expletives also reveal an inexcusable intellectual laziness.

I grew up learning that certain words should not be spoken. Having one's mouth washed out with soap implied that there must be dirt in there somewhere. But when parents weren't listening, kids would often utter the forbidden phrases in rebellion.

This childish fetish survives to adulthood in many whose vocabulary should've grown richer with age. Words mean things, and often words DO mean (bad) things to people.

In a curious linguistic twist, there are some words that are acceptable in the pulpit but are frowned upon when uttered in the pew. The words "damn" and "hell" never found their way into my vocabulary, but I wondered why my pastor could say them in a sermon without a good soapy mouth washing.

These two words are sprinkled strategically throughout the Scriptures. They're part of the inspired record of God's dealings with humankind. They're not "taking the Lord's Name in vain," nor are they sexually explicit. So what's so bad about using these words in casual or even angry conversation?

Well, apart from the afore-mentioned intellectual laziness, there are some serious considerations here. The thoughtless use of words that carry such awesome meaning does have consequences worth considering.

There's the matter of authority. You or I do not have the authority to damn anyone or anything. Such a request misrepresents the nature of God and the mission of Jesus. *For God did not send His Son into the world to condemn the world, but that the world through Him might be saved.* (John 3:17)

Also, the casual use of words like these trivializes the most serious matters facing mankind – the judgment of God for sin, and the eternal abode of the lost. If I were the devil, I would take great pleasure in people taking hell and damnation with a grain of salt. In fact, I would encourage their misuse – were I the prince of darkness.

Let the words of my mouth and the meditation of my heart be acceptable in Your sight, O Lord, my strength and my Redeemer. (Psalm 19:14)

Follow Through *1/18 – January 18*

It's a puzzle to me! It's the same with every game I've ever tried to play. They keep telling me that my follow-through needs improving. It was that way in tennis: you've got to follow through with the racquet. It was the same with basketball: your follow-through is weak. Baseball, same thing: follow through with the bat.

And now it's golf. I hear it all the time. "It's the follow-through that makes the ball go straight," they say. Why should it matter what happens after I make contact with the ball? Why can't I just get up there and hit the thing?

Well, since I've heard this so many times, I thought there might be something to it. And it's true – the path of the ball is aided, not only by what happens before contact, but by what happens afterward, too. The desired results can only be achieved by following through properly after initial contact.

It doesn't surprise me that this is a principle of life and relationship as well. How many times have I, with compassion and good intent, made contact with someone saying, "Let's get together for lunch?" Or, "I'd really like to get to know your family." Or, "I'll be praying for you."

I leave the encounter, as they do, feeling good about the contact we've made. But time passes and there's no lunch and no prayer and no knowing the family. The desired results, the good intentions, never were realized. I end up feeling guilty every time I see that person, and a wedge of distrust is forged between two people who once had meaningful contact.

It's all in the follow-through, isn't it? Just like in golf, or tennis – its not just making contact, it's what happens afterwards that determines success.

I'm not knocking good intentions. No sir! It's true that good intentions never got anybody to Heaven, but no one ever got there without them either. So let's hear it for the good intentions that we all have.

However, good intentions sometimes lead us to promise things that we have neither the time nor the energy to fulfill. Maybe we ought to intend a little less and follow-through a little more.

God has good intentions where we're concerned. And He has great follow-through, too. Paul knew this when he said, *I am confident of this very thing, that He Who began a good work in you will perfect it until the day of Christ Jesus.* (Philippians 1:6)

January 19 – 1/19 *Hitherto...*

Hitherto the Lord has helped us..." says the prophet in I Samuel 7:12.

Samuel was offering sacrifice to the Lord at Mizpah when the Philistine army showed up ready to pick a fight with the Israelis. But before the battle could begin the Lord spoke with the voice of mighty thunder from heaven. The enemy was thrown into confusion and was driven off by the Israeli army.

On the spot, at Mizpah, Samuel erected an altar and called it "Ebenezer," which means – a stone of help. It was a way of memorializing the Lord's help and that's when he said, "hitherto the Lord has helped us."

The language of King James may confuse us. Other translations simply say "thus far" or "heretofore." But "hitherto" simply means "from there to here – and from here to there, (wherever there is) God is our helper."

It's also interesting to me that he built his altar at Mizpah, the place of a watchtower. That's what Mizpah means. It was high above the surrounding territory so Samuel could see in all directions.

I have a deep suspicion that most of the Lord's help in my life goes completely unnoticed by me. I had reason to think that a few years ago when I was in an accident. A man in a pickup ran a red light and broadsided my car at about 35 mph. It totaled my car but left me with a shoulder injury.

I don't blame anyone. I have only gratitude in my heart for that incident. If I'd been a split second further into the intersection, I could have been killed.

So I build an altar today, I raise my Ebenezer, in deep gratitude for the Lord's help in preserving my life then and many times since, for whatever reason He has in His infinite wisdom.

Altars are made of hard things – stones – and this was a hard thing. But I lay it before the Lord as an altar, and offer upon it my sacrifice of praise.

Pray For Our President *1/20 – January 20*

On this day every four years a president is inaugurated for another term. The nasty business of politics tends to draw emotional lines among us, but above partisan considerations, we are commanded to pray for our nation's leaders.

I exhort therefore, that... supplications, prayers, intercessions, and giving of thanks, be made for all men; for kings, and for all that are in authority; that we may lead a quiet and peaceable life in all godliness and honesty. For this is good and acceptable in the sight of God our Savior; Who will have all men to be saved, and to come unto the knowledge of the truth. (I Timothy 2:1-4)

Paul writes this to Timothy, who was leader of the Church in the Roman city of Ephesus, a center of persecution and the scene of the martyrdom of thousands of Christians in the 1st Century. Yet Paul exhorts the people to pray for the very leaders who were perpetrating violence against them.

How we pray for our President is important. We tend to pray simple prayers depending on our like or dislike of the one God has ordained for this time and place. If we like him we pray, "Dear God, bless the President." If we don't like him we pray, "Dear God, get the President."

We are called to deeper stuff than that. Paul calls for "supplication, prayers, intercession, and giving of thanks." That's a lot more than bless him, or get him! We're part of a kingdom that's not of this world, but is above this world. Our actions, words and prayers should reflect our citizenship in the Kingdom of God's dear Son, Jesus Christ.

Paul writes in the same book to Timothy some important words for us to consider at this time in our political environment.

I charge you in the presence of God, Who gives life to all things... that you keep the commandment without stain or reproach until the appearing of our Lord Jesus Christ, which He will bring about at the proper time - He Who is the blessed and only Sovereign, the King of kings and Lord of lords; Who alone possesses immortality and dwells in unapproachable light... To Him be honor and eternal dominion. Amen! (I Timothy 6:13-16)

The church isn't a political action committee, nor a branch of a political party. It's the dominion of King Jesus, the "blessed and only Sovereign, the King of kings and Lord of lords," and President of presidents. We owe supreme allegiance to King Jesus in whose name we minister and in whose name we pray for our President.

"Rosita is dead!" The announcer's voice interrupted a basketball game to which I was listening. A two-month vigil was over. She was kidnapped from her bedroom at knifepoint in October. This was December. The basketball game continued under a cloud of grief.

They caught the man who did it. He had done it before. His arrest made international headlines. His trial was a media circus. Hundreds of hours and millions of dollars were spent in the search for Rosita. Celebrities kicked in reward money and posters with Rosita's picture covered the western states.

Rosita's funeral was held on December 9. 1,500 people attended. A choir sang. The Governor and our Senators were there. The President sent a note.

At the moment of Rosita's death, another child's life was ending not far from the crime scene. No one was looking for her. No one wanted her, and no one mourned her passing. She was aborted just a month before she was to be born.

What's wrong with this picture? What rationale rules here? Why is Rosita's death a national tragedy and another child's death business-as-usual? I don't suggest that we trivialize this tragedy but can't we also mourn the loss of unborn children whose lives are sacrificed on the altar of convenience?

One reason Rosita's death impacted so many was the violent nature of it – the break-in, the knife, the abduction, the killing – all in a frenzy of violent activity. We pretend to abhor violence, but our abhorrence is selective. When a baby is aborted there is a break-in, an abduction – and there is a killing.

The reason for the difference in how we view these two deaths is that Rosita had a history and a future, an identity, a name and a face. There were lots of visual images – pictures of Rosita's childhood antics, Rosita at the piano, Rosita at the beach, Rosita with her friends. She was a beautiful twelve-year old. She had her mother's eyes – her father's nose. She had a genetic identity.

An aborted fetus has no identity, no name, and no face. There are no pictures. They're forbidden. If there were any pictures they would not wind up in anybody's family album. But every child conceived has a genetic history and a future. The genetic code is all there at conception. She has her father's eyes. He has his mother's hair color, his grandfather's height. She has her mother's build. He will grow bald just like his dad – if given the chance.

Rosita was known and loved. Millions rightly mourn her death. But, while millions mourn one death, few mourn millions of deaths. What's wrong with this picture?

It is a fact that every child conceived has an identity with God. *Before I formed you in the womb, I knew you.* (Jeremiah 1:5) Each one has a face and a future with Him. They are not forgotten. He remembers – and so do we.

Whose Life Is It? *1/22 – January 22*

What do we mean when we talk about the sanctity of life? If we're going to stand for something we should know what we're standing for. I looked it up. Sanctity is the state of being sacred, "consecrated or belonging to God; made holy." It's from the Latin word "sacre" – to set apart, consecrate.

Do we believe that all life is sacred? Some people believe that, and risk their lives to save toads and birds. Hindus in India believe that all life is sacred to the extent that animals are given divine status. Where do we draw the line when we speak of the sanctity of life? Is all life sacred? What about plants and insects, and microorganisms? I can see it now – some group is going to march to save microscopic life from being destroyed when someone uses Lysol. People don't agree on where the line between sacred and not-so-sacred life is.

What is life anyhow? In a primitive sense life is defined as the ability to grow, assimilate food, and reproduce. But there's got to be more to sacred life than that. According to Scripture, life in human form didn't occur until God breathed into man the breath of life, and man became a living soul. He didn't do that to toads and birds and amoebas. Only man received the breath of life from God. Everything else that's alive has another kind of life that must not be in the same category as human life.

The issue is, of course, unborn babies who are aborted without considering whose life it is that's being taken. If we believe in the sanctity of life and sacred means "belonging to God," then in a sense we're taking God's life and He only chose to give up His life once – at the cross!

Says the Psalmist in 139:13,14: *You created my inmost being; You knit me together in my mother's womb. I praise You because I am fearfully and wonderfully made.* I am His by an act of creation, and His by an act of redemption. All that remains is for me to be His by an act of my own will. Then I'm His by creation, by redemption – and by choice.

Life is a wonderful thing. As I write the guns and bombs of war are blasting away in Iraq. As a believer in the sanctity of life I fall to my knees and pray that it will end soon because Iraqis, Iranians, Kuwaitis, Saudis, Jordanians, Israelis, Russians, Americans, and all who breath the air of planet earth – share the same sacred breath of life from God. We all came from Adam and will all give account of our stewardship of the life we've been given.

If there is sanctity to life – and there is – then our commitment is to the pre-born and the post-born, the young and the old, red and yellow, black and white, that we may all come to know Him, the well-spring of life – to Whom life ultimately belongs.

Today is "Sanctity of Life Day." It's the anniversary of Roe v. Wade. What makes human life sacred isn't how productive, or how cute, or how rich, or how smart a person may be. What makes human life sacred is that God breathes life into every "zygote" conceived.

What's a "zygote" (pronounced zy-goat)? No, a zygote is not a Himalayan mountain creature. A zygote is the name used by scientists to describe the cell formed by the union of the female egg and the male sperm in the uterus. The amazing thing about a zygote is that all the genetic information for a fully-grown human being is in this microscopic wonder. The color of the eyes, hair, and skin, as well as all the information needed to form a healthy person with everything in the right place.

I get a kick out of the animal rights people and their not-so-subtle attempts to humanize the animal kingdom. A phrase that I heard the other day on TV was "animals are people, too." The statement was accompanied by touching pictures of cute little animals doing people-like things, like waving and playing with toys. This proves, they say, that since a dog can wave like a human he must be in the same category. That logic leads me to conclude that if I could make a choo-choo sound, I would be a train.

The sad truth is, that while some people are genuinely concerned about cruelty to animals, the net result is not to humanize animals but to animalize humans. In recent years the trend has been to raise lower forms of life to the level of the God-breathed family of mankind. God didn't breathe into cattle and make them in His image; He simply made them.

By all the current evidence, men, women, infants and old people who are not "productive" are considered as expendable as an unwanted litter of kittens. We have devalued human life in a misguided attempt to value equally all forms of life. Nowhere is this more apparent than in the matter of abortion. And I say, "Zygotes are people, too!"

Jesus didn't die for kittens or cuddly puppies. He died for men and women and boys and girls who have the awesome power of choice and can reject or accept His offer of grace. One of the tragic consequences of abortion is that the right to choose is denied the principle character in this drama.

I'm sorry Mom, but you're not the principle character in this drama. You're in the supporting cast. Daddy's on stage, too, but the baby's the star. But in millions of cases, the star never has a chance to make an entrance – or a choice – or a difference.

I pray to be able to say with compassion, as Jesus did for those who aborted His life, *Father, forgive them, for they know not what they do.* (Luke 23:34)

Take Out The Garbage *1/24 – January 24*

The strength of the laborers is failing and there is so much rubbish that we are not able to build. (Nehemiah. 4:10)

A frequent request heard around most households is "Take out the garbage." It's a never-ending chore that's seldom appreciated for its importance to the health and sanity of everyone in the house.

I, for one, am grateful for the garbage collectors or sanitary engineers, or whatever is currently politically correct to call them. They do us all a great service by taking all of that stuff someplace other than where we live.

Some years ago a barge carrying 3000 tons of garbage left New York harbor. Its usual dumping site was full, so after two unsuccessful attempts on the East Coast, it sailed to New Orleans, where they threatened to call out the National Guard to prevent the release of its cargo. It then sailed south and was rejected by Mexico and Belize. It finally returned to where it came from and found a suitable spot to dump its very foul smelling load.

We all have the same problem: what do you do with the rubbish of life? When Israel was rebuilding the wall of Jerusalem they came to the point of having to deal with the rubbish. This is a spiritual problem, too. There must be a way for me to systematically dispose of the accumulated rubbish in my life or I will be consumed by it and my growth will cease.

What is spiritual garbage? It consists of several things:

1. Un-consumed things. I'm exposed to an incredible amount of teaching, most of which I receive gladly. If I don't take it in and respond to it, it can spoil and become a source of ungodly condemnation to me.

2. Broken things. Broken vows, broken relationships and broken dreams can contaminate my life. And broken vows to me can taint my life with bitterness.

3. Rotten things. My actions and words can stink of the awful presence of sin. Death, decay, and rottenness follow sin wherever it goes. Sin contaminates the best of intentions and kills the seeds of abundance in me.

4. Packaging. I must learn the difference between product and package. Truth is what I need, but sometimes I'm enamored by the package it comes in. This may be a person, an experience, or a tradition, etc. which I may need to let go of in order to retain the truth that the Spirit brought to me in that package.

So, it's time to take out the garbage! And we've found a place that will accept our garbage – all of it. We can dispose of it at the cross, and then rise up to worship Him Whose blood can keep us clean and growing.

January 25 – 1/25 **Heavenly Seed**

You have been born again not of seed, which is perishable but imperishable, that is, through the living and abiding word of God. (I Peter 1:23)

The Scripture speaks of the new life, which we have in Jesus as being born again, or born from above or newborn. The writer says that the seed that conceived us and brought us new life was no perishable or corruptible seed.

The seed of life that came to birth in us was not conveyed by relationship with any earthly agent – not the church, not an organization, not a pastor, not a father or mother. I am newborn by a heavenly seed, and the newborn me is a glorious and often troubling combination of flesh and spirit.

In a sense, the church is just the stable in which this "virgin birth" took place. It provides shelter and warmth and interaction with those who come to share the glory but I am not newborn because of a relationship with a church, any more than Jesus was born because He was in a stable.

Years ago I applied for a passport to travel to the Middle East. The people at the agency asked me for a birth certificate. It took some doing to get it because of some difficulty in the courthouse back in Illinois, but it finally came through.

For a while I wondered if they would ever come up with it and I felt as though I was being treated as a nonentity. I wondered why they needed a birth certificate to tell whether I existed or not. I am! That should be proof enough.

Many Christians can't produce a certificate of their new birth. They don't remember details like some people do, or exactly when it happened. Some say, "Well, if you don't remember when it happened, it probably didn't."

That response is sort of stupid. I don't remember details of my natural birth either but I'm alive. What if we insisted that everyone be able to come up with details of their natural birth from the baby's point of view before they were accepted as a living being?

How do I know I was born? I know I was born because I'm alive, not because I can document the details for you. In the same way I know I am born again, not because I can remember the time and the place, but because I'm alive to spiritual things. I am alive to God. I love the family of God. I worship in spirit and in truth – that's how I know I was born again.

Incidentally, I do remember the time and place of my new birth, but that's not what proves it happened. I know I was newborn because I'm alive!

The Shaking — *1/26 – January 26*

A few weeks ago an earthquake, centered on the Central Coast, did some damage and there were two lives lost. It measured 6.5 on the Richter scale.

Just a few days later in Iran, there was a quake of the same magnitude of 6.5 that, incredibly, took the lives of more than 20,000 people. What a tragedy. We sent massive aid to that country which hasn't been a friend in the recent past. But it was the time to reach with tangible love to the dear Iranian people.

Every year there are about 500,000 detectable seismic disturbances in the earth's crust. Approximately 100,000 of these can be felt and about 1,000 of them cause damage of some kind. An earthquake is a particularly frightening occurrence because that which we assumed was stable, which we have built our homes and lives upon, proves to be wholly undependable as a foundation.

A primitive tribe on the Satpura plateau of India responds to an earthquake strangely. The men of the tribe go outside and drive nails into the earth to make it firm again. I've had the same feeling after an earthquake – like everything nailed down is coming loose. But there are times when the earth is quite still and my life is shaking with emotional and spiritual tremors.

Hebrews 12:26, 27 describe this shaking: *Yet once more will I make to tremble, not only the earth, but also the heavens. This means that in this shaking all that is not permanent will be removed, that is, everything that is merely made, and only unshakable things will remain.*

There is a shaking that's not sent to destroy us, but to establish our lives upon things that are not "merely made" – things that can't be shaken. The quaking helps discern the difference between the firm and the flimsy, the eternal and the temporary.

For me this shaking hasn't been a jolting 8.2-on-the-Richter-scale earthquake. It's been more like the shaking I did when I was a kid in a sand pile or at the beach. I'd take a piece of screen wire and sift the sand through it. As I shook the screen, the smaller particles would fall through and the larger pieces would remain on top.

That's what happens in a steady shaking that sees many small things fall through, so to speak, and we're left with that which has eternal substance. And that's a very good thing!

Incidentally, God chooses the size of the holes in the screen; I don't get to do that. I don't fear that, because I know that the hand that made the sifter – and holds it – and shakes it – is the good hand of my good Lord!

At a recent conference in the Midwest on Worship in the Church, the floor was opened for comments. One man waved his hand frantically to get the moderator's attention. "There's one thing about our worship service which really bugs me," he complained. "To me it's like fingernails being scraped across a blackboard."

"What's that?" the leader cautiously asked, fully expecting him to say something about new fangled songs or loud instruments. But it wasn't one of these issues at all. "The announcements," he said. "I just hate it when the mood of worship is spoiled with all those announcements." Heads bobbed in agreement all around the room. Announcements were out of favor in that corner of the world, no question about it.

We have similar concerns in this corner of the world. You're soaring above the clouds on Sunday, your wings catching the strong breeze of the Spirit carrying you upward with "God of Wonders" and then, thud… "The Neighborhood Outreach Dinner will be on Monday…" and you're back to a world of flesh – and meetings.

The announcements do seem like a mundane moment wedging its way into an hour of inspiration. But the announcements are one of those places where the rubber of the church's worship life meets the earthy road of the details of its common life. In fact, with the dreaded announcements, the church is expressing in its worship (not apart from its worship) one of the most basic and yet most profound truths about the character of the God we worship: "The Word became flesh and dwelt among us…"

Worship is inspiring. But think about what that means. Inspire means to breathe in. The opposite of inspire is expire, which means to breathe out. But you can't continually breathe in. You have to breathe out, too. If you breathe out without breathing in you die. But if you only breathe in, you also die.

What's that got to do with announcements? The events that make it through the screening process to be presented to your eyes and ears, and hopefully your heart, are part of breathing out the life of the Body of Christ.

I suspect that the Body of Christ, in America especially, has been doing too much breathing in and not enough breathing out. It could also be said that we eat too much spiritual food and don't exercise our muscles enough in spiritual productivity. And we know all too well what that can lead too.

Faith without works is dead, says James 2:17. Could it be that faith comes to death by suffocation or obesity? I wonder…

Clap Your Hands! — *1/28 – January 28*

Psalm 47:1 says, *Clap your hands, all you nations; shout to God with cries of joy!*

The hands are used for all kinds of expression, but the highest use of these extensions of our personalities is in worship. There's a kinship between the physical and the spiritual that's obviously involved in praise. It has always been and will always be so.

Clapping the hands to praise music or offering holy applause to the Lord are acceptable forms of worship. But they are more than that. Clapping hands is an object lesson, a parable, about the Body of Christ.

First, when I clap my hands, two parts of my body agree to meet at a certain place. That's basic, but it's important. You'd have a problem if you set about to clap, and your hands didn't meet. Embarrassing! When we worship, parts of the Body of Christ from all over agree to meet at a certain place to the glory of God. We really do need each other to make a joyful noise to the Lord.

Second, opposite parts of the body agree to meet. My two hands are not the same; they are mirror images of each other. One is left and the other is right but they agree to let their differences fit together to make a sound for the glory of God in worship. We're not all the same, but our differences enhance the expression of our worship.

Third, I notice that when most people clap, their stronger hand is lower than the weaker one in order to make the sound of clapping. This is also a picture of our coming together. Submitting one to another in love makes for a joyful noise in the ears of the Father.

Fourth, one cannot clap with clenched fists. The two different parts of my body that have agreed to meet to make a clap must have an open relationship with each other. Otherwise, there is little expression. An open hand is the expression of an open heart. If there are any clenched fists among us, the joyful noise will be muffled, as surely as if we tried to clap with our fists.

When our kids were young we used to play "patty cake" with them. "Patty cake, patty cake, baker's man. Bake me a cake as fast as you can." It was an exercise in coordination as my big hands met the tiny hands of our children.

I've seen young people play a similar, though much faster and more intricate, game with each other's hands. They stand facing each other and, with perfect timing, do a rhythmic exercise with each other's hands.

I know this sounds ridiculous, but if you and I could ever be that together in purpose and expression, it would bring great glory to our Lord.

This was a favorite expression of my dear grandmother. Whenever anything unusual happened she would say, "Well, my stars, what do you think of that?"

She was a delightful lady and a devoted follower of Jesus, but this expression had fastened itself in her vocabulary. I never thought about its origin then but I'm thinking about it now. It's from the world of charts and observations of the stars called astrology that supposedly shapes our lives. If something out of the ordinary occurs, it was "my stars" that caused it, so they say.

Does it concern you, as it does me, to learn that one-third of Americans believe this astrological gibberish, that even presidents of our nation in the past have consulted astrologers. I can't dismiss this possibility as being simply an amusing diversion; there's more to it than that. The force behind it has an ancient feud with Almighty God and is committed to destroy anything and everything that bears His blessing.

What does the Bible say about this? It's not silent on the matter. Deuteronomy 18:9-13 says it clearly: *When you enter the land which the LORD your God gives you, you shall not learn to imitate the detestable things of those nations. There shall not be found among you anyone who makes his son or daughter pass through the fire, one who uses divination, one who practices witchcraft, or one who interprets omens (an astrologer), or a sorcerer, or one who casts a spell, or a medium, or a spiritist, or one who calls up the dead. For whoever does these things is detestable to the LORD; and because of these detestable things the LORD your God will drive them out before you. You shall be blameless before the LORD your God.* There it is!

This passage gives us a clue to the massive conflict in the Middle East today. The big question is, "Whose land is it anyhow?" This passage says that God gave it to Israel, not because they were so good, but because the inhabitants of Canaan practiced astrology, witchcraft, and other satanic, Babylonish rituals; things that were an abomination to the LORD. Therefore, they lost their right to the land. The message of this passage is: If a nation condones and practices things that are detestable to the LORD, they will not enjoy their land for long. "Therefore, the LORD drove them out!" says the Scripture.

Some of the greatest losers in history have been devotees of astrology. Most notable among them was Adolph Hitler. He consulted the stars daily in the management of the Third Reich and the conduct of the war in Europe. We all know what a howling success that was.

Incidentally, about the stars and my dear grandmother's expression, "My stars" – they are hers, and mine, and yours, and His. We are fellow heirs with Jesus of all things – and that includes the stars.

Remember Who Made You — *1/30 – January 30*

Ecclesiastes 12:1 says this: *Remember now thy Creator in the days of thy youth.* A loose translation: "remember who made you while you're still young enough for it make a difference."

How different would your life be today if you'd been conscious of your Creator's presence when you were young. It's significant that Solomon places such emphasis on being aware of Creator God while we are young, in light of the overt attempts by secular society to get us to forget Him in our youth.

If there was no creation, there is no God, and our destiny is left to the winds of fate, or worse yet, to our own devices. If there was no creation, there is no redemption, and we are lost in our sins. While our faith does not rest on the word of scientists, even believing ones, it is good to know that thinking men are reaching the same conclusions that simple faith has led us to embrace; that *in the beginning God created the heavens and the earth.* (Genesis 1:1)

I heard one astronomer say recently, "It appears now that scientists have been like a group of mountain climbers, searching for the origin of the universe. They have painfully scaled a series of difficult peaks and as they ascend their final peak, they find a group of theologians who've been there for centuries."

There are many sincere men and women who've thoughtfully searched the record of the physical universe for answers to honest questions. We could learn much from them. I pray that a climate of humility and openness will prevail in the interface between the scientific community and the church.

The ancient Egyptians believed that a flat world rested on four pillars of stone. The Hindus believed that a flat world rested on the back of a huge elephant, and the elephant stood on the back of an enormous turtle, and the turtle stood on an immense coiled snake. But we are asked to believe some equally incredible theories that involve spontaneous generation and lower life forms becoming higher life forms. It does require a lot of faith doesn't it?

About the same time the Egyptians were talking about the flat earth resting on pillars of stone, Isaiah was saying things like, *He rides upon the circle of the earth,* (Isaiah 40:22) and *He stretches the north out over the empty place and hangs the earth on nothing.* (Job 26:7) I'll never forget the first time I saw a picture of earth from space. There it was, an orb hanging on nothing, and an empty space above the north, just like the Word said five thousand years ago.

I can get very excited about creation, but I must remind myself that God's greatest work was not the universe. All of that He created by the words of His mouth and with His fingers. But He couldn't redeem us so easily. This required the shedding of blood, and the death of His only begotten Son.

January 31 – 1/31 *Taught Of The Lord*

All your children shall be taught of the Lord, and great shall be the peace of your children. (Isaiah 54:13)

For many years I've taken great comfort from this promise for my children. But something about it began to trouble me the other day as I was praying for them. I've always assumed that this promise meant that God was going to teach them – "they will be taught of the Lord." I found, however, that all of the translators don't agree on the wording here. While many do say they "shall be taught by the Lord," some of them say they "shall learn of the Lord." That's different! This difference may not be significant but it's interesting.

If my children are going to be taught by the Lord, then why should I worry about them learning anything? On the other hand, if it means simply that they shall learn of Him, then someone has to do the teaching. This is, in fact, closer to the whole counsel of God on the matter. God has chosen to do all of His work here on earth through human instruments. To say that our children will be taught of the Lord without dedicated teachers is to misunderstand the intent of this and other passages in the Scripture. Thank God for teachers!

What does it mean to be a teacher? Well, I learned early on that one is not a teacher unless something is learned. Wherever, whenever, however, anything is learned, teaching is happening. If it happens through you, you're a teacher. In the nursery, or with two-year-olds, or sixth graders, or senior citizens, if something is communicated, received, and added to another, you're a teacher. And sometimes the only thing learned is love.

To be a vessel through whom the Lord teaches is one of life's great joys. But to be one who teaches others to know God as He truly is – and not as the world has perceived Him – is a joy beyond comprehension.

Here how God says it in Jeremiah 9:23 and 24:

"Let not the wise man boast of his wisdom or the strong man boast of his strength or the rich man boast of his riches, but let him who boasts boast about this: that he understands and knows me, that I am the LORD, who exercises kindness, justice and righteousness on earth, for in these I delight," declares the LORD.

Proverbs 9:10 says, *The fear of the LORD is the beginning of wisdom, and knowledge of the Holy One is understanding.*

All your children shall be taught of the Lord, and great shall be the peace of your children. (Isaiah 54:13)

And when they had been brought safely through, we found that the island was called Malta. And the natives showed us extraordinary kindness; for because of the rain that had set in and the cold, they kindled a fire and received us all. (Acts 28:1, 2)

This scene takes place after Paul's shipwreck in the Mediterranean and, while I can't be sure, it seems to me that it must have been February. Maybe not, but the words "rain" and "cold" give us a clue.

A person needs extraordinary kindness in February. Garfield, that feline philosopher, calls February "the armpit of the year." It couldn't be – armpits are warm. In reporting a cold wave that swept down from Alaska, a newsman said, "If the year were taken to court, February would be the charge against it." February gets no respect. Thankfully it only has 28 days except for Leap Year.

February has always been cold and rainy or snowy. Growing up in Illinois exposed me to its maximum bleakness. And twenty-five years on the north coast of California did nothing to change my mind about this month. While we're grateful for the rain, couldn't it be a little less like all the other Februarys I've known? I suppose that into each life some February must fall.

My complaint is tongue-in-cheek; February does have its good points. I'm alive in it, for one. Then there's Valentine's Day. Without the warmth generated by millions people on the 14th, February would not survive until March. And many famous Americans were born in February, like George Washington, Abraham Lincoln, Erma Bombeck and Tim Howard.

The name of this month comes from Roman times. There was a Roman festival called Februa, which was for purification. The word februa means expiation or cleansing. Evidently, there was so much revelry in January that they needed a special time of austerity and discipline to keep from fouling up the whole year. This is what February was to the Romans.

The Book of Romans was written to Christians in a culture that gave February its name. *Let us therefore lay aside the deeds of darkness and put on the armor of light. Let us behave properly as in the day, not in carousing and drunkenness, not in sexual promiscuity and sensuality, not in strife and jealousy.* (Romans 13:11-13)

So we lay aside the deeds of darkness. This is februa, expiation – atonement, and it is a prelude to the refreshing renewal that comes with repentance and forgiveness. The dark skies that hung over the necessary Cross of Jesus gave way to the rising of the Son of Righteousness.

It's that way with February, too. The cold, rain and snow of this bleak month are necessary parts of the sunshine, warmth, and of Springtime and harvest. This almost makes February bearable.

"When was the last time you had a good conversation about sin?" Who said that? Was it a TV evangelist, or the Pope? Or was it a pastor? It was none of the above. It's from an editorial in the Wall Street Journal of all places.

That's a good question. We don't talk about sin much for fear of being prudish or intolerant. But this is a time for rethinking matters of sin and embracing wisdom of holiness. It is, after all, wise to be holy.

The above-mentioned Journal article titled "The Joy of What?" was about the popular book "The Joy of Sex." Somebody should write a book and call it "The Joy of Holiness." It would be much closer to the truth. It's great joy to worship the Lord and love each other in the beauty and wisdom of holiness.

The awakening of the moral sense of the Wall Street Journal perhaps has more to do with the bottom line financially, than any religious convictions. Sin is costly; it eats into the profits of corporations and kingdoms. Scandals are very upsetting to stockholders and citizens alike, and it just isn't fiscally or politically correct to get caught in the act of indulging one's baser desires.

The church hasn't been silent on sin but it hasn't been heard. Its voice is like that of a parent warning kids of the dangers of substance abuse or sexual sin. Parents speak but are not heard – until the consequences of sin are felt. Sadly, the law of sowing and reaping is the ultimate teacher for kids and kingdoms.

We've seen the scandals of church leaders, athletic wonders, media stars, and other public figures. I grieve for the jokes and slurs about gifted people who were once identified with integrity and morality. Comedians have a field day when the moral and the mighty are fallen.

It isn't comedians who are laughing at God, however. It's anyone who thinks they are exempt from moral law because they have the privilege of power of one kind or another. These are the ones who laugh at God – and He will not be mocked. God doesn't have to do anything but withhold His blessing for their house of straw to crumble in the inevitable storm.

Psalm 29:2 says this: *Ascribe to the LORD the glory due His name; worship the LORD in the splendor of His holiness.*

I take from that the sense that holiness is a splendorous, beautiful thing; a highly sought after, immensely desirable, joyous – and a wise thing.

Is it that to you?

Where Sin Abounds... *2/3 – February 3*

Once upon a time there was a sweet little girl named Karla. Life was good for Karla, her mommy and her daddy until she was five-years old. That's when daddy left. Then life began to turn very dark for Karla and her mom. By the time Karla was a teenager her mom was a prostitute and taught Karla to turn the tricks of that trade.

She began drinking and selling herself to anyone with money to pay for her services. She became part of the wild drug culture of the Southwest. When she was in her early twenties, she and her boyfriend planned to steal a motorcycle and things got radically out of hand. In the melee that followed the failed robbery attempt, Karla brutally murdered two people with a pickaxe.

She and her friend were arrested, tried, and sentenced to death for their horrible crimes. Karla was taken to the Texas State Women's Prison to await execution. She entered prison an unrepentant, hardened criminal. People said that if anyone ever deserved the death penalty, it was Karla.

A few months after she entered prison she got bored sitting alone in her cell and decided to join the rest of the inmates at a puppet show put on by a local church. She was touched by the love she saw in the people that did the show. She stole a Bible, not realizing that they were provided free to all inmates.

Back in her cell, she read it. And for the first time in her memory, she wept uncontrollably as a ray of healing love-light penetrated the hardness of her heart. Karla became a truly repentant new creation in Jesus Christ.

Karla's story became national news and Larry King interviewed her for two hours. My wife and I watched in amazement as this articulate, humble, radiant sister in Jesus told of her transformation. "Jesus has already saved my life," she said, "so it doesn't matter what happens to my body."

"Everybody gets born again on death row," people said. But Karla lived her new life for fourteen years, ministering to other inmates and impressing even her captors with her grace and peace under the sentence of death.

I can't remember being so impressed with evidence of God's redeeming grace. We prayed for God to spare her life, reasoning that her new life would do more good than her death. All appeals failed and on February 3, 1998, Karla Faye Tucker was given a lethal injection. She died with her eyes wide open and a smile on her face, anticipating seeing her Redeemer face to face.

This is not about capital punishment; it's about capital redemption. It's about abundant life that survives lethal injection. "If Jesus can save me, He can save anybody," Karla said. The soul that sins shall die, God says. But, as Karla knows, where sin abounds – grace much, much more abounds!

February 4 – 2/4 *IWNDR*

I never thought I would do it – but I did. When I recently purchased a car I decided to take the plunge. I bought some of those personalized license plates. My wife and I discussed what we wanted on them and we both agreed that our choice expressed something about how we've come to view life. We decided on "I WNDR" (it's wonder, not wander), and for our other car "I WNDR 2".

"What does that mean?" you ask. Well it means that a sense of wonder is very important to me and I want to encourage a wonder view of life in everyone. When I say, "I wonder!" I don't mean it in the skeptical, questioning sense in which it is often used, as in, "Sometimes I wonder about him!" Or, "I wonder if he'll make it." There's not a trace of skepticism in my use of the phrase. As a matter of fact, it's probably just the opposite. It's more like openness – simplicity, curiosity, when approaching any person, place, or thing.

I wonder a lot about God; what's He really like? He's not being represented very well these days. But He can be known in increasing degrees of intimacy. It's also true that how I think about God is probably the most revealing thing about me or anyone else, for that matter. I love to meditate upon His nature. The best thoughts I think are about Him. He is wonder-full.

I wonder about His creation. "Mother Nature," is said to be the force behind everything in the natural world. But all that is complex and ordered and beautiful and fruitful is, in fact, the Father's Nature revealed in ways we can understand. There's so much to wonder about in the whole wide universe. It's wonder-full.

Things are a wonder. We often protest the preoccupation with "things." But things are a part of life on planet earth, and they reveal the infinite character and variety of life as God has given it to us. It's only when we see a thing in a very limited way and focus on the created thing and not the Creator that we get into difficulty.

A flower is a thing; a galaxy is a thing; a bird is a thing; a tree is a thing; a river is a thing; an ocean is a thing; a mountain is a thing, even a computer is a thing; but what things these are! They are wonder-full.

I pray that today you will be filled with a sense of wonder. If you can cultivate this sense of wonder you will never be bored.

IWNDR. Indeed, life is WNDRFL! I hope U WNDR 2.

Eden's Legacy — *2/5 – February 5*

The LORD God planted a garden eastward in Eden; and there He placed the man whom He had formed. A river flowed out of Eden to water the garden; and from there it divided and became four rivers, Pishon, Gihon, and the name of the third is Tigris; it flows east of Assyria. And the fourth river is the Euphrates. (Genesis 2:7-14)

According to this description, the Garden of Eden was probably located in the area just to the north of the Persian Gulf in the watershed of the Tigris and Euphrates rivers. That puts it in what is now Iraq.

In 1972 the oil producing countries of the Persian Gulf raised prices causing major panic and gas lines around the world. It was then that I began to see a connection between the huge deposits of oil in that region and the Garden of Eden. I have a theory about this whole scenario.

Here it is: since oil is a "fossil fuel," (made of organic substances subjected to time, heat, and pressure) and since the Garden of Eden was the plushest garden ever on the face of the earth, it makes sense to me that the oil beneath the region of the Persian Gulf may well be the fossilized Garden of Eden.

I can't prove that theory, but given the location furnished in Scripture it seems likely. The oil had to come from somewhere and where else on earth was as rich in organic material as this place.

So the oil that brought the world to the doorstep of the Gulf States may be from the Garden of Eden. God knew what He was doing when He planted the garden there. The scramble for the black gold of the region comes as no surprise to Him.

While oil is a powerful factor it today's world, it's not the most significant legacy of Eden. Something else came from the garden eastward in Eden that has impacted the entire human race millions of times more than oil. That legacy of Eden is sin.

Sin puts every, man, woman, and child in the place of needing a Savior. And as surely as God has made provision for the energy needs of the world with the deposit of oil beneath the sands of the Gulf States and elsewhere, He has made provision for man's need of forgiveness at the Cross of Jesus.

For God so loved the world (all of it) that He gave His only Son that whosoever (all races, colors, tribes, nations) believes in Him will not perish but have everlasting life. (John 3:16)

And that provision pre-dates Eden!

February 6 – 2/6 *Pleasant Boundaries*

Lord, you have assigned me my portion and my cup; you have made my lot secure. The boundary lines have fallen for me in pleasant places; surely I have a delightful inheritance. (Psalm 16:5, 6 NIV)

What's your favorite scripture verse? Chances are it's one that God made real to you in a crisis, which brought hope and comfort when you needed it most.

Sometimes the least likely passages are the source of strength. Take the psalmist David, for example. Can you guess what David's favorite Scripture was? Judging from the many references and the words he uses to describe his favorite theme, I'd say that Psalm 119 gives us a clue as to what it is.

Psalm 119 has 176 verses. Amazingly, each of the 176 verses makes some reference to the law of God. You get the idea that David's favorite portion of Scripture was the Law of God – the Commandments. He says as so in verse 97, *O how I love Thy law.*

This is what David refers to, or at least what it says to me, in Psalm 16 in the above mentioned verses... *the boundary lines have fallen for me in pleasant places; surely I have a delightful inheritance.*

How does one come to love the Law – the boundary lines? How does one begin to see that they are fallen in pleasant places and that life within those boundaries is delightful? The Law seems so restrictive, so rigid, so Old Testament. "I gotta be me! You can't tell me what I can or can't do!"

I grew up in the Midwest, in the era of the steam engine. I have fond memories of standing beside a huge black beauty, making all sorts of strange noises. I often watched in awe as the engineer pushed a lever and the huge giant breathing dragon began to move.

But the train couldn't go anywhere it wanted to go. It couldn't go out across the cornfield; it couldn't go down the busy highway. If the train were to arrive safely at its destination, it had to stay on the track because the train was made for the track. But the track is so restrictive, so limiting.

But here's the good part; the track is also made for the train. It makes the way smooth. The train was made for the track, and the track was made for the train. The Law wasn't made for God, but for man. It's how life works best. It's how a society prospers. It's how the weak are protected, and the strong restrained. And it is "our schoolmaster" to bring us to Jesus.

If I am ever to love the Law, as David did, I must see that I was created for it, and it was created for me. It's my friend. It comes from a God of infinite goodness, who loves me eternally, and has a plan for my life that doesn't include the ravages of sin.

Pleasant boundaries – delightful inheritance – *O, how I love Thy law!*

Until He Comes **2/7 – *February 7***

Once again, by grand design, we're brought to the sacred table of communion to not only remember, but to contemplate with deepest awe and proclaim the Cross upon which Jesus died for us all. I say "by grand design" because of the instructions the Holy Spirit gave to Paul in I Corinthians 11:24-26:

The Lord Jesus in the night in which He was betrayed took bread; and when He had given thanks, He broke it, and said, "This is My body, which is for you; do this in remembrance of Me." In the same way He took the cup also, after supper, saying, "This cup is the new covenant in My blood; do this, as often as you drink it, in remembrance of Me." For as often as you eat this bread and drink the cup, you proclaim the Lord's death until He comes.

"Until He comes," did you catch that? God has ordained that we periodically proclaim the truth of the His death until He comes back to earth. It must be extremely important to God for Him to establish such a pattern for us.

He didn't say, "read your Bible until I come." He didn't say, "Sing until I come." He didn't say, "have good Christian fellowship until I come." These are good things that we should continue to do until he comes. But His special emphasis is upon proclaiming His death until He comes back.

What are we to think about the Cross? What are we to proclaim about it? The Cross is a somewhat fuzzy concept to Christians today. The Cross is not about fun and enjoyment. It's about sacrifice and death – and then – resurrection.

It's often been said that we are at a crossroads, meaning that we have a choice to make. Will we go one way or the other? But it's often more than just your average crossroad in life. It may really be Cross Road that we must choose. It is the way of the Cross, or the status quo.

The Cross Road isn't for thrill seekers. It's not for the faint of heart, the casual spectator, or the curious. It is a narrow way and not all will choose to travel there. But, as the old song says, "The way of the Cross leads home."

And wherever He entered villages, or cities, or countryside, they were laying the sick in the marketplaces, and entreating Him that they might just touch the fringe of His cloak; and as many as touched it were being cured. (Mark 6:56)

"The marketplace" is a common phrase heard in sermons that encourage Christians to get out into the world and touch people with the love of Jesus. But what does this expression mean in our time and our town.

The word "marketplace" conjures up thoughts of a supermarket or the mall in our minds today. That's not far from reality but its actual meaning is much broader. It's the Greek word agora, a place where people meet.

The agora was the scene of action for any town. Business was conducted there, (Matt. 20:3) debates were held there, (Acts 17:17;) judicial proceedings were held there, (Acts 16:19;) and children played there, (Luke 7:32.)

Jesus spent lots time in marketplaces because that's where the people were. When He came to the villages, people knew where He could be found so they brought their sick people to the marketplace. His life and ministry was primarily there, and not in the synagogues of His day.

I've been to marketplaces in Cairo, Egypt; Amman, Jordan; Beirut, Lebanon, and Old Jerusalem in Israel. They're fascinating places. The narrow passages and teeming crowds make it impossible to navigate without being jostled about by the masses. Marketplaces are havens for pickpockets and thugs. It's risky to venture into this strange world. But that's where the people are.

There's a condition that affects some people called agoraphobia. It's from the Greek "agora" – the marketplace, and "phobos" – fear. It's the fear of the marketplace; fear of contact with people who may cause pain. My heart goes out to those who live in the nightmare of agoraphobia. May the Lord give them the comfort of His presence.

Many Christians suffer from a spiritual form of this malady. We love the comfort and security of our home and our church. We've grown accustomed to the place and the people, and things are predictably safe. But when we think about going to the streets or the mall or next door to share Jesus' love, we have a spiritual panic attack. It's risky business to step from the safety of the sanctuary to the mania of the marketplace. But that's where the people are – the people who need Jesus.

We'd like it very much if they all came to our church, but that's not likely. That would be nice and safe for us, but not for them. Jesus went where people were and if we are to be followers of Him – we will, too.

He said, *Go into all the world and proclaim the good news to everybody... and I will be with you, even to the end of the age.* (Matthew 28:19, 20)

Dedication *2/9 – February 9*

We say, "She's really dedicated!" An athlete proclaims, "I want to dedicate this game to my mother." "Is this a dedicated line?" asks the computer technician about to connect a modem to a telephone line. "Today we dedicate this building," says the pastor at a ceremony for a new building.

What does it mean to dedicate? "To set apart and consecrate to God or to a sacred purpose; to devote to a sacred use, by a solemn act," says the dictionary. Dedication can't be done in isolation; dedication must be to something or someone, and for something or someone; an object and a purpose are required. As Christians, we don't just dedicate a thing; we dedicate it to God for His sacred purpose.

The origin of the word as it is used in Scripture is even more emphatic. It means, "Cursed in the Name of God!" In other words, whatever I dedicate to God for His purpose is cursed for any other use. Dedication is costly.

Louis XI of France had a solemn deed drawn up in 1478. It was signed, sealed, and recorded. In it he conveyed the entire section of Boulogne, France to the Virgin Mary, but he reserved for his own use, all the revenues thereof. He deluded himself with the idea that he had done a generous thing, a pious thing, when he had done nothing at all. It had cost him nothing.

As King David said when he bought the land upon which the temple would eventually be built, *I will not offer to the Lord that which costs me nothing!* (II Samuel 24:24)

A judge, of the US District Court some years ago, ruled that the Salvation Army erred when it fired a twenty-eight year old employee after she admitted using the Army's photocopier to reproduce pages of satanic rituals. The judge ruled that her Constitutional Rights had been violated, and ordered the Army to pay her $1,250,000. The photocopier was dedicated to the Lord.

Sometimes it seems that the bad guys are winning. I played basketball in high school, and when we played on our home court, the crowd cheered us even when we were behind. But when we went on the road, we could be twenty points ahead, and it seemed like we were losing; nobody cheered.

This isn't our home court. We're on the road here. Even the referees seem to favor the home crowd. This is not a friendly place for the people of God. Only dedication to God's purpose will win the victory and see us home.

Exodus 32:29 says this: *Then Moses said, "Dedicate yourselves today to the LORD - in order that He may bestow a blessing upon you today."*

February 10 – 2/10 **Wonder**

They were filled with wonder and amazement... (Acts 3:10) The occasion was the healing of a lame man at the gate of the temple, but these words describe something of great value to us in our day.

For the most part, we've lost a sense of wonder. We've been exposed to so many marvelous things in our lifetime that nothing seems to amaze us anymore. I was in Bishop California some time ago. Bishop is over 4000 feet above sea level and the air is crystal clear. I asked if we could go out away from the lights of the town and see the stars Saturday night.

So we went part way up White Mountain to about 8,000 feet. I'd forgotten how marvelous the sight of the heavens really is. Such magnificence could never be seen from the Valley. I was filled with wonder at the sight of thousands of stars and the bright cloud of the Milky Way!

I wonder a lot. I don't mean that in the sense of doubting, or suspecting as in, "I wonder about that." I mean that lots of things stir me deeply with wonder and amazement. I've even felt that I was a little strange, at times, for being caught up in wonder over something that most normal people take for granted.

It's easy to be amazed by a miracle. Any rare or unexpected thing excites wonder in most people. But it's a special gift to be stirred to wonder over familiar things. Jesus has this gift and would give it to anyone who would receive it. He was often filled with wonder, even though He created all that is He still wondered at a child, the lilies of the field, the birds of the air, etc.

I wonder about words. They're wonderful! They're like little boxes that contain truth. It's fun to work with them, turn them around and see them from every conceivable angle, and then see them appear on paper, or hear them uttered through yet another marvel – speech.

I wonder about things – created things. I wonder about their purpose and their value in the eyes their Creator. I wonder about atoms and molecules and planets and stars and galaxies. I'm amazed that God has given us such abundant resources and has trusted us to make good things out of what He has given. I wonder at the gift of thought; God gave me a brain that's created in such a way that it can wonder.

I wonder about God, most of all. What He is like has captured my interest and inspired me with awe. I understand the heart of the psalmist when he said, *O LORD, our Lord, how majestic is Your name in all the earth!* (Psalm 8:9)

"Majestic" is a wonder-word. His majesty is amazing! But I'm also amazed that God could express Himself completely in the form of a man in Jesus Christ and yet still be the majestic God Who fills the universe.

Anything Goes! *2/11 – February 11*

Forty, or so, years ago there was a popular song that went like this: "In olden days a glimpse of stocking was looked on as something shocking, now heaven knows, anything goes."

That was then – this is now, and things have gotten worse than our ancestors thought possible. Now everything goes, and not much of value is left.

A few years ago a previous President was suspected of having numerous sexual liaisons with women in the course of his time in public office. Even though we didn't really know anything but what the news media told us, the nation reacted in some very interesting and revealing ways.

A senator said, "Even if he did all that he's being accused of, he's still a great leader and a good man." Am I missing something here? How can one be "good" and do all of that stuff? And how can one lead a nation on the high road of truth and peace while personally walking the low road of deception?

Another statement: "I don't ask my dentist, or my plumber, or my mechanic about his sex life so why should I care about the President's?" Excuse me! I'd like to know if my plumber might be trusted in my house while I'm gone.

It's like this episode in the life of our United States has put our society through a moral CAT-scan. The diagnosis: a terminal case of Moral Relativism. What is moral relativism? Well, it's the idea that what is right and wrong varies from situation to situation. We once called it "situation ethics."

Several years ago, I was driving to the office one morning, listening to the radio when the traffic report came from a helicopter vantage point. He said these words, which I wrote down immediately: "The signal lights at the intersection of Chestnut and Tulare are green in all directions."

That dangerous situation is upon us. Everybody has a green light to do whatever. That's the danger of moral relativism. But when our lives intersect – and they surely will – and no one stops, someone gets hurt.

An encouraging word from the song I mentioned at the beginning of today's meditation: "Now Heaven knows." God does know what's going on and He is poised to come to a world where anything goes – and save us from ourselves.

February 12 – 2/12 *Happy Birthday, Abe*

February is the month in which we celebrate the birthdays of two of our greatest Presidents, George Washington, the Father of our Country, and Abraham Lincoln, the Great Emancipator. Today is Abe Lincoln's birthday.

I'm more familiar with Abe Lincoln than I am Washington because my roots are in the heart of Illinois, The Land of Lincoln. A measure of the respect, which our family has for this man, is that we named our only son Lincoln.

It may come as a shock to realize that the man who could write the Second Inaugural Address and the Gettysburg Address had no more than four months of formal education. And this was in a one-room country schoolhouse where students ranged in age from 5 to 25.

When he was seven years old, his family was forced out of their home, and he had to work to help support them. At age nine, his mother died. At 22, he lost his job as a store clerk. He wanted to go to law school, but his education wasn't good enough. At 23, he went into debt to become a partner in a small store in New Salem, Illinois, just two miles from our first pastorate.

At 26, his business partner died, leaving him a huge debt. At 28, after courting a girl for four years, he asked her to marry him. She said no. At 37, on his third try, he was elected to Congress, but two years later, he failed to be re-elected. At 41, his four-year-old son died. At 45, he ran for the Senate and lost. At 47, he failed as the vice-presidential candidate. At 49, he ran for the Senate again, and lost. At 51, he was elected President of the United States. Some people get all the breaks.

In Lincoln's younger days, he served as a Captain in the militia during the Black Hawk Indian War. Because he was inexperienced in the formalities of military drill, he often blundered. Once, while marching a line of more than twenty men abreast, he came to a long fence with a single narrow gate.

For the life of him, Abe could not remember the proper command to get his company endwise so that it could go through the gate. Finally, as the troops neared the gate, Lincoln ordered. "This company is dismissed for two minutes. It will fall in again on the other side of the gate."

Abraham Lincoln was a man of faith and wisdom. He once said, "We have forgotten the gracious Hand which has preserved us in peace and multiplied and enriched and strengthened us, and have vainly imagined, in the deceitfulness of our hearts, that all these blessings were produced by some superior wisdom and virtue of our own." Forgive us, Lord.

Happy birthday, Mr. Lincoln.

Swifter, Higher, Stronger — *2/13 – February 13*

The Winter Olympics brought the world together in Salt Lake City in 2002 with the Olympic motto ringing in the ears of the contestants in the games — "Swifter, Higher, Stronger."

This lofty goal was to be assaulted on skis, skates, and sleds in the cold snows of the Wasatch Mountains and the icy arenas of the city. But one is compelled to ask, "Swifter, higher, stronger than what – or who?"

While we're encouraged to excel in the kingdom of God, we're not to strive to be swifter, higher, or stronger than another brother or sister. My measure of success isn't another person, but it's in overcoming my own limitations.

Speaking of the Olympics, perhaps you've heard of some of the more obscure events, or even participated in them yourself:

There are the "Pass-The-Buck Relays" where the baton of responsibility is passed from one person to another. This race began when Adam passed the baton to Eve and it hasn't slowed down since. The pass-the-buck relay ends only when someone takes the baton home, and claims it as his own.

In the swimming competition, there's the ever-popular "O-For-The-Good-Old-Days Backstroke." This was first performed by the entire Israelite nation. They'd come through the Red Sea without even getting wet. Then when things got rough, they longed for Egypt and began to execute this difficult maneuver, trying to get back into what God had delivered them out of.

How about the "False Conclusion Ski Jump." In this event contestants ski headlong down a long ramp of rumors and half-truths and leap to hasty conclusions. There's never been a lack of contestants. They line up for the chance to jump to conclusions.

Well, so much for Olympic silliness. It was the Olympics in Greece to which Paul referred in I Corinthians 9:25-27:

Everyone who competes in the games goes into strict training. They do it to get a crown that will not last; but we do it to get a crown that will last forever. Therefore I do not run like a man running aimlessly; I do not fight like a man beating the air. No, I beat my body and make it my slave so that after I have preached to others, I myself will not be disqualified for the prize.

Not by skis, skates or sleds – but by the power of the Holy Spirit, the grace of God, and the blood of Jesus, we will be swifter, reach higher and grow stronger than we have ever been before.

February 14 – 2/14 — *A Scrap of Paper*

Today is Valentine's Day. People send love notes to one another; some will be silly, some serious, but all will be sent to emulate a man named Valentine.

Valentine was a Roman follower of Christ, who lived in the 3rd century A.D. Emperor Claudius II martyred him in the persecution of Christians. Some years later, he was made a saint in the Roman Catholic Church.

Another martyr named Valentine, who was bishop of Terni, a region in present-day central Italy, has also been suggested as the inspiration for our modern celebration of Valentine's Day.

It's interesting that both of these men named Valentine were martyred for their faith in Jesus Christ. The wonder is, not that they were willing to die, but that there was something – Someone – for whom they were willing to die.

There's not much that people are willing to die for these days. Oh, we're quite willing to let someone else die – like unborn babies – but we know little of the selfless love and dedication of the namesake of Valentine's Day.

Love has been trivialized in our society, and we've been affected by it more than we know. Love songs (I call them "luv songs") fill the air with distorted messages of the meaning of true love. One can't speak of love's trivialization without recognizing its implications in marriage today.

"Nothing but a scrap of paper – that's all a marriage license is!" This kind of extravagant statement is a symptom of the spirit of our age. With increasing frequency, marriage is being put down, cast aside, and overturned.

But wait just matrimonial a minute! Aren't scraps of paper important? Is it not one of the marks of civilized men that they protect themselves against fraud and savagery by mere scraps of paper?

Sure, a wedding license is a scrap of paper, but so in an employment contract, your paycheck, a twenty-dollar bill, the deed to your home, the Constitution of the United States, and the Bible you hold in your hand. Scraps of paper – indeed! But there is authority and power in the paper.

Here's Gods idea of marriage: *Let marriage be held in honor esteemed worthy, precious, of great price and especially dear - in all things*. (Hebrews 13:4 Amp)

Shalom, Jerusalem — *2/15 – February 15*

I'd like to tell you about my most favorite place on earth, Jerusalem. I've been there many times and hope to return there soon. This city is the earth's center of gravity. Not a day passes but that it's on the front pages of the newspapers of the world. Jerusalem is like no other city on earth.

That isn't just my opinion. Apparently, it's how God feels, too. I found these expressions of just how significant Jerusalem is to the heart of God.

In this house, and in Jerusalem, which I have chosen out of all tribes of Israel, will I put my name for ever: (II Kings 21:7)

As the mountains are round about Jerusalem, so the Lord is round about his people from henceforth even forever. (Psalm 125:2)

If I forget thee, O Jerusalem, let my right hand forget her cunning. If I do not remember thee, let my tongue cleave to the roof of my mouth; if I prefer not Jerusalem above my chief joy. (Psalm 137:5, 6)

Come ye, and let us go up to the mountain of the Lord, to the house of the God of Jacob; and he will teach us of his ways, and we will walk in his paths: for out of Zion shall go forth the law, and the word of the LORD from Jerusalem. (Isaiah 2:3)

And I will rejoice in Jerusalem, and joy in my people: and the voice of weeping shall be no more heard in her, nor the voice of crying. (Isaiah 65:19)

Thus saith the LORD; I am returned unto Zion, and will dwell in the midst of Jerusalem: and Jerusalem shall be called a city of truth; and the mountain of the LORD of hosts the holy mountain. (Zechariah 8:3)

And I will bring them, and they shall dwell in the midst of Jerusalem: and they shall be my people, and I will be their God, in truth and in righteousness. (Zechariah 8:8)

Yea, many people and strong nations shall come to seek the Lord of hosts in Jerusalem, and to pray before the Lord. (Zechariah 8:22)

And I will pour upon the house of David, and upon the inhabitants of Jerusalem, the spirit of grace and of supplications: and they shall look upon me whom they have pierced, and they shall mourn for him... (Zechariah 12:10)

O Jerusalem, Jerusalem, thou that killest the prophets, and stonest them which are sent unto thee, how often would I have gathered thy children together, even as a hen gathers her chickens under her wings, and ye would not! (Matthew 23:37)

Pray for the peace of Jerusalem: they shall prosper that love thee. (Psalm 122:6)

I love this place! Shalom.

February 16 – 2/16 **Greater Than Our Hearts**

Dear children, let us not love with words or tongue but with actions and in truth. This then is how we know that we belong to the truth, and how we set our hearts at rest in His presence whenever our hearts condemn us. For God is greater than our hearts and He knows everything. (I John 3:18-20 NIV)

Most of us have a deep sensitivity about our flaws and inadequacies. We're our own worst critics when it comes to sincerity and our motives for doing things. I can only speak for myself, but sometimes I don't feel like a Christian and I think that I'm being a hypocrite. Have you ever felt that way?

We humans seem to be programmed for condemnation. Our hearts condemn us because sometimes we don't feel like a saint, or like doing Christian things. We live in fear that someone may find out the truth about us.

Well, the truth about us is encouraging. First of all, we all have this problem. We secretly suspect our motives at times, and wonder if we may turn out to be one of those dreaded hypocrites that Jesus dealt with so harshly.

Second, doing things you don't feel like doing isn't hypocrisy, it's discipline! A hypocrite is one who is trying to be something he isn't. A pig trying to be a swan – that's hypocrisy.

Third, if you've been born again by the Spirit of God, to act like a Christian in all circumstances and situations, isn't hypocrisy. It's being what you are – a child of God, and it doesn't always feel good. It's called obedience.

The Scripture we just read says that the test of our spirituality is whether we love in deed and in truth. Love isn't a feeling here, it's an action – a choice.

Often, when we serve the Lord and His people, the subtle voice of the Accuser says, "Sure, you're doing a good thing, but why are you doing it? Your motives are selfish; you're enjoying yourself way too much. And you're not supposed to enjoy doing God's will. You hypocrite!"

Through many bouts with the Accuser on this matter of motive, I've discovered that if he can't keep me from doing a good thing, he will say that I'm doing a good thing for a bad reason. And if I stop doing the good thing because I fear I'm doing it for a bad reason, he has won.

We must not stop! God simply calls for pure actions. Besides, how does one change his reason for doing something? Like, "Oh, I think I'll change why I'm doing this now." Good luck. I can change what I do, but I'm not sure how to change my reason for doing it. It's God's business to change my heart. And that He does.

We're called to be and do – not to feel. If my heart condemns me, God is greater than my heart – and He knows all things! Be at rest in His presence.

Walking In Light *2/17 – February 17*

God is light; in Him there is no darkness at all. If we claim to have fellowship with Him yet walk in the darkness, we lie and do not live by the truth. (I John 1:5, 6)

The other night I watched with fascination as a narrow beam of light pierced the darkness of the winter sky of our Valley. It was just a shopping mall trying to attract attention to a grand opening.

I remember when giant searchlights scanned the night sky looking for enemy aircraft during the WW II. I've seen those huge arc lights up close. They are white hot and would certainly blind anyone if aimed horizontally.

God is that kind of light multiplied by millions, in whom no darkness can possibly survive. Consider the glaring search light of these words... *If we claim to be without sin, we deceive ourselves and the truth is not in us.* (I John 1:8)

We often prefer the darkness of denial to the light of reality. Sin does that to us. It loves darkness and fears light. Sadly, our darkness is often self-imposed, as we prefer to deny the truth about our sin. Self-righteousness is denial and merely another kind of sin to be confessed.

Identifying an action or an attitude as sin is not our first inclination. We call it a habit or a weakness or a hang up. But what do you do with a hang up? But when I call it sin, I know what to do with it. Confess it. And a whole lot of good things start to happen to free me.

My dear children, I write this to you so that you will not sin. But if anybody does sin, we have one who speaks to the Father in our defense–Jesus Christ, the Righteous One. He is the atoning sacrifice for our sins, and not only for ours but also for the sins of the whole world. (I John 1:9-2:2 NIV)

Denial hardens. Denial narrows my life. Denial separates me from friends, loved ones – and God. It's impossible to see with your eyes closed. It's difficult to receive with your fists clenched. It's impossible to embrace with your arms crossed. It's hard to discover when your mind is made up.

Confession changes all that. It turns the light of God's healing love upon my heart. The searchlight that revealed the sin becomes a surgical laser cutting away the cancer of my iniquity. His love-light opens my eyes and my hands and my arms and my mind.

No wonder God says, "When we walk in the light... we have fellowship with one another." And fellowship is sweet in the light.

February 18 – 2/18 ***Preposterous!***

And behold, some are last who will be first and some are first who will be last. (Luke 13:30)

Jesus often refers to this contrast between first and last in His teaching. It's an interesting concept. In the literal meaning of the word, it is "preposterous." Let me explain what I mean.

I have one of those big, heavy, four-inch-thick (I measured) unabridged dictionaries, with the root meanings of words. I looked up preposterous. It's from two Latin words, "pre" – before, and "posterus" – coming after.

We're familiar with these words. They're added to other words like previous, presume, and prefix, having to do with something beforehand; or postpone, postscript and postwar, having to do with something that occurs afterward.

Preposterous, however uses pre and post, before and after, as if they occurred at the same time – something incredible, outrageous or impossible. "That's preposterous!" we say, meaning that it just can't be that way.

There are many things that Jesus calls us to that are preposterous. When He says, "The last shall be first, or the greatest among you shall be your servant," He's asking something incredible and outrageous, by the standards of this world system. We are called to be preposterous.

This is not at all surprising. He Himself is preposterous. He is called Alpha and Omega in Revelation 1:8, the first and the last – pre and post. *I am the Alpha and the Omega, Who is and Who was and Who is to come, the Almighty.* Incredible! Astounding! Preposterous!

In Revelation 1:17 John says, *And when I saw Him, I fell at His feet as a dead man. And He laid His right hand upon me, saying, 'Do not be afraid; I am the first and the last.'* There's something about the first-lastness, the Alpha-Omega-ness of Jesus that does answer to my fear. A chorus we sing expresses the peace that comes from knowing He is the first and the last. It says:

"He is Alpha and Omega, the beginning and the end.
He's behind me, He's before me, He's ever my Friend.
Whatever I do, wherever I go, Jesus is my source and my goal."

That just about covers it. He's behind me, taking care of my past. He's ahead of me, taking care of my future. And He is walking with me right now as my Redeemer-friend. I'm grateful beyond words for Jesus.

He's Preposterous!

An Active Faith-Shield *2/19 – February 19*

Above all, take the shield of faith with which you will be able to extinguish all the flaming missiles of the evil one. (Ephesians 6:16)

The picture that comes to mind in this passage is of a Roman soldier, fully armored, carrying a large metallic object that we recognize as a shield. When I was a kid, in mock (and not-so-mock) street battles, a garbage can lid did quite nicely to divert rocks and whatever else came flying from the bad guys. It even had a handle – and I was once small enough to hide behind it.

In today's warfare, a shield is not an object that one carries around for protection, it's an aggressive force that moves out to meet an incoming missile and destroys it in mid-flight. The Patriot, as it's called, was deployed as a shield against the Scud missiles fired by Sadaam Hussien in the Gulf War. The Patriot is not an offensive weapon but an aggressive, mobile, and very effective defensive force that shot down dozens of flaming missiles.

The technology of the Patriot is fantastic. As I understand it, this is the process: A satellite or an AWACS plane picks up the evidence of a missile being fired. A message is sent halfway around the world to Washington and to Colorado Springs where computers analyze the trajectory and determine the point of impact. Then, another message is sent by satellite to the Patriot with the co-ordinates that will intercept the missile in the air.

One problem with the Patriot is that, even though contact is made with the missile, it's often so close to populated areas that considerable damage is done by debris and unexploded munitions in its warhead. It would be better if the interception could take place earlier in the process.

There are spiritual lessons here. Because of the image of the Roman soldier standing there with his shield fending off fiery darts, we have come to see the shield of faith as a passive thing, effective at close range if one knows how to handle it. The problem is the same, as with the Patriot – by the time the enemies flaming missiles get close enough for the shield to be effective, a lot of collateral damage can occur.

For instance, when your enemy, the devil, fires a missile of temptation to commit adultery in your direction, it must be extinguished early. If not, it will do some damage to you and those you love, even if the flaming thing doesn't succeed in destroying you completely.

Another thing, as the Patriot doesn't rely upon its own information but responds to commands from headquarters, so a Christian must not rely upon his or her own judgment in defending against flaming missiles of temptation.

We must hear the word of the Lord from "on high," and respond before we can even see the danger.

During the cultural revolution of the 1960's, the cry from the youth of our land was, "You gave us roots, now give us wings." It was a quest for freedom from anything that restricted expression. Well, the sexual revolution followed and we have flown, with our new wings, into the side of the mountain, morally.

During this time the church was saying the same thing, basically. The cry of many congregations across the land was just that, "You have given us roots, now give us wings." And a great spiritual renewal resulted as the church became free from powerless tradition and empty form.

Now we are seeing the reverse of that revolution in the nation's youth and, perhaps, even in the church. "You gave us wings, now give us roots," is the message one hears from hurting souls. Roots don't have the dramatic appeal that wings do, but one cannot fly forever without purpose and direction and a sense of reality, all of which roots deliver in abundance

One truth that is a deep root of our faith is expressed many places in Scripture but nowhere quite so simply as Luke 19:10, *The Son of Man is come to seek and to save that which was lost.*

A sense of lost-ness – the prerequisite to being found – is not popular with the "me generation." But sin had separated me from the source of life it was not until I knew of my desperate need that I had any inclination toward the grace that Jesus offered to me. I needed to know that I was lost before being saved had any meaning for me.

It may sound like the A, B, C's, but the foundation of our faith is simply this, *For God so loved the world that He gave His only Son that whoever believes in His should not perish but have everlasting life.* (John 3:16) Without Him we perish! That's what being lost means. And the Father's love reached to us in time.

A father had a son who was constantly getting into trouble. All efforts to change the situation seemed futile. Finally, one of his friends said, "If that were my son I would wash my hands of him." The father answered, "If he were your son, so would I – but he is my son."

Jesus came to seek and to save all who are lost – and make them sons of God.

Under God — *2/21 – February 21*

With the war in Iraq and President's Day this month there's a lot of patriotic feeling on the streets of America's cities these days. If any cause is worth the sacrifice of a few, it's probably worth the sacrifice of many. The moral strength of all of us may be severely tested before this war is over.

Our Pledge of Allegiance has, for years, contained the phrase, "one nation, under God." That phrase expresses the spirit of the earliest days of our nation. The Declaration of Independence contained three references to God: the first in the opening paragraph where, "the laws of nature and the laws of God," are evoked; the second in the next paragraph where, "we hold these truths to be self-evident, that all men are created equal and are endowed by their Creator with certain unalienable rights…" and the third when the signers appeal to "the Supreme Judge of the world for the rectitude of our intentions."

The draft of the Declaration closed with this sentence: "And, for the support of this declaration, with firm reliance on the protection of Divine Providence, we mutually pledge our lives, our fortunes, and our sacred honor."

During the Constitutional Convention, when the Declaration was to be adopted, there was a time when it appeared that passage was going to fail. Then Ben Franklin, one of my favorite people, made the greatest speech of his distinguished lifetime.

He said, "I have lived, sirs, a long time, and the longer I live the more convincing proof I see of this truth: that God governs in the affairs of men. And if a sparrow cannot fall to the ground without His notice, is it possible that an empire can rise without His aid? We have been assured in the sacred writings that 'except the Lord build the house, they labor in vain that build it.' I firmly believe this! And I also believe that without His concurring aid we shall succeed in this political building no better than the builder of Babel…

"I therefore, beg leave to move that henceforth prayers imploring the assistance of heaven, and its blessing on our deliberations, be held in the Assembly every morning before we proceed to business, and that one or more of the clergy of this city be requested to officiate in that service." It was done as he suggested and the Declaration of Independence passed.

The men and women who planted the seeds of this great nation and watered them with their own blood believed that, *Blessed is the nation whose God is the Lord...* (Psalm 33:12)

February 22 – 2/22 *The Toothpaste Principle*

And the Word became flesh and dwelt among us, and we beheld His glory, the glory as of the only begotten of the Father, full of grace and truth. (John 1:14)

I once made a trip to San Francisco to see a man that I dearly love. I was his pastor for several years, so when I became aware of his crisis I was compelled to go to him. He was an athlete, a swimming instructor at a university, and has always taken very good care of himself. But he had diabetes.

He became aware of a problem in December. In January he was hospitalized. After several tests and treatments, it was determined that his left leg would need to be amputated. Several days later, his right leg was also amputated.

When I came into the room we embraced and sobbed together. No words could express either my joy or my grief upon seeing him. We talked about the Lord and how good He had been to us. There were questions in his mind about why this happened and what its purpose was, but he was trusting.

His wife joined us and told me that when Larry (great name) came out of surgery he was singing, "Praise the Name of Jesus." I told him that he had just demonstrated "The Toothpaste Principle." He laughed and asked what that was, so I told him.

You squeeze a tube of toothpaste and what's inside comes out. The principle: when we are squeezed – under pressure – what's inside of us will come out. It could be anger, profanity, or bitterness. Or it could be peace, praise or joy.

Jesus is the chief exponent of this principle. He expressed it this way: *Out of the abundance of the heart the mouth speaks.* (Luke 6:45) He was full of grace and truth so that's what came out of Him when He was squeezed.

The Pharisees pressured Him, and truth came out of Him. Crowds of people pressed upon Him, and grace and truth came out of Him. Sinners came to Him and grace flowed from Him to them. The ultimate pressure was the cross. He was falsely accused, mocked and ridiculed, beaten beyond recognition, nailed to His cross and hung out to die!

What came out of Him, as men squeezed the life from Him, is testimony to what was inside of Him. He said, *Father, forgive them for they know not what they do.* (Luke 23:34) I'm in awe of the cross, not only the fact of it, but also the manner of it. With His last breath, He taught me how to handle pressure.

Jesus' action under pressure is not just an example; He has come to reside in me. He wants to be what comes out of me when I'm squeezed. It doesn't always happen that way, because there is a lot of me in there, too.

John the Baptist said: *He must increase and I must decrease.* (John 3:30) That way more of Him and less of me will come out when I'm squeezed.

Theyology *2/23 – February 23*

Theyology is the latest study course in many of our institutions of learning. I made up this word to describe a system of thought that equates the opinions of mere mortals with the utterances of Almighty God. We espouse theyology when we refer to an illusive, unnamed source referred to as "they." "They say…" is one of the telltale phrases of theyology.

The lifestyle of adherents to theyology is marked by preoccupation with what "they" think, what "they" are doing, or saying, or wearing. This mind-set is on a collision course with true theology – the knowledge of God and His ways.

There was a time when one of God's great prophets fell victim to theyology. His name was Elijah. Romans 11:2-5 says, *Do you not know what the Scripture says in the passage about Elijah, how he pleads with God against Israel? "Lord, they have killed Thy prophets, they have torn down Thine altars, and I alone am left, and they are seeking my life.' But what is the divine response to him? 'I have kept for Myself seven thousand men who have not bowed the knee to Baal.'*

Elijah was overcome by the doctrine of theyology. "They" were offended when he embarrassed their gods. He ran for his life because "they" were after him. "They" had forsaken the altars of the Lord. "They" were, in fact, ruling his life! But before we point the finger too long in Elijah's direction, let's consider the impact that "they" have upon our own lives.

More than we know our lives are shaped by what "they" do and say. The advertising field is committed to the gospel of "they" to get us to buy one product or another. If it can be shown that everyone is doing something they have a winner. Call it peer pressure – call it mass appeal – call it majority rule, it all boils down to theyology!

We're seeing a great revival of theyology in the political arena. One of my pet peeves is the way candidates, media, and leaders of our nation are influenced by public opinion polls. There's a new one out every day. It's sickening! Television exists on a rating system that estimates what "they" are watching. Politicians give speeches based on what "they" want to hear.

There has developed a breed of experts in this field, which could be called theyologians. These are the polltakers, which gather and interpret what "they" are feeling. Decisions of great international significance are made on the basis of polls taken of people who are simply willing to express an opinion.

There's something very wrong about this. It's another form of idolatry that the Most High God will not tolerate in His people or in the world for long.

God isn't taking a poll to see what His next move will be among the nations. Hallelujah!

We have some friends – former co-workers – who now live in Illinois. She was our pianist and he was my right hand man with multimedia. We stay in touch with these dear people for they are a part of our lives.

One thing we've always gotten a kick out of is her love for parsley. We would often save ours for her. She's been known to dip her parsley in chocolate and eat it as a snack. But aside from this bit of strangeness, these two qualify for the designation of what I call Parsley People.

Parsley is full of good things and makes your breath smell sweet, but it has only one function for most cooks. It's there to make the rest of the food look good.

That's what parsley people do best. They make someone else look better, just by being there and doing what they do. They adorn that which is around them without drawing attention to themselves.

Queen Victoria of the British Empire had two famous prime ministers during her reign; William Gladstone and Benjamin Disraeli. When she was asked to describe the difference between these two men she said, "When I am with Mr. Gladstone, I feel I am with one of the most important leaders in the world. But when I am with Mr. Disraeli, I feel as if I am one of the most important leaders in the world."

Disraeli, and his kin, are the Parsley People. The world needs lots of Parsley People. Anyone for the job?

Let There Be Light! **2/25 – February 25**

It's hard to imagine a world without light, but that was the state of things before God said, in Genesis 1, *Let there be light.* And the prenatal universe knew the impact of His words – *And there was light!* I don't know if God spoke Hebrew, but this language says simply, "Light, BE! - And light was!"

I can imagine a well-timed dramatic pause between "Light," and "BE!" And the Book of Job says, of this occasion, *The morning stars sang together and the angels shouted for joy!* (Job 38:7) What a moment! With these two words, the dominion of darkness was forever doomed, the rest of creation was made possible, and God's children would never be slaves to darkness.

I've had it up to here with talk of the power of darkness. It's time to speak of the power of light. Since the moment that God said, "Light, BE!" and light was, there has been no contest. Light is never threatened by darkness. Never has been; never will be! It's just the nature of light to dominate darkness.

Any power that darkness has is in its mystery and obscurity. When the light comes on, there is no mystery any longer, and nothing is hidden from view. The figures that dominate darkness are seen for what they are, frauds and impostors, children of their father, the Devil, who still whines over the entrance of light into the cosmos.

My family took to Carlsbad Caverns in New Mexico when I was a boy. The guide took us deep into the earth and turned out all the lights. He said that there was no way that any light could get into the cave at that point, so what we were experiencing was total darkness. Even after several minutes for my eyes to become accustomed to the darkness, I couldn't see my hand in front of my face. It was a bit frightening, and some people started to panic a bit.

The guide then lit one small candle, and the darkness fled as light flooded the cave. The fear left and we proceeded with our tour. I'll never forget that experience. It taught me something important about the power of light – not the power of darkness.

How does light respond to darkness? It doesn't. It just shines! Light doesn't tremble in fear that the darkness will overcome it.

And the Light shines on in the darkness, for the darkness has never overpowered it... (John 1:5, Amp)

February 26 – 2/26 *Revive Thy Work, O Lord!*

O Lord, I have heard the report of You, and was afraid. O Lord, revive Your work in the midst of the years, in the midst of the years make Yourself known! In wrath remember mercy. (Habakkuk 3:2) This is a prayer of the prophet at a time when the people he loved were in bondage and exile, far away from their homes.

Revival is an old-fashioned word. It brings back childhood memories when an evangelist would come to our town, and we'd have meetings every night for two weeks or more. When the meetings were over, everything seemed to go back to normal, whatever that was.

Just because the term revival is old-fashioned, doesn't mean it's something to be relegated to the past. Lots of things are old-fashioned – like eating and sleeping that are essentials for life. You can eat different foods, and sleep on different beds, but food and rest are not optional; but they're old-fashioned.

Call it what you will – revival, renewal, or whatever – it's as essential to the body of Christ as food and rest is to the human body. If we're to survive the influence of the spirit of the age, we must be renewed from above – often.

We're as much in need of reviving as the people to whom the prophet was speaking. We, too, are captive to this world's values and ways and we, too, are exiled from our homeland of God's presence and power. We're as much strangers in this land as Israel was in Babylon, yet we've set up housekeeping and our roots run deep into the soil of an alien land.

With the passing of time we lose our distinctive identity as God's people and adopt the values of this alien land. God longs to draw His people back to Himself. This is called revival. It's not just a time for meetings. It's God's means of restoring His people to the things that make them different from the world around them.

Revival can't be scheduled. When God intends to move upon His people His timing will be perfect. Someone has said, "God alone can cause the winds of renewal to blow upon His people. We cannot. But we can and must set our sails to move when the breeze begins to blow."

Revival can't be invoked. It can't be claimed or commanded. It's not enough to simply ask. II Chronicles 7:14, a verse that has had great impact on my life says, *If My people who are called by My name, will humble themselves and pray, and seek My face, and turn from their wicked ways, then I will hear from heaven, forgive their sin and heal their land.* There's more involved than asking.

Revival can't be denied. When God's people take seriously the words of II Chronicles 7:14 we will place ourselves directly in the path of God's rushing mighty wind. Set your sail and enjoy the trip.

Revive Thy work, O Lord!

Chaos *2/27 – February 27*

I followed, with great interest several years ago, events in the states of the former Soviet Union. The word that characterized nearly every level of life in Russia in those days is "chaos."

Americans took the demise of their former enemy as the end of the struggle for freedom, but in that part of the world political instability has been the order of the day and it didn't get better with the fall of the government. Chaos!

The conditions that millions of people experienced were many times worse than the Great Depression, which devastated our nation in the nineteen-twenties and thirties. Economic hardship threatened to send many former Soviet Republics back to Communism. Chaos!

Moral confusion led to high crime rates, and violence controlled the streets of major cities. Alcoholism, always a problem in Soviet society, was completely out of control. Divorce multiplied, and abortion was rampant. Chaos!

I did not take any satisfaction in these conditions. Millions of good people were crying out for peace and safety, and they were not neglected in my prayers. What I saw happening in Russia will happen to any nation, even ours, if we leave God out of our national life. Chaos!

The sad fact is that Russia, and its sister nations, are still in a state of spiritual chaos. While there is some strength in the church, there is also an immense fertile field for cults and "isms" of all kinds. There is, for instance, a frightening rise in occult and psychic activity in these states.

What does this have to do with us? Well, from my vantage point, three things have to do with us. First, the faith of our fathers has been the moral rudder for our ship of state. There, but for the grace of God – we go.

Second, in the USSR, decades of Godless government and atheistic teaching in schools and universities, have brought economic, moral and spiritual chaos; a direct result of a rudder-less society, adrift on an uncharted sea. There, but for the grace of God – we will go.

Third, observing the events in Russia linked my heart in prayer with these people whom Jesus loves. I grew to love them. They need the pure Gospel. They're starving for Jesus. There – by the grace of God – we must go!

Solomon said, *There are three things which are too wonderful for me, yes four which I do not understand: the way of an eagle in the air, the way of a serpent on a rock, the way of a ship in the midst of the sea, and the way of a man with a maid.* (Proverbs 30:18,19)

I share Sol's wonder. I don't know much about the serpent on the rock but I do know a little about the other three. I suggest that they answer to the same principle, expressed in nautical terms as "the set of the sail."

The eagle is master of the air currents by adjusting the set of his wings. A sailboat can go anywhere on the sea by setting its sails properly, no matter what the direction of the wind. And perhaps this principle applies somehow to the way of a man with a maid. Think about it.

Many of us think that progress can be made in our lives only when the winds of circumstance are blowing favorably for us. But if we wait for favorable winds, we'll hardly ever go anyplace worth going, or be anything worth being.

God gave the eagle and me a similar gift – the ability to set my wings, or the "sail of my soul," so that I can reach my goal whatever the wind is doing.

The ultimate goal for me is to be like Jesus, at all times, in every place. I can set my sail to head in that direction no matter what happens. Navigation is the skillful art of moving to a known destination. This may be our problem. We don't know where we're going so we're at the mercy of the winds.

Paul talks about this in Ephesians 4:14: *We are no longer to be children, tossed here and there by waves, and carried about by every wind of doctrine...*

I'm not much of a goal-setter, and I'm a bit intimidated by those who are. It's not that I've drifted though life without reference points, but it seems to me that the only goal worthy of complete devotion is, in fact, to be like Jesus.

God help us to set our course to be like Him, and then set our sail – no matter which way the wind is blowing.

Leap For Joy! *2/29 – February 29*

There's one of these unique dates every four years in a Leap Year. Why are leap years needed? The short answer is that leap years are needed so that our calendar is in alignment with the earth's motion around the sun.

The long answer: the average time between two successive vernal equinoxes is about 365.2422 days long. This means that it takes 365.2422 days for the earth to make one revolution around the sun. This is one year.

Using a calendar with 365 days would result in an error of 0.2422 days or almost 6 hours per year. After 100 years, this calendar would be more than 24 days ahead of the seasons – which is not good.

By adding an extra day every 4th year, the calendar will follow the seasons much more closely than without leap years. It makes it possible for our calendar, our timetable, to catch up with God's.

I don't know about you, but I need those catching-up times in my spirit. It's a fact of human nature that we tend to lag behind God's schedule and drag our feet, or we run ahead of God's schedule and need to slow down to catch up.

Not only is this a time for us to realign with God's timetable, it's a time for us to leap for joy! This year can be, not only a Leap Year in an astronomical sense, but a "leap-for-joy year" in a spiritual sense, for the things God will do in our lives. He honors us with His presence and that's a leap-for-joy thing!

Even when things don't go well, Jesus said that it's a leap-for-joy time.

Blessed are you when men hate you, and ostracize you, and cast insults at you, and spurn your name as evil, for the sake of the Son of Man. Be glad in that day, and leap for joy, for behold, your reward is great in heaven... (Luke 6:22, 23)

So, in a Leap Year of the earth's journey around the sun, let us leap for joy that the Son of Righteousness is with us – and our reward in heaven is great!

"The Lord is good," we often declare; and then we add, "Because He has healed me." Or, "The Lord is good because He saved our marriage." Or, "The Lord is good because He provided the rent money this month." Or, "The Lord is good because He has redeemed my life from destruction."

We mean well when we say these things; we mean to praise Him for His kindness toward us. But, since it's my job to look at words more closely than most, I would take issue with the because-and-effect of these statements.

When we say, "The Lord is good because..." we're saying, though we may not intend to, that our happy condition is the cause of His goodness. "Because" is a word that defines the cause of a condition or an effect in my life. It would be more accurate to say, "I had a good day today because God is good." "I am healed because He is good."

The goodness of God is that which disposes Him to be kind, benevolent, and full of good will toward us. He is tenderhearted and compassionate, and His attitude toward all, is open, frank, and friendly. By His nature, He is inclined to bestow blessing, and He takes holy pleasure in the happiness of His people.

The goodness of God has great personal implications for me that I am reminded of at this time of year. In March of 1986, I went with a friend to the Middle East. It was a very confusing, painful time for me.

I spent a week in Beirut Lebanon at the time that extremists were kidnapping Americans. There I was – tall, fair-skinned, blue-eyed, among short, olive-skinned, dark-eyed people. I could hardly pass for a native. I walked the streets of Beirut thinking, "wouldn't it be great to be kidnapped." The thought of someone else taking over my life was a relief. It didn't happen.

I called my wife from Jerusalem and told her that I was sure of only three things: that Christ died for my sins, that He rose again from the dead, and that God is good. She didn't ask questions, though she knew I was in a dark place. She later told me that if I was sure of those things, then nothing that she valued was in jeopardy.

I came to know in the depth of my being that God is good, even when everything's falling apart. I would be restored to wholeness because He is good – and He remains forever good.

Our lives would be forever changed if we believed that the God of heaven, though exalted in power and majesty, is eager to be friends with us. The greatness and power of God rouses fear in us, but His goodness encourages us not to be afraid. To fear and yet not be afraid – that is the paradox of faith.

Our faith is simply confidence in the goodness of God!

The Inner Man *3/2 - March 2*

The Bible speaks often about the inner man. It uses terms like "the hidden man of the heart" (I Peter 3:4), or the "innermost being" (John 7:38). Paul prays for those he loves, in Ephesians 3:16, that they would *be strengthened with power through His Spirit in the inner man.*

A contrast is made here between the outer, visible person and the inner, not-so-visible person. All of us have both an outer and an inner identity. What other people see may not be what we're really like on the inside. Part of that may be their perception of us, but part of it is also that sometimes the inner man does not keep pace with the surface, visible image that we let people see.

Something happened some time ago that brought this home to our family. We were in the process of moving from one part of the city to another. One evening we were moving some boxes to the new place. I had three of my grandchildren with me while their mother drove a van to be unloaded. I parked across the way to allow the van to get close to the door for unloading. We got out of the car and all of us went in to unlock the doors.

No more than 45 seconds later I came out to start unloading when I heard what sounded like wood cracking. I turned and watched as a forty-foot-tall tree crashed into my car. The "CRUNCH" I heard when it hit the hood and the roof was sickening. I stood there in shock for a few seconds and then said – to nobody in particular, "That tree fell on my car!"

The next morning I took pictures and surveyed the damage: a broken windshield, crushed hood, dented fenders and a 4" branch driven between the right fender and the front bumper. I saw a bit of humor through the lens of my camera as I framed the picture to include the damage and my license plate, which reads, "I WNDR".

Inspection of the tree trunk was revealing. Twelve years ago (we counted the rings) when the tree was planted, a nylon cord was tied around the root ball. As the tree spread its root system, it also grew taller and wider, reaching over forty feet high and about two feet in diameter at the base, but the core of the tree did not grow larger than the nylon cord allowed. Recent rains were drawn up into the tree, and the thin core inside the trunk – only 8" wide – could not support the tree. It was only a matter of time until it crashed.

We're like that. Our inner man, our spiritual man, must be fed and free of bondage to support the weight of our life. If we're not, it's just a matter of time until the pressure of life becomes so great that we crash, one way or another.

It isn't that the pressure of life is too great, it's that our inner man – our core – isn't strong enough to bear it.

Let us cleanse ourselves from all defilement of flesh and spirit, perfecting holiness in the fear of God. (II Corinthians 7:1)

The blood of Jesus Christ... cleanses us from all sin. (I John 1:7)

The more I learn about the physical characteristics of human blood, the more I understand why the blood of Jesus is so powerful in the spiritual dimension.

There are almost six quarts of blood in the average human. Each time the heart beats, about five ounces of blood are pumped through the veins, arteries and capillaries of the circulatory system. At a rough estimate of 70 beats per minute (105,000 beats per day), this works out to more than 1,800 gallons of blood pumped every day through the body's 60,000 miles of blood vessels.

Blood has been called "fluid tissue" and by some is considered to be another organ of the body, a liquid organ. It is about 55% liquid and 45% solids – red cells, white cells and platelets.

The blood regulates temperature, and moves energy, minerals, hormones, and various chemicals to exactly the right place on time, with efficiency envied by Federal Express.

The red cells (about 25 trillion) in the blood carry nutrients and oxygen all the cells. If one part of the body is cut off from the blood for a while – it dies. On the other hand, the parts of the body that have the highest exposure to blood heal the fastest and are the healthiest.

On it's journey through the body the blood passes through the lungs where there's an amazing exchange of gases. The blood dumps carbon dioxide it has picked up from burned fuel, and takes on oxygen, which it carries to the cells to help the conversion of food into energy. These red cells are replaced at a rate of about 3 million new cells every second, in the marrow of the bone – the "blood factory" of the body.

The white cells (only 3 trillion) perform an absolutely fantastic function. They are the disease fighters of the body. They produce antibodies against viruses, detoxify foreign substances, and literally eat up and digest bacteria.

The blood keeps my body alive and well without any effort at all on my part. I don't have to think, plan, organize or try to make the blood do all that it does.

More about amazing blood – mine and His – tomorrow.

The Cleansing Blood ***3/4 – March 4***

Human blood is an amazing substance. A major purpose of blood is cleansing. The by-product of the conversion of food into energy is carbon dioxide, much the same as when one burns wood in the fireplace. The red cells take carbon dioxide from the cells of the body so that they don't smother in their own exhaust, so to speak, and feed the cells with life-giving oxygen. Without this exchange we wouldn't live long.

The cleansing power of blood is focused on the kidneys. These two organs, about the size of a child's fist, are where the blood dumps the impurities it has picked up in it's journey through the body.

Every second of every hour of every day there is a cleansing process going on inside of me keeping me clean and free from disease. All I have to do to make it work is eat reasonably well, exercise moderately, and not do anything stupid, like take poison.

All of these things and more are true of the blood of Jesus. I'm overwhelmed with gratitude for the cleansing of the blood of Jesus. It not only washed me clean from my sins when I accepted Jesus years ago, it keeps me clean now – as surely as the blood flowing in my veins cleanses my body.

And I don't have to try to make it happen. If Jesus lives in me, His blood is at work in me now – cleansing at the deep level of my flesh, reaching the imbedded impurity, and washing it away!

And according to the Law, all things are cleansed with blood, and without shedding of blood there is no forgiveness. (Hebrews 9:22)

We have confidence to enter the holy place by the blood of Jesus, (Hebrews 10:19)

If we walk in the light as He Himself is in the light, we have fellowship with one another, and the blood of Jesus His Son cleanses us from all sin. (I John 1:7)

Let it be so, Lord. Hallelujah for the Blood of Jesus!

March 5 – 3/5 *Bee All That You Can Bee*

It's a quiet Spring-like Saturday morning in the Valley. For some people it's a day away from the daily grind. But for some very important "citizens" of these parts, it's business as usual.

It's blossom time and as we speak, something is happening that's essential to most of our agricultural products. It's about bees and what they do to make fruit, nuts and vegetables abundant in this, the world's most productive region.

Pollination by honeybees is as vital to the production of many crops as water and sunlight. Almonds, cherries, plums, cucumbers, melons – fifty-eight crops in all – rely completely on bee pollination. These plants are unable to produce a commercial crop without cross-pollination.

My curiosity was stirred when I saw all of the white boxes on the edge of orchards. I had no idea, until I started to research the matter, that so much of our economy depends upon what these little creatures do. How does it all happen? How is fruit produced in such abundance as a result of little bees flying from one blossom to another dragging pollen with them?

One can imagine a scenario back at the hive. The head drone calls an early morning meeting of the worker bees to inspire more aggressive pollination. "The farmers are counting on us. We must not let them down. Go, go, go! Pollinate the world!"

Obviously, that's not how it's done. But that's how we'd do it if we were concerned about fruit in our lives, or producing fruit in the world. We'd go to seminars and listen to sermons on how to evangelize the world. We'd buy books on fruit bearing and make conscious efforts to be more productive.

But how do the bees do it? How does life bear fruit so abundantly in this agricultural paradise? Basically, it happens when bees simply do what they're created to do. They don't set out to pollinate the world.

Bees pollinate blossoms on the way to fulfilling their instinctive purpose – to serve the queen. All the other stuff is serendipitous. The nectar the bees gather from the blossoms goes back to the hive to make honey to feed the next generation of bees. Pollination happens incidentally.

I wondered how this applies to the command of the Lord to be fruitful and multiply. As new creatures in Christ Jesus, we have a new purpose – "to be to the praise of His glory." (Ephesians 1:12) That purpose is as instinctive in a Christian's heart as the bees drive to gather nectar for the queen. And when we live to fulfill that purpose, lots of good things happen along the way.

If bees can pollinate the Valley, we can touch this world with the life-giving grace of God. The best way to do this is by doing what we are created to do – serve our King.

Follow Jesus, love Him completely – and bee all that you can bee!

Propitiation *3/6 – March 6*

I John 2:2 and 4:10 says, *He Himself is the propitiation for our sins; and not for ours only, but also for those of the whole world... In this is love, not that we loved God, but that He loved us and sent His Son to be the propitiation for our sins.*

Propitiation – there's a twenty-dollar word with a million dollar meaning. It's used three times in the New Testament to describe an amazing fact about the death of Jesus. It means, "to turn away wrath through sacrifice." Judgment for sin and the curse of sickness are turned through the sacrifice of Jesus.

The best way to describe propitiation is to recall something about World War II. The Germans developed a bomb that could home in on a radio signal. So they smuggled homing devices into buildings targeted for destruction. The bomb homed in on the device and destroyed the building it was in.

Sin is a homing device for God's judgment. His judgment is not aimed at people – it targets sin. But if sin is in me, it's going to be judged. But at the Cross, God moved the object of judgment, my sin, onto the body of Jesus, and now He bears in His body the judgment for my sin.

Isaiah wrote: *He was wounded for our transgressions, bruised for our iniquities, and the chastisement for our peace was upon Him and by His stripes we are healed.* (Isaiah 53:6)

This amazing promise sums up, in a few golden words, a two-fold wonder of the cross. There, by one sacrifice, the sin and the sickness of the world rests fully upon the Lamb. And we are forgiven and healed.

For three years, Jesus walked the earth and demonstrated openly the power of God to heal and forgive. Even in the last hours before His death He healed. Under the shadow of the cross He restored the ear of the High Priest's servant, which Peter had impetuously lopped off.

He will soon be led away to His own wounding; time is short, yet there is time for tenderness. His brow and hands will soon be pierced, His heart will break, but the lesser wound of a serving man must still receive attention.

It is God's nature to heal. He is Jehovah Rapha – The LORD that heals. But the healing He bestows, as with the forgiveness He offers, does not come without price. One would think that He could just command healing to happen or simply cancel all the sin in the world.

But sickness and sin are forever linked to sacrifice. The hurt and the healing are linked together – His hurt for my healing – His death for my forgiveness.

This is grace. This is propitiation.

How dare you! One usually hears this phrase after he or she does something so outrageous that it defies belief. It's sure to follow an action undertaken without authority or reason, as if one assumed what he had no right to assume.

I've been on the receiving end of "how dare you" a few times, and it wasn't pleasant. Twice I heard God say it. I don't mean I heard a voice from heaven or anything weird like that. But, in a way that I've come to know, He spoke and said, "How dare you." It wasn't an angry, arrogant tone. Nor was it condescending or condemning. The words were compassionately framed to get my attention at critical times in my life.

The first time I heard it was through the experience of a pastor who shared his pain. He was in the study in his home early one Saturday evening. He had been preparing for the next morning when he heard the screeching of tires and a horrifying thud.

He rushed out the door to the street in front of his home. There, to his utter horror, he saw his six-year-old son lying in the street in front of a car. He was bleeding and very badly injured.

The ambulance came and he and his wife rushed to the hospital, only to discover that their dear son did not survive the trip. He was instantly with Jesus. It all happened so quickly. They were devastated.

The trip back home late Saturday night was very painful. After comforting his grieving wife he retreated to his study to pour out his heart to the Lord. It was too late to call anyone to take the service next morning, but how could he stand before the people he loved and have anything to give him or her?

Consumed with grief and unable to think clearly, he glanced at a plaque on the wall that said, *My grace is sufficient for you.* (II Corinthians 12:9) In desperation he cried, "O God, please make your grace sufficient for me." That's when he heard God say, "How dare you ask me to make what IS."

Since I heard that story, I have never asked God to make what is. I've learned that His grace is sufficient. I got the point.

More about "How dare you!" tomorrow.

How Dare You-2! *3/8 – March 8*

How dare you! The second time I heard that phrase was about 20 ago. I was struggling with forgiveness, and the person I couldn't forgive was me.

My actions and my attitude were sinful in God's eyes and I felt condemned and unworthy to bear His name, let alone stand before His beloved people and speak to them in His name. I'd been struggling with this for many months.

It was a Saturday night for me and I was preparing a message, and trying to prepare my heart, for the next morning. I paced the floor of the sanctuary, walking between the aisles crying to God to help me. But I couldn't break through the darkness.

Then, in a way that I've come to recognize Him speaking to me, in firm, yet compassionate tones, He said, "How dare you try to be holier than I am"? I was shocked. He went on, "I've forgiven you, yet you can't forgive yourself. How dare you assume a higher standard than I. Go in peace, my son, you're clean in my sight."

I got the point… again. I haven't been the same since. I have no plans to sin again, but I may be presumptuous, or vain, or just plain stupid at any time. If so, God knows how to get my attention… How dare you!

In whatever our heart condemns us; for God is greater than our heart, and knows all things. (I John 3:20)

March 9 – 3/9 *Woe Is Me!*

A famous message by Jonathan Edwards was titled, "Sinner In The Hands Of An Angry God." I downloaded this message from the Internet the other day; it was an amazing sermon. Jonathan Edwards read his message. He was near-sighted and held the paper close to his eyes as he read. It's said that people in the congregation wept profusely and many clung to the posts in the church, fearing they were sliding into hell that very moment.

Where did we leave the gift of Godly sorrow? A gift? Yes, Godly sorrow is a gift as surely as pain is a gift to tell us that something threatens the body. II Corinthians 7:10 says, *For godly sorrow produces repentance leading to salvation, not to be regretted...*

Where has all the sorrow gone? Perhaps we left it at the place we picked up our obsession with happiness. Godly sorrow and happiness didn't go together very well so we laid it down to pick up happiness – now we have neither.

Where there is no remorse, there can be no repentance; and where there is no repentance, there can be no forgiveness. And where there is no forgiveness, there can be no healing. Where there is no healing, the pain continues unabated and there can be no joy!

"Don't worry, be happy!" It sounds so good, doesn't it? Whatever your problem – not to worry, or, as they say in Australia, "no worries, man!" That's the philosophy of our day. But if your problem is sin, you do have something to worry about. My sin affects the lives of others. My sin affects my relationship with God. My sin affects my forever life!

In Isaiah 6:5, the prophet repented of his uncleanness when he saw the glory of the Lord: *Woe is me! For I am undone; because I am a man of unclean lips, and I dwell in the midst of a people of unclean lips: for mine eyes have seen the King, the LORD of hosts.*

"Woe is me" was Isaiah's response to the glory of God. In our day, we have seen neither the gore of sin nor the glory of God. We may see the gore of sin in the news of the day, but we never relate it to our own sin. After all, I'm no murderer, or adulterer. But Jesus made it very clear that to entertain a thought of hatred or lust is to be guilty of the sin.

All have sinned and fallen short of the God's glory. Isaiah felt the immense distance between his heart condition and the glory to which he was exposed.

"Woe is me," isn't part of our vocabulary these days. Sadly – coincidentally – neither is "glory."

The Treasures of Darkness *3/10 – March 10*

I will give you the treasures of darkness and the hidden riches of secret places, that you may know that I, the LORD, who call you by your name, am the God of Israel. (Isaiah 45:3)

We tend to think of darkness as being synonymous with evil, and yet the Lord promises that He will give us its treasures. I don't think He is referring to the darkness of evil but perhaps to the darkness of "unknowing".

I've learned a lot through the lens of a camera. Unbelievable beauty lies undiscovered all around us. But one element essential to photographing that beauty is light. You can't take pictures without light of some kind. But once the picture is taken, the developing process that brings them to the finished product requires darkness. If light shines on the film at the wrong time it could ruin the picture.

There's a spiritual lesson in this. When I look through the lens of a camera, I see a picture I want to take. I snap the shutter and go about my business. Later, sometimes much later, the film will go into a darkroom, be developed, and then I hold the picture in my hand and say, "That's what I saw in my lens, and now I have it!"

It's like that with faith. *Faith is the substance of things hoped for, the evidence of things not seen.* (Heb. 11:1) So when my faith sees some good thing that God promises, I snap a "faith picture". But that's not the end of faith's expression. I must also have faith that when the darkness comes, my faith picture will come through intact.

In good time we'll see that the darkness of unknowing is an essential element in the developing of our faith and the realization of things that faith sees. It may not be that there are treasures hidden in the darkness, but that the darkness itself is the treasure.

Let's trust Him in the dark – and see what develops.

Someday my prints will come!

March 11 – 3/11 *The Cloud of Unknowing*

They should seek God, if perhaps they might grope for Him and find Him, though He is not far from each one of us; for in Him we live and move and exist, as even some of your own poets have said, 'For we also are His offspring.' (Acts 17:27, 28)

One further thought about darkness. There are times when we're prone to think of people who do not see as we do as being blind. If someone doesn't worship, or believe, or teach as we have come to appreciate, the too common label of "spiritual blindness" is attached to them.

There are other reasons for not seeing. They may not be blind at all. There just may not be enough light for seeing. In the Scripture for today, Paul the Apostle is in Athens and he recognizes that the Greeks are a very religious people. They have lots of gods and one of them is "The Unknown God." Paul proceeds to tell them about the God of the Bible.

He says that He was not far from each of them and describes their search for Him as groping in the darkness. In fact, the One for whom they were searching was nearer to them than the breath they breathe. "In Him we live and move and exist." So, their spiritual condition was darkness because they didn't see what is all around them. Paul gives them light enough to see God as He is revealed in Jesus Christ.

John of the Cross wrote a book many centuries ago that impacted my life greatly. The book was titled, "The Cloud of Unknowing." In it he talks about God, Who dwells in the darkness of our unknowing. It is spiritual arrogance to think that any of us have superior knowledge of Jehovah God, Whose transcending nature is all together other than we are. Humility requires that we bow before our God, Who is far greater than our understanding.

Even though I live and move and have my being in Him, I'm convinced that there are hidden riches in Him that I've not yet seen. It's not because I'm blind, but because God has not shown His light upon them for me yet. Let's not too quick to call it blindness, when it may be just a shortage of light.

Into such a condition the Lord speaks His original words, "Let there be light!" Let there be darkness too – the treasured darkness that's required to develop our faith pictures – and challenges me to search for Him Who dwells in my cloud of unknowing. Amen!

Underneath 3/12 – March 12

There is no God like the God of Israel - He descends from the heavens in majestic splendor to help you. The eternal God is your Refuge, and underneath are the everlasting arms. (Deuteronomy 33:26, 27)

There's much wisdom in the old joke about the man who falls off a cliff and is on his way down a two-hundred-foot drop. At about one hundred feet he grabs a single un-sturdy branch. As he hangs there he cries for help. A voice comes over the side of the cliff, saying, "Yes, My son." The man yells up to the voice, "Who are you?" The voice answers, "I am God." The man pleads, "Help me!" The voice says, "Certainly." The man asks, "What do I have to do?" The voice says, "Let go of the branch." The man looks down, looks up, and says, "Is there anyone else up there?"

The reason we smile at this joke (you did, didn't you?) is that it's human nature to cling to whatever we have a grip on, however insecure it may be. We do not easily let go of anything, or anyone for that matter, that offers even the slightest hope, in favor of a leap into the unknown. So, when God says, "Let go," we invariably ask, in our own way, "Is there anyone else up there?" "Isn't there another way?"

In fact, there's always somebody else up there – with advice on how we can survive our dilemma. It may be friends or family, counselors or comforters, or the devil himself to offer alternatives to God's way. They may say, "Hang in there a little bit longer," as if the frail twig you cling to will grow stronger in your hands. They may say, "We'll rescue you." But if the truth were known, they're clinging to their own branches and are themselves in jeopardy.

These other voices may mean well but they don't know what God knew full well when He said, "Let go," – that underneath are His everlasting arms. Underneath what? Underneath you. Underneath your family. Underneath everything that is.

You can't fall far enough to go beyond underneath. You can't sink so low that His loving arms cannot lift you – they are underneath. And His arms are not made of stone so that we are crushed by the fall. They are the loving arms of Father God who absorbs in His own body the shock of our fall.

Well, what if I let go and He yanks His arms out at the last second. That may have happened before when someone other than God said, "Let go." Like the father whose son was in a tree who said, "Jump." His son jumped, and the father stepped aside and let his son fall to the ground. He said, "That will teach you – never trust anyone!" Just how long will His arms be there? Forever – they are everlasting arms. He will be there!

In the final analysis, it's not letting go that's threatening to us, it's hanging on to what will never change and can't save us. God isn't asking us to fall into the unknown. He is asking us to know – to be confident – that underneath are the everlasting arms!

I get a kick out of this thing called "political correctness." It's not considered appropriate anymore to call things by their simple, descriptive, well-known names. To be politically correct one must avoid, at all costs, telling it like it is. You've got to dress up the obvious in proper attire lest someone be offended by naked truth. And it isn't just politicians that seek to re-define reality with pseudonyms; theologians are pretty good at it, too.

Some examples of this psychobabble are not so bad. For instance, a handicapped person is called "physically challenged." It certainly is a physical challenge, which many face heroically without the full use of some part of their body. I have deep admiration for those who serve Jesus among us with the expenditure of much more energy than I.

But what's wrong with the term handicapped? We know what it means and we share the condition; it's just a matter of degree. None of us is physically un-challenged. We're in the same boat; we all take our turn at the oars.

It's the re-defining of reality that gets to me. Just when you think you know the rules and the frames of reference, someone changes them. People aren't just poor; they're "financially challenged." Join the club. You're not just blind; you're "visually challenged." Again, having to change the prescription on my glasses, join the club.

I heard about someone the other day that was called "vertically challenged." She was just short. A dead person may someday be called "horizontally challenged." A bald man is called "follicly challenged," obviously so-called because of his loss of hair follicles. Is that supposed to make me feel better?

The world-view that gave us these versions of reality would refer to the starving children of the Sudan as "nutritionally challenged." They're dying of hunger. The ones who are challenged are those of us who have plenty to eat. Let's feed them. That's the challenge.

I was hungry, and you gave Me nothing to eat; I was thirsty, and you gave Me nothing to drink; I was a stranger, and you did not invite Me in; naked, and you did not clothe Me; sick, and in prison, and you did not visit Me.

Then they themselves also will answer, saying, "Lord, when did we see You hungry, or thirsty, or a stranger, or naked, or sick, or in prison, and did not take care of You?" Then He will answer them, saying, "Truly I say to you, to the extent that you did not do it to one of the least of these, you did not do it to Me." (Matthew 25:42-45)

Challenged-2 *3/14 - March 14*

Here's more about "political correctness." In the arena of political correctness, if you can use emotionally neutral words you're acceptable. Well, emotion is an important element of communicating the truth about the human condition.

Jesus was a master of words that carried an emotional and an intellectual message of the truth. He called the Pharisees "white-washed tombs," and "a generation of snakes." In today's re-defined reality they would be called "morally challenged."

When He spoke of eternal punishment for sin He used terms like hell, *where the worm dieth not and the fire is not quenched,* and a place of *weeping and wailing and gnashing of teeth.* That's pretty emotional and much too graphic for modern ears. We would prefer to speak of hell as a "thermal challenge."

There are just too many challenges. Give me a break. Why not call sin by its real name. It is a wonderful thing to be able to correctly identify an action or attitude as sinful. Then you know exactly what to do about it. Repent and be forgiven. But how do you deal with an ethical weakness or a moral challenge? There is no challenge in sinning. It's a man-sized challenge not to sin.

What's the point of all of this? Words mean things; they convey emotions as well as data, and both are vital in motivating action. I Corinthians 14:8 says, *For if the trumpet give an uncertain sound, who shall prepare himself to the battle?*

One reason I'm concerned about this is that we, who are privileged to have people listen to us, or read what we write, spend a lot of time and prayerful consideration in the choice of the right words. It's frustrating for words to change their meaning with the political climate. You might say we are "vocabularly challenged."

It's enough to drive a man to think!

March 15 – 3/15 *The Ides of What?*

Well, here we are – at the Ides of March. "Beware the Ides of March," Julius Caesar was warned in act one, scene two of Shakespeare's play "Julius Caesar." Caesar's bloody assassination on March 15, 44 B.C., forever marked the Ides of March as a day of infamy. It has fascinated scholars and writers ever since.

For ancient Romans living before that event, however, an ides was merely one of several calendar terms used to mark monthly lunar events. The ides simply marked the appearance of the full moon, and every month had one.

Superstition says, "Forget Friday the 13th. Ignore ladders, black cats, broken mirrors and spilt salt. Think instead of today, March 15, and beware." Beware of what? All because of something that happened in 44 B.C. "What fools we mortals be," to quote another of Shakespeare's lines.

Superstition introduces a fear factor into our lives that has no place in the heart of a follower of Jesus Christ. Terror thrives in this anxious atmosphere. It reminds me of a character from our own national history.

Black Bart was a professional thief whose very name struck fear as he terrorized the Wells Fargo stage line. From San Francisco to New York, his name became synonymous with the danger of the frontier. Between 1875 and 1883 he robbed 29 different stagecoach crews.

Amazingly, Bart did it all without firing a shot. Because a hood hid his face, no victim ever saw his face. He never took a hostage and was never trailed by a sheriff. Instead, Black Bart used fear to paralyze his victims. His sinister presence was enough to overwhelm the toughest stagecoach guard.

The fear factor paralyzes faith. Jesus is, in fact, in the darkness in which fear thrives. He is here now; He is there tomorrow – and fear is no factor to Him.

The Ides of March harkens back to a date in 44 B.C. The B.C. stands for "before Christ." After Christ, everything changed.

Do not be afraid, little flock, for your Father has chosen gladly to give you the kingdom. (Luke 12:32)

Spring Training *3/16 – March 16*

"We don't do Lent." I heard that in my growing-up years in our church back in Illinois. Lent was for Catholics, and we were not of that persuasion.

From Ash Wednesday to Easter, many in the Christian world mark their foreheads with ash and begin to abstain from certain foods or physical pleasures for 40 days, not counting Sundays. This is called Lent.

They do this to imitate Jesus Christ's 40-day fast in the wilderness. Some give up smoking. Others give up chewing gum. Still others give up overeating or cursing. I know of a man who gave up watermelon, even though there are no watermelons in sight at this time of year. People vow to give up anything, as long as it's supposed prepare them for Easter.

Lent comes from an ancient word, meaning "Spring." Christians in the 9th century said, "Let's celebrate. Let's prepare for Easter. Let's prepare for Good Friday and have a time in the Spring that we set apart for that purpose."

According to the Catholic Encyclopedia, "the real aim of Lent is to prepare men for the celebration of the death and Resurrection of Christ. The purpose of Lent is to provide purification by weaning men from sin and selfishness through self-denial and prayer..."

The problem with Lent, and any other human attempt to achieve holiness, is that it doesn't work that way. The Bible says that we are purified – cleansed, set apart and made pure in God's sight – by the shed blood of Jesus Christ (Hebrews 9:11-14, 22; 13:12). No amount of fasting, abstaining from physical pleasures or any other form of self-denial can purify us.

There is, however, something to the idea of preparing our hearts to celebrate the most important events in the history of the universe – the death and resurrection of Jesus Christ. Some heart preparation can greatly enhance our celebration of this glorious season.

Can I draw upon my interest in the upcoming baseball season for an analogy? I'm a Giants fan and I'm still somewhat in mourning over last year. They should have won the World Series – but I'm not bitter. Anyhow, this year holds great promise. But it involves a period of preparation of body, mind, and soul. It's called Spring Training, which is going on right now.

Lent is like Spring Training for Easter, the celebration of Jesus Christ's victory over death, hell, and the grave, which marked the beginning of a new and living way in our relationship with the living God.

It's right that we prepare to celebrate with joyous Hallelujahs!

Although it's not a national holiday in the United States, many communities across the country celebrate St. Patrick's Day with parades, festivals, and "wearing of the green." The first parade honoring the day occurred in Boston in 1762. Over the years, parades and other celebrations on St. Patrick's Day became a way for Irish immigrants to remember their roots.

Who was Patrick? While much of his life is clouded by legend, there are some generally agreed-upon facts. He was born in Scotland or Wales around 370 A.D. and that his given name was Maewyn Succat. His name sounds like something out of "The Lord of the Rings." His parents, Calpurnius and Conchessa, were Romans living in Britain.

As a teenager, Maewyn was kidnapped and sold into slavery in Ireland, where he worked as a shepherd. During that time he began to have visions and dreams. In one dream, he saw a way to escape from Ireland – by going to the coast and getting on a ship. He acted upon his dream, and after a perilous journey, he arrived at the coast and discovered a ship bound for Britain.

Back in Britain, Maewyn's dreams continued. One vision summoned him to return to Ireland, where he'd been a slave. Although this vision moved him, Maewyn didn't feel himself worthy of returning to Ireland in his non-believer state. So, he journeyed to France where he entered a monastery and began studying for the priesthood. There he changed his name to Patrick (meaning "father of his people" in Latin).

It was only after his true spiritual conversion that Patrick felt he could answer the call to return to Ireland to "care and labor for the salvation of others." He returned as a bishop around 432 A.D., traveled throughout Ireland spreading the word of God, and building churches and schools.

Patrick's humility, engaging personality, and knowledge of ways of the Irish, which he learned while he was a slave, helped his mission succeed. He made his headquarters in present-day Northern Ireland. By the time of his death on March 17 between 461 A.D. and 490 A.D., Ireland was almost entirely Christian. St. Patrick is Ireland's patron saint.

What does St. Patrick's Day have to do with our life in Jesus today? Well, he is one of a host of men and women who have been devoted to the spread of the gospel to the world. I honor him for that. Our concept of life in 5th century Ireland is clouded by what we know of recent history.

While I may not be able to identify with Patrick at every level of my walk with Jesus, I can appreciate his genuine concern for people who are lost in their sins. March 17 was not his birthday, but his death day.

Perhaps I will see him in heaven.

Generational Faith *3/18 – March 18*

Well, if you woke up this morning it means you're getting older. Every tick of the clock means you're getting older. Let's accept the fact that all of us are, in fact, getting older. That's not news.

This was driven home to me a few months ago when our granddaughter gave birth to our first great-grandchild. I'm not nearly old enough to have a great-grandchild. My wife is, but not me, even though I'm two years older than she.

What's newsworthy about this blessed event is that another generation will know of the Lord's faithfulness. And how will she know of the Lord's faithfulness? Her parents, grandparents, and great-grandparents will tell her. With their mouth they will make known God's faithfulness to all generations.

The word "generation" is an interesting one. From the same root we get the words "generate" and "generator." A generation, then, is that which has been generated. In the case of the human family, what are generated are children.

The common root of these words is the Latin word "genus," meaning kind or family. The word "gene" is obvious in the word generation. Not until fairly recently did we know that genes are the carriers of vast amounts of information that gave a new born his or her physical and family identity. The marvelous fact is that our great-grandchild, and every other child born of woman, is the product of many generation of genetic input.

Therefore know that the LORD your God, He is God, the faithful God who keeps covenant and mercy for a thousand generations. (Deuteronomy 7:9)

I'm proud to be a father, a grandfather, and now a great-grandfather. If it means I'm getting older, so be it. My children and grandchildren have blessed my life in hundreds of ways that I couldn't have known without them. I look forward to the next adventure.

And I will establish My covenant between Me and you and your descendants after you in their generations, for an everlasting covenant, to be God to you and your descendants after you. (Genesis 17:7)

March 19 – 3/19 *Surrounded By Mercy*

He who trusts in the Lord, mercy shall surround him. (Psalm 32:10)

What a promise! I desperately need mercy. I know I have it from God, but I need it from you, too. I need to be surrounded by it. I don't deserve it from God or from you either, for that matter. But then mercy is never deserved.

I – we – need mercy all around us so that we can become what God intends for us to be. This is a cold, cruel world. It's dog-eat-dog out there. But it shouldn't be that way in here – in the family of God.

James 2:13 says, *Judgment is without mercy to the one who has shown no mercy.* That's a remarkable statement. It makes it clear that unless I show mercy toward those who've sinned against me, I will stand before God in judgment and I will not find mercy from Him. Such a fate is terrifying indeed!

It's natural for us to demand justice when we are wronged. It's super-natural to offer mercy. We say that the offender ought to feel the full force of the consequences of their actions. "He deserves what he's getting, after all he was wrong and I was right. Throw the book at him!"

If there's any book throwing, let it be the Word of God. Mercy is its theme song from cover to cover. In Exodus 34:6 the scene on Mt. Sinai is described, the place of the law carved in stone. Here the LORD passes before Moses and declares Himself to be *merciful and gracious, longsuffering, and abounding in goodness and truth.*

The Psalms are rich with the theme of God's mercy. *The Lord is merciful and gracious, slow to anger and abounding in mercy... As high as the heavens are above the earth, so great is His mercy toward those who fear Him. As far as the east is from the west, so far has He removed our transgressions from us.* (Psalm 103)

That's extremely good news. It's not good news that I am a lost sinner. It's good news that lost sinners find mercy in the Lord Jesus Christ.

A wise saint of years gone by said, "He who cannot forgive another breaks the bridge over which he himself must pass." It's imperative that we get off the judgment seat and onto the mercy seat if we are to find mercy with the Lord.

If I get what I deserve, that's justice. If I don't get what I deserve, that's mercy. If I get what I don't deserve, that's grace!

After the promise of surrounding, abounding mercy, the Psalmist continues with this admonition: *Be glad in the Lord and rejoice, you righteous; and shout for joy, all you upright in heart!* (Psalm 32: 11)

What a way to live. Praise the LORD!

What Made Jesus Cry? *3/20 - March 20*

And when He approached, He saw the city and wept over it, saying, "If you had known in this day, even you, the things which make for peace! But now they have been hidden from your eyes... (Luke 19:41, 42)

What made Jesus cry? Palm Sunday usually brings to mind His triumphal, joyful entry into Jerusalem, but on the way from the top of the Mount of Olives to the city, He stops the procession.

He looks over the city, which His Father chose as His dwelling place – *But I have chosen Jerusalem, that my name might be there forever.* (II Chronicles 6:6)

The view from that hillside is still breathtaking, to this day. Jesus looks long at the city He loves – and He cries. Most translations say He wept but the Greek word "klaio," (klah'-yo) is used here and it means, "to sob, i.e. wail aloud."

The reason He sobs is stated clearly – they didn't know "the things which make for peace." What a thought-provoking statement! The city is in political, religious, and social turmoil and the people and their leaders are blind to the things that would bring peace. This makes Jesus cry.

There is no other place like Jerusalem. It's still a city divided. For Jews, it's the dwelling place of Yaweh – Jehovah God, the site of Solomon's Temple and the home of the Ark of the Covenant. Abraham offered Isaac here; David's golden reign was here. Centuries of bloody battles have been fought here. The bond between Jews and Jerusalem is deeper than politics or reason.

Muslims believe that prayers said in Jerusalem "weigh a thousand times more than prayers said in any other place." Mohammed is supposed to have ascended to Heaven on his white horse from Mount Moriah. He came back down, however – and died like the rest of us.

Christians, like me, make pilgrimages to this city because of the city's significance in the life, death and resurrection of Jesus Christ. I love this place! I understand perhaps a fraction of what Jesus may have felt that day.

This was the day of His triumphal entry into Jerusalem – the city of peace – but they didn't know peace. The Prince of Peace was among them but they were about to crucify Him.

Nothing has changed from then to now – with human nature – or God's tears.

John 14:27 says, *Peace I leave with you; My peace I give to you; not as the world gives, do I give to you. Let not your heart be troubled, nor let it be fearful.*

Jesus wept on His way into Jerusalem because they didn't know the things that make for peace – and they still don't. Peace treaties don't make for peace. Suicide bombers don't make for peace. Economic aid doesn't make for peace. Strong armies don't make for peace. Walls don't make for peace.

Jerusalem is special, partly because it's a microcosm of all humanity, and whatever makes for peace here, makes for peace everywhere. Jerusalem could also be said to be like the human heart – designed for God's dwelling place, but fragmented, confused, terrorized, and at war with itself.

Evidently there are some things that do make for peace, or else why would Jesus weep? So, what are they?

First, forgiveness for sin makes for peace. Sin is the great disturber of the peace. It destroys peace with God and with other people, which is essential for abundant life.

Second, healing of wounds makes for peace. In the Middle East, as in every human heart, there are painful wounds from the past. There are memories of generations of injustice and people's sinful actions leaving gaping scars, which must be healed.

Jesus, the Weeping Savior, offers both of these by one sweeping act of sacrifice. There, anyone who seeks will find forgiveness for sin, and wholeness – healing for the wounds of war.

Isaiah says it best: *He was wounded for our transgressions, bruised for our iniquities and the scourging for our peace was upon Him.* (53:5)

It Is Enough... *3/22 – March 22*

As we near the celebration of Easter, my heart is filled with a greater joy and praise than I have known for some time. The images of Calvary and the Empty Tomb are still fresh in my mind from my visits to Jerusalem. Those places and what happened there have deep personal meaning for me.

I think I've finally come to rest about some basic things in my walk with Jesus. A hymn I love sums it up for me.

> "My faith has found a resting place, not in device nor creed;
> I trust the ever-living One; His wounds for me shall plead.
> I need no other argument; I need no other plea;
> It is enough that Jesus died, and that He died for me."

That sounds so simple. You'd think I'd have settled that long ago, since I've been a Christian for sixty years. But the awesome implications of the death of Jesus Christ and His resurrection from the dead are just now beginning to sink into my heart.

A resting place – in the Cross of Jesus. What a strange place to find refuge; an instrument of execution. But it's more than that, of course. It's the place where the Lord laid upon Jesus my iniquity and the sins of the whole world. And He died there in my place.

A person doesn't have to know much more than "Christ died for my sins..." to enjoy this resting place. And there's room for us all at the foot of the Cross.

If I can rest in what Jesus did for me at the Cross, it makes a difference here and now. His death secured for me complete acccss to God now, and entrance into heaven later. My prayers are heard and my eternal destination is settled.

I despise airplanes. I'm too big for the seats, and often the view from where I sit is not very good. I am usually extremely uncomfortable in an airplane. But my ticket said I was going home, just like the folks in first class.

The destination is the thing – not the current view out the window, or my present state of comfort. I'm going home!

> "I need no other argument; I need no other plea.
> It is enough that Jesus died, and that He died for me."

March 23 – 3/23 *It Was Not a Pretty Thing*

Almost from its beginning, Easter was a season rather than a single day. The celebration of Easter began forty days before Resurrection Sunday and included a time of self-examination, fasting, and other forms of spiritual preparation for the climatic observance of the death and resurrection of Jesus Christ. That period came to be known as Lent.

The events we celebrate, the awful agony of Jesus in the Garden of Gethsemane, His bloody crucifixion, and His glorious resurrection, are too important to approach with the same pace by which we live every other day. The events of those three days forever changed the world.

The focal point of the world's destiny is the Cross of Jesus. It was just a wooden instrument of capital punishment – an equivalent of an electric chair, the gallows, the gas chamber, or the firing squad. It was not a pretty thing.

But what happened at the Cross has never found a parallel in the history of humankind. Jesus, God in flesh, was laden with the sins of every human being who has ever lived and there, suspended between heaven and earth, He died to pay the price, once for all the sins of all men in every time and in every place.

At the cross we understand both God's judgment and His mercy. We are humbled to the dust, and at the same time raised up and comforted. As we see the horror of our sin brought down upon the loving heart of God, we cry: "How hateful I must be to God! Surely I am fit only for death!" And we hide our faces in shame.

But at the same moment, we see Jesus deliberately bearing it all for our sake, standing on our side of the gulf between God and man, willing rather to be separated from the Father. And we cry in amazement: "How precious I must be to God! Surely He, Who has done this for me, will never let me perish."

We don't wallow in sackcloth and ashes to mourn the memory of a fallen hero, as many do. We celebrate the awesome victory of our risen, ever-living Lord, Who somehow managed to get hold of the right end of the device upon which He died, and beat up on death, hell, and the grave with it.

Think of it! All sins forgiven, the slate wiped clean, that old arrest warrant canceled and nailed to Christ's Cross.

He stripped all the spiritual tyrants in the universe of their sham authority... and marched them naked through the streets. (Colossians 2:13-15, The Message)

The First In Line *3/24 – March 24*

He went a little farther and fell on His face, and prayed, saying, "O My Father, if it is possible, let this cup pass from Me; nevertheless, not as I will, but as You will." (Matthew 26:39)

The garden of Gethsemane was a favorite retreat for Jesus and His disciples, but it is most remembered as the setting for these words. In this place Jesus, being as much human as divine, actually considered the cost of what was about to happen to Him.

He prayed for the cup of agony to pass from Him, if it were possible. This would mean the end of God's redemptive initiative and, in fact, the end of you and me. Notwithstanding a film version of a few years ago to the contrary, this was the last temptation of Christ – the temptation to let the world literally go to hell, and consider only His own life and comfort.

Thank You Jesus, for choosing to suffer and die so that we could know resurrection and life. Incidentally, it was in another garden where the Adam was faced with the same basic option – his way or God's. In Gethsemane, Jesus Christ, the Second Adam prevailed over temptation and canceled the effect of the first Adam's failure.

The cup that Jesus drank was no cup of tea or pleasant repast. It was a cup of blood and pain that no man, before or since, has been able to drink in full.

I'm reminded of a way the Romans used to make a sort of game of public executions. When crucifixion grew wearisome they added other innovations, like "the passing of the cup."

A crowd gathered to witness the festivities and cheered as the criminals were marched into the arena and stood shoulder-to-shoulder before the magistrate. A cup of deadly poison was given to the first in line. He was required to drink from it and pass it on to the next one in line. The crowd roared its approval as one by one, the offenders fell dead from the poison. To add a bit of sport to the event, the Romans said that if the cup was empty when it came to you, you got to go free. Your crimes were forgiven.

It's not out of context to suggest that Jesus, like the criminals in the arena, stood first in line, bearing the sins of the world. He was given the cup first – and He drank it all! Now all of us sinners in line for judgment can go free, because He drank the full measure of God's judgment for our sins.

All I need do is confess that I am a sinner and accept the fact that He died for my sins. Then I am free.

If the Father had let the cup pass from Jesus, it would be left for me to drink it. Thank you, Jesus, for taking the cup and drinking it all!

March 25 – 3/25 *Conception Day*

Last Christmas season I pondered one of the most awesome wonders that my curious mind has ever considered. My musing went something like this:

God's entrance into the human condition, the Incarnation, could have been in the form of a full-grown bearded Israeli man – but it wasn't. He could have come as a handsome young man of twenty-six – but He didn't.

The Almighty could have assumed human form as a precocious twelve-year-old – but He didn't. And God could have sent His Son to earth as a tiny baby – but He didn't. Read on.

The moment of the Father's introduction into human flesh was not on the day we celebrate as Christmas, and it was not in a little town called Bethlehem of Judea. It happened in Nazareth in the Galilee, in the womb of Mary. That's when the Word became flesh and dwelt among us.

The angel, *You will conceive in your womb and bring forth a Son, and you shall call His name Jesus... and He will be called the Son of the Highest.* (Luke 1:31, 32)

I vowed, as I continued to ponder the wonder of this miracle, that our family would celebrate, not only the birth of Jesus, but His conception as well. I marked the day on my calendar nine months before Christmas, and that was March 25th, today.

When I first told my family about this we gathered at the table and recalled the miracle when God became flesh, and we celebrated "Conception Day."

I personally think it should be a national holiday. But that will never happen. I do, however, plan to make it a personal holiday to remember when Almighty God became a human being so tiny He could not be seen without the aid of a microscope. He is an awesome God.

We love to quote the Scripture this time of year that most of us know from memory – John 3:16, (which I learned in the King James version)

For God so loved the world that He gave His only begotten Son that whosoever believeth in Him should not perish but have everlasting life.

Well, God gave His Son before He died on the cross. He gave Him in the womb of Mary. That's when God so loved... that He gave.

Now we celebrate the death and resurrection of Jesus. These events were seen ahead of time by the Father and were planned and executed by His Almighty hand. Jesus Christ came in flesh – to die in flesh that we may live.

O, Sacred Head, Now Wounded *3/26 – March 26*

I'm not much impressed by sacred places and shrines. Jerusalem has hundreds of sites where somebody did something significant. Big deal. So what if Peter ate fish here, or Jacob drank water here, or Jesus walked here. But I tread softly upon the site of Calvary and the Garden Tomb. Standing on this ground declares to my whole being that my faith rests not in a concept or a doctrine, but in an actual historic event that happened here.

This week the Christian world will think about the Cross. Good Friday forces us to think about it, at least in passing. But, to those who have accepted the death of Jesus as atonement for sins, it is more than a passing fancy. I invite you to meditate upon the cross with me through the words of hymn that dates back to the Dark Ages.

The church, which Jesus established 1000 years earlier was, for the most part, degenerate and corrupt. The moral standards of its leadership were disgraceful and utterly shameful. Out of such darkness shone a few points of light. One of these was Bernard of Clairvaux.

At age twenty he devoted himself to follow Jesus and founded an order of monks called the Cistertians. They were so called because he felt that God's people should not be pipe-lines or for the grace of God but cisterns which became filled themselves, and then overflowed upon the world around them. Bernard was full of love for Jesus and it overflows to this day in two of his hymns; "Jesus, The Very Thought of Thee," and "O Sacred Head."

I can't escape the impact of these hymns upon my life. They speak words I wish I had originated about my dear Lord. I borrow them often in worship.

"O, sacred head, now wounded, with grief and shame weighed down;
Now scornfully surrounded with thorns Thine only crown.
O, sacred head, what glory, what bliss 'till now was Thine.
Yet though despised and gory, I joy to call Thee mine.

"What Thou, my Lord hast suffered was all for sinner's gain;
Mine, mine was the transgression, but Thine the deadly pain.
Lo, here I fall, my Savior. 'Tis I deserve Thy place;
Look on me with Thy favor, and grant to me Thy grace.

"What language shall I borrow to thank Thee, dearest Friend?
For this Thy dying sorrow; Thy pity without end?
O, make me Thine forever; and should I fainting be,
Lord, let me never, never outlive my love for Thee!"

That last line has great meaning for me, having had a brief brush with death. Bernard said it well, and I repeat it as my own:

"Lord, let me never, never outlive my love for Thee!"

March 27 – 3/27 *The Land of Beginning Again*

Blessed be the God and Father of our Lord Jesus Christ, Who according to His great mercy, has caused us to be born again to a living hope through the resurrection of Jesus Christ from the dead. (I Peter 1:3)

At Easter of 1988 I memorized this verse (I really did type it today without looking, trust me) and it has become a strong support for a new hope that was born in me then and lives in me now, sixteen years later.

It describes new life made possible by the resurrection of Jesus, which we celebrate today. It speaks of the Land of Beginning Again. This is no fairy-tale kingdom of wands and wishes and kisses that turn frogs into princes. There's no fairy godmother here. But there is the God-Father of our Lord Jesus Christ, Whose mercy made possible the purchase of my share of the Land of Beginning Again.

This land was created by the Father long ago and given to His children. We lost title to it by sin and neglect. But the Father's mercy redeemed it. The price was the blood of Jesus. Title to the land was held in escrow for three days and then – Jesus rose from the grave! And escrow closed. The land is ours. Now it is for us to occupy and build upon. Here we really can start over.

There are times when we all need to be brought back to life and start living again. There is such a place as the Land of Beginning Again, and that the sleepless nights won't last, the days consumed with despair will become easy again, the world goes on – and us with it, changed, and alive again.

The darkness does not last forever. We begin to live again in very quiet ways. There are few lightening flashes or glorious visions. There are many less dramatic agents of resurrection. There's a phrase in a conversation with a friend that all of a sudden opens up a way that wasn't there before.

There's the relationship, broken for years, that somehow finally finds the grace to start to heal. There's the one who asks you for help, and in the midst of ministry, you suddenly realize it's yourself you are ministering to, and you must be alive or you couldn't be doing these things.

Simple gifts, so much a part of ordinary life that you could miss them if you blink – and sometimes we do miss them. But they never stop happening. The gift of life fully restored in the Land of Beginning Again – this is the work of the Risen Savior.

He is risen! — He is risen, indeed!

Resurrection and Springtime *3/28 – March 28*

Last week about this time we experienced the Vernal Equinox. Did you feel it? It marks the point in time when the sun is directly over the equator in its apparent movement northward. In the life of planet earth it's the beginning of Spring. The message of Spring is, has been, and always will be, that THE LORD IS GOOD.

The Lord did not suddenly become good when the sun passed over the equator. Spring is here because God is good! *Lo, the winter is past, the rain is over and gone. The flowers appear on the earth; the time of singing has come, and the voice of the turtledove is heard in our land. The fig tree puts forth her green figs, and the vines with the tender grapes give a good smell.*

These words from the Song of Solomon 2:11-13, could've been spoken of the San Joaquin Valley this time of year. Spring has come to the valley! Someone said that Spring is "God thinking in gold, laughing in blue, and speaking in green!" That's not literally true but I do know that God in His mercy, has placed boundaries upon winter and has renewed the face of the earth every year at this time since creation. Life springs forth in abundance all around us. That's why they call it Spring.

It's also significant that Jesus rose from the dead at this season of the year. We know, of course, that it happened just after Passover, which was a Spring feast of the Jews. The timing was beautiful! It was the special touch of the God of all seasons to bring Jesus out of the tomb at a time when life was springing from death in joyous profusion everywhere.

Furthermore, if the King of Life didn't rise from the dead, there would never be another Spring. One hundred and fifty miles east of here is a baked-out gorge called Death Valley – the lowest place in the U.S., dropping to 276 feet below sea level. It's also the hottest place in the country, with an official recording of 134 degrees.

Streams flow into Death Valley only to disappear, and a scant two and a half inches of rain falls on this barren wasteland each year. But, a few years ago, an amazing thing happened. For nineteen straight days rain fell onto that bone-dry earth. Suddenly, all kinds of seeds that lay dormant for years burst into bloom. In the valley of death there was life!

This is the message of the resurrection. A desert becomes a garden. Beauty transcends the ugly. Love outwits hatred. Grace outlasts greed. A tomb is emptied. The grim and haunting outline of a cross disappears in the glow of Easter morn.

There are seeds of incredible beauty lying dormant in the soil of our lives, awaiting the rains of the Spirit and the warmth of the risen Son.

Resurrection and Springtime – they go together quite nicely.

March 29 – 3/29 *Another Ewe?*

Cloning – it was the talk of all the talk shows. What is all the fuss about? Well, some genetic engineers figured out a way to make an exact genetic duplicate of a sheep.

They did this by taking the genetic material, the nucleus, out of an egg from the ovary of a female sheep – an ewe – and replacing it with the nucleus of a cell from a second ewe. This egg was then impregnated with material from another cell of the second ewe. This egg, with identical genetic material from the second ewe, was then placed back into the uterus of the first ewe. Amazingly, after many years of trial and error, this time it worked.

A lamb was born in the usual manner that was a carbon copy of the adult ewe from which the cells were taken. The lamb was, in effect, the twin of the ewe – only seven years younger.

What does God think about all of this? I asked Him but He hasn't gotten back to me yet. But I think we can take a cue from history and His dealings with similar "break-through" events in man's quest for knowledge.

When I see the big picture, I'm not worried. God has not only put a stop to man's quest at times, as in the Tower of Babel, etc. but He has also been the inspiration for many, if not all, of the major discoveries that have brought healing and genuine progress to us earthlings.

Identical twins are born frequently. They have the same genetic make-up and the same parents. What's different in the cloning of the ewes is that one twin is an adult and the other is a baby.

A misinformed journalist reported that man has finally been able to generate life. This is utter nonsense. No one has created life – they've taken advantage of life, they've exploited life in these experiments. They weren't using rocks here – they were using living cells.

If there is anything to get excited about from a Christian perspective it's that life is such a wonder. Though not sacred, even animal life has the Creator's unique touch upon it. The question many are asking is this: "If they can do this with sheep, how long will it be until they can do it with humans?"

With knowledge increasing so rapidly, God may very well say what He said to Babel and to the oceans of the world, "Thus far shall you go and no farther."

Until then it's safe to say they may clone another ape, or bird, or rat, or ewe – but there will never be another you.

A Titanic Challenge *3/30 – March 30*

The phenomenal success of the movie Titanic reveals a deep interest in the tragic demise of the unsinkable ocean liner. I've not seen the movie version of this horrible disaster but I know the story well. 1,500 people lost their lives in the cold waters of the North Atlantic when The Titanic struck an iceberg.

There were a few hundred who escaped in lifeboats and lived to tell the story. The sinking of this grand creation of "modern" engineering has been called the greatest single tragedy of the last century.

The tragedy raises a titanic challenge to the faith of some. The challenge – how to explain why some people died while others lived. Were the living ones somehow more worthy to be alive? Or did the dead ones do something that made them more worthy of death?

And who decided who should live and who should die? And what if you were almost worthy enough to survive but not quite? You needed just one more good deed or one less bad one. Perhaps God had arranged for all the people fated to die on that day to book passage on the ill-fated voyage, along with those who were destined for merely a cold, wet brush with death.

Or maybe the determination of life or death was just the luck of the draw or the roll of the dice. If you survived you were in the right place at the right time. If you died – well, you get the picture.

I confess that I've not lost much sleep over this apparent dilemma. I've long since resolved the questions in my own mind. But I reconstructed this challenge to make a point about an even greater issue.

Last week we celebrated the death and resurrection of Jesus. What happened in Jerusalem 2,000 years ago is linked to the destiny of everyone on the Titanic and every human being since the beginning of time.

The wall of a tomb in Egypt tells a story of an ancient and modern concept of life after death. Osiris, the god of the after-life, stands beside a balance scale. The heart of the pharaoh is placed on one side of the scale, and a feather on the other side. If the heart is heavier with bad deeds than the feather, the pharaoh is, pardon the expression, history.

That isn't justice; that isn't righteousness; and that isn't the way of a loving God. God's way has nothing whatever to do with whether your good deed outweigh your bad deeds. If that were true you could be almost, but not quite saved. Or make it into heaven by the skin of your teeth.

The only just answer to the question of one's eternal destiny is the grace of God. We're not saved by the skin of our teeth, but by the blood of Jesus. All other answers are just rearrangements of the deck chairs on the Titanic.

March 31 – 3/31 **A Watched Pot**

An old proverb says, "A watched pot never boils." This seems to imply that if you stand there and watch the pot on the stove, something mysterious occurs that keeps it from boiling.

This isn't true, of course. It only appears that the water won't boil because the watcher can't predict exactly when it will start to bubble. This says more about human impatience than the effect of human eyesight on the boiling process.

Sometimes it seems to take so long for things to change when we pray. We stand by and watch, hoping that our pot will boil. But there are facts we don't have, and influences we can't know about that affect the outcome.

Time is a factor; there are no "microwave answers" to prayer. And yet, as surely as water boils at a certain temperature at sea level, with fervent prayer and sufficient time, the promises of God will be fulfilled.

I Kings 8:56 says, *There has not failed one word of His good promise!* Jesus said in Mark 11:24, *Whatever you ask for in prayer, believe that you have received it, and it will be yours.*

The boiling point of water at sea level is 212° Fahrenheit, or 100° Centigrade. If sufficient heat is applied to the bottom of a pot of water it eventually must boil, whether you watch it or not. It's a natural law.

To be able to predict the precise moment of boiling you would have to know the intensity of the heat, the nature and thickness of the pot, the amount of water in the pot, its previous temperature, and the temperature of the surrounding air. If you had these facts you could predict when the pot would boil, but the water would probably boil away before you could make all of your calculations.

It's also difficult to predict when prayers will be answered or when God's promises will be fulfilled. But there are laws at work here, too – spiritual laws – that will one day become evident. *The effective, fervent prayer of a righteous man avails much,* the Word says in James 5:16.

Fervent means hot, and fervent prayer is like a fire under the pot of our circumstances. If we knew all the factors in the matter for which we are praying, we could predict accurately, applying spiritual law, when our prayers would be answered. We think we know – but we don't.

Watched pots do boil, eventually – and God answers prayer.

These Foolish Things *4/1 – April 1*

God has chosen the foolish things of the world to shame the wise.
(I Corinthians 1:27)

This being April Fools Day, it seems appropriate to shed some light on the matter of foolery. In sixteenth-century France, the start of the New Year was observed on April first. It signaled the visible onset of Spring. It was celebrated then in much the same way as the New Year is today.

Then in 1562, Pope Gregory introduced a new calendar for the Christian world, and in it the New Year fell on January first. There were some people, however, who hadn't heard about the change, since communications left a bit to be desired in the those days.

There were also others that heard about the change but didn't believe it or didn't accept the change, so they continued to celebrate New Year's Day on April first. They called them "April fools." People would make fun of these people and play tricks on them. Thus April Fools Day began.

Foolery is a subject the Bible has lots to say about. In Solomon's writings alone there are 120 references to fools, foolishness, folly, etc. In the New Testament there are a variety of Greek words translated "fool" or "foolish" in our English Bibles.

For instance, in Ephesians 5:15, Paul says, *See then that you walk circumspectly, not as fools, but as wise.* The word "fool" here is "asophos" – unwise.

In I Corinthians 1:23, the apostle says, *but we preach Christ crucified, to Jews a stumbling block, and to Gentiles foolishness...* Here the word for "foolishness" is "moria" – silliness, absurdity, far out. Even today, the Cross is seen as absurd and foolish in the eyes of the world. Paul then says, *the foolishness (absurdity) of God is wiser than men.* I Corinthians 1:25

Foolishness, in the Scripture, runs the gamut from unwise, to silly, to stupid, to insane. "He's nobody's fool," it is said, but in fact, everybody is somebody's fool, by these definitions from the Scripture.

What kind of fool am I? I've probably been all of the above, at one time or another. But there's one kind of fool I don't mind being called: *We are fools* (absurd, far out) *for Christ...* (I Corinthians 4:10)

What kind of fool are you?

April 2 – 4/2 *Are You Listening?*

Speaking to His disciples after the miracle of the loaves and fishes, Jesus addresses the problem we all have when it comes to receiving spiritual things. He said, *Having eyes to see, do you not see? And having ears to hear, do you not hear?* (Mark 8:18)

Later in the narrative He asks, *how is it that you do not understand?* (8:21) as if, incredibly, He actually expected them to get what He was driving at. He did then, and He does now!

While ears have nothing physically comparable to eyelids, they can be just as effectively closed as eyes. Hearing is an activity of the mind and not just those two strange looking appendages on either side of your skull.

We all know what it's like to speak to someone clearly and directly, only to learn later that they didn't hear a word we said. If that's true, then it's also likely that we have been the unhearing one also. Our "earlids" were closed.

It's Spring and the time of my favorite pastime, baseball, which brings to mind an analogy of the relationship between speaking and listening.

The pitcher is the speaker; the listener is the catcher. The catcher behind the plate must be as active as the pitcher on the mound. Receiving the ball requires an action on his part. He reaches out to complete the play.

Just so, communication between speaker and listener doesn't occur unless the listener's mind and spirit are actively engaged in the receiving process. He or she must reach out to catch what comes from the speaker.

When communication fails, the fault may not always be with the "catcher". Wild pitches sometimes come from the pitcher's mound – and the pulpit. I've thrown a few knuckle balls myself, which nobody could catch. Most of the time, however, communication fails when listening isn't as active as speaking.

Well, we have a pitcher and a catcher in the speaking/listening process, so just who's the batter we're trying to keep from knocking the ball out of the park? The obvious answer is "It's the devil, of course."

While it's true that *we wrestle not against flesh and blood,* (Ephesians 6:12) the fact of the matter is that one of the strongest "hitters" in his lineup isn't the devil or a ghoulish demon from hell, but our own fleshly nature, which does not receive spiritual things with great excitement, to say the least.

The sad truth is that we could stop the afore-mentioned verse with "we wrestle not" when it comes to our fleshly desires.

Batter up! Are You Listening?

Do Touch That Dial *4/3 – April 3*

Lately, I am struck by how much impact a fairly modern innovation has had upon our lives. I'm talking about television. Hardly anyone alive today remembers what life was like before TV.

It's not just the sex and violence either, as influential as those things are upon our values. It's the endless stream of images and sounds that we know as commercials, that both reflect and influence what we are becoming, and how we are known.

I've had occasion to see behind the scenes of television advertising, and I'm deeply concerned that Christians are largely unaware of the awesome power of this medium. In the first twenty years of an American kid's life, he or she will see one million television commercials. This makes the TV commercial the largest information source in the education of your child.

"And now a word from our sponsor," is followed by the command, "Don't touch that dial." Well I say, "DO touch that dial!" It's hard to imagine a more effective mechanism for brainwashing a society than television advertising.

A commercial teaches a child three things. The first is that all problems are resolvable. The second is that all problems are resolvable fast. And the third is that all problems are resolvable fast through some technology.

It may be a drug or a detergent. It may be an airplane, an automobile or computer. The essential message is that the problems that beset people are entirely solvable if only we will allow ourselves to buy into a technology or a product of some kind.

Commercials teach these themes through parables. The problem is stated, and then in eight to ten seconds, the middle part comes – which is Hawaii or a new car or a drug. The moral is nailed down at the end where we're shown what happens if a person follows this advice. And the actor, of course, is ecstatic.

At the heart of this elaborately engineered system of persuasion lies one fundamental premise: Each group in our society has its weakness, and deep-seated emotional need. Agencies make big profits by isolating and identifying each population segment's vulnerabilities.

Our Sponsor, The Lord God, says, *Be not conformed to this world, but be transformed by the renewing of your mind.* (Romans 12: 2) Far more than we know, we're being conformed to this world by 30-second ads on TV.

The life style of the rich and famous is replacing the life force of the meek and lowly. Beware the power of "a word from our sponsor."

And go ahead – DO touch that dial.

April 4 - 4/4 *It's Not the Stupid Economy*

It's the economy, stupid!" is a phrase from a past presidential election. It was spoken to point out that elections are won or lost on the basis of economic issues, and you are stupid if you think that anything else really matters to American voters.

Well, call me stupid, but I believe that other things matter a great deal more than gross national product, stock market or super market prices. Morality matters, and character counts.

Check out the words of the prophet Amos. In chapter one he addresses his message to Jeroboam, King of Israel. Jeroboam's reign was a prosperous one. People had nice homes and drank expensive wine. Amos is not impressed with the health of the economy of Jeroboam's kingdom.

He writes in 5:10-13: *You hate the ones who reprove in the court, and despise him who tells the truth. You trample on the poor... For I know how many are your offenses and how great your sins. You oppress the righteous and take bribes, and you deprive the poor of justice in the courts. Therefore the prudent man keeps quiet in such times, for the times are evil.*

We are living in such times. Righteousness is synonymous with intolerance, and integrity is seen as narrow-minded-ness. Spin merchants have twisted the truth until things are grossly out of balance, and when your dryer goes on the spin cycle with an unbalanced load, or your tires wobble because they're out of balance, the dryer, or your car can't last long. Neither can a society.

Americans, it seems, have determined that it's the economy, their personal economy, that matters – and that's what's stupid! It's stupid for millions of Californians to contribute over $100,000 a minute to the lottery. But no one ever says, "I just don't like the lottery, they're always asking for money."

People feed state coffers on the faint hope of gaining something. Yet, when it comes to contributing to God's Kingdom, we're reluctant to even talk about it.

But God does promise that there'll be a certain return on whatever is given in His name. *Give, and it will be given to you; good measure, pressed down, shaken together, running over, they will pour into your lap. For by your standard of measure it will be measured to you in return.* (Luke 6:38)

That's God's economy – and that's not stupid.

The Square Root of Evil — *4/5 – April 5*

Timothy 6:10 says, *For the love of money is the root of all kinds of evil.*

The Scripture teaches that there is an even deeper root than money for all the evil in the world. The root of the root, so to speak, is pride or self-love. I call this, to borrow a term from mathematics, the "square root" of evil.

We love money because it can buy things to satisfy self-love. We love power because it feeds our pride. We love things because they gratify our egos. Yes, the root of the root – the square root of evil – is self-love.

A few years ago a 40-year-old single woman in Santa Monica, California made headlines by the ultimate act of self-love. She proposed to herself, she accepted herself, and she married herself – and now she has to live with herself. This seems bizarre, but deep down in our hearts burns a flame of self-love that warms us all.

This self-love business has political implications with the emphasis on health care and welfare, etc. Government of, by, and for the people works only as long as the deep root of self-love is subordinate to the common good. That's not happening here.

Alexander Fraser Tytler, (1748-1813) at the end of the 18th century, wrote a book titled "The Decline and Fall of the Athenian Republic." Long before the American Democracy had been tested he made the following observation about the ancient Greek democracy: "A democracy cannot exist as a permanent form of government. It can only exist until the voters discover that they can vote themselves money from the public treasury."

Every political issue, every marital problem, every crisis in relationship, and every war, for that matter, has as it's bottom line cause – self-love. God has only one way to deal with self-love – the Cross. Only a return to the redeeming work of Calvary can save us from bondage to the chains we ourselves have forged by our self-love.

The Cross lays the axe of God's judgment to the root (the square root) of the tree of flesh. That's why, *the message of the Cross is foolishness to those who are perishing, but to us who are being saved it is the power of God.* (I Corinthians 1:18)

If self-love is the square root of evil, then the Cross, to borrow another mathematical term, is the scene of exponential grace – grace^{10}.

And that's grace enough!

April 6 – 4/6 *The Cost of Caring*

And he came to him, and bandaged up his wounds... and he put him on his own beast, and brought him to an inn, and took care of him. And on the next day he took out two denarii and gave them to the innkeeper and said, "Take care of him; and whatever more you spend, when I return, I will repay you." And Jesus said, "Go and do the same." (Luke 10:34-37)

I've visited the scene of this story – the road to Jericho. The old road is a very narrow footpath, which winds among the imposing rocks of the Judean Wilderness. A man fell victim to thieves here, and while others passed by, a Samaritan stopped and stooped to help, and thus became a famous example of what it means to care.

Jesus went so far as to say that this kind of action is expected of those who follow Him. It is the minimum required; it ought not be the exception.

But there are risks; and there's the rub. The Chinese language has an interesting word for "crisis." It's made from two characters pronounced "way" and "gee". The first is a word for danger; the other is a word for opportunity. So, in Chinese, a crisis is a dangerous opportunity.

The Samaritan and all those who "go and do the same" are subject to danger hidden in opportunity. Consider that, to stop, get off your donkey, and stoop down to help a fallen man on that road put one at great risk of attack from the very ones who caused the wounds. It could be a trap.

I speak from experience when I say that reaching to help someone in need is far more painful than staying on your donkey and moving on. If it's safety you require, then don't go near people in need; it may cost you your comfort.

The road is crowded with passers-by, like the priest and the Levite, who are experts on what ought to be done, but are doing nothing. It doesn't cost anything to have an opinion. It's the doing that's dangerous!

There is a substantial cost to caring in one's own heart, soul, and body. It's not for the faint of heart or the lazy to bind up the messy wounds the thief has caused. Beginning the healing process in the wounded one can be messy.

More about the cost of caring tomorrow.

Downward Mobility *4/7 – April 7*

In Luke chapter 10 Jesus tells the story of what we now call "The Good Samaritan." A Samaritan was an alien to Jewish life and an outcast in Jewish society. But he took the man, a Jew, who was a victim of a viscous attack, to an inn and stayed with him overnight. It cost him time and fouled up his schedule, not to mention the money spent to care for the half-dead man. If the man had died, and that was a possibility, the Samaritan risked the criticism that he hadn't done enough.

I've known the agony of seeing someone die, or a marriage fail, for whom I cared in similar ways as the Samaritan in the story. You always think you could have done more, or gotten to them earlier, or called someone with more expertise. So we often hold back our caring impulse for fear that what we have will not be enough. Well, something is better than nothing any day.

There is also the risk of bearing the burden too long. The Samaritan left the wounded man with another and came back to check on him later, at which time it is assumed that the man was well enough to care for himself. There is danger in assuming too much responsibility for another.

Every human being has limits. Only God is capable of bearing the weight of the total, everlasting dependency of His people. None of us are able. Knowing when to let go is as important as knowing when to get involved.

When caring costs, remember that not caring is even costlier; it's disobedience to the command of Jesus. The risks of reaching are nothing compared to the risk of offending the One Who has called us to be His Body in the earth.

Today's young urban professionals have coined the phrase – upward mobility. It means, evidently, that one is on a ladder of success, moving upward in the company or institution at a steady pace.

Jesus Christ calls us to "downward mobility" – stooping, reaching, binding wounds and caring for people He loves.

He did it first; it's our joy to follow Him.

The Dead Sea fascinates me. Since it's the lowest spot on earth, at 1,300 feet below sea level, it has no outlet. Where could the water go when every place is uphill from there? The only way water exits the Dead Sea is by evaporation, which leaves behind all the minerals carried into it by the Jordan River.

The concentration of salt in the Dead Sea is ten times higher than any other body of water on earth. Its water is twenty-seven percent salt of one kind or another. No plant or animal can exist there.

The wealth of the Dead Sea is enormous. All the fruits, vegetables, cut diamonds, technology and manufactured goods exported from Israel are nothing compared to the mineral wealth in the Dead Sea. Its tremendous reserve is estimated at 22 billion tons of magnesium chloride, 12 billion tons of sodium chloride, 6 billion tons of calcium chloride, 2 billion tons of potassium chloride, and 1 billion tons of magnesium bromide. The value of these chemical salts is over 2 trillion dollars. That's a lot of salt!

Jesus lived in the land of the Dead Sea when He said to His followers, *You are the salt of the earth; but if the salt has become tasteless, how will it be made salty again? It is good for nothing anymore, except to be thrown out and trampled under foot by men.* (Matthew 5:13) They knew what He meant.

Salt was a preservative then. Salting meat was the only way to retard spoilage and decay. They understood that Jesus was saying their presence in the earth was a preserving influence. We see that today. What would our nation be without the church to challenge the decay and rottenness all around us?

They must have understood, also, that salt seasons and imparts a desirable flavor. We do this where we work, and where we live, and where we shop, primarily by our words. *Let your speech be always with grace, seasoned with salt,* says Colossians 4:6. Thank God for the special flavor the followers of Jesus give to this community by peaceful, loving, grateful, graceful words.

They must have known that salt is an irritant, also. It hurts when it's applied to an open wound, but it heals when it hurts, as it disinfects. Sometimes we must confront an open sin, but the healing begins when the germ is destroyed.

Jesus was surely aware of one important quality of salt when He made this comparison. It's simply that salt creates thirst. He was saying that we are to be making people thirsty for Him. Sadly, many Christians either remain confined to the "salt shaker" or, when they are touching the world, they are repulsive influences. We must live to make people desire what we have tasted in Jesus.

Perhaps Jesus was saying, "You have great value; I have come to take you from the Dead Sea of your sins, and scatter you into all the earth to preserve, season, heal, and create a thirst for Me. You are the salt of the earth."

A Monument to Triumph *4/9 – April 9*

Shout in triumph, O daughter of Jerusalem! Behold, your king is coming to you; He is just and endowed with salvation, humble, and mounted on a donkey, even on a colt, the foal of a donkey. (Zechariah 9:9)

On the main road into Baghdad there is a huge arch of crossed swords, which Saddam Hussein caused to be built to celebrate his vicious exploits. Our marines drove their tanks and marched through that arch in defiance of his authority in the war in Iraq.

Napoleon Bonaparte, the French emperor had conquered most of Europe in the early 19th century. In 1806, he decided to build a big arch, which stands today in Paris – The Arc de Triomphe, or The Arch of Triumph.

His victorious troops, he surmised, would soon march through the arch cheered by the population of Paris. This never happened thanks to General Wellington who defeated Napoleon at Waterloo in 1815

Napoleon's arch was patterned after a much older one in Rome, Italy – Trajan's Arch. Here, on the Via Appia (Apian Way), one finds an impressive triumphal arch erected around 114 AD in honor of Trajan.

Another such arch, Hadrian's Arch, still stands in Athens, Greece. This arch lies on an ancient street that led from the old city of Athens to the new, Roman section. It was constructed A.D. 131, in honor of Hadrian.

Jesus Christ, on the day that we celebrate as Palm Sunday, also went through an arch with shouts of "Hosanna to the King." The arch still stands – it's the Eastern Gate of the temple, known as the Golden Gate (not the one in San Francisco, although the thought of Jesus riding in triumph into "Baghdad By The Bay" is an exciting one).

The thing about Jesus' triumphant ride is that He did it before the battle was fought and won. He hadn't died and risen from the dead yet. But He accepted the celebration as if it were a done deal. And, in point of fact, it was a done deal – from the foundation of the world. (Revelation 13:8)

There is something in the human spirit that must build something when a victory is won. Napoleon, Hadrian, Trajan, Hussein, and countless others, have had a compulsion to make something that will outlast them to punctuate their exploits. It must be a man-thing – or a pride-thing.

What did Jesus build to celebrate His defeat of death, hell, and the grave, and the ignominious dethroning of the god of this world? Is there a monument somewhere that marks His victory?

Yes indeed! Jesus said I'm going to build something that the gates of hell will not be able to withstand. I will build My Church! And so He did.

If the descendants of Jacob DeHaven have their way, the federal deficit will increase by $141.6 billion. That's what they claim the U.S. government owes them. It stems from a loan of $450,000 that Jacob DeHaven made to the Continental Congress to rescue George Washington and the troops at Valley Forge. Apparently the debt was never repaid. His descendants claim that the loan, at 6% interest compounded daily, is now worth $141.6 billion.

In the winter of 1777-78 General Washington sent this urgent appeal to the governor of Pennsylvania. "Unless aid comes, our affairs must soon become desperate beyond the possibility of recovery. The army must disband or starve." Jacob DeHaven lived near Valley Forge. He believed strongly in freedom and lent Washington $50,000 in gold and $400,000 in supplies. The army survived. Independence triumphed.

DeHaven tried to collect the debt after the war, but was offered only worthless paper Continental money. He held out for gold. He was never repaid and died in poverty in 1812. Did DeHaven's loan save the cause of freedom? We will never know for sure, but if it did, we owe him a debt worth more than the money. All of us are in his debt.

There is a far greater debt that we owe – the debt of our sin. The interest on this debt is compounded daily by repeated transgressions until the weight of it is enough to destroy body, soul and spirit. There's no way that any of us can pay for our sins; we can't do enough, be enough, give enough, pray enough, live or die enough to pay the debt, which our sin has heaped to our account.

A hymn comes to mind – Jesus Paid It All. Here are the 3rd and 4th verses:

"For nothing good have I whereby Thy grace to claim,
I'll wash my garments white in the blood of Calv'ry's Lamb.
And when before the throne I stand in Him complete,
Jesus died, my soul to save,' my lips shall still repeat.
Jesus paid it all, all to Him I owe.
Sin had left a crimson stain, He washed it white as snow."

We will soon celebrate the Lord's death and resurrection – the payment in full for our sins. For this alone He is worthy of our devotion and praise everyday.

Searching For Theudas *4/11 – April 11*

Without Easter, the Church never would have come into existence. Without Easter, the name of Jesus Christ would be about as recognizable as the name Theudas. Who, you may ask, is Theudas? Good question.

He lived in Israel several years before Jesus. He was, in his time, a very popular prophet and teacher. He attracted hundreds of followers, and then, when he offended the wrong people, he was put to death.

So why haven't we heard of Theudas? Because after his death his followers scattered and went on to other things, and the world soon forgot about him. When Jesus died, it looked like the same thing would happen. Before he was even dead the overwhelming majority of his followers had deserted him.

The apostle Peter was one of Jesus' key disciples. Jesus had said to him earlier, "You are a rock, and on this rock I will build my church." But Peter, the rock, crumbled like sand when Jesus was facing death. He denied ever having anything to do with him, and he went back to his fishing boat.

When Jesus died, it appeared that His cause would die with Him and that He would become as obscure as Theudas. But it didn't happen that way. The followers of Jesus didn't fade into oblivion. In fact, they came back bolder and more courageous than ever before. What happened? What made the difference? Easter Sunday, that's what.

Jesus died, they put Him in a tomb, and everyone assumed that that was that. Then, He came back to life. He was dead and gone, and then He was alive and with them again. That's what made the difference.

But on the first day of the week, at early dawn, they came to the tomb, bringing the spices which they had prepared. And they found the stone rolled away from the tomb, but when they entered, they did not find the body of the Lord Jesus.

While they were perplexed about this, behold, two men suddenly stood near them in dazzling apparel; and as the women were terrified and bowed their faces to the ground, the men said to them, "Why do you seek the living One among the dead? He is not here, but He has risen!" (Luke 24:1-6)

Searching for Theudas? You'll find him among the dead. Searching for Jesus? You'll find Him among the living! He is here, now.

He is risen, – He is risen, indeed!

At the very heart of our faith is the Cross of Jesus Christ. If the Cross is the heart, then the blood that issues from it is our life. Without the blood of Jesus we'd be as dead spiritually as a corpse drained of this precious "fluid tissue."

The sight of blood makes many of us feel weird, but we all have occasional scrapes and lacerations that remind us that it's there inside of us all the time doing its job even when we don't think about it. It's like that with the blood of Jesus. It does its work all the time whether I think about it or not.

I once read a story that brings some understanding as to how the blood of Jesus works for us. Over a century ago in France, Dr. Felix Ruh and Louis Pasteur worked together on what was then called the "germ theory."

Dr. Ruh, a Jewish doctor in Paris, watched helplessly as his granddaughter died of black diphtheria. He vowed with fierce determination that he would find what killed her and prove that the germ theory was correct. The medical society of Paris disapproved of Pasteur and Ruh and exiled them from the city. They built a lab in a forest there and continued their research.

Twenty beautiful horses were led into an enclosure near the lab for a test of the germ theory. Scientists and doctors came and watched as Dr. Ruh opened a steel vault and took out a large pail filled with black diphtheria germs, which he had cultured for months. There were enough germs in that pail, he said, to kill everybody in France.

Dr. Ruh went to the horses and swabbed their nostrils, tongue, throat, and eyes with the deadly germs. Then they all waited to see the outcome. Several days later every horse developed a high fever – and all but one soon died.

Most of the doctors and scientists got tired waiting for the last horse to die and left. For days the horse lingered, lying pathetically on the ground. At two o'clock one morning the horse's temperature went down a half degree. The nurse awakened Dr. Ruh. By sunrise it had dropped two full degrees. By that night the fever was gone and the horse could stand, eat and drink.

Then Dr. Ruh struck the horse a deadly blow and drew out all the blood from this animal that had overcome the disease. They took the blood to the Paris hospital, and into the ward where 300 babies were dying from the plague.

They inoculated every child with the blood of the horse. All but three of the babies recovered completely. The blood of the overcomer saved them.

And so are we! Jesus took the full weigh of the sins of the world upon Him and overcame death, hell and the grave. His blood contains the anti-body for the deadly disease of sin. Now all of us, who are cleansed by His blood, are free of the curse of sin and death. Praise the Lord!

How Shall We Then Think? *4/14 – April 13*

A few years ago Hollywood produced a movie with a plot so bizarre that every newspaper, magazine and talk show was filled with references to it. I'm talking about "Indecent Proposal," in which a man who needs money real bad is offered a million dollars to let a rich man commit adultery with his wife.

I resent with a passion, the ease with which the world plants its ideas into our brains. They are using our brains as billboards for whatever they're selling. If you watch television, listen to the radio, or read a newspaper, you're forced to think things that ought not be thought. These thoughts have been planted in our little brains at the whim of some writer or producer, so it's vital that we challenge conventional wisdom on matters of morality.

Francis Shaffer said that what was unthinkable in one generation became thinkable in the next generation and accepted practice in the next. That's how civilizations collapse. That pattern prompted Dr. Shaffer's question, "how shall we then live?" To paraphrase the good Doctor I would suggest, in light of the flood of ideas gushing from the minds and mouths of the gurus of garbage, an appropriate question is "how shall we then think?"

How should we think about a man selling his wife, or a wife offering herself in such an insidious proposal? Once it is established that there is an acceptable price for moral compromise, it's just a matter of negotiating the amount and awaiting the opportunity. And you can be sure that someone will come up with the incentive, and the opportunity is just around the next choice.

It's said that every man has his price. Most of the time the price isn't money – it's pleasure, or a high of some kind. For a Christian, there can be no price of any kind. He or she is already bought and paid for. I Corinthians 6:19 and 20 says, *Do you not know that your body is a temple of the Holy Spirit who is in you..., and that you are not your own? For you have been bought with a price...*

If I really believe that I've been bought with the precious blood of Jesus no one else has a right to make an offer for me. There are some things that are not options. I'm not my own. I've been bought. Jesus is my new owner – My price has been paid. No one this side of heaven can match it.

April 14 – 4/14 *Where Was God?*

I've been grieved by the sight of a helpless man on the ground, being beaten with clubs and feet. The violence of that scene is very much like that of another time and another place. The scene was graphically portrayed in Mel Gibson's "The Passion of the Christ." Jesus is being beaten senseless.

There is the unmistakable sound of fist against face, and whip striking flesh betray the presence of deep anger and deadly hatred. There are those who walk by the Man and spit upon in His face. They rip His beard out by the roots and as a mocking gesture they fashion a sort of crown out of thorns and crush it into His skull. His blood stains the pavement of the courtyard.

Then they demand crucifixion. The charges are politically motivated and false, but He offers no defense. He is summarily convicted and sentenced to die that very day on a hill outside the city with two common criminals. Most criminals are tied to their crosses; this One is nailed – hands and feet. The entire weight of His body rests on those nails as a creepy darkness covers the region. In one last gesture of contempt a spear is thrust into His side. No one could survive such an ordeal, and He eventually sighs deeply and dies.

Where was God while all of this was going on? That's a good question and one that deserves an answer. Where was He then and where is He now when injustice and violence prevail? Was He – is He now – powerless to stop the carnage in the world?

To answer the question, "where was God?" – *God was in Christ reconciling the world unto Himself.* (II Corinthians 5:19) That's where He was! He was there.

But what about now? Where is God when violence breaks the peace of the night? Where is He when injustice threatens the stability of our times? He is now where He was then – in the body of Christ, reconciling the world unto Himself. We are the body of Christ now and God has taken up residence in us. And His mission hasn't changed – to save that which was lost.

The purpose of God was accomplished when Jesus breathed His last on the cross. The cry "It is finished" was not the mere gasp of a worn out life; it was not the cry of satisfaction with which a life of pain and sorrow is terminated. It was the deliberate utterance of a clear awareness on the part of God's appointed Redeemer that now all had been done that could be done to make God known to men, and save them from death hell and the grave.

But where was God three days later when the grave gave up its captive and Jesus rose from death to live forever? He was in Christ then, too. And now the risen Lord is in His people, still reconciling men unto God.

You just can't keep a God-man down.

Over Taxed — *4/15 – April 15*

Haggai 1:6 reads: *You have planted much, but harvested little. You eat, but never have enough. You drink, but never have your fill. You put on clothes, but are not warm. You earn wages, only to put them in a purse with holes in it.* Can you relate?

It's April 15 and some of us are feeling a bit over-taxed. The Internal Revenue Service takes a bigger bite every year out of our resources and has long ago replaced the church as the recipient of the tithe. This isn't God's idea. The demands of government and its agencies are indeed god-like while the blessings that flow from this semi-supreme being are sparse indeed.

One man expressed the frustration of many in response to a demand for payment of dues: "In reply to your request for my dues, I wish to inform you that the present condition of my bank account makes it almost impossible. My shattered financial condition is due to federal laws, state laws, county laws, city laws, corporate laws, in-laws, and outlaws.

"I am expected to pay a business tax, amusement tax, school tax, gas tax, food tax, furniture tax, excise tax and income tax; even my brains are taxed! I am required to get a business license, hunting and fishing license, car license, truck license, not to mention a marriage license and a dog license. The only reason I am clinging to life at all is to see what is coming next."

Unlike the kingdoms of this world, the Kingdom of God is ruled by the principle of giving, not paying. This makes the motivation internal – not external, and that's God's way.

Give and it will be given to you; good measure, pressed down, shaken together, running over, they will pour into your lap. For whatever measure you deal out to others, it will be dealt to you in return. (Luke 6:38)

April 16 – 4/16   *Four Verbs of Easter*

As the first day of the week began to dawn, Mary Magdalene and the other Mary came to see the tomb. And there was a great earthquake; for an angel of the Lord came and rolled back the stone from the door, and sat upon it....

And the angel said, 'Do not be afraid, for I know you seek Jesus Who was crucified. He is not here; for He is risen, as He said. Come and see the place where the Lord lay. And go quickly and tell His disciples that He is risen from the dead.' (Matthew 28:1-7)

In four words, the angel encompasses the whole of Christian experience; four verbs, four imperatives. Come and see! Go and tell!

Come! A warm invitation; you're welcome here. Come! This was our first exposure to the Holy Spirit as He invited us to know Jesus. *Come, let us reason together, says the Lord, though your sins be as scarlet, they shall be as wool; though they be red like crimson, they shall be as white as snow.* (Isaiah 1:18) *Come unto me all you that labor and are heavy laden, and I will give you rest.* (Matthew 11:28)

See! Don't take the word of another; use your own eyes; gain personal experience. See the place where He once laid. See for yourself that Jesus is alive. "God has no grandsons," it is said, meaning that each one who comes must be directly related to the Father. Come and see!

Go! The temptation is to come and see – and stay in the glow of resurrection morning. But all who are warmly received are as warmly invited to go and tell. We don't go from Him – we go with Him. *I am with you always,* He said.

Tell! We don't go empty handed. We have something to tell; that Jesus Christ is risen from the dead and is alive today to save, heal and be now all that He ever has been. Not every one is called to preach, but we are all commissioned to bear witness of what we have seen. And if you haven't seen, you can't tell. If you don't have it, you can't share it!

On the Easter just before he died, Dr. William Sangster painfully printed a short note to his daughter. Dr. Sangster had been used powerfully in a time of renewal in England just after WW II.

Then his ministry was ended by a disease that progressively paralyzed his body, even his vocal chords. But the last Resurrection Sunday he spent on earth, still able to move his fingers, he wrote: "How terrible to wake up on Easter and have no voice to shout, He is risen! Far worse, to have a voice and not want to shout, Hallelujah! He is Risen!"

Come and See! Go and Tell! He is risen! He is risen, indeed!

Dead or Alive? *4/17 – April 17*

In the course of the year I find myself gearing up for important holidays and then breathing a sigh of relief when they're over and done. Things get rather hectic around a church at Easter and Christmas, for instance. But this year I'm not quite finished with Easter, yet.

I'm captivated with the fact that Jesus is alive now. But I fear that many of us, including myself, live our lives as though He were not.

Do we think he is dead or alive? If He's dead, I can only learn about Him; the way He lived, and taught, and eventually died. But if He's alive now, I can learn from Him. He can teach me now – from His living room inside of me.

If He is dead and gone we may learn a lot about Him, just as we would any other person who lived and did some good stuff, or some bad stuff, for that matter. I can't learn directly from a dead person. He or she can be an example for me but cannot be a teacher to me. But Jesus is alive now, and every day I learn – not just about Him – but I can sit at His feet and learn from Him.

How does He do that? He does it because of His Spirit, who is not confined to a certain geographical area as His physical body was. It is the Spirit of the living Jesus who lives in us.

I will not leave you as orphans; I will come to you. After a little while the world will behold Me no more; but you will behold Me; because I live, you shall live also. In that day you shall know that I am in My Father, and you in Me, and I in you...

But the Holy Spirit, whom the Father will send in My name, He will teach you all things, and bring to your remembrance all that I said to you. (John 14:18-20, 26)

Dr. Joseph Hartounian was a professor at a theological seminary who came to America from Armenia. One day a well-meaning friend said to him, "Your name is difficult to pronounce and difficult to spell – it could hurt your professional career. Why don't you change your name to Harwood or Harwell or something like that?"

Dr. Hartounian asked, "What do those names mean?" His friend said, "Well, nothing. They're just easier to remember."

Dr. Hartounian said, "In Armenia, when my great-grandfather was baptized, they named him Hartounian which means 'Resurrection.' I am Joseph Hartounian and I will be a son of Resurrection all my days."

And so are we all. And since we are sons and daughters of Resurrection, then the One, who gave us life, lives now to teach us how to act and speak and love and live – like Him.

April 18 – 4/18 *In Praise of Dirt*

I rise today in praise of dirt. Why would anyone in his right mind want to say good things about dirt? It's something we try to keep our cars and carpets free of, not to mention our kids. But, in its place, dirt or soil is a wonder.

This time of year the valley we live in is bursting with green and red and gold from things that draw their life from the soil. The degree to which we depend upon dirt cannot be overestimated.

All over the world it's the same. Men have always depended upon the soil for food and commerce. God's promise to Noah after the flood assures us that, *while the earth remains, seed-time and harvest... shall not cease.* (Genesis 8:22) This means that God has created a marvelous system, in which decaying matter goes back into the soil from which it came, to form the basis of another cycle of seed-time and harvest.

Genesis 2:7 records the formation of man *from the dust of the ground and God breathed into his nostrils the breath of life; and man became a living being.* And in Genesis 3:23 man is sent out of the Garden of Eden, *to till the ground from which he was taken.* This amazing fact is recorded long before anyone knew that the elements that compose the human body are the same elements in the soil. The Hebrew word for the ground is "adama." The word for man is Adam.

The food we eat comes directly or indirectly from the soil. That's easy to see with potatoes or lettuce or carrots, but it's also true of milk and meat and eggs. They come from the soil, too. A cow eats grass, a chicken eats seed, and their bodies convert what came from the soil into other forms of food. Even fish survive on minerals washed into the water from the soil. The dirt you wash off of your hands after you've worked in your garden is the stuff of life.

I'm grateful for two of my teenage years spent on a farm. It gave me a deep appreciation for the soil and the wonder of growing things. I spent many hours alone in a forty-acre field on a tractor; the plow churning up the rich black soil of Southern Illinois in preparation for the seed. The smell of it comes back to me as a pleasant memory. I saw the whole process work before my very eyes – seed to harvest and back again. Many of you know what I mean.

Ecclesiastes 12:7 says, *our bodies will return to the earth as it was, but our spirit will return to God Who gave it* – a reversal of the creative process. The breath or spirit, which God breathed into man, expires and returns to Him. The cycle is then complete – and the beat goes on.

I'm grateful for soil, dirt, earth – whatever it's called. I speak words of praise to the Lord God in worship today for the wonder of the earth beneath my feet.

In the words of David, *The earth (soil) is full of the goodness of the Lord!*

Fill In The Blanks *4/19 – April 19*

"For to me, to live is _______, and to die is _______." How you honestly fill in the missing words for yourself is a penetrating commentary on your life and your future.

We know how the apostle Paul filled them in. He said, *For to me, to live is Christ, and to die is gain.* (Philippians 1:21) In other words, "My life is all about Him, and dying will only be more of Him."

We are so much affected by our culture that we don't realize how self-centered our life really is. If the truth were known, too many of us would say, "My life is all about me." Or, "My life is all about my work." Or, My life is all about my family." At the root of all these statements is a self-centered life.

Regrettably, there's been some teaching in the church-at-large that legitimizes the idea that God's purpose in the earth is to take care of me and mine; my sickness, my needs, my blessing, my future, my family, etc.

God's purpose is all about Jesus. God wants many sons just like Him; always has, always will. For the Church, Jesus Christ is the Center around which everything turns, the Foundation upon which everything rests, and the supreme Head under Whose direction everything moves. Life works best that way. It's the way the manufacturer's handbook recommends.

I read the tragic story of Rico, an eighteen-year-old senior at a high school in Maryland. Rico had everything going his way – a full scholarship to the University of South Carolina, a first-place award in the school's talent contest, and popularity among his peers.

Rico was driving home from a basketball game one Friday night when he was stopped by a county patrol car. On the seat beside him lay a bag containing several chunks of crack cocaine. To avoid arrest, he swallowed the drugs. Later that night he went into convulsions, and his parents rushed him to the hospital. Early Saturday morning Rico died.

On the wall of Rico's room was a poster of his hero – basketball star Len Bias. Len was the star of the University of Maryland basketball team drafted by the Boston Celtics. The night he was drafted, Len Bias died of an overdose of crack cocaine.

Is that a sad story? Yes. Is it surprising? Not really. Rico's model was Len Bias. He looked at that poster every day. Len was his hero.

Question. Whose picture is on the wall of your heart? Who do you want to be like? Who's your hero?

Let us fix our eyes on Jesus, the Author and Perfecter of our faith. (Hebrews 12:2)

Life is all about Him!

April 20 – 4/20 **His Wounds Still Plead**

After eight days again his disciples were inside, and Thomas with them: then came Jesus, the doors having been shut, and stood in their midst, and said, Peace be with you. Then He said to Thomas, Reach here your finger, and see My hands; and reach here your hand, and put it into My side: and be not faithless, but believing. And Thomas answered and said to Him, My LORD and my God. (John 20:26-28)

If you'd gone to the Upper Room in Jerusalem on Good Friday night, you would have found the door shut and barred "for fear of the Jews." Inside were eleven despairing humiliated men. Their world had caved in upon them. They had hoped Jesus would have been the Messiah to redeem Israel. He had promised so much; His words had been so powerful – His deeds so gracious. And now He was dead, and they were stuck there, deluded, frightened fools, in real danger from those who had put their Master to death.

Suppose you had gone back to the same house a week later. Nothing had changed as far as the outside danger was concerned. The windows would have been shut, the doors still closed. But through them you might have heard laughter and the singing of joyous psalms, and had you listened closely, you would have heard Jesus invite Thomas to reach out his hand and touch Him.

Thomas' joyous response, "My Lord and my God," must have evoked hilarious praise from the others assembled there. You might have said to a friend, "We must have come to the wrong house." But no, something had happened. Almost everything in the world was different. It was after Easter.

I like Thomas; I can identify with him. He's not willing to open himself to more disappointment by taking another's word for something as important as his faith. While Jesus commended those who believe and don't see, He was patient with Thomas, and all of us whose hearts have been broken, who needed to touch – or be touched by Jesus.

There's a bit of Thomas in all of us. But I've wondered about something. If God raised Jesus from the dead, why didn't God fix Him up? Why did the nail prints remain? And why does it picture, in Revelation, "the Lamb as it had been slain?" Evidently the scars in Jesus' hands and feet and side were not healed in the process of resurrection.

Could it be that they remain for the Thomas in us all to witness? Could it be that the scars of our Wounded Healer still stand against the sickness and death of my life?

His wounds still plead – and by them we are healed.

Collateral Blessing *4/21 – April 21*

We've recently passed some important anniversaries in our nation's history of terrorism. Two of these dates are strangely tied together on the same date.

On April 19, 1993, federal agents stormed the compound of the Branch Davidians who were followers of David Koresh, killing 80 people, 27 of them children. This was the first time I heard the term "collateral damage."

On Friday, April 19, 1995, Timothy McVeigh bombed the Murrah Building in Oklahoma City on the second anniversary of the Waco massacre. 168 people died, 19 of them children. "They were collateral damage" – McVeigh said of the children.

I grieve for the loss of innocent life in our war on terrorism in Afghanistan and Iraq. Hundreds of innocent human lives have been sacrificed in an attempt to stamp out the scourge of Al Queda and Osama Ben Laden. Collateral damage has been great in this gigantic effort.

Collateral damage happens to children when fathers and mothers decide to divorce and go their own ways. The battle of the sexes brings tremendous harm to those who are simply spectators to the carnage.

Lest we point the finger of blame outward forever, we've all sinned and fallen short of God's glorious purpose for us. All sin generates collateral damage. There's just a whole lot of it in this world.

But, if there's collateral damage, there's also collateral blessing. If collateral damage means that there are unintended victims of hostile action, collateral blessing means that there are unexpected beneficiaries of benevolent action.

In other words, whenever I do something good in the name of Jesus, there are those who are blessed without me intending or even knowing about it.

Check this out: A 19th century Sunday School teacher named Kimball led a shoe clerk to Christ named Dwight L. Moody, who became an evangelist and led Frederick B. Meyer to the Lord, and he preached on college campuses.

Meyer led Wilbur Chapman to the Lord. While working with the YMCA, Chapman arranged for Billy Sunday to come to Charlotte, North Carolina, to hold revival meetings where Mordecai Hamm was called to the ministry.

Under Mordecai Hamm's preaching, Billy Graham gave his heart to Jesus Christ. And Billy Graham has preached to more people than any man in history. I'm sure that Sunday School teacher named Kimball had no idea what would result from leading a shoe clerk to Christ.

Collateral blessing is God's answer to collateral damage.

April 22 – 4/22 | *Come, Let Us Worship*

O, come let us worship and bow down; let us kneel before the LORD our Maker. For He is our God, and we are the people of His pasture, and the sheep of His hand. (Psalm 95:6, 7)

Worship is so vital to our walk with God that the enemy will do anything to discourage, deter, distort, delay, displace, dispute, and/or disturb my worship of Almighty God.

What breathing is to my body, worship is to my spirit. I must worship or die! As I grow in the Lord it's enjoyable to gather with other saints and worship, but it's also absolutely vital to my life in Him.

I've observed that when people are exposed to expressive worship for the first few times they are a bit uncomfortable. It's all so different from what they expect. Some even say, "You'll never catch me raising my hands and talking out-loud in church, even to God."

But something about the vitality of a worshipping congregation keeps them coming back. Pretty soon they raise their hands about half-mast. Then, as they continue to hunger after God, they begin to utter a few sounds of praise. It isn't very many weeks until they are one with the body in spiritual worship.

It reminds me of a caterpillar said to another caterpillar as a beautiful butterfly flew overhead. He said, "You'll never get me up in one of those things."

The fact is that, in the normal metamorphosis of the caterpillar, he will be "up in one of those things." So it is with worship. The normal growth of a child of God makes him into a worshipper of his God.

The battle of the ages is for the worship of mankind. That which belongs to Jehovah, Satan wants for himself. Recognizing the tactics of the enemy will help us in our worship.

I noticed, in my former pastorate, that at nearly every service about one-fourth of the congregation would be from ten to twenty minutes late in arriving.

That meant that they missed a substantial part of worship. I saw the effect of this in their lives. The enemy was causing any kind of delay he could to keep people from worshipping. Anything from traffic jams to family spats, to even ministry activity was keeping them consistently from worship.

It became a mark of growth for them to overcome things that delayed them and be there, even before service to prepare their hearts to come before the King. It wasn't long before they were free to worship in spirit and truth.

Exalt the LORD our God, and worship at His footstool; holy is He. (Psalm 99:5)

Counterfeit Hope *4/23 – April 23*

The mass suicide of 39 people, who wanted to leave their "containers" a few years ago to meet up with an alien spacecraft, was a terrible travesty. It was superimposed upon the celebration of Easter at the time, and that seemed to me to be very ironic.

These poor souls acted upon the hope that there would actually be something out there in the tail of a comet. They spent their entire reservoir of hope on a lie. Their hope was counterfeit. Talk shows, news magazines, and the tabloid press lumped all of those whose hope lies beyond the grave into one big bag, and called that bag the far-out fringe of sanity.

One commentator poked fun at Christians who celebrate the resurrection of Jesus Christ. He likened us to the followers of the demented purveyor of counterfeit hope, the leader of the Heaven's Gate suicide cult.

This is one of the devil's most successful tactics: to make people suspicious of the genuine because of the dramatic nature of the bogus. In fact, there could be no counterfeit if the real thing didn't exist. Even the stupidest crook doesn't print Monopoly money.

Bank tellers learn to spot a counterfeit, not by studying all of the counterfeits, but by being intensely familiar with real money. The only reason that false hope can exist at all is that there is a genuine hope of life beyond the grave in Jesus Christ.

The Apostle Paul gives sound counsel in II Corinthians 2:11 *...in order that no advantage be taken of us by Satan, ...we are not ignorant of his schemes.*

We're on to you, Mr. Devil. We know that the ultimate purpose of your scheme is not to destroy the few, but to attack the multitudes whose faith and hope is in Jesus Christ. Your jealousy is showing; you wanted to be like God, and Jesus Christ is God, and you've never gotten over that.

Well, you have no advantage here. We're not ignorant of your schemes. Translation: we're not stupid. Our hope is in our Living Savior.

A child and a philosopher both ask the same question: "What is God like?" The most revealing thing about us is what we conceive God to be.

This is what He is like:

• He is Self-existent and Self-sufficient. He needs nothing of His creation with which to sustain Himself. See Exodus 3:14, John 5:26, and Acts 17:25, 28.

• He is Eternal. He is without beginning or end. He always was and always will be. See Psalm 93:2, and 102:27, and Revelation 4:9, 10.

• He is Omniscient. He has perfect knowledge of everything. There is nothing that He does not know about anything or any one. See I John 3:20, Psalm 139:1-6, and Romans 11:33-36.

• He is Omnipotent. He is The Almighty God. He is all-powerful. There is nothing that He cannot do. See Genesis 17:1, Genesis 18:14, Jeremiah 32:17, Luke 1:37, and Revelation 19:6.

• He is Omnipresent. He is present in all places at once. And He is all that He is in every place and time. You cannot be where God is not. See Psalm 139:7-10, Jeremiah 23:23, 24, and Matthew 18:20.

• He is Sovereign. He is the Supreme Ruler of the universe. He is over all and can do what He wants without explanation, permission or apology. See Daniel 4:34-35, Isaiah 46:10, and Ephesians 1:11.

• He is Immutable. He does not change in His being, His attributes or His purpose. He cannot improve – He is perfect. See Malachi 3:6, Psalm 102:24-27, Hebrews 13:8, and James 1:17.

• He is Holy. He is morally perfect and united in all of His thoughts, deeds and motives. There is no darkness in Him. See Isaiah 6:3, I John 1:5, Habakkuk 1:12-13, and Exodus 15:11.

• He is Righteous. He always acts with fairness, justice, and equity. He always, in every time and place, does what is right. See Psalm 119:137, Daniel 9:7, 14, and Isaiah 45:21.

• He is Faithful. He is absolutely trustworthy in all His ways and true to His word. No promise of His can ever fail. See Deuteronomy 7:9, Lamentations 3:22, 23, Psalm 36:5, and 119:90.

• He is Good. He is kind, merciful, gracious, loving, and patient... He is completely free from malice or evil intent. It is His goodness that makes all that He is work for our good. See Psalm 119:68, 33:5, 145:9, and Nahum 1:7.

For this is God, our God forever and ever. He will be our guide, even to death. (Psalm 48:14) He is worthy of our praise.

Tongues of Fire *4/25 – April 25*

There are two places in the New Testament, which mention prominently the words "tongue", or "tongues." One mention occurs in Acts 2, *...there appeared to them divided tongues, as of fire. And they were all filled with the Holy Spirit and began to speak with other tongues, as the Spirit gave them utterance.* (Acts 2:3, 4)

It must have been something to see little flames of fire coming to rest above the heads of each of the 120 people gathered in that second story room. And then something very unusual happened; their tongues began to form words of praise to God in languages they hadn't learned.

The other place that features the tongue is in James chapter 3, and that's what this "Tongues of Fire" business is really all about. Here's what it says:

... the tongue is a little member and boasts great things. See how great a forest a little fire kindles! And the tongue is a fire, a world of iniquity. The tongue is so set among our members that it defiles the whole body, and sets on fire the course of nature; and it is set on fire by hell. (James 3:5, 6)

The tongue is not only pictured here as a raging fire, but a world of iniquity, and in verse 8, a restless evil, and full of deadly poison. These are very strong statements. Surely my little tongue is not that lethal – or is it? The inspired Word of God does not exaggerate for emphasis. Sticks and stones may break my bones but words can kill people, marriages, and churches.

The church is a particularly vulnerable arena for tongues of fire to do their damage. In the warmth of loving relationship, spiritual worship, and inspired teaching one would think that gossip, backbiting, lying, tale-bearing, and other sins of the tongue would not thrive. But they do!

What makes a flaming tongue so dangerous is that it doesn't flare up in public; it most often burns a brother or sister outside of their hearing in private. But like kids playing with matches in the closet, the flame started in private creates a very public blaze that destroys the whole house.

I'm the master of my unspoken word, but once that word is spoken, I become its slave. We think that sharing a bit of juicy gossip is harmless at best, and a weakness of the flesh at worst – "PG" rated. But God calls it sin. Given the enormous damage caused through the centuries by the sins of the tongue, they should all be "X" rated!

This is serious business because everyone reading these words has one of these lethal weapons in his or her mouth. It could go off without warning.

Like our brothers and sisters on the Day of Pentecost, we stand in need of an outpouring of the Spirit, to cause us to speak with "other" tongues; tongues that warm and not burn; that heal and not harm; that comfort and not curse – tongues of grace and mercy and peace – not tongues of fire.

Truly I say to you, unless you are converted and become like children, you shall not enter the kingdom of heaven. (Matthew 18:3) This is serious business. If I can't enter heaven unless I'm converted, I'd better be pretty sure I know what that means. The word is a strong one – it means, "to change the mind." I can't do that without saying that I am wrong – I have sinned – and this is repentance. Conversion is turning from "the way that seems right to men," and going another direction – God's way.

Modern methods of dealing with human problems exclude the possibility of such conversion. To the practitioner of science today, the past is an accurate predictor of the future. One's problems of yesterday are destined to worsen tomorrow. The Good News is: things don't always have to be the way they've always been. Conversion is not only possible; it's essential for entrance into the kingdom of God.

The stories of God's grace transforming lives are common in the kingdom. One man, a professional diver, was diving on the coast off California when he saw an oyster on a rock with a piece of paper clenched between its shells. He detached the oyster and commenced to read the paper through his goggles. It was a gospel tract, and in that strange setting, his heart was opened. He prayed, "Lord, I can't hold out any longer against Your mercy, it pursues me to the bottom of the sea. Be merciful to me, a sinner!" And he was converted.

Then there was Ty Cobb, the great baseball player of fifty years ago. He led the league in hitting four years in a row, hitting over .400. On his deathbed, July 17, 1961, he was converted to Jesus Christ. He had lived a rough life, but Jesus changed his heart and his mind. He said, with tears, "Tell the boys that I'm sorry it was the last of the ninth that I came to know Jesus. O, how I wish it had been in the first inning of my life."

The hardest words to pronounce in any language are, "I was wrong!" They do not come easily for they strike the root of the tree of pride. But those words are the beginning of being right – right with God and right with people. *Unless you be converted - you shall not enter the kingdom of heaven.*

An aggressive Christian asked a man, "Are you a Christian"? The man stopped and thought for a moment. He was asked again, insistently, "Are you a Christian?" The man gave one of the best answers I've heard to this question, and it relates to the matter of conversion. He took a piece of paper and wrote some names on it. He gave it to the questioner and said, "I'm not the best person to ask that question. These are the names of people who know me. This name is my son – and this one is a business associate – and this one is my neighbor. Ask them if I'm a Christian!"

Those who know us best will confirm true conversion.

God's Yellow Ribbon is Red *4/27– April 27*

The yellow ribbon has become the symbol of the welcome extended to those we love who are defending freedom around the world. There weren't many yellow ribbons after Viet Nam – the idea just didn't catch on.

The following is from an unknown author and appeared in *Illustration Digest*, the July/August 1989 issue. It's one of many versions of this urban legend.

"Tie A Yellow Ribbon 'Round The Old Oak Tree" was a song sung by Tony Orlando in the late '60's and early '70's. It became very popular, but the idea goes way back before Mr. Orlando came on the scene. As a matter of fact, one C.C. McCabe, a chaplain in the civil war and later a Methodist minister told the story first. He was traveling down the coast of California in 1881. As he rode along, a young man near him was quite nervous and fidgety. He explained that he had just been released from prison and was headed home.

He wasn't sure if his parents would welcome him back. So he had written them a letter asking them to let him know if he could come by the house after he was released. He told McCabe that he had said, "If it is OK to stop by the house for a visit, just tie a rag in the old tree by the back porch." He would be able to see the tree from the train as he passed by the family farm. "If there is not a rag in the tree, I'll just keep going."

As the train approached the farm, the young man could not bring himself to look for the signal. He asked McCabe if he would look and let him know if he saw a cloth in the tree. As the train rounded a turn, McCabe saw the tree and, leaping to his feet screamed out, "Look, look! The whole tree is covered with yellow rags. Hundreds of them! Look! Look!" The young man who had spent years in prison knew he was welcome home.

The story tugs at the emotions and one is tempted to quickly refer to the story of the prodigal son and the waiting father, which, of course, is an obvious parallel. But it goes deeper than that. The spiritual parallel of the rags tied to the tree is a Man nailed to a tree – the Cross. The universal symbol of Christianity, despised by many, ignored by some, abused by others, still declares to those in bondage, "All is forgiven, welcome home!"

God's yellow ribbon is red – with the blood of Jesus. It's God's indication that the vilest sinner and the "goodest" sinner need not fear approaching Him. *The one who comes to Me I will certainly not cast out!* (John 6:37)

"Come now, and let us reason together," says the Lord, "Though your sins are as scarlet, they will be as white as snow; Though they are red like crimson (double-dyed in Hebrew) they will be as wool." (Isaiah 1:18)

The bombing in Oklahoma City in an April past killed over 200 men, women, and children. Scenes of the bloodshed shocked a nation already hardened to violence. It was the worst terrorist attack in American history.

A memorial prayer service was held where heart-felt words of comfort flowed freely, along with solemn vows to bring the perpetrators to swift and certain justice. It was part of the healing process.

Assurances were given that God understood the pain of those who lost loved ones in the tragedy. He does. Children were comforted with the promise that God would protect them. He will.

But the unspoken question in the hearts of hundreds of those whose lives were shattered by the evil action must have been: Why didn't God prevent it?

We've been brain washed. Movies, comic books, and video games have convinced us that, no matter what the danger, the script calls for last-second rescue. We've watched the Terminator save the day in the nick of time. Nobody gets hurt but the bad guys. God must be no less heroic and timely in His defense of the righteous.

Our fascination with last-second rescue and Superman-like deliverance is the product of our fear and wishful thinking, not our faith and truth-centered hope. The Scriptures do not promise immunity to pain and tragedy for followers of the Crucified One. That's what grace now and heaven later are all about.

In the real world, if someone chooses to lie, steal, commit adultery or make a bomb in defiance of all the laws of God and man, and the promptings of their own conscience, it's going to be a day of disaster. Someone made a choice.

Every human has the awesome right of choice. God's grace will not violate my power to choose. He gave us the force of commandment and the guidance of conscience to influence our choices.

Man's way of dealing with this danger is to pass more laws, enlarge the police force, build more prisons, and enforce the death penalty. Promise these things and you can be elected to almost any office in the land.

God's plan to change society and prevent the bombing of innocent people is simple. It's in Jesus' profound statement of purpose in Luke 19:10, *The Son of Man has come to seek and to save that which was lost.*

Destructive choices are the product of our lost-ness. We must reach every lost man, woman, and child with Gospel of Jesus' love, because it changes the chooser. And if the chooser is changed, his new choices can heal and not hurt, build and not destroy.

James 5:20 says, *Remember this: Whoever turns a sinner from the error of his way will save him from death and cover a multitude of sins.*

The Path of Wrath *4/29 – April 29*

Marian Anderson died today. I grieve the loss of this woman. She was one of my childhood heroes. I was 5 years old when she was refused entrance into a public meeting because she was black. She handled herself with amazing grace. I've followed the life and career of Miss Anderson, an opera singer, who touched my young heart with her warm voice and her love for Jesus.

I can tell you why she made an impression on me; she reacted to injustice the way I thought people should. She didn't respond with anger when she was refused access to the arena for which she had trained. She eventually sang, to the standing ovations, at the Metropolitan Opera. Marian Anderson knew that the wrath of man does not work the righteousness of God. *But let everyone be quick to hear, slow to speak and slow to anger; for the anger of man does not achieve the righteousness of God.* (James 1:19, 20)

What has happened to us? Some are applauding the actions of a mother who shot a man in the head whom she believed molested her son. Others spout a dangerous rationale for the shooting of an abortionist. We are encouraged to "understand" the pressures these self-styled, self-consumed "victims" must have felt. It's most troubling that fanatics and terrorists in the name of God here and in Iraq and in Jerusalem perpetrate many such actions. This is the essence of blasphemy and the misuse of His holy name.

Hasn't anybody read Romans 12:17-21 lately? Here's what it says: *Never pay back evil for evil to anyone. Respect what is right in the sight of all men. If possible, so far as it depends on you, be at peace with all men. Never take your own revenge, beloved, but leave room for the wrath of God, for it is written, "Vengeance is Mine, I will repay," says the Lord... Do not be overcome by evil, but overcome evil with good.*

That's pretty clear – never pay back evil for evil. And this was written to believers living in the pagan culture of First Century Rome. Thousands of Christians hid in the Catacombs and were the objects of deadly sport in the Circus Maximus. That was the moral climate that provoked the words Paul wrote in his letter to the Christians in Rome. I've known injustice and I confess that the idea of getting even appeals to the darker side of my nature, but there is absolutely no place for revenge in the mind, heart, or hand of a disciple of The Crucified One.

The path of wrath does not lead anywhere worth going. The path of wrath does not lead to victory – only to more wrath, more vengeance, more bloodshed. Hear it again from the mouth of God – *The anger of man does not achieve the righteousness of God.* And, *Never, never, - pay back evil for evil!*

Or, to put it another way – two wrongs don't make a right.

Sam Donaldson of ABC News asked Ted Turner, the network giant, what he wanted on his tombstone. Ted's answer was, "I have nothing more to say." The message of the Easter season is a bit different. It declares that God has a lot more to say and is alive forever to say it.

"History is just news from the graveyard." So says a character in a poetic novel. When you think about it, he's right.

The best news in all of history is from a graveyard outside Jerusalem with a tomb that's empty. The One Who had occupied the tomb temporarily, stands before all humanity for all time with the assurance:

I am the resurrection and the life. Whoever believes in me, though he were dead, yet shall he live; and whoever lives and believes in me shall never die. (John 11:25, 26)

This is what the Scripture refers to as a living hope. Expressing the state of mind of his day, Sophocles wrote, "Not to be born at all – that is by far the best fortune; the second best is as soon as one is born with all speed to die."

A believer, in the ancient world, shone as a bright beacon in on a dark night because he had hope, a living hope. His hope came from two things.

First, the Christian believed that he was born again, and his new birth had the very life of God in it which neither time nor eternity could destroy.

Second, his hope came from the resurrection of Jesus Christ. The Christian had within him – this Jesus Who had conquered death and, therefore, there was nothing he needed to fear.

What was true for our brothers and sisters in the 1st century is true for us in the 21st century because Jesus lives! We, too, have the life of God within us and we, too, are the dwelling place of the risen Lord, Who has conquered death, hell, and the grave.

It's not only the hope of heaven in the sweet bye-and-bye. Resurrection makes a difference here on planet earth now! Resurrection is what God does when we've done all we can do, and it turns out to be death.

Resurrection is what God does when we have exhausted our attempts at freedom. Resurrection is God's freedom from everything that binds us to earth and we can know His freedom now!

Double Vision *5/1 – May 1*

Where there is no vision, the people perish. (Proverbs 29:18 KJV)

Other versions of Scripture say it differently, but the key thought is conveyed however you may say it: the men and women of God must have a vision, or someone's going to perish.

The vision in practical terms is a kind of "double vision;" a sense that God, first of all, brought us to our present place and, second, He will take us from here to another point of growth in Him. It is as much a part of "vision" to see that God has led thus far, as it is to see His leading for the future.

In I Samuel 7:12, the prophet built an altar between Mispah and Shen and said, *Thus far the LORD has helped us.* He called the altar "Ebenezer," "a stone of help." We will go on from here by the same power that brought us to here.

If we have the facet of vision that sees that we've been led to where we are now by the Lord, then we should have a sense that we're moving into new challenges in the future by the same gracious guidance.

A shipload of travelers, about 360 years ago, landed on the shore of America. The first year, they built a town site. The next year they elected a town council. The third year the town council planned to build a road five miles west, into the wilderness.

In the fourth year the people tried to impeach their town council because they thought it was a waste of public funds to build a road five miles westward into a wilderness. Who needed to go there anyway?

Here were people who had the vision to see across three thousand miles of ocean and overcome great hardships to come to a new land. But in just a few years they were not able to see five miles out of town.

They were satisfied with where they were. They settled for what they had. They failed to see that the great God who brought them to the new world was surely capable of taking them further into the new world.

With a clear vision of what we can become in Jesus Christ, individually and collectively, no ocean of difficulty is too great. Without it, however, we will not move beyond our current boundaries.

Without people to care and work, pray and give, however, the double vision (seeing what God has done and will yet do) will come to nothing. Without a vision people perish; without people – visions die an ignominious death.

May 2 – 5/2 — *You're a Winner!*

You're a winner! This isn't one of those positive thinking pep talks to convince you to have a winning attitude. It's about a brightly colored envelope I got in the mail recently. The envelope said, "You're a Winner! And you have never been closer to winning five million dollars." I read on.

I had been selected as a "designated participant." All I had to do was to return the winning card. As I read through the double talk, I discovered that all I had really won was the chance to spend money for substandard merchandise at inflated prices.

The double-speak of the world may seem convincing, but the end of it is debt, and ultimately death. There ought to be a law prohibiting the waste of perfectly good trees to make the paper on which this junk is published. Except that now there're coming to me in paper-less droves in my e-mail.

Satan sends messages in the same spirit as the junk we all get. The first message he sends is the opposite of the junk mail I got. It says, "You're such a loser." "You'll never amount to anything." "You might as well give up."

Then, when the time is right and we're desperate for good news, he sends this brightly colored one: "You can be a winner. All you have to do is do what you always wanted to do anyhow, and wealth, happiness, popularity, and complete fulfillment will be yours."

Isaiah 55:1-3 says, *Come, all you who are thirsty, come to the waters; and you who have no money, come, buy and eat! Come buy wine and milk without money and without cost. Why do you spend money on that which is not bread and your labor for that which does not satisfy? Listen, listen to Me, and your soul will delight in the richest of fare. Give ear and come to Me, and I will make an everlasting covenant with you, My unfailing kindnesses promised to David.*

There's a question right in the middle of these powerful words; *Why do you spend money on that which is not bread and your labor for that which does not satisfy?* Good question. Why indeed? God calls us to find our satisfaction in Him and He will delight our soul with the richest of fare. That sounds pretty good to me, and in fact, it has proven to be true.

So you want to be a winner. The real winners are those are not consumed with getting things, but with sharing things with others that are just too important not to share. The greatest among these share-ables is the Gospel of Jesus Christ. The real Good News is too important to keep to ourselves.

Something *5/3 – May 3*

If anyone thinks himself to be something, when he is nothing, he deceives himself. (Galatians 6:3) Paul's admonition to the Galatians is worthy of examination.

Life has a way of humbling those who think they're really something; like the pastor who spoke at a certain charitable organization. He felt that he had done rather well. After the meeting the chairman handed him a check. "Oh, I couldn't take this," the pastor said with proper humility. "I appreciate the honor of being asked to speak. Put it someplace useful."

The chairman asked, "Do you mind if we put it into our Special Fund?" The pastor replied, "Of course not. What's the Special Fund for?" He replied, "It's so we can get a better speaker next year."

I have, upon leaving a job or a city, felt that the true value of my "many self-less, humble, efforts" would not be appreciated fully until I was gone. Then they would miss me. "You don't miss the water until the well runs dry," was the rationale behind this faulty thinking.

Well, I've found that it's not true; the water was still there. I was just the guy that operated the pump. There was still plenty of water in the well, and if I wasn't there to draw it, someone else would.

Humiliating, isn't it? I have a theory about the rushing mighty wind that came on the Day of Pentecost. It's based on the principle that nature abhors a vacuum. The idea is that Jesus is of such substance to the natural and the spiritual world that when He left earth a huge vacuum was formed.

A few days later, His Spirit rushed in to fill the void left by His physical departure and the result was a rushing mighty swish, like when you open a can of coffee, only magnified millions of times.

When He ascended to heaven, Jesus left a hole in people's lives that His Spirit rushed in to fill. "And they were all filled," and quite satisfied with the Holy Spirit's Presence, for He is the Spirit of Jesus.

I don't know about you, but my departure from any place has never caused a rushing mighty wind. But then, when nothing leaves, nothing rushes in to fill its place. Yet there is a sense that the only time we are ever "something" is when we know that we are nothing – without Jesus.

Without Me, you can do nothing, (John 15:5) He said. And He's really Something! The only Something in the universe.

May 4 – 5/4 *Blessed*

The document that our founding fathers drafted two hundred years ago, The Constitution of the United States of America, has been the foundation of our nation since its inception. Revisionist judges are challenging it, but it stands firm as the basis of our government.

There's another document that goes much further into the past than our Constitution. This document has been called the "Constitution and By-Laws of the Kingdom of God." It's the Sermon on the Mount.

This "Manifesto of the King" is in Matthew 5, 6, 7, and it describes a radically different way of life, as compared to the prevailing values of the world and the religious community of Jesus' day. Matthew 5:2 in the original Greek says, *Having opened His mouth He went to teaching them saying...*

The phrase "opened His mouth" isn't just a fancy way of saying, "He said." This phrase means two things. First, it marks the expression of something of solemn importance, and second, it's a picture of one who opens his mouth and lets his heart come pouring out of his mouth.

So Jesus is speaking things of solemn importance from His heart. He's describing what human life and human relationships look like when they come under His gracious rule. The "Preamble" to this Constitution is called the Beatitudes. I call them the Be-Attitudes, because they speak of attitudes that ought to be. Here's Matthew 5:1-10.

And seeing the multitudes, He went up on a mountain, and when He was seated His disciples came to Him. Then He opened His mouth and taught them, saying, "Blessed are the poor in spirit, for theirs is the kingdom of God. Blessed are those who mourn, for they shall be comforted. Blessed are the meek, for they shall inherit the earth. Blessed are those who hunger and thirst for righteousness, for they shall be filled.

Blessed are the merciful, for they shall obtain mercy. Blessed are the pure in heart, for they shall see God. Blessed are the peacemakers, for they shall be called the sons of God. Blessed are those who are persecuted for righteousness sake, for theirs is the kingdom of heaven."

The word, "blessed", has been translated, "happy," but there's more to it than that. Literally it means – spiritually prosperous. We miss the point entirely if we think of Jesus' message setting forth the principles of His kingdom only in terms of happiness as the world sees it.

In God's eyes, happiness is linked to spiritual values, not material things. It's expressed in John's third letter. He says, *Beloved, I pray that in all respects you may prosper and be in good health, just as your soul prospers.* (III John 1:2)

Cinco de Mayo *5/5 – May 5*

Cinco de Mayo is not an American holiday, but it should be. Why Cinco de Mayo? And why should Mexicans and Americans celebrate this day? Because 4,000 Mexican soldiers smashed the French army of 8,000, at Puebla, Mexico, on the morning of May 5, 1862.

The French had landed in Mexico five months earlier on the pretext of collecting Mexican debts from the newly elected government of democratic President Benito Juarez. Under Emperor Napoleon III, who detested the United States, the French came to stay.

They brought a prince with them to rule the new Mexican nation. His name was Maximilian. Napoleon's French Army hadn't been defeated in 50 years. It invaded Mexico with the finest modern equipment. The French weren't afraid of anyone, especially since America was embroiled in a bloody Civil War.

The French Army left the port of Vera Cruz to attack Mexico City to the west. The French assumed that the Mexicans would give up, should their capital fall to the enemy – as European countries traditionally did.

Under the command of Texas-born General Zaragosa, the Mexicans awaited. Brightly dressed French Dragoons led the enemy columns. The Mexican Army was less stylish.

General Zaragosa ordered his cavalry, under the command of General Porfirio Diaz, out to the French flanks. In response, the French did a most stupid thing; they sent their cavalry off to chase Diaz and his men, who proceeded to defeat them soundly. The remaining French infantrymen charged the Mexican defenders through sloppy mud from a thunderstorm and through hundreds of head of stampeding cattle stirred up by Indians armed only with machetes.

When the battle was over, the Mexicans had won a great victory that kept Napoleon III from supplying the confederate rebels in the United States for another year, allowing the Union to build its army, thus smashing the Confederates at Gettysburg, essentially ending the Civil War.

Union forces were then rushed to the Texas/Mexican border under General Phil Sheridan, who made sure that the Mexicans got all the weapons and ammunition they needed to expel the French.

It might be a stretch to credit the survival of the United States to those brave Mexicans who faced an army twice as large in 1862. But who knows?

Cinco de Mayo is important; it celebrates freedom and liberty. These are two ideals for which Mexicans and Americans have fought shoulder to shoulder to protect – ever since the 5th of May, 1862.

Besides that, it's my son's birthday.

While we're on the subject of things Hispanic, let me introduce you to Simon Bolivar, one of South America's greatest generals. His victories over the Spaniards won independence for Bolivia, Panama, Colombia, Ecuador, Venezuela and Peru. He is called El Liberator and the "George Washington of South America."

Bolivar was born in July 24, 1783 at Caracas, Venezuela. His parents died when he was a child, and he inherited a fortune. As a young man, he traveled in Europe. As he returned to Venezuela, Bolivar joined the group of patriots that seized Caracas in 1810 and proclaimed independence from Spain.

The Spaniards forced Bolivar to retreat from Venezuela to New Granada (now Colombia) also at war with Spain. He took command of a Colombian force and captured Bogotá in 1814.

Bolivar marched into New Granada in 1819. He defeated the Spaniards in Boyar in 1819, liberating the territory of Colombia. He then returned to Angostura and led the congress that organized the original republic of Colombia. Bolivar became its first president on December 17, 1819.

Why am I talking about this man today? Two reasons: because he was committed to liberty, and because of the following account.

In 1824 Peru won its independence from Spain under the leadership of General Bolivar. Bolivar called a convention for the purpose of drafting the constitution for the new country. After the convention the general was approached by a delegation suggesting that he be their first president. Bolivar declined saying that he felt someone else deserved the honor more than he did.

The people still wanted to do something special for Bolivar to show their appreciation for all that he had done for them, so they offered him a gift of 1,000,000 pesos, a very large fortune in those days.

Bolivar accepted the gift and then asked how many slaves there were in Peru. He was told there were about 3,000. "And how much does a slave sell for," he wanted to know? "About 350 pesos for an able-bodied man", was the answer.

Then, said Bolivar, "I will add whatever is necessary to this million pesos you have given me and I will buy all the slaves in Peru and set them free. It makes no sense to free a nation unless all its citizens enjoy freedom as well."

Simon Bolivar is a hero in South America. He's one in my heart, too.

The Deborah Factor *5/7 – May 7*

Village life in Israel ceased, ceased until I, Deborah, arose, until I arose a mother in Israel. (Judges 5:7) *Up! For this is the day in which the Lord has delivered Sisera into your hands.* (Judges 4:14)

This is from "The Song of Deborah" written in the 12th century B.C. after she had led the battle against a confederation of five kings led by Sisera.

In her song of victory, however, Deborah describes herself as a "mother in Israel," not as a warrior. She was one of the judges who functioned before there were kings in Israel. Her daily activity included sitting in the city street acting as an arbitrator in disputes. Her wisdom came at a time of great crisis and her godly judgments preserved the nation for an entire generation.

With all that Deborah did, the way she saw herself, and the one thing she wished to be know for, was that she was a mother in Israel. That's what I'm calling The Deborah Factor – Motherhood.

What Deborah did was to clean up messes; settle disputes between angry people. Maybe that's why she called herself a mother in Israel. That's what mothers do.

History records that village life had ceased, for all practical purposes, until Deborah came on the scene. The situation was of such a fearful nature that villagers fled to nearby walled cities for protection against invading armies.

At one point Deborah yelled, *Up!* (That sounds like what mothers say to their kids every morning.) She rallied the people, even the "mighty men of valor," to trust and not be afraid. And that's what mothers do.

The last line of the Song of Deborah says, *So the land had rest for forty years.* What a legacy! Her influence cleaned up and preserved a nation. That's what mothers do.

The image of Deborah as a mighty Xena-like warrior in the battle against Sisera may be a bit deceiving. To accomplish all that she did as leader among her people she must have also been a woman of great compassion.

There's a vital link between motherhood and compassion. In the Hebrew language of the Old Testament the word for "compassion" comes from the root word, "womb." And there's the mother-link.

It means that my compassionate acts give a person another chance. I don't hold past failures against them. I forgive them; I offer a "fresh start." That's what mothers do.

We honor mothers partly for all battles they've fought for us, and the messes they've cleaned up for us, like Deborah. But we can honor them even more by doing battle ourselves, and cleaning up our own messes.

May 8 – 5/8 **Honor to Whom Honor is Due**

Render to all what is due them: honor to whom honor is due. (Romans 13:7)

For years we observed Mother's Day because it was there. But something happened one Mother's Day that made me take a good hard look at this tradition in the church.

We did the standard things: honoring the oldest mother; the one with the most children, etc., when a young man loudly objected to what he considered idolatry. He bellowed out scripture about having no other god's before Jehovah and suggested that we were guilty of mother worship by our acts of respect. It was quite disruptive.

The next week, the young man came in to see me. I learned that he didn't know who his mother was and, after some painful disclosures, he confessed he was reacting to the pain of his own life. But his challenge caused me to examine the practice of honoring anyone in general, and mothers in particular.

The term "honor" is not synonymous with worship in the Scripture, for the Lord tells us to honor elders, parents, and all men, but to worship only Him. It simply denotes respect; "to acknowledge what is right or due."

Such action obviously blesses the recipient, but it's also a point of growth for me to recognize and honor those who've contributed substantially to my life. It's right that we honor faithful spiritual leadership. It's right that we honor mothers as God's gracious provision. It would be disobedience, not idolatry, to withhold such honor.

So mothers, we honor you today with the full approval of the Lord of the Church. You're respected and loved as the channel through which God chose to bring us into being, as He did His own Son. More than that, you have been an incredible influence upon all of us, your children.

We need you, Mothers! We respect and honor you – in Jesus Name!

The Arena of Faith *5/9 – May 9*

Therefore, since we have so great a cloud of witnesses surrounding us, let us run with endurance the race that is set before us, fixing our eyes on Jesus...

This passage from Hebrew 12:1, 2 was the subject of a book, which I read many years ago by Eric Sauer titled, "The Arena of Faith." The book pictures the characters in Hebrews chapter 11, (Enoch, Abraham, Jacob, Moses, to name a few) as former runners in the race, and they are now spectators in the arena as we run our particular race today. (Whether this is to be taken literally or not, is open to debate, but it suggests an interesting scenario.)

In any athletic endeavor, the greatest fans are those who've played the game. They understand the rigors of the race. They appreciate the subtle nuances of competition. Hebrews 12:1 pictures those whose race is over, cheering us on. They don't gloat in their accomplishments nor rest on their laurels, but instead identify with those who struggle against great hardship to endure to the end, and are great fans of the race.

The writer of Hebrews also admonishes us to draw inspiration from the lives of those who've gone before us. Their example establishes a standard of performance that should motivate us to do better. I thought it might be helpful to cite a few other examples you may not have heard about, of those who've competed in the Arena of Faith long before we got to the track.

Ignatius lived late in the first century. He was Bishop of the church at Antioch in Syria and was about to be devoured by wild beasts in Rome for his profession of faith. He wrote to the church in Rome, "Now I begin to be a disciple. I care for nothing of the visible so that I may win Christ. Let fire and the cross, let the companies of wild beasts, let the breaking of bones and tearing of limbs, and all the malice of the devil come upon me; be it so, only may I win Christ Jesus!"

In the sixteenth century William Tyndale, English reformer and martyr, declared: "If God spares my life, I will cause a boy that driveth the plow shall know more of the Scripture than a learned man dost." Tyndale made a translation of the Bible in the English language secretly in exile. When it was completed, it was smuggled into England where many copies were burned by order of the Bishop of London. Hundreds of common people, however, got copies of Tyndale's translation before he was burned at the stake in 1536.

Under the picture of missionary Peter Milne in the church he founded on the little island of Nguna in the New Hebrides are these words, "When he came there was no light; when he died there was no darkness."

All of these and millions more followed the admonition of the second verse, *Fixing our eyes on Jesus, the author and perfecter of our faith...* As we run our race, we must do the same. He's our greatest example.

He's also our biggest fan!

May 10 – 5/10 *Move It or Climb It?*

I've been fascinated by the words which Jesus spoke to his disciples after they had failed top cast a demon out of a young man. He said, *If you have faith as a grain of mustard seed, you shall say to this mountain, "Move from here to there," and it shall move; and nothing shall be impossible to you. But this kind does not go out except by prayer and fasting.* (Matthew 17:20)

The idea of moving mountains appeals to me. Especially if it's as easy as some people make it sound. I like things easy. "Just believe God," they say, and then they quote this passage to show how easy it is to deal with any obstacle in my way. What could be easier than saying, "Mountain, move!" Then stand back and watch it go from here to there? But when it doesn't move, I'm left to conclude that I didn't even have mustard-seed-size faith.

We miss the point of Jesus' words if we think the message is about how easy it is to move big mountains. It's not about that. It's about growing big enough that mountains become like clods of dirt that we kick out of the way as we walk by faith. Jesus ended His statement about mountains by saying that this kind of demon did not go out except by fasting and prayer. That's hard work! But it makes one big in the realm of the spirit, big enough to kick demons from here to there!

I've got a few mountains I've been yelling at for years, but they don't seem to get the message. They're too big to go around. They're made of hard stuff, too hard to go through without some real dynamite power.

What am I talking about? I'm talking about unresolved relationship conflicts, areas of weakness in my flesh, promises to the Lord I didn't keep, and a huge mound of things that loom larger over time, that stand as obstacles to my spiritual progress.

Stacey Allison and Peggy Luce became the first women to climb Mount Everest on March 6, 1989. Stacey had tried it before and had failed. She was asked if succeeding had taught her anything about her character. "No," she said, "getting to the summit didn't. Winning is easy. Not getting there the year before did."

I've learned a lot from my mountains. Some of my mountains will never move because God put them there for me to climb. I will get big enough in Him to handle them, and the view from the top will be fantastic!

Environmental Grace — *5/11 – May 11*

Can a litterbug go to heaven? To hear some environmentalists talk you'd think not. Along with oil spillers, tree choppers, gas-guzzlers, pesticiders, non-recyclers, and CFC sprayers, litterbugs are doomed to perdition (or will doom the rest of us) by their dastardly deeds. Saving the earth has taken on a religious tone, it seems to me.

We tend to dismiss the speeches as part of a liberal agenda that seems bent on making life difficult for conservative Christians. To say the least, evangelical Christians haven't been leading the march to save the planet, but is it just so much left-wing political hype to speak of taking good care of the earth? Or do we, who claim to know the Creator, have something to say and do about our environment? I think we do.

First, the earth is the Lord's, but the earth is not the Lord! Many have made the earth a god and worship at its altar. The Creator of heaven and earth is no more pleased when men worship a tree, an ocean, or a bird than He is when they worship a graven image. I'm a lover of created things, but my first love is the Creator of all things bright and beautiful. The Lord God made them all.

Second, a spiritual understanding of this matter begins with stewardship. Another word for it is management. While the earth is the Lord's, He has entrusted the management of it to us. Adam and Eve were given commands to "be fruitful and multiply," but they were also told to "cultivate and keep the garden," (Genesis 2:15). One look at the San Joaquin Valley will show that we've done quite well at being fruitful. But another look at the Amazon rain forest will show that we've not tended very well to parts of this earth.

Third, we're not managing our resources, but the resources of the One to Whom the earth belongs. The earth is the Lord's! Jesus speaks about this in Luke 16: *There was a rich man whose manager was accused of wasting his possessions. So he called him in and asked him, "What is this I hear about you? Give an account of your management, because you cannot be manager any longer."*

There is, along with genuine concern, some unfounded fear in the issue of the environment. The word "chemical" is loaded with irrational implications. A company whose logo said "Better Living Through Chemistry" had to change it because of the fear of chemicals. But in fact everything that exists can be defined in chemical terms.

One obvious example is H2 O, dihydrogen oxide – water. It's amazing what God did to make water. He took two highly flammable gases, hydrogen and oxygen and made something with which to put out fires. With sodium chloride, He took sodium, an extremely volatile substance, and chlorine, a poisonous gas, and made something to season and preserve and heal – salt.

If God can make water and salt from elements that by themselves are volatile, then perhaps He can cause people come together who strongly disagree about how to take care of the God's earth. Lord, give us wisdom!

What will they think of next? An entry into what's called "Reality TV" is a glorified quiz show called "The Weakest Link." I've watched it a few times, mainly because I'm a Jeopardy junkie, and I like the challenge of answering stupid questions.

The host of this hour-long ordeal is a stern, crusty English woman who has absolutely no compassion for those who don't know the answers. At the end of each round of questions, the contestants choose the one they feel has fouled up the most and is "the weakest link." He, or she, is dismissed with a cruel, curt "good bye."

I don't know about you, but I've sometimes felt like the weakest link in the Church because I didn't know enough, or wasn't fast enough, or experienced enough, or spiritual enough. Basically, I just wasn't enough. And so, I waited for the inevitable, "good bye," from above.

But it never came. It never came because the Church is not a chain with links. It's the Body of Christ, and the weakest parts are protected and honored.

Just look at what it says in I Corinthians 12:22, 23: *...those parts of the body that seem to be weaker are indispensable, and the parts that we think are less honorable we treat with special honor. And the parts that are unpresentable are treated with special modesty, while our presentable parts need no special treatment.*

Wow! That means I'm not going to get voted off because I'm not enough. And neither are you. We're all important parts of His body, and the power to perform and be what we can be is not our own – it's His.

This idea that the weakest part of any earthly entity is valued and indispensable is radical. Government agencies, corporations and institutions function by weeding out unproductive members and by promoting those who meet specific performance standards.

But this is not so in the Body of Christ. But then, the Church is not an earthly entity. It's God's thing – not ours. God has arranged the parts in the body, every one of them, just as he wanted them to be. *But now God has placed the members, each one of them, in the body, just as He desired.* (I Corinthians 12:18)

More about "The Weakest Link" tomorrow.

The Weakest Link-2 *5/13 – May 13*

But God has combined the members of the body and has given greater honor to the parts that lacked it, so that there should be no division in the body, but that its parts should have equal concern for each other. If one part suffers, every part suffers with it; if one part is honored, every part rejoices with it. Now you are the body of Christ, and each one of you is a part of it. (I Corinthians 12:24-27)

The Holy Spirit makes it clear that "the weakest links" among us have a unique place in God's order of things – a place of equality and honor.

Since we are the body of Christ, it stands to reason that we should, at some point, begin to look like Him. While each part may not resemble Him completely, together we should be showing the world what Jesus looks like.

Do you remember going to an amusement park and putting your face above a headless frame painted to represent a muscle man, a clown, or even a bathing beauty? Some of us have had our pictures taken this way, and the photos are humorous because the head doesn't match the body.

I wonder, if we could picture Jesus Christ as the head of our local body of believers, would the world laugh at the mismatch? Or would they stand in awe of a human body so closely related to a divine head? I pray that they would see at least some reasonable likeness.

Well, my fellow weakest links, we've found a home in God's family. The good news is– *His power shows up best in weak people.* (II Corinthians 12:9) (Living Bible)

Good-bye!

May 14 – 5/14 **Citizens of Heaven**

For many walk, of whom I often told you, and now tell you even weeping, that they are enemies of the cross of Christ, whose end is destruction, whose god is their appetite, and whose glory is in their shame, who set their minds on earthly things. For our citizenship is in heaven, from which also we eagerly wait for a Savior, the Lord Jesus Christ... (Philippians 3:18-20)

The word, “citizenship”, is the Greek noun “politeuma.” This word referred to a body of people constituting a nation or a state, or a body of politic. It also meant a body of people who were residents in a foreign city while their citizenship and allegiance was elsewhere.

I thought it would be interesting to look up the oath that people from all over the world take when they become U. S. citizens. It’s fascinating reading. Here’s what they swear to:

“I hereby declare, on oath, that I absolutely and entirely renounce and abjure all allegiance and fidelity to any foreign prince, potentate, state, or sovereignty of whom or which I have heretofore been a subject or citizen; that I will support and defend the Constitution of the United States of America against all enemies, foreign and domestic;

“That I will bear true faith and allegiance to the same; that I will bear arms on behalf of the United States when required by law; that I will perform noncombatant service in the armed forces of the United States when required by law; that I will perform work of national importance under civilian direction when required by law; and that I take this obligation freely without mental reservation or purpose of evasion; so help me God.”

That’s pretty amazing. I wonder how many people who were born in this country would be willing to take such an oath. Maybe it would be a good idea if we all did.

However, that part about renouncing one’s allegiance to any sovereign to whom I have been subject is potentially a problem for those who have also sworn allegiance to the Lord Jesus Christ.

It has been a bit easier to resolve any conflict of allegiance because our nation was founded upon Godly principles. The Dome of the Capitol in Washington D.C., for instance, has this inscription: “One God, one law, one element; and one far off, divine event to which the whole creation moves.”

But in recent years our nation has strayed so far from its Godly roots that we can no longer claim, with any degree of credibility, to be a “Christian nation.”

So we who have sworn allegiance to King Jesus will have some interesting choices to make in the months and years to come. We are, after all, citizens of a heaven kingdom, and we ought not to forget that for a moment.

I'll Be Switched *5/15 – May 15*

My grandmother had many colorful expressions that come creeping back into my thoughts from time to time. No one could say them quite like she could. She had a way with words.

One of these expressions came to mind when I was reading about the "caning" of a young man who was convicted of malicious vandalism in Singapore. He was given a reduced sentence of four strikes with a rattan cane, after intervention by our President, instead of six, as originally prescribed.

The whole thing is a tempest in the proverbial teapot, threatening to affect America's relations with the government of Singapore for years to come. And, sadly, the media gave more coverage to this minor incident than the horrible massacres in Rwanda. Ethnic cleansing, they call it.

Evidently four well-deserved whacks on the backside of one rebellious American are of more consequence than the senseless slaughter of a quarter of a million Africans. That's terribly frightening!

I digress. The phrase my grandmother used when she was faced with some unbelievable or outrageous circumstance was this: "Well, I'll be switched!" I often wondered what it meant.

It's a phrase reminiscent of the days when switches were used to spank disobedient children. I doubt if very many of you have ever heard it uttered. Sometimes, just to make it interesting, the offending one was required to cut the switch from the tree that would be used to administer the punishment.

Punishment... now there's a unique idea. You don't hear much about it these days. I'm certainly not advocating abusive measures in the discipline of children. But the pendulum has swung so far that punishment for wrong conduct is itself seen as wrong conduct.

Wrong... now there's another unique idea. How many times have you sensed that someone you care about was upset and you asked, "What's wrong?" And they said, hoping to avoid confrontation, "There's nothing wrong." That sums up the moral climate of America these days. "There's nothing wrong."

No action, however immoral or repulsive, is wrong." Vandalism isn't wrong, adultery isn't wrong, lying isn't wrong, murder isn't wrong. The problem with nothing being identified as wrong in a civilized society is that nothing is right either. Honesty, fidelity, purity, and holiness are not "right." They're simply your choice of ways, given your situation, of interfacing with your world.

But wrong is real – and time will prove it. Wrong seeds produce bad harvest, even it you didn't think they were wrong seeds when you planted them.

Well, I'll be switched!

May 16 – 5/16 *Who's Life Is It Anyhow?*

Don't you know that your body is the temple of the Holy Spirit, who lives in you and was given to you by God? You do not belong to yourself, for God bought you with a high price. So you must honor God with your body. (I Corinthians 6:19, 20)

There's a popular TV show called "Whose Line Is It Anyway?" It features four zany regulars who are presented with hypothetical situations to which they must make up dialogue and actions on the spot, apparently without preparation of any kind.

It's rather amusing to watch as they ad lib their way through a half-hour of improvisational nonsense. The spontaneous nature of it encourages expression to whatever lurks just beneath the surface in the minds of the players.

Like the cast of "Whose Line Is It Anyway?" many of us live our lives in a kind of ad-lib fashion. We have no script to guide us so when situations arise we are left to improvise our responses to life's little (and big) surprises.

It follows that, when we are left to ad-lib our way through life, we often express what lies just beneath the surface of our thoughts and emotions. And that can get us into a heap of trouble.

Take the matter of our sexuality, for instance. Most people of the world, and many Christians, ad-lib their way through the maze of immoral options that are available in our society. When confronted with temptation, we improvise since there is no script to which we feel bound. And more often than not, improvisation leads to sin.

God has not left us to improvise and ad-lib our way through life. He has given us a script to follow – His word. In it He gives us the plot and the dialogue and reveals the right way to make it through to the last scene.

Even more incredibly, He assumes ownership and takes responsibility for getting us through life. He purchased us with His blood and we belong to Him.

So the question now is: "Whose life is it anyhow?" This is a big deal; it makes all the difference in the world (and I do mean in the world) that I am His.

God has plans for me, plans for good and not evil. And He has given me His word to guide me, and His Spirit to fill me.

Whose life is it anyhow? It's not mine, it's His, and – to borrow another famous line – "it's a wonderful life!"

Life Without Brakes *5/17 – May 17*

I was stopped at a red light at Olive and Palm when something happened that I would never forget.

I was in the middle lane with a car on either side of me at the line of the crosswalk when I heard the sound of screeching tires behind me. I looked in my side mirror and saw an old blue Oldsmobile coming toward me in my lane at high speed.

The left front wheel of the car was locked and smoking in a vain attempt to stop this heavy vehicle. Without thinking, I quickly pulled my car as far to the right as I could and almost in front of the car on my right, leaving a very narrow lane for the run-away car to pass through.

He made it through the opening I had created for him and ran the red light at about thirty miles-per-hour. It was something of a miracle that I didn't get rear-ended and that he didn't get clobbered by cross traffic at this busy intersection. Then I did something stupid.

When the light changed, I caught up with him to see what kind of idiot would do such a thing. I pulled along side and looked into the run-away car and was met with the most evil stare I have ever seen.

It was a car full of guys laughing at having a grand time because they had escaped tragedy again. They appeared to be capable of inflicting severe damage to my person so I backed off a block or two, and saw them run stop signs three more times because they simply couldn't stop.

Only one wheel of the car had any braking power and the other three didn't, but they were driving as though they could stop any time. If you're going to stop your car, it's going to take a total commitment from your brakes.

There are examples, in our national and personal history, when we were like the run-away car, without total commitment – to stop – or go. The results are very painful and continue to trouble us.

Jesus has called us to forsake all to follow Him. But many of us live with brakes-on-one-wheel commitment, and can't stop what we're doing to follow Him completely.

We think we can stop sinning any time and follow Him. But the longer and faster you go without stopping, the harder it is to stop.

We may get away with it for a while, but eventually there will be a crash.

Lord, how they have increased who trouble me? Many are they who rise up against me. Many are they who say of me, "There is no help for him in God." Selah. But You, O Lord, are a shield for me, my glory and the One Who lifts my head. (Psalm 3:1-3)

Selah – a word shrouded in mystery; a Hebrew word that's never translated into English. It appears seventy-three times in Psalms and three times in Habakkuk. The Latin Vulgate, which was an early translation of the Old Testament into Latin by the Catholic fathers, ignored the word altogether as if it were not a part of the text of Scripture. I think the Holy Spirit meant this word to be included in the sacred writings. It is a word for today!

Selah is probably best understood as we realize that all of the Psalms were intended to be sung and accompanied by instruments. It's most likely that Selah is an instruction to the singers to pause while the instruments played an interlude, or modulated to a higher key.

Some scholars say that it's simply a musical interlude while others say that it means, "Pause and think about it." My humble opinion is that it's both. It's a musical interlude, which gives occasion for contemplating the words. It could be called a meditation pause.

I've checked out most of the occurrences of Selah in Psalms and a pattern is evident to me. Most of the time the tone of the Psalm is similar before and after Selah – the meditation pause – as in Psalm 46:7, 8: *The Lord of hosts is with us; the God of Jacob is our refuge. - Selah - Come, behold the works of the Lord.*

But sometimes the tone changes after Selah as in the verse at the top of this page. *Many are they who say of me, "There is no help for him in God." Selah. But You, O Lord, are a shield for me, my glory and the One Who lifts my head.*

The background of the 3rd Psalm is that David is fleeing from his own son, Absalom. He's discouraged and listens to the voices of those who say that even God can't help him now.

But when David observes the Selah pause, and the musicians play an interlude, he comes out on the other side changed. "But You, O Lord, are a shield for me…" This pattern occurs many times. The meditation pause – Selah – makes a difference in how the psalmist sees his condition.

Our lives need the "Selah" pauses, especially when trouble comes. The Lord can speak peace and counsel when the music of life comes to rest.

Quiet At The Core *5/19 – May 19*

Strangers have risen against me, and violent men have sought my life; they have not set God before them. Selah. Behold, God is my helper; the Lord is the sustainer of my soul. (Psalm 54:3, 4)

There's so much noise in the world. It doesn't seem possible for it to stop long enough for us to meditate upon the Lord, and see our condition in the light of His truth. The chaos of this world drowns out the still small voice of the Spirit.

We need Selah pauses every day. As a matter of fact, we need a Selah at the core of our being – a quiet place where we can retreat to in times of noise and stress. We need to be quiet at the core.

That's so different from the world, even the natural world. Planet earth is anything but quiet at the core. If it were possible to go to the center of the earth, one would find a caldron of molten rock. This churning, boiling mass sometimes breaks to the surface as volcanoes spew tons of ash and lava. The earth is chaotic at the core.

The world's systems are chaotic at the core. The closer one gets to the major centers of the world's activity, the more chaotic it is. The New York Stock Exchange, for instance, the center of the financial world, is chaotic at the core.

A trip to the hallowed halls of Congress in Washington D.C., the center of the political world, reveals chaos at the core. The noise and clamor of heavy metal music, and the screams of crazed mobs reveals the chaos at the core of the entertainment centers of the world.

There just aren't any Selahs in the world. It can't afford them. If there were pauses in the revelry and clamor long enough for anyone to think about what's happening, the world wouldn't be able to maintain its hold upon its prisoners.

I'm grateful for the Selahs in the Scripture and in my life. I've been able to identify quietness at the core of my being that is an anchor in times of stress. Invariably, my Selahs have made a difference in how I view my crisis.

I'm grateful that the translators left the Selah pauses in the Scripture, and the Lord has put one at the core of my being!

May 20 – 5/20 — *Canceling Cancer*

Some people I care about have cancer. The very word strikes fear into our hearts. Chances are pretty good that every one of us knows someone who has been given this news. But chances are also pretty good these days that every one of us knows someone who's in remission or has been free of this disease for some time.

I got to thinking about this matter and wondered why the word "cancer" carries such power. The word, "automobile", doesn't terrorize us like "cancer" but more people die from automobiles than cancer, especially when you factor out the preventable kind such as lung cancer caused by smoking.

I have no desire to trivialize or minimize the anguish many feel when confronted with the fact that cancer has a foothold in their body, but something must be done to take the sting out of this word for believers in Jesus Christ. To fear anything too much is to trivialize and minimize the power and hope in the name of Jesus.

The way I go about seeing words may seem a little strange. "Words are my game," I've been know to say. I often use the letters to make an anagram by using the letters of the word to form different words. I tried that with "cancer" without much success. Not many words can be made from those six letters.

Then I sometimes make an acrostic that relates to the word. For instance:

Christ's Atonement Nullifies Cancer's Evil Ravages! Or, how about this one: Christ's Almighty Name Conquers Enemy Rule!

You can probably make up your own, too. It's one of the ways that words can be given different impact. Any time I can impose the name of Jesus upon a problem, I've begun to conquer it. The name of Jesus is a name above all names – even the name "cancer"!

One reason that it's important to take the sting out of fear-filled words is that fear itself often becomes a factor in the crisis. If "a merry heart does good like a medicine," as the Scripture says, then a fearful heart has the opposite effect. Fear gives disease, or whatever crisis I'm facing, more power than it has in and of itself. There are 365 "fear-nots" in the Bible and Jesus said, "Fear not!" more often than anyone else.

I pray that we can cancel cancer's petrifying power with the light of truth and the power of the name of Jesus!

Praise To Thee! *5/21 – May 21*

It was my privilege to participate in the graveside service for a veteran of World War II a few years ago. He was a major is the United States Air Force and flew missions for three years between Burma and China over the Himalayas, or "The Hump," as they called it. I will never forget the ceremony.

A company of fifteen from Castle Air Force Base came to give honor to their fallen comrade. Six of them marched in strict military order to the casket – three on each side – and carefully took the flag which was covering the casket by its four corners and its middle and raised it horizontally above the casket.

That was my signal to begin. I spoke for ten minutes of the man and his many years of military service, and of Jesus, our Captain of the Armies of Heaven. When I finished, six riflemen raised their weapons and fired, on command, a three-gun salute. Then a bugler, a young lady, blew Taps. It was impressive.

Then the six men holding the flag all this time over the casket began to fold it. Every movement was crisp and coordinated and had to be perfectly executed. They took a full eight minutes to fold the flag. It was an exercise designed to give honor to a fallen hero and the Flag of Freedom for which he served.

When the flag was folded satisfactorily, it was presented to the family. The whole thing was like going back in time to when great respect and honor was given those who fought and died for our freedom.

From Bunker Hill to Desert Storm and Bosnia freedom has found its noble defenders. I knew, as I stood watching the flag being folded, that such honor was a holy and righteous thing. God was pleased.

Oliver Wendell Holmes wrote a hymn for the military over a century ago. It couldn't be sung in the "politically correct" atmosphere today, but thousands who lifted their voices in praise to Almighty God once sang it.

Here are the words to The Army Hymn.

O Lord of Hosts! Almighty King! Behold the sacrifice we bring!
To every arm Thy strength impart, Thy Spirit shed through every heart.
Wake in our breasts the living fires, the holy faith that warmed our sires.
Thy hand hath made our Nation free: to die for her is serving Thee.
Be Thou a pillared flame to show the midnight snare, the silent foe,
And when the battle thunders loud, still guide us in its moving cloud.
God of all Nations! Sovereign Lord! In Thy dread name we draw the sword.
We lift the starry flag on high that fills with light our stormy sky.
From treason's rent, from murder's stain, guard Thou its folds
Till peace shall rein, till fort and field, till shore and sea,
Join our loud anthem – Praise to Thee!

May 22 – 5/22 *I Love a Parade*

Parades have been around for a long, long time. Parades have welcomed home conquering heroes, proclaimed the coronations of kings and queens, and celebrated the dynamic life of a community for thousands of years.

Something about a parade mirrors life. One can stand on the sidewalk and watch it go by, or get out there and march. I've done both and, since I've been taller than most people for most of my life, I prefer watching to marching. I was conspicuous marching, but I had a definite advantage watching.

For several years our city witnessed what was known as a March for Jesus. I participated in it, and it was a blessing. The Body of Jesus Christ took to the streets for all the reasons that parades have always happened: for our conquering hero, our King of Kings, and for an expression of the life the Christian community in Fresno.

"We will march for an audience of One" was the theme of this event for many years. This meant that taking to the streets was not playing to the crowd or courting the attention of media cameras and microphones. It was for Jesus.

I like this idea. I think it's what the Kingdom of God is all about. We are called to live our whole lives for an audience of One. Didn't Jesus say, in His Kingdom Manifesto called the Sermon on the Mount, *Seek first the kingdom of God and His righteousness and all these things will be added to you.* (Matthew 6:33)

It's all about relevance. Preachers are challenged to be relevant. Success in ministry is judged by relevance, but relevant to what? Relevance does not exist in isolation.

The dictionary says: "Relevant – adj: having a bearing on or connection with the matter at hand." For the Christian, the first matter at hand is Jesus. We must first be relevant to Him. We'll never touch our world with life-changing power by being relevant to it. We must be "irrelevant" to the world – outside of it – to change it.

Man reasons that the Church must be relevant to the world. It sounds good and even compassionate. But empathy has no power to affect change unless the Church is first in living relationship – relevant – to God in Christ Jesus.

It's always been so. *The LORD appeared to Abram, and said unto him, I am the Almighty God; walk before Me, and be blameless.* (Genesis 17:1) Walk before Me is the active phrase – and then Abraham went out and changed his world.

The salt is out of the shaker. I can see and touch my world in Jesus' name. To see with His eyes, care with His heart, and touch with His grace; there's great power in that! But you have to be out there to do that.

I love that parade!

Abounding Hope 5/23 – May 23

Blessed be the God and Father of our Lord Jesus Christ Who, according to His great mercy, has caused us to be born again to a living hope through the resurrection of Jesus Christ from the dead. (I Peter 1:3)

This passage has invaded my thoughts hundreds of times since I committed it to memory years ago. I refer to it and write about it frequently. There are few scriptures that contain as much fundamental truth as this one.

The key word of this passage is "hope." What is hope? We say, "I sure hope tomorrow is a nice day." Or, "I hope my boss will give me a raise." Or, I hope I can make it through this semester." That's not hope as the Bible defines it.

Hope is the expectation of an absolute certainty. It's the patient anticipation of what we know will be; the difference between "I hope so" and "I know so!"

Hebrews 6:17-19 says this, *In the same way God... interposed an oath, in order that by two unchangeable things, in which it is impossible for God to lie, we may have strong encouragement, we who have fled for refuge in laying hold of the hope set before us. This hope we have as an anchor of the soul, a hope both sure and steadfast and one that enters within the veil.*

That's what I'm talking about; hope as an anchor of the soul, sure and steadfast, attached to something eternal beyond this realm – within the veil, in the Holy of Holies of God's abiding Presence.

Now the God of hope fill you with all joy and peace in believing, that ye may abound in hope, through the power of the Holy Spirit. (Romans 15:13)

What does it mean to have an abounding hope? The Apostle Paul describes the world as being without hope in Ephesians 2:12, *remember that you were at that time separate from Christ, excluded from the commonwealth of Israel, and strangers to the covenants of promise, having no hope and without God in the world.*

Now the opposite is true: we are included in the covenants of promise, and we are with God and He is with us. The basis for abounding hope is the abiding presence of the living Jesus within us by the power of the Holy Spirit.

We have the life of God within us and we are the dwelling place of the risen Lord Who has conquered death, hell, and the grave.

This is what abounding hope is made of.

Jesus, knowing that all things had already been accomplished, in order that the Scripture might be fulfilled, said, "I am thirsty." A jar full of sour wine was standing there; so they put a sponge full of sour wine upon a branch of hyssop, and brought it up to His mouth. When Jesus therefore had received the sour wine, He said, "It is finished!" And He bowed His head and gave up His spirit. (John 19:28-30)

With a clear voice Jesus uttered His last word from the cross. It was just one word in the language He spoke, "tetelestai!" – in Aramaic – "It is finished" in English. Thousands of small pieces of evidence from the first century shed light on how this word was used.

If a promissory note were paid in full, the holder of the note would write across the face of it "tetelestai." When a king sent a soldier on a mission to a distant country and the soldier completed his work, he sent back the message to the king, "tetelestai." When a field was planted and the last seed was covered, the farmer would say to his family, "tetelestai," it is finished!

There's great joy in work when it is done, and done well. Jesus drank deeply of this well of pleasure even while He was dying in great anguish. As He saw each part of it falling into place, this must have been part of "the joy that was set before Him," as Hebrews says.

What was it that was finished? The very first recorded words of Jesus are found in Luke chapter two when He was separated from Mary and Joseph in the temple, *Did you not know that I had to be about My Father's business?* (Luke 2:49) And His last words before His death were, "It is finished." It was the Father's business to, once and for all, destroy the power of sin. This was accomplished, done, completed, wrapped up, perfected – finished!

But there's more. The cross is a place of death and by His death there, Jesus created a place where anything that I take to it can be finished. It's a place for finishing anger and bitterness, despair and frustration, sickness and bondage, sin and guilt.

It's no accident that the cross forms an intersection by the way it is made. The cross of Jesus forever stands, as a place of meeting with God, for it was there that Jesus reconciled man to God. *God was in Christ reconciling the world unto Himself.* (II Corinthians 5:19) When God and man are at peace, nothing is impossible and everything is possible.

As Christians, we have a place where, for all things that need to come to an end and need closure, – "it is finished!"

Flowers — *5/25 – May 25*

When Jesus wanted to teach His disciples to trust The Father for everything they needed, He used a flower to illustrate His point. He said, *Observe how the lilies of the field grow; they do not toil nor do they spin, yet I say to you that even Solomon in all his glory did not clothe himself like one of these.* (Matthew 6:28)

This time of year we're blessed with such a profusion of beauty all around us that we may not see the lesson of the flowers. So let me pick a posy and postulate a parable.

The less romantic among us may think that flowers are optional in God's scheme of things. Not so! No flowers – no fruit. No fruit – no seed. No seed – no new life. And all life, as we know it, would cease in one flowerless season.

A flower is the promise of life. We like their fragrance and their beauty and florists make millions on them, but they are first and foremost essential to the propagation of the species.

I wondered: what is it in my life in Jesus that is comparable to the flower? It must be something described in the Scripture as beautiful, attractive, fragrant, and having the seed of life in it. I think the quality that answers to all of these is holiness. We're called to worship God "in the beauty of holiness."

Holiness is like "a sweet smelling savor of Christ" to the world. And true holiness is attractive because it's like Jesus. And all we need do to populate the world with a new species of humanity is be like Jesus all the time.

So, if it's fruit I want, I can either tie some on or ask the Lord to let me flower into holiness. And isn't it interesting that in the Scripture, Jesus is called "The Rose of Sharon" and the "Lily of the Valley."

Lord, may my life have about it the aroma of Your presence in me. And, please, Lord, let it be the seed of life that I can share with others. Amen.

In 1956, during the Mau Mau uprisings in East Africa, a band of roving Mau Maus came to the village of Lauri, surrounded it and killed every inhabitant including women and children, 300 in all. Not more than three miles away was the Rift Valley School, a private school where missionary children were being educated away from their parents.

Immediately upon leaving the carnage of Lauri they came with spears, bows and arrows, clubs, and torches to the school with complete destruction in mind. You can imagine the fear of those little ones and their instructors housed in the boarding school. Word had already reached them about the destruction of Lauri; there was no place to flee with the little children. All they could do was pray. The whole school went to prayer.

As they prayed, out of the darkness of the night, lighted torches were seen coming toward the school. Soon there was a ring of Mau Maus around the school, cutting off all escape. Shouting and cursing could be heard as they began to advance on the school, tightening the circle and coming closer.

Suddenly, when they were close enough to throw a spear, they stopped. They began to retreat and ran into the jungle. By the time the army arrived, their would-be assassins had dispersed. The army spread out in search of them and captured the entire band of raiding Mau Maus.

Later before the judge at the trial, the leader was called to the witness stand. The judge questioned him: "On this particular night, did you kill the inhabitants of Lauri?" Came the reply, "Yes." "Was it your intent to do the same at the missionary school in Rift Valley?" The answer was "Yes."

"Well, then," asked the judge, "why didn't you attack the school?" The leader of the Mau Maus said: "We were on our way to destroy all the people and the school, but as we came closer, all of a sudden, between us and the school there were many huge men dressed in white with flaming swords, and we became afraid and ran to hide!"

He shall give His angels charge concerning you, to guard you in all your ways. (Psalm 91:11) *See that you do not despise one of these little ones, for I say to you, that their angels continually behold the face of My Father.* (Matthew 18:10)

One night the king of Syria sent a great army with many chariots and horses to surround the city (of Dothan). When the prophet's servant got up early the next morning and went outside, there were troops, horses, and chariots everywhere. "Alas my master, what shall we do now?" he cried out to Elisha. "Don't be afraid!" Elisha told him. "For our army is bigger than theirs."

Then Elisha prayed, "Lord, open his eyes and let him see!" And the Lord opened the young man's eyes so that he could see horses of fire and chariots of fire everywhere upon the mountain! (II Kings 6:14-17, Living Bible)

The Power of Books *5/27 – May 27*

Between the lines of the fourth chapter of II Timothy is a touching glimpse of the heart of Paul the Apostle. He's writing to his son in the faith, Timothy. After some words of instruction, he throws open the windows of his soul.

He says, beginning with verse 6, (I will leave out some words to show a train of thought) *I am already being poured out as a drink offering, and the time of my departure is at hand. I have fought the good fight, I have finished the course, I have kept the faith. Be diligent to come to me quickly. Bring the cloak, and the books, especially the parchments. Do your utmost to come before winter. The Lord be with your spirit. Grace be with you.*

The great English preacher Charles Spurgeon said of Paul, "The man is about to die; yet he wants books! The Spirit inspires him, yet he wants books! He's been preaching for 30 years, yet he wants books! He's seen the Lord, yet he wants books! He's had a wider experience than most men, he's been caught up into the third heaven and heard things unlawful to utter, yet he wants books! He's written a major part of the New Testament, yet he wants books!"

The people, whom God has chosen to use including Jesus Christ Himself, have been readers of good books, especially the Sacred Scriptures. We must not underestimate the power of a book, even a bad one. According to one authority, for every word in Hitler's "Mein Kampf," 125 lives were lost in the horror of World War II.

The written word has had great power since the first human recorded his thoughts with a stick in the dirt. But today, with a flood of information so easily available through television, radio, the Internet, and other forms of sometimes-mindless media, books are an often-neglected resource for the growing Christian.

Someone has suggested that, if you could build a package, small enough to carry in your pocket, a machine which would instantly stop and start, in which you could instantly reverse yourself or go forward, which would require no batteries or other energy sources, and which would provide you with full information on an entire civilization, and truth to make you free, what would you have? You'd have a book!

But the man who does not read has no advantage over the man who cannot read. First, I thank my Creator God for giving me the amazing capacity to read. Second, I thank Him for giving some the ability to express truth on paper. Third, I offer both of these gifts for Him to use in growing me into the likeness of His dear Son.

Good books have shaped my life; may I recommend a few – like Isaiah, Romans, Jeremiah, John, Psalms, II Timothy… Grace be with you.

May 28 – 5/28 | *A Young Cloud of Witnesses*

Therefore, since we have so great a cloud of witnesses surrounding us, let us run with endurance the race that is set before us, fixing our eyes on Jesus... (Hebrews 12:1)

On this Memorial Day weekend I thought it might be helpful to cite a few examples of those who surround us with their witness of faith in the living Jesus. It may seem strange to recall these names from the Columbine High School tragedy of some years ago, but these kids have joined the ranks of those that Hebrews 11 and 12:1 talks about. Their lives bear witness to Jesus.

From Littleton, Colorado come these accounts – things you won't hear in the news about those who were killed there April 20, 1999:

John Tomiln, a committed believer – age 16. At his memorial service John's best friend shared that although John was a great guy, he was not going to heaven because of that. He was going to heaven because of his trust and fellowship with Jesus Christ. There were a number of first time commitments to Christ at his memorial service.

Rachel Scott, a committed believer – age 17. She wanted to be a missionary in Africa. Her boy friend shared how her faith had impacted him and those around her at school. 15 commitments to Christ occurred at the service.

Cassie Bernall, a committed believer and martyr for Jesus – age 17. Cassie was totally anti-Christian 2 years before. She was involved in witchcraft and very suicidal. Her parents forcibly drug her into the youth pastor's office.

When she walked out of his office, his reaction was, "Wow, she is a lost cause..." Cassie, about 6 months later, walked back up to the youth pastor and said "You'll never guess what I did today... I gave my life to Christ."

From that point forward, Cassie was a radical evangelist on her campus. And because of this, her killer asked her if she believed in God. She replied, "Yes, I believe in Jesus Christ." For that she was killed.

At Cassie Bernall's Memorial Service 75 kids made commitments to Christ.

These testimonies say one thing loud and clear: Jesus Christ was – and still is – worth dying for.

Heroes Of The Faith *5/29 – May 29*

Hebrews chapter 11 is an inspiring record of saints "of whom the world was not worthy." The Spirit reminds us of the casualties in the Battle of the Ages. The tendency is to canonize these people on the one hand, or forget about them entirely on the other. We will do neither. We will simply remember and honor them as soldiers in a war that continues to this day.

Those mentioned in Hebrews 11 were not the only casualties in those early days of the war. There were an estimated four million nameless Christians interred in the Catacombs of Rome in the first three centuries of the church.

More than fifty million Christians died for their faith in the Dark Ages, and more than two million were killed when the Communists seized China in the late 1940's. These all share one crime – a living faith in the risen Lord.

We remember their courage and their faithfulness. They were not a special breed of human beings; they were just like us. They were no more or less brave or spiritual than we are. But as we remember them, we must remember the most important matter of all. There was something that warranted their courage. There was Someone worthy of his or her faithfulness.

When the sword is raised or the fire is lit, that's the moment of truth. If what you've been living for is a lie, that's the time to say, "Let's talk, I don't really believe all that stuff." But they didn't, they died praising Jesus.

This chapter reminds me of an old but still penetrating question: "If I were put on trial for being a Christian, would there be enough evidence to convict me?"

With Abel and Enoch and Abraham and Noah from Hebrews 11, the disciples of Jesus lives ended in martyrdom. Matthew was slain with a sword in Ethiopia. A horse dragged Mark through the streets of Alexandria, Egypt until he was dead.

Luke was hanged on an olive tree in Greece. John was boiled in oil, survived, and was banished to Patmos. Peter was crucified upside-down. James, the son of Alphaeus, was beheaded in Jerusalem. James, the son of Zebedee, was thrown from the pinnacle of the temple and beaten until dead. Jude was shot to death with arrows.

Bartholemew was flayed alive. Andrew was crucified on an X-shaped cross and he preached to his persecutors until he died. Thomas was run through with a lance in India. Matthias was first stoned, and then beheaded. Barnabas was stoned to death at Salonica. Paul was beheaded at Rome.

The war between light and darkness has many casualties, some even from friendly fire. The Church is famous for killing its wounded. It ought not be so. But when the war is over, friendly-fire casualties get crowns too.

Joe Knapp, Jack Anderson, Mason Hughes, Ken Erickson, and Bob Pierce – I remember you today with gratitude. You shaped my world vision.

May 30 – 5/30 **An Illustrious Warrior**

A university alumnus, shown a list of examination questions by his old economics professor, exclaimed, “Those are the same questions you asked when I was in school 20 years ago!” “Yes,” said the professor, “we ask the same questions every year.”

The alumnus said, “But surely you know that students pass along the questions from one year to the next.” “Of course”" said the professor, “But in economics, we change the answers.” That’s the way of the world. Its moral compass is all out of whack. Its values change, and the people that embody those values change.

I grew up in a world of super-heroes: Superman, Wonder Woman, Captain Marvel, and Batman. Ordinary people like me can’t be heroes. Or can they?

Hebrews chapter 11 presents a long list of heroes of the faith and it contains a significant phrase: *They were weak, but became strong*. (Hebrews 11:34) It seems that strength and super powers are not prerequisites to hero-ness. God’s heroes are weak people who’ve simply made themselves available.

God gives the heroes of the Bible very little comfort. Comfort is the theme of so many of the hymns and choruses we sing. The “comfortable words” are the ones we select from the Scriptures. They’re there and they ought to be read.

But also read the stories of the heroes in the Bible. Surprisingly, God treats them quite roughly. To the complaining Job, God says, “Stand up on your feet like a man. I have something to show you.”

To Elijah, hiding from Jezebel in a cave, God says, “Get out of here. I have something better for you to do with your life.” To Moses, hiding on a farm in Midian, complaining that he can’t be a leader, God says, “I don’t care if you don’t think you’re a leader, I’ll tell you what to do.”

Then to Paul, plagued by a thorn in his flesh for which he was given no answer, just the words, “Keep going. My grace is sufficient for you.”

The dictionary defines a hero as “one greatly regarded for his achievements or qualities; the chief man in a book or a story; an illustrious warrior.”

Without meaning to sound unearthly, I confess to you that Jesus is my only Hero. He is highly esteemed by me for His qualities. I greatly regard His achievements on the cross for me! He is the Chief Man in the story of the ages, and He is, indeed, an illustrious Warrior.

More than any comic book hero of my childhood or creation of a Hollywood producer, Jesus Christ embodies the qualities I admire; and I want to be just like Him when I grow up!

Have a blessed Memorial Day.

Living Dihydrogen Monoxide *5/31 – May 31*

Every week it seems that there's another chemical substance getting into the ecosystem that threatens to destroy life on planet earth as we know it. We've become easy prey for the "experts" who foster fear and confusion in order to promote an often hidden agenda.

A freshman at Eagle Rock Junior High School won first prize at the Greater Idaho Falls Science Fair recently. He did it by urging people to sign a petition demanding strict control or total elimination of the hazardous chemical "dihydrogen monoxide."

The reasons to ban dihydrogen monoxide were:
1. It can cause excessive sweating and discomfort.
2. It is a major component of acid rain.
3. It can cause severe burns in its gaseous state.
4. Accidental inhalation can kill you.
5. It contributes greatly to erosion.
6. It decreases the effectiveness of automobile tires.
7. It has been found in the tumors of cancer patients.

The student was trying to show how conditioned we are to accepting any thing that sounds scientific. He asked fifty people if they supported the ban, and forty-three said, "yes." Six people were undecided about the ban, and only one knew that the chemical in question was – water – H^2O.

How gullible are we? The substance that our very lives depend upon – water, can be made to be a dreaded hazardous chemical.

What would our valley be without water? What would planet earth, for that matter, be without this liquid miracle? And yet there are, in fact, dangers associated with it. Thousands of people will drown this year in waterways all over the world. Some will die because their tires will skid on rainy streets. Others will be killed or injured by water in its gaseous state – steam.

I might add that 1,500 people were killed by dihydrogen monoxide in its solid state when the Titanic hit an iceberg.

There is, however, a water supply that is not in any way hazardous to your health. I know of no one who has drowned in it or been burned by it or other wise maimed or bruised by it.

It's the living water Jesus promised to those who will come to Him and drink from His well of salvation. And, if you're thirsty, it's yours for the asking.

Jesus stood up on the last day of the Feast of Tabernacles and cried out, "If any man is thirsty, let him come to Me and drink. He who believes in Me, as the Scripture said, 'From his innermost being shall flow rivers of living water.'" But this He spoke of the Spirit... (John 7:37-39)

June 1 – 6/1 *Satisfying Long Life*

The fear of death has held people in its paralyzing grip since Adam. Jesus, By His resurrection, *released those who through fear of death were all their lifetime subject to bondage.* (Hebrews 2:15)

I know that this is true in my head, and I've been given everlasting life by trusting in Jesus. And I know, in the words of an old spiritual, "I'm gonna live forever!" But there's still a nagging fear that my time here on earth may end prematurely. As the man said, "I'm not afraid to die, I just don't want to go on the next bus load."

The Bible has some promising things to say about long life here on earth. *I will fulfill the number of your days!* (Exodus 23:26) *Because you have set your love upon Me... with long life will I satisfy you and show you My salvation.* (Psalm 91:14,16) *Those who are planted in the house of the Lord shall flourish, they shall still bear fruit in old age, they shall be fresh and flourishing.* (Psalm 92:13, 14)

Even to your old age, I am the LORD, and even to gray hairs I will carry you! I have made, I will bear; even I will carry, and will deliver you! (Isaiah 46:4) *My son, do not forget My law, but let your heart keep My commands; for length of days and long life and peace will they add to you.* (Proverbs 3:1, 2)

The fear of the Lord is the beginning of wisdom and the knowledge of the Holy One is understanding. For by Me your days will be multiplied and years of life will be added to you. (Proverbs 9:10, 11) *The fear of the Lord prolongs one's days.* (10:27)

From these promises it's clear that the Lord wants us to live long on the earth. But quantity of days is not all He promises; He promises quality, too. He said He not only would fulfill the number of my days, but He will also "fill full" all of my days. He promises to satisfy me in my long life.

He says that I will flourish, be fresh and, incredibly, still bear fruit in old age like the palm tree. Ordinary fruit trees diminish their yield as they grow older. But as the palm tree ages, its fruit grows sweeter and more abundant.

Moses was 80 when God called him. Michelangelo painted the ceiling of the Sistine Chapel lying on his back on a scaffold at near 90. Those who have lived long, full lives challenge me to believe that I have only just begun.

I like the way Rev. Arthur Brown, at 103, put it when asked for his long-life formula. He said simply, "Don't die." Sadly, for many however, fruitful life is over long before death comes.

Help me Lord, that I don't stop living before I die. Lord, help us all.

Billions and Billions *6/2 – June 2*

One billion minutes ago was some time around the year 102 A.D. It's believed that the Apostle John was still living in Ephesus in Asia Minor at this time, and died a natural death not long after this date.

It's been said that the average man has no working concept of any number larger than 500. I doubt this is true today with the talk about the national debt. Nevertheless, it's difficult to deal with such abstract figures as millions, billions, and trillions, when most of us are concerned fives, tens, and twenties.

For instance: there are now 6 billion people on the earth; 25 percent of whom live in China, and 5 percent of whom live in the U.S. It's hard to visualize such vast numbers of people.

Let me take you a little deeper into the world of numbers, and let's try to gain some perspective. For example: a billion seconds is equal to 31.71 years. If you are younger than 31 years 8 months 15 days, you have not yet lived a billion seconds.

A billion minutes is equal to 1,902.59 years. A billions hours ago was in the prehistoric past, 114,155 years, 146 days, and 3 hours ago, sometime mid-year in 112,150 B.C, perhaps before creation.

At the average rate of 70 beats per minute, the human heart beats 4,200 times an hour, 100,800 times a day and 36,817,200 a year. At that rate it reaches the 1 billion beat mark in 27 years, 58 days, 21 hours, 15 minutes and 17 seconds. If you are younger than, that your heart has not yet beat I billion times.

My mind cannot grasp the majesty of His grace in my little world, let alone the grandeur of His universe with its billions and billions of galaxies, each with billions and billions of stars. For instance, on a clear night, beyond city lights, with the unaided eye, one can see only about 1,160 stars in the northern hemisphere. If we could survey the entire celestial sphere, northern and southern hemispheres, we could still see only about 3000.

The heavens, indeed, declare the glory of God, and one of the ways they say it is in the language of numbers. To more adequately describe the vast numbers of objects in the telescopic and microscopic universe, scientists have coined the word googol. A googol is a one followed by 100 zeros.

All things great and small, the Lord God made them all. Such quantities boggle the mind, but the Scripture says that God has done such great things that numbers cannot define them, even with computers.

But as for me... to God I would commit my cause, Who does great things and unsearchable, marvelous things without number! (Job 5:8, 9)

The people of the land have practiced oppressions and committed robbery, and they have wronged the poor and needy and have oppressed the sojourner without justice. And I searched for a man among them who should build up the wall and stand in the gap before Me for the land, that I should not destroy it; but I found no one.

The Lord spoke these words in Ezekiel 22:29, 30. They are among the most troubling and challenging words in the Scripture.

God is calling for intercessors – gap-standers. That's the simple meaning of the word intercession; one who stands between two parties bridging the gap. An intercessor is a go-between, a mediator, and a proxy on behalf of another.

Intercessors are powerful. Intercessors pray for others until God releases His grace and resources upon them. Intercessors wage spiritual battles with the unseen forces of darkness – and win! Intercessors sometimes rise early, or stay late, or get up in the middle of the night to pray. And they believe!

Blessed is the church that has an army of intercessors. Blessed is the person who has an intercessor for a friend, and calls for help when needed. Intercessors touch the world. Their ministry leads to changed lives in Nepal, Malawi, China, Pakistan, and Poland, wherever a nation is targeted in prayer. Intercessors change world events. People in power rise or fall with their prayers. Even the demons of darkness flee in fear when an experienced intercessor invades their territory.

Dr. Raymond Edmond had not been in Uruguay as a missionary very long when he became deathly sick. In fact, the Uruguay nationals had dug his grave and were waiting close by to take his body away. Suddenly, Dr. Edmond sat up in bed. He called to his wife, "Bring me my clothes. I'm getting up!" He had instantly recovered, and nobody knew what had caused his recuperation.

Many years later, he was retelling the story of his remarkable recovery to a church in Boston, Mass. After the service, a little old lady with a small dog-eared, beaten up prayer book came up to him. She said, "What day did you say you were dying in Uruguay? What time would it have been in Boston?"

They figured it would have been 2:00am on a specific date. He wrinkled face lit up. Pointing to her prayer book she exclaimed, "There it is, you see? At 2:00am on that date, God said to me, 'Get up and pray – the devil's trying to kill Raymond Edmond in Uruguay!'"

Those who stand in the gap between heaven and hell, life and death, God and man – intercessors – are like the Dutch boy with his finger in the dyke. They are holding back the judgment of God upon a world consumed with sin and oppression. The problem with this picture is that there's more than one hole in the dyke – and there aren't enough fingers.

Take Care Of The Blossom *6/4 – June 4*

Can you believe it? It's June already, and by the stack of wedding invitations, you know it's going to be a busy month for brides and grooms, and the families of such. Love is in bloom and the fragrance of roses, carnations and violets is mingling with all the other aromas of life in these parts.

Speaking of blooms and blossoms reminds me of an incident a number of years ago. I was called to mediate a dispute between opposing factions in a neighboring church. The rift between them had grown to the extent that one group was going to leave the church and begin another work. As I tried to heal the wounds that words had caused, the Lord let me see an unusual picture.

I saw a blossom on an apple tree, and a moth landing on the blossom and laying its eggs in the fragrant bloom. Then I saw the apple that would come from that blossom and a worm crawling out of the apple. I realized then that the worm crawling out of the apple was from the eggs that were laid in the blossom weeks earlier.

When you see a wormhole in an apple, it's evidence of this process. The worm doesn't crawl into the apple; it crawls out of it from the eggs that were laid in the blossom stage.

The meaning of the parable was clear to me. The group that was going to start a new church was doing so in anger and rebellion, and seeds of future disaster were being laid in the blossom of their work. It wasn't wrong to begin a new church, but they would find that an impure blossom begets impure fruit. Time proved this to be true.

It's like that in love relationships, too. Love blooms and it's wonderful! The future is bright with the hope of a long and happy life together. And then, sometimes – more times than we know – the seed of future conflict is laid in the blossom of courtship.

Later, we may blame current circumstances or other outside influences for the conflict, but it has its source in blossom time when compromises were made morally and spiritually.

This is why God commands sexual purity in the blossoming stage of a relationship. He is concerned with the worm that will emerge later and contaminate the fruit.

And nobody likes a wormy apple.

June 5 – 6/5 **Forever More**

Thou wilt show me the path of life: in thy presence is fullness of joy; at thy right hand there are pleasures forever more. (Psalm 16) *I am he that liveth, and was dead; and, behold, I am alive forever more, Amen; and have the keys of hell and of death.* (Revelation 1:18 KJV)

I was born and bred on the King James Version of the Bible. Most people don't remember a time when that was all there was. I appreciate the new versions which make God's Word more readable, and I have no quarrel with the wide acceptance they now enjoy, but somehow I managed to get the message through the "thees and thous" of the language of 1611.

Over eighteen years ago Pastor Roger Whitlow asked if I would write some articles for the bulletin. I accepted the privilege as a sacred trust and have deeply enjoyed this means of expression. My original intention was to shed light upon a few words that we read in the Scriptures but don't stop to think about very much.

The first one I did was on the King James phrase used hundreds of times in the Scripture, "It came to pass." I saw this phrase as God's way of saying that bad things don't come to stay – they come to pass, and if I can patiently endure, I can outlast anything that comes to pass. The new translations say, "happened" in place of "it came to pass;" more up-to-date but not as colorful.

The second word I wrote about was on the Old English word "untoward" as it's used in Acts to describe the world as an "untoward generation." (Acts 2:40) It's the same as saying "without direction", aimless – not toward anything. The Lord wants to save us from "un-toward-ness," and give us direction for our lives. The new translations say "perverse"; newer but not as descriptive as "un-toward."

My latest curiosity is a combination of words that we often think of as one word but is two words in the Scripture, and really a combination of three words. It is "forever more." We sing it in some of our choruses and hymns and we sing it as one word – forevermore. In the Hebrew and Greek you will not find a word for "forevermore" but you will be referred to "forever" and "more." The word that stirred my curiosity for the words "forever more."

In Psalm 16:11 David says, "at Thy right hand are pleasures forever more." It is saying that in our future with Him there will be pleasures forever – more than we have now, more than I could contain now. In Psalm 86:12: "I will glorify Thy name forever more," the implication here is that in my future I will glorify Him more than I do now, more than I can now.

In other places the word means "to the vanishing point," as in Revelation 1:18 when Jesus speaks and says, "I am alive forever more!" He is alive, to the vanishing point of everything else.

All of us who are in Him share His "forever-more-ness."

Confidence Casting *6/6 – June 6*

Cast not away your confidence! These words are from Hebrews 10:35. They have been great strength to me in recent years. But misplaced confidence can have disastrous effects. We've all had the sad experience of trusting someone or something only to find that there was no basis for our trust.

Confidence has value only as it embraces that which is worthy. Faith in faith is folly; to be in love with love is equal folly. Faith and love must embrace a worthy person before any meaning can be given to their expression.

In this verse, that which is worthy of confidence is the promise of God. Verse 36 says, *You will receive what God has promised.* We can stand confidently upon the promise of God because the God of the promise is faithful.

In the early days of our country a weary foot traveler came to the banks of the Mississippi River for the first time. There was no bridge. It was early winter, and the surface of the mighty stream was covered with ice. Could he dare to cross over? Would the ice be able to bear his weight? Night was falling, and it was urgent that he reach the other side.

Finally, after much hesitation and fear, he began to creep cautiously across the surface on his hands and knees so as to distribute his weight as evenly as possible, and keep the ice from breaking. About halfway over, he heard the sound of singing behind him. Out of the dusk there came a man, driving a horse-drawn load of coal across the ice, singing merrily as he went.

Here he was, on hands and knees, trembling lest the ice be not strong enough to bear him up. The same ice on which he was creeping upheld a man, his horses, his sleigh and his load of coal – and the man was singing!

Like the weary traveler, some of us creep upon the promise of God. Cautiously, timidly, with fear and trembling, we venture forth as though His promise may fail at any time. Or perhaps we imagine that the lightness of our step may make His promise more secure, as if we could contribute even in the slightest to its strength.

God's promises have stood the test of millions of confident saints before us. What God has promised has borne the weight of kingdoms. What God has promised He will do! We're not "skating on thin ice" when we trust Him! And when we walk in confidence, we can sing in the shadows!

I John 5:14,15 says, *This is the confidence that we have in Him, that if we ask anything according to His will, He hears us. And if we know that He hears us, we know that we have the petitions that we have asked of Him.*

Are you creeping – or standing on the promises of God?

According to the Scripture, my love for God is an effect of something else. I John 4:19 says, *We love Him because He first loved us.* In other words, His love for me gives birth to, or causes, my love for Him.

Therefore, if I want to love Him more, I should concentrate on the cause, and discover new dimensions of His love for me. If I try to love Him more, I cannot. But if I let Him love me, I cannot help but love Him more. It works!

"Whatever a man sows, that shall he also reap." "For every action, there's an equal and opposite reaction." These well known axioms apply to more than physics and farming. They describe the universal law of cause and effect. Effects have causes; they do not stand alone.

A speaker sympathized with wives who get blamed for everything that goes wrong around the house. He cited the television spot in which the husband is upset because of "ring around the collar." The wife is nearly in tears because her detergent hasn't removed the dirt from her husband's shirt. The ring around her husband's collar is seen as evidence of her failure. The speaker said, "Nobody asks the obvious question – 'Why doesn't he wash his neck?'"

Cause and effect! We spend too much time fighting effects when our time, energies, money, and prayers would be more fruitful if directed at causes. Herein lies wisdom – to discern one from the other. The man or woman who can begin to separate cause and effect, action and reaction will find it helpful in relationships, in business, and in their walk with the Lord.

We're told in Ephesians 6 that our battle is not with "flesh and blood" (effects), but with "principalities and powers and the rulers of the darkness of this world" (causes). Why not address the cause of disruption, destruction, and death, rather than waste our energies fighting the people who are affected by Satan's power plays.

In a positive application of this truth, Romans 14:19 commands us *to follow after the things that make for peace.* In other words, peace is the effect of something else and will come only if I follow what causes peace. Many are chasing after peace when simple obedience to God would result in peace.

Joy is an effect whose cause is the abiding presence of the Lord Jesus. Self-control is an effect caused by the rule of King Jesus in my life. As a matter of fact, all of the things identified in Galatians 5 as the "fruit of the Spirit" are not to be sought after.

They are "fruit" – effects of the life of the Spirit of Jesus Christ in me.

No Left Turn *6/8 – June 8*

Let's hear it for the road builders of the world, the engineers, laborers and heavy equipment operators who spend their time (and our money) smoothing out the rough places on the streets and roads upon which we must travel. I've had an up-close look at their work recently, which prompted this writing. For well over a year a major road has been under construction and it's finally about to come to a conclusion.

It was a major project for two reasons. First, this was no re-surfacing job; they tore up the old road and started from the base. I thought of the times when I tried to re-surface when I should have re-built. The tendency is to smooth the surface when the real problem may lies deeper.

Their second problem: the work had to be done while maintaining a flow of traffic. To do this they shifted all traffic to one side of the road making one lane each way while they worked on the other side.

To make this difficult process go as smoothly as possible the city posted "No Left Turn" signs at every intersection. If you wanted to turn left you had to turn right and make a "U" turn to get going in the direction you wanted. I was appalled and somewhat frustrated by the number of people who disregarded the "No Left Turn" signs and turned left anyhow.

Some mornings the road would be littered with broken "No Left Turn" signs, which had been trashed by angry motorists. More than once this mostly mild-mannered motorist vented his fleshly frustration with a longer than necessary blast of the horn. I drew pious spiritual analogies to the "spirit of lawlessness" that was rampant in our land. So I changed my course and have not used that road until recently.

Left turns are perilous, unfriendly, invasive, abrasive things, especially on the "straight and narrow." Turning left means crossing some one else's path. Left turns are 90° of danger which risk collision with another's right of way. There are appropriate times and places to make left turns in life – to make a change of direction – but proper signaling is required so that others can be prepared for your radical departure from the common flow.

Right turns, on the other hand, are gentle, friendly, merging, safer kinds of things. Generally speaking, you don't have to cross anyone's path to make a right turn. You can even do it on a red light, if you're careful. A right turn does mean a change of direction, but it's not nearly as dangerous as a left turn. I like right turns best.

Well, enough of my ramblings. And all of this logic goes out the window if you're driving in England or Japan. But changes of direction can be good for us when directed by God. But they can be dangerous if we strike out on our own and disregard the laws of God.

We're not alone on this road of life, you know. Others are following us.

This is about the season that is celebrated around the world as Pentecost. It is so called after the Jewish Feast of Pentecost or "First Fruits," which was fifty days after the beginning of Passover. Many of us have been conditioned to think of Pentecost in very limited terms, mostly centering around a "mighty wind" and "tongues of fire" in an upper room on the Day of Pentecost.

But there is more to it than that. There had been a Day of Pentecost since there had been Passover. It was mainly an agricultural festival celebrating the appearance of "first fruits" or the visible evidence that it was going to be a good year for the crops. When the blossoms faded on the trees and the vines took time to produce leaves, there was a sense of apprehension as to whether the fruit would actually appear. When it did, it was cause for celebration.

Another important feast in the Jewish calendar is the Feast of Tabernacles or "In-gathering." This fall festival celebrated the last fruit harvested and was a time of rest and rejoicing for the blessing of the Lord upon their labors. These two feasts were the major agricultural celebrations of the year. They were every bit as sacred as Passover or the Day of Atonement.

The connection between the Day of Pentecost as a Jewish feast day and the Day of Pentecost as a spiritual landmark for the church has to do with this matter of "first fruits." Much like the process of growing things, Jesus planted the seeds of His Kingdom during His three years of ministry to His disciples. The seeds began to sprout as He taught and the blossom of hope appeared – then faded with the tragic crucifixion of Jesus the Christ.

But then He rose from the dead! He was alive! But what of the seeds He planted? What about the fruit? Was there to be anything of lasting value to come of His life – and death? His followers waited and "when the Day of Pentecost had come they were all together in one place." Then it happened – the promised Holy Spirit came with spectacular manifestations of power.

One of the blessings of that day was the evidence that there would be a kingdom after all! The seeds that Jesus planted would produce fruit that would remain. Those gathered in that room were the "first fruits" of a vast harvest of blood-bought souls. The Church, the Body of Christ conceived in the love of Calvary, was born that day.

Lost in the fervor of rushing a mighty wind, tongues of fire and the miracle of language not learned, is the creation of a loving community of interacting personalities – not just a mere collection of saved souls. This worshiping, loving, and sometimes-struggling body would change its world – not by force or techniques, but by its very presence in the midst of a pagan society.

This is what Pentecost is about. The Church was born then – the first fruits of Calvary. And it's alive and well in every part of the world!

Prehistoric Grace *6/10 – June 10*

Everywhere you look these days there's a dinosaur. I ate a hamburger the other day with the exotic name of an extinct reptile. The meat, I assume, was ground beef and not minced pterodactyl. Why the fascination with creatures that supposedly lived and died millions of years ago?

I strongly suspect that when you get to the bottom of the revival of interest in things prehistoric, you will find a sizable wad of money. Books, cartoons, fast food, movies, toys, and even theme parks are bringing in millions of dollars for the promoters of dinosaur mania.

Did these creatures really exist in the form in which they are depicted today? How does anyone know what they really looked like? Where does prehistoric flora and fauna fit with the Biblical record of creation? If they actually existed, what happened to them? Why aren't they around today?

No one, not even the most brilliant paleontologist, can say with certainty what these creatures looked like. Pieces of bone or a tooth or two are used to build a model of what the creature may have looked like. Some scientific principles are applied along with lots of imagination. There were no photographa-saureses then. There're no movies of the playful antics of tyrannosaurus-rex.

Some Bible scholars theorize that between Genesis 1:1 and 1:2 there's an implied time gap where there's room for the prehistoric menagerie that modern earth-scientists say existed. This theorizing, while hinted at in Scripture, amounts to a defensive scramble for credibility in response to pseudo-science. For a Bible scholar to construct a gap scenario from bits and pieces of Scripture is little different than what a scientist does with bits and pieces of bone.

My faith doesn't rest in the gap theory, nor is it challenged by the possible existence of dinosaurs. My faith rests in something that pre-dates the prehistoric. A lot was happening "before the foundation of the world."

Just look at this: *Blessed be the God and Father of our Lord Jesus Christ, Who has blessed us with every spiritual blessing... just as He chose us in Him before the foundation of the world.* (Ephesians 1:3, 4)

You were not redeemed with perishable things like silver or gold, but with the blood of Christ. For He was foreknown before the foundation of the world... (I Peter 1:18-20)

Revelation 13:8 speaks of *the Lamb slain from the foundation of the world.*

Before there were dinosaurs, God thought of me – and you. Before there was sin, God had a Lamb prepared as the perfect sacrifice for sin. Before there was anything – there was God.

With Him, nothing is prehistoric – and nothing pre-dates His grace!

The baseball season began with the promise of Spring. When the umpire yelled "Batter up!" in April, all the teams believed they could win it all. But by the time June arrives, the realities of life become painfully evident and many teams take a nosedive. This phenomenon is so common that it's been given a name – it's called the June Swoon.

The forces at work on the baseball diamond are loose in the world at large. Any enterprise worth the investment of time and energy begins with great promise. And when the glow of first hope is gone and the humdrum of maintaining excellence sets in, there is a predictable downturn in the happiness quotient. The June Swoon in the seasons of the soul can occur in a friendship, a business, a church – or a marriage.

There is a scientific law called the Second Law of Thermodynamics. This law states that any closed system left to itself tends toward greater randomness; that is, it breaks down. It takes a conscious, ordered input of energy to keep anything together.

Any homeowner knows that to maintain a house, one must daily, monthly, and yearly invest time and energy to keep the house enjoyable to live in. If no energy is expended on the house, it eventually comes to the point of needing a complete home makeover, or it gets torn down.

Although it's a law of material systems, the Second Law of Thermodynamics obviously describes other systems as well. Consider the marriage relationship. June is traditionally the month of love and romance. Many young hearts are captivated by the promise of true.

There's nothing quite like loving and being loved. We celebrate the act of creation, which brings into being something that did not exist before the wedding. Hope springs eternal in the heart of each member of the wedding party, including the M.O.B. (mother of the bride) and the F.O.G. (father of the groom.) But the Second Law of Thermodynamics will make itself known.

The June Swoon of a marriage doesn't happen in June; it may not come for five or six years, but it will come. Marriage is a "closed system," so to speak. Each marriage is an exclusive relationship in which only two people on earth can participate. A married couple may have many friends or relatives or even children, but only they can participate in the dynamics of "holy matrimony."

When baseball teams go through the doldrums of a slump, the good ones go back to the fundamentals of the game. A neglect of the fundamentals – the basics – probably led to the slump in the first place.

Marriage is like that. It must have a daily investment of time and energy so it can survive the slump. If no energy is added, the relationship deteriorates. It may not be easy, but when the old June Swoon hits a marriage, it's back to fundamentals, like – "I Love You!"

A Dilemma of the Heart *6/12 – June 12*

I consider myself a caring person. I'm sure that you would say the same for yourself. But lately it seems that there are just too many things, and too many people to care about. I catch the news on TV and radio, I read the newspaper every day, and there's always another crisis some place in the world to wring compassion out of my heart.

This dilemma has caused me to ask, "Lord, just what am I supposed to spend my heart upon? My heart's not big enough for all the need in the world. Lord, how do I keep my caring-heart balance in a world of crisis?"

Years ago a story broke that captured the compassion of the nation. Jessica McClure, a two-year-old from Midland Texas, was trapped for two days at the bottom of an abandoned well. The whole country stood at the edge of that well watching around-the-clock coverage of rescuers attempting to free her. I prayed for her.

Yet at about the same time, earthquakes in the Soviet Union and Costa Rica killed hundreds, and it hardly got anybody's attention. In five South American countries, a cholera epidemic killed about 1,500 people and infected another 145,000. And now more than 1,000 Americans have been killed in Iraq.

150,000 people drowned in Bangladesh in the aftermath of a devastating cyclone. In Africa, 27 million people faced death from famine; a crisis many times worse than the one a few years ago that gave us "We Are The World."

What is it about my heart, and perhaps yours, too, that gets caught up in the Jessica McClures of the world and can't seem to grasp the enormity of the current genocide in the Sudan?

My well-developed sense of guilt tells me that, if each soul is precious in the sight of God then I should care 27 million times more for the starving Africans than for one Jessica McClure. I should care 150,000 times more for the dead in Bangladesh than for a young boy rescued from a pond and brought back to life. But it doesn't work that way, does it?

We all tend to spend our caring on the things closest to us, and I'm not sure that's a bad thing. I've almost concluded that God intends for me to care most about the things for which I have direct responsibility, an accompanying authority to act, and resources to meet the need.

God knows how to awaken me to that for which He holds me responsible. I don't want to miss His wake-up call. That is my heart's dilemma.

June 13 – 6/13 *The Eye of the Beholder*

We're all familiar with the story of Beauty and the Beast, especially since the Disney people have made it into a cartoon classic and a stage extravaganza. The movie version, not surprisingly, is a bit different from the French fairy tale from which the story is taken, but the essential elements are there.

A beast, the incarnation of ugly because of a spell upon him, meets a young maiden who is the epitome of beauty. In time, she sees through the gross exterior to the heart of the beast. To make a very long story short, her love for the beast breaks the spell and – Shazaam! – She's got herself a handsome prince instead of an ugly beast.

It's really a classic morality play, which reflects life in some important ways. Obviously, the story teaches us to see beyond outward appearances to the inner character and heart of a person.

We've been duped, all of us, into accepting standards of beauty which value only appearance. Hollywood and the media in general have marketed beauty and twisted our national psyche to sell everything from movies to cars.

One study reveals some interesting numbers. Eight-percent of the world is considered really beautiful. And eight-percent of the world is considered really ugly. The rest of us fill up the other eighty-four-percent.

The study also said something that makes one think. It said that both the eight-percent beautiful and the eight-percent ugly had some single outstanding feature that set them apart. This distinguishing feature in the beautiful group may have been big eyes or a long neck or a mole in a strategic location. For the ugly group it may have been a genetic defect or a result of disease or injury. The point is that a single feature often defined beauty or ugliness.

If the truth were known, the eight-percent ugly people would be beautiful to you if you loved them. And, sadly, the eight-percent beautiful people may turn out to be really ugly if you got to know them.

Love does make a difference. It doesn't break a spell so much as it lifts a veil over our eyes so that we begin to see as God sees. Beauty is, indeed, in the eye of Great Beholder of us all.

Kids once memorized this definition of beauty from McGuffey's Reader.

"Beautiful faces are they that wear
The light of a pleasant spirit there;
Beautiful hands are they that do
Deeds that are noble, good and true;
Beautiful feet are they that go
Swiftly to lighten another's woe."

A Star And Some Stripes *6/14 – June 14*

I was just five feet from the most powerful man in the world the other day. President George Bush came to our city, and I stood by the road while his limousine drove by. I saw his arm. I watched from a distance as he climbed the stairs of Air Force One parked at the airport. It was impressive. He's a nice man. That much power should be in the hands of a nice man.

The most impressive sight of all to me wasn't the motorcade of twenty motorcycles, and dozens of other various and sundry vehicles. It was the flag on the tail section of Air Force One. It was immense! It has to be one of the largest American flags in the world. "Old Glory" was never more glorious. The Stars and Stripes have been seen around the world by millions who would breathe free. It was impressive!

The stars on the blue background stand for the states of the union. In my lifetime the number has grown from forty-eight to fifty. It began with thirteen, for the original colonies that won independence from England. The red stripes stand for the blood that's been shed to obtain and retain our freedom. The white stripes stand for the bandages that have bound up the wounds of war.

I'm grateful and humbly proud to be an American. I'm also embarrassed and grieved for the sins of our land – past and present. It seems to me that another banner must be lifted in our neighborhoods and communities. It would be the flag of the One Who said, "Whom the Son sets free is free indeed!"

We could use the stars and stripes motif for this flag, too. Only this flag would have only one star. That star would be Jesus, the Bright Morning Star. All other luminaries cease to shine in the presence of His glory. He said, *If I be lifted up from the earth, I will draw all men unto Me."* (John 12:32) That's speaking about a banner or a flag that's unfurled for all to see.

The red stripes would stand for the blood of Jesus, which takes away the sin of the world. There is no other way to get rid of sin. You can't talk it away, or scare it away, or legislate it away, or kill it. A substance that's stronger must wash it away – and that's the blood of Jesus.

The white stripes would stand for the purity which all men will own when they are forgiven and washed clean by His blood. It would instantly resolve a thousand points of crisis if the hearts of men were clean and free.

I'm not naive enough to imagine that this is going to happen today or anytime on planet earth. We're talking about heaven here. But we can get heaven to earth in little person-sized pieces.

When one soul is cleansed, the Kingdom of God is established on earth and the flag – the Star and some Stripes – flies proudly over head.

June 15 – 6/15 **We Don't Know How to Blush**

They dress the wound of my people as though it were not serious. "Peace, peace," they say, when there is no peace. Are they ashamed of their loathsome conduct? No, they have no shame at all; they do not even know how to blush. (Jeremiah 8:11, 12 NIV)·

William Bennett wrote a little book a few years ago, which he named, "The Death of Outrage." Things have gotten much worse since he wrote his book. Outrageous things happen every day and outrageous images fill our TV screens and newspaper pages. We've been so exposed to outrageousness that we are inflicted, it seems to me, with a kind of outrage fatigue.

There was a time when society showed outrage at people's misconduct, but no more. We dismiss the sins of others and accept their misconduct without hesitation. It isn't that we forgive their behavior – we simply excuse it.

We don't only dismiss the sins of others, we're easy on ourselves, too, and excuse our own sins as weakness or the fault of someone else. In the words the prophet Jeremiah, we have forgotten how to blush. We have no shame.

What happens when people have no sense of shame? The result is Hitler's Germany where 6 million Jews and 2 or 3 million others were gassed to death. The result is Jeffrey Dahmer who killed and ate 15 victims. The result is Columbine High School where young boys kill classmates, teachers, and police officers.

Is there room in the heart of a follower of Jesus for outrage? I'm deeply troubled by 9/11, and events in Iraq and other places where terrorism rules. I'm deeply troubled by the gathering storm of outrageousness in the political arena this election year.

Most troubling to me is the feeling of outrage that lies just beneath the surface of my own heart when innocent people are victimized. What's a follower of the Prince of Peace to do in the face of outrageousness? What's a nation to do? Wouldn't it be better if we all just got angry enough to do something? Anything! – Wrong answer.

I often recall James 1:19, 20, *But let everyone be quick to hear, slow to speak and slow to anger; for the anger of man does not achieve the righteousness of God.*

What happens when people have no sense of shame? They have no sense of forgiveness, either. They have no sense of gratitude or love. They are, in fact, dead to all but their sin.

But Jesus is the Resurrection and the Life.

Communication *6/16 – June 16*

A professor began a lecture to his class on Communication with these words: "Communication is any modus operandi by or through which eventuates the reciprocal transposition of information between or among entities or groups via commonly understood systems of symbols, signs or behavioral patterns of activity." "Huh?"

Communication is vitally important to every relationship that I can think of. Its importance is dramatized by its lack, in most cases. Marriages end for want of it. Kids and parents are estranged, friends go separate ways, governments collapse, and nations go to war when communication breaks down.

God and man must also communicate well if God's will is to be carried out on earth and man is to be redeemed and walk in fullness. It's hard to imagine any single element as important as communication.

It boils down to this: hearing and being heard, listening well and speaking so as to be understood. It's as simple as that. But, as someone said, "There are three rules for communication. Unfortunately, no one knows what they are."

Two of the followers of Jesus were walking to Emmaus the day of the resurrection. As they conversed, Jesus drew near and walked with them, although they did not recognize Him. His question to them, in Luke 24:17 (KJV), seems appropriate for us to ask of ourselves. He said, *What kind of communication is this that you have with one another as you walk?* Good question!

How are we doing in the "hearing-and-being-heard" department? How we do at this skill, for that's what it is, will shape all of our relationships. My growth in my walk with God will be as I hear Him and am heard by Him. I hear Him through His word and His Spirit living within me. I hear Him through His expression in the created world.

God hears me when I pray. He hears me when I cry. He hears me when there are no words to express my deepest need. He hears me, not from His lofty throne in far-off heaven, but from His dwelling place inside of me. I need not shout, He hears my faintly uttered whisper.

How do you answer Jesus' question: "What kind of communication is this that you have with one another as you walk?" Think about it.

My Father's God

When Moses led the Israelites through the Red Sea, they paused on the far shore and celebrated. Exodus 15 records the song they sang: *The Lord is my strength and song, and He has become my salvation; He is my God, and I will praise Him; my father's God, and I will exalt Him!* (15:2)

After affirming his personal relationship with God, Moses makes a link with the past with the phrase – "my father's God." He says, in effect, "My God was my father's God and my father's God is my God also." The chain of faith linked Moses to many generations of men who worshiped the Living God.

As Moses moved into strange, untested territory, he affirmed the continuity of generations of trust in the living God. This was not a wild, weird, hair-brained venture of a new generation seeking freedom. This move into the unknown had its roots in a promise to Abraham, Isaac, and Jacob. And it would succeed by the faithfulness of their God to keep His promise.

A father's personal relationship with God is not hereditary, but father's faith in God, through good times and bad, is a rich heritage for his children. As Moses entered the Wilderness of the Unknown, as our children eventually must, his point of reference was to his father's God. We can and we must give our children the same.

Sometimes – most of the time – a father is not aware of his godly influence upon his children. In fact, he often feels that he falls far short of his role model, Father God Himself. Father God is a tough act to follow. But the unconscious influence of a life of faith is always there.

Some fathers boast that they have "quality time" with their children as opposed to "quantity time." That sounds good, but I wonder about its value from a child's point of view. You can't plan wonder or the spontaneous moment when a child sees God in daddy's eyes. It takes a lot of time for godly influence to happen.

It must have been important to Moses to be able to speak of his father's God. But I will tell you, from a father's experience, it's also satisfying to know that my God is the God of my children. They have chosen to serve Him, and this father's heart is full of joy for this.

My father's God has become my children's God. Hallelujah!

A Father's Blessing *6/18 – June 18*

David said, *You are my Father, my God, and the Rock of my salvation.* Psalm 89:26
Jesus said, ...*Yet I am not alone, because the Father is with me.* (John 16:32)

The concept of "father" was God's idea first. He was the first one to do it and be it, and He is a tough act for us mortals to follow, for sure. But we don't have to do it without Him. In fact, we can't.

In Deuteronomy 11:26-28 the Lord said, *Behold, I set before you today a blessing and a curse: the blessing, if you obey the commandments of the Lord your God... and the curse, if you do not....*

Blessing and curse... the Scripture is filled with examples of God placing a blessing upon someone or pronouncing a curse upon a person or a city or a nation. These actions have far-reaching implications.

A blessing, once bestowed by God, is a pre-determined outcome of good. A curse, once pronounced by God, is a pre-determined outcome of evil.

This means that if God has blessed a person or a people, no matter what happens between point A and point Z – the end result is blessed goodness. And, if God has cursed a person or a people, it doesn't matter what happens between point A and point Z. The end result will be accursed evil.

Now here's an amazing thing – God declares in Genesis that we are created in His own image so it is apparently in our power to bless and curse. By the power of our words we can cause good or evil to happen. That's awesome!

In Bible times a father gathered his children around him, placed a hand upon their head, and pronounced a blessing upon them which God honored in their lives. On the other hand, a curse was sometimes uttered and ultimately realized in that child's life, which God also honored. We can, in fact, affect the destiny of our children by what we speak.

We can and must speak blessing to our children. I don't just mean to casually compliment them. The act of blessing our children is worthy of thoughtful prayer and preparation.

We, fathers, tend to sell ourselves short and so we live short of the privilege and authority which God has given to us. William Wordsworth said, "Father; – to God Himself we cannot give a holier name."

If we understand the power God has given us, it's unthinkable that a father would ever curse his children. But thankfully, the blessing of God cancels the curse of man.

The United States is one of the few countries in the world that has an official day on which children honor their fathers. On the third Sunday in June, fathers all across the United States are given presents, treated to dinner or otherwise made to feel special.

The origin of Father's Day isn't clear. Some say it began with a church service in West Virginia in 1908 – a kind of equal time for Mother's Day. Others say the first Father's Day ceremony was held in Vancouver, Washington.

Regardless of when the first Father's Day occurred, the strongest promoter of the holiday was Mrs. Bruce John Dodd of Spokane, Washington. Mrs. Dodd felt that she had an outstanding father. He was a veteran of the Civil War. His wife had died young, and he had raised six children without their mother.

In 1909, Mrs. Dodd approached her minister and others in Spokane about having a church service dedicated to fathers on June 5, her father's birthday. That date was too soon for her minister to prepare the service, so he spoke a few weeks later on June 19. From then on, the state of Washington celebrated the third Sunday in June as Father's Day.

States and organizations began lobbying Congress to declare an annual Father's Day. In 1916, President Woodrow Wilson approved the idea, but it wasn't until 1924 that President Calvin Coolidge made it a national event to, "establish more intimate relations between fathers and their children, and to impress upon fathers the full measure of their obligations."

Since then fathers have been honored by their families throughout the nation on the third Sunday in June.

In a society that often considers a father's presence optional, it's worthy of note that even worldly wisdom honors him. An English proverb says, "One father is worth more than a hundred schoolmasters."

The last verse of the Old Testament speaks of the work of the Holy Spirit in these last days. *And He will restore the hearts of the fathers to their children, and the hearts of the children to their fathers, lest I come and smite the land with a curse.* (Malachi 4:6)

The Climate of Life — *6/20 – June 20*

It was a Saturday night in June. It was a busy day and we were relaxing before going to bed when it started to rain. This was no ordinary late Spring shower. It was raining as hard as I've ever seen. El Niño had struck again.

I said to my wife that it was a shame to let such a beautiful storm go to waste. So we got in the car and ventured out into the downpour. We got soaked just running eight feet from the house to the garage.

My family has accused me of wanting to be one of those storm chasers like in the movies. I can't deny that the awesome power of a thunderstorm, or anything else in God's creation fascinates me and activates my substantial wonder mechanism.

Anyhow, we enjoyed it, ending up at our grandkid's home where they, too, were excited about the storm. I know that rain at this time of year isn't good news for some. I wouldn't want to be homeless at such a time. But we had fun.

There are spiritual lessons here. I came to realize long ago that storms are part of the normal climate of life. "Into each life some rain must fall," they say. We should not expect constant sunshine and trouble-free lives while we live here on planet earth.

And, just as certain places in the world get more rain than others, some lives seem to have more dark clouds and stormy conditions than average. The climate of their lives is just more conducive to storms.

Conversely, some people seem to live their lives without much storminess at all. They seldom have a bad day, and if they do, they make a big deal out of it. And those who live under a dark cloud of turmoil have little sympathy for their fair-weather friends.

The difference should not be a surprise to us. Why some have lots of trouble and others don't may be as simple as the climate of life. If you live where you do, you're going to get rained on, or maybe not. We certainly shouldn't get all pushed out of shape because someone else has it sunny and we have it stormy.

Financial, physical, emotional, relational, storms just keep coming. The long dark night of the soul, the season of despair and depression – some of us have been there and done that, or are there now – and are doing that.

I have some folks in mind as I write this who are in the middle of an El Niño pattern of trouble in their lives right now. We care about you, dear ones. Jesus is with you in your storm, and so are we.

May the Lord of the wind and the waves grant you His peace. Amen.

June 21 – 6/21 **Seasons**

Psalm 1 describes the godly man: *He shall be like a tree planted by the rivers of water, that brings forth its fruit in its season...* Did you get that? "In its season."

Today is the beginning of Summer – the Summer Solstice – the most daylight of the year. Yesterday we considered that storms are part of the climate of life. Climate is the day-to-day conditions that affect life on planet earth. But, there's another factor that affects or lives, and it's worth a look – the seasons.

There's a season for fruit, but there isn't fruit in every season. Most Christians don't believe in seasons, only harvest time. We want fruit all the time, but there just cannot be a perpetual harvest.

With high purpose, God created seasons in nature that have a parallel in the seasons of the soul. There's the Winter of quiet reflection when things that were once vibrant with beauty lie dormant, stripped of vital signs of life. There's the Springtime of refreshing when *flowers appear on the earth; the time of singing has come, and the voice of the turtledove is heard in our land.* (Song of Solomon 2:11-13)

Then there's the Summer of re-creation when blossoms of hope begin to produce tangible, growing results. Then comes the Autumn of reaping when the rewards of labor are realized. Each season has its purpose, and there could be no season of harvest without the others in succession.

I wondered about a connection between the noun "season", a time of the year, and the verb "season", to add flavor. I found that they are closely related. A substance known as a "seasoning" takes its meaning from that which has been matured and brought to full flavor through the passing of many seasons.

Parsley, sage, rosemary, and thyme draw their distinctive flavors from hot and cold, wet and dry, dark and light – seasons. It's a fact that climatic sameness does not make for distinctive flavor when it comes to herbs and seasonings.

One famous coffee maker boasts that its coffee beans come from a place in the mountains of Colombia that knows the cold of winter and the heat of summer. The implication is that this contrast adds to the full, rich flavor of their coffee.

In just such a way, the seasons of the soul add full, rich flavor to life. The point is this: in the seasons of life we are seasoned for life. God has designed the seasons of the soul to deepen us, to instruct us in wisdom, and to help us grow strong; "like a tree planted by the rivers of water." (Psalm 1:3)

It's in the seasons of life, the Winter of reflection, the Spring of refreshing, the Summer of re-creation and growth, and the Autumn of reaping, that we come to mature, full flavor, well seasoned, ready and able to bear fruit that is worthy of the Master – Who is Lord of the seasons.

A Growing Season *6/22 – June 22*

He who gathers in summer is a wise son, says Proverbs 10:5. In our valley summer isn't normally harvest time but the word "gathers" used here doesn't so much speak of harvest as much as it does increase. So it could read, "he that increases in summer is a wise son."

The idea is that we will take account at the end of summer and be able to say that we have increased since Spring. Summer is a growing season. That's how it is with grapes and figs, and peaches and almonds, and corn and wheat. And that's how God intends it to be for our families and our walk with Jesus.

Often summer isn't a growing season. It's a time of pleasure and the pursuit of things that diminish us spiritually. I'm all for fun but I've noticed that I, and those I love, neglect the basics when there are so many options. We come to the end of this season gasping for breath and starved nearly to death for nourishment in our spirit.

The time to think about this is at the beginning of summer so that we can take steps to insure growth this year. Just yesterday we crossed into Summer – the Summer Solstice, it's called. It was the day with the longest hours of daylight in the year. From here to December 21, the Winter Solstice, daylight hours will slowly decrease.

When I was a child in Illinois, three words were drilled into us in grammar school. These three words were at every railroad crossing, (there were lots of those then.) They'd be the last words the teacher spoke as she dismissed the class every day, and especially when school was out for the Summer.

These three words have probably saved thousands of lives over the years. The words are: Stop, Look, and Listen! And these three words can insure that this summer will be a growing season for you and yours.

More about this tomorrow.

"Three little words..." That was the title of a popular song decades ago. The three words were, "I love you." They're still effective today. They can make a difference in someone's life, maybe even yours.

There are also three little words that can make Summer a season of spiritual growth for you and your family.

STOP! Resist the tendency to go through summer nonstop. Take time to be quiet. What we call recreation is supposed to be re-creation – new life! That requires rest and relaxation as well as activity and exertion. At the beginning of summer, take note of the momentum that builds in an attempt to get too much into not enough time. Stop! Evaluate. Meditate. Change directions if necessary. Stop trying to keep up with everyone else.

LOOK! Observe the passing scene. Take time to notice people. Look at your kids – just look at them! Aren't they special? These years are precious. Take lots of pictures – mental, and otherwise.

Look at the magnificent world that God has created. He intended that we see Him in it. Don't miss Him there. He's beautiful! Look at the heavens that declare His glory. Look for opportunities to share God's love.

LISTEN! Hear the sounds of laughter, the birds singing, and the wind in the trees. A doctor told a man with life-threatening hypertension to go to a certain spot in the forest and sit down on a log.

He gave him an envelope that wasn't to be opened until he got to the log. Arriving there the man opened the envelope. Inside was one word – "listen." The man spent five days there – listening, and came back a well man.

Listen to what the Lord will say to you. It's certain that He will speak; it's not certain that you will hear.

Stop - look - and listen; three words that can insure a safe crossing of the middle of the year. When we come to September, let it be said that we were wise and increased in summer. *He who gathers (increases) in summer is a wise son,* says Proverbs 10:5.

Summer is a growing season. Let's grow for it!

Honorable Marriage *6/24 – June 24*

Let marriage be held in honor, esteemed worthy, precious, of great price and especially dear - in all things. (Hebrews 13:4 Amp)

"Marriage is honorable," says the King James Version of the Bible. Most people don't see marriage as being honorable, precious, worthy of high esteem, or especially dear.

Society has promoted marriage as an alternate life-style, along side of other options available to people these days. But God says it's more than a social convenience or one of many options for people who want to be together. He says it's worthy of great honor to be married.

Do you feel honored to be married? God Himself holds in honor those who choose to live in accordance with the Word of God and commit themselves to their mate for the duration of their lives. That's something of far greater value than the esteem or rejection of mere men.

Married people need other married people. This is one of the strengths of the church. Someone has said that we all need three types of relationships to make our lives meaningful. First, we need those who are further along the way, who give us hints of the next step. Second, we need those who are our peers, with whom we share mutual discovery. Third, we need those who are not so advanced, friends we can nourish and sustain.

Married life in the church provides all three types of relationship. There are those who are further along the road of life, whose lives we observe for guidance in our own journey together. The experience of many years has made them a special treasure. We need them.

There are those who are our peers. It's fun to be with them because we're near the same place on the road of life. We have mutual interests and common challenges. We need them, too.

Then there are those just starting on the journey of wedded bliss, who still wear the freshness of new discovery and believe that, in all the world, there has never been a love like theirs. We need them, too. And they need us!

God intended that every married couple know all three types of relationship and not get locked in on one type only. Usually couples limit their contacts to the second group, their peers. So much is lost in this exclusiveness, not only in what could be received, but also in what could be given.

Marriage is honorable, precious, worthy of high esteem and especially dear. God said so – and, after fifty years of marriage, so do I.

June 25 – 6/25 *O. J. Samson*

Many years ago growing up in Sunday School, a series of lessons was introduced called "Heroes of the Faith." These were lessons about the lives of Old Testament men like Joshua, Daniel, Gideon, and Samson.

I don't know how old I was then, but I was old enough to question whether Samson should really be included in the list of heroes. The lessons presented him in the best possible light, but I could read for myself the exploits of this man of God with great strength, long hair – and feet of clay.

It's said that modern sports competition such as football, basketball, baseball, soccer and hockey mirrors warfare. In other words, taking the ground of the opposing team on the football field is a kinder, gentler equivalent of the D-Day invasion of Europe.

To Samson war was sport, and he was a first round draft choice of everybody. With one act of holy rage he changed the course of Israel's history. But lust and greed proved to be his downfall. You do remember Delilah, don't you?

Well, in June of 1994, O.J. Simpson, a football player of considerable skill, was arrested for a double murder. The whole nation watched the unfolding drama of his capture and his trial. I saw a parallel between Simpson and Samson and merged the two personalities into one named – O.J. Samson.

They both had it all and were idolized by their contemporaries. Both were rich and famous and great fun at parties. Both were impressive physical specimens and dominated the headlines of their day.

But, if you check the record in Judges chapters 14-16 for Samson, and the Los Angeles Police Department for Simpson, you will find that both were the slaves of their own lust and violence. Delilah was not the first woman in Samson's bed, and Simpson's record of spousal exploits is long.

In recent memory we've seen sports stars and TV evangelists fall like flies because of moral failure. These people are not heroes; they're celebrities. And the difference is important. A celebrity may excel in one field of endeavor, but moral excellence is not implied. Celebrities live the good life; they're sought after for endorsements. They have a following – but they're going nowhere.

A hero on the other hand, carries the burden of being emulated; they're role models, and ought to be. They often lead honorable lives in obscurity until moral conviction leads them to act heroically against injustice and evil.

Who are the heroes today? They're men and women who conduct themselves with honor; who resist sexual temptation with heroic consistency; who channel their rage to productive ends; who bow at the nail-scarred feet Jesus Christ, Lion of Judah, Lord of Lords – and my only Hero.

Road Rage *6/26 – June 26*

"Road Rage!" That's a new syndrome that's turning highways nationwide into bumper-car rides and shooting galleries.

We've all felt it at one time or another. You get cut off in traffic by a reckless jerk that violates the law and common decency, and you feel the temperature rising inside of you. What was he thinking?

If you're like me, you have to decide, in the heat of that moment, whether to lay on your horn and challenge his actions or, in automotive terms, turn the other fender and get on down the road.

For many, the freeway has replaced the sports arena as the site of frenzied competition. What should be the reaction of the people of God as we travel the highways and byways of this land when we observe reckless stupidity?

Well, obviously the first thing that comes to mind is that followers of Jesus Christ ought not to be the recklessly stupid ones. How I drive should be an extension of the Lordship of Jesus in my life.

Turning the other cheek or fender does not come naturally to most of us but this principle of the Kingdom of God marks a major point of difference between the kingdoms of the world and the way of the cross of Jesus.

Soviet leader Nikita Khrushchev once said, "There is much in Christianity that is in common with us Communists, but I cannot agree with Him when He says when you are hit on the right cheek, turn the left cheek. I believe in another principle. If I am hit on the right cheek, I hit back on the left cheek so hard I will knock your head off. This is my difference with Christ." And long live the difference, Nicky!

While Khrushchev and fanatic Islamists may disagree with Jesus at this point, we who've been redeemed by His blood are bought and paid for. We're called to obey Him, whether we intellectually or emotionally agree or not.

The Lord says to all who follow Him, *Beloved, do not take revenge, but leave room for God's wrath, for it is written: 'It is mine to avenge; I will repay,' says the Lord. On the contrary, If your enemy is hungry, feed him; if he is thirsty, give him something to drink. Do not be overcome by evil, but overcome evil with good.* (Romans 12:19-21)

God can handle vengeance; I can't. His vengeance will be just. It will not consume Him, and it will be final; there will be no re-vengeance.

By doing good to the one who hurts me I overcome my enemy's evil. So, even in the event of reckless stupidity on the road, I must cleave to that which is good. Sometimes doing good – is as simple as not blowing my horn.

Amen!

This is about the awesome power of blessing. All through the Scriptures, the following utterances changed lives and influenced nations.

• Then the Lord spoke to Moses, saying, *"Speak to Aaron and to his sons, saying, 'Thus you shall bless the sons of Israel. You shall say to them: The Lord bless you, and keep you; the Lord make His face shine on you, and be gracious to you; the Lord lift up His countenance on you, and give you peace.* (Numbers 6:22-26)

• *Blessed shall you be in the city, and blessed shall you be in the country. Blessed shall be the offspring of your body and the produce of your ground and the offspring of your beasts, the increase of your herd and the young of your flock. Blessed shall be your basket and your kneading bowl. Blessed shall you be when you come in, and blessed shall you be when you go out.* (Deuteronomy 28:3-6)

• *Blessed is everyone who fears the Lord, Who walks in His ways. When you shall eat of the fruit of your hands, you will be happy and it will be well with you. Your wife shall be like a fruitful vine, within your house, your children like olive plants around your table. Indeed, may you see your children's children.* (Psalm 128)

• *I bow my knees before the Father, ...that He would grant you, according to the riches of His glory, to be strengthened with power through His Spirit in the inner man; so that Christ may dwell in your hearts through faith; and that you, being rooted and grounded in love, may be able to comprehend with all the saints what is the breadth and length and height and depth, and to know the love of Christ which surpasses knowledge, that you may be filled up to all the fullness of God.* (Ephesians 3:14-19)

• *Now may the God of peace Himself sanctify you entirely; and may your spirit and soul and body be preserved complete, without blame at the coming of our Lord Jesus Christ. Faithful is He who calls you, and He also will bring it to pass. The grace of our Lord Jesus Christ be with you.* (I Thessalonians 5:23, 24, 28)

• *Now the God of peace, who brought up from the dead the great Shepherd of the sheep through the blood of the eternal covenant, even Jesus our Lord, equip you in every good thing to do His will, working in us that which is pleasing in His sight, through Jesus Christ, to whom be the glory forever and ever. Amen.* (Hebrews 13:20-22)

• *Now to Him who is able to keep you from stumbling, and to make you stand in the presence of His glory blameless with great joy, to the only God our Savior, through Jesus Christ our Lord, be glory, majesty, dominion and authority, before all time and now and forever. Amen.* (Jude 1:24-25)

These blessings are ours to speak in faith. They are founded in truth and represent the heart of God toward all of His people. May you know the power of God's blessing in this beautiful day.

Concupiscence *6/28 – June 28*

"Concupiscence" is an antiquated word from the King James Bible that has a modern expression in our society. It's the Greek word "epithumia" – "a longing for that which is forbidden." Some 35 times it's translated "lust" or "evil desire." It applies most directly today to the use of pornography.

What does the Bible say about pornography? I Thessalonians. 4:3-5: *For it is God's will that you should be holy; that you should avoid sexual immorality; that each of you should learn to control his own body in a way that is holy and honorable, not in passionate lust (concupiscence).*

While there were no magazines or movies in Bible days, pornography is prostitution, according to the Scriptures. The word for "harlot" is "porne" – the selling of the body for the purpose of sex – pornography. Take money out of the equation and pornography would cease to exist.

Proverbs 6:23-27: *For the commandment is a lamp; to keep you from the harlot. Do not lust after her beauty in your heart, nor let her allure you with her eyelids. For by means of the harlot a man is reduced to a crust of bread. Can a man take fire to his bosom, and his clothes not be burned?* Good question!

Pornography is adultery. Jesus said, *You have heard that it was said, "You shall not commit adultery." But I say to you that whoever looks at a woman to lust for her has already committed adultery in his heart.* (Matthew 5:27, 28)

Whoever commits adultery lacks understanding; he who does so destroys his own soul. (Proverbs 6:32) In addition to these truths, pornography is hedonism, secular humanism, and just plain self-indulgence to the ultimate.

Pornography's appeal is the promise of satisfaction. But no appetite is ever satisfied by endless feeding, but by controlling it. I Thessalonians 4:4 says, *to possess his own vessel in sanctification and honor.* This is satisfaction!

What can we do? Perhaps you're like the man who was told that his little efforts would never tip the scale of justice. He replied, "I don't think I ever thought they would. But I am prejudiced beyond debate in favor of my right to choose which side shall feel the stubborn ounces of my weight!"

What is the rock upon which objection to pornography rests? Is it law? Laws change. Is it the standard of a community? That changes, too. Isn't there something that I can rest my case upon that's outside the tyranny of change?

The only thing that qualifies is God's Word! II Peter 1:4 says, the Word of God is so incorruptible that by it we are able to *escape the corruption in the world caused by lust.*

While the world doesn't recognize its authority now, someday it will be judged by God's word.

June 29 – 6/29 *Altars*

Just before crossing Jordan into the Land of Promise, Moses gave instruction to the people about living in the land. In Deuteronomy 27:5, 6 he says something that interests me about altars.

Build there an altar to the LORD your God, an altar of stones; do not use an iron tool upon them. Build the altar of the LORD your God with fieldstones and offer burnt offerings on it to the LORD your God.

May I suggest that, if we are to live abundantly in the land into which the Lord has brought us, we must learn to build altars? Altars, first of all, are made of stones; hard things. The Lord gives us a place for the hard things that come into our lives; build an altar out of them. But iron tools must not touch the hard things, according to the reference. What does that mean?

It means that the stones are not to be cut to the shape that we desire, but are to be built into the altar just as they are found in the field of our lives. We tend to shape our hard things to make them fit us, don't we?

Second, the hard things are to be laid in order before the Lord. Lying in the field where we stumbled upon them, they do not make an altar. Carrying them around with us doesn't make them an altar. Only when they're brought together and laid in order before the Lord, do they make an altar. A kneeling position works best here.

Third, once the stones are laid in order, something is to be laid upon them and sacrificed. What is to be laid upon our hard things made into an altar? The answer? Romans 12:1 says, *I urge you, brothers, in view of God's mercy, to offer your bodies as living sacrifices, holy and pleasing to God - which is your spiritual worship.* Our bodies, our flesh, ourselves must be offered upon the altar of hard things in worship to the Lord.

Altars are about worship, to be sure, but they're also about pain; for the sacrifice, the sacrificer, and even the Lord, Who takes no pleasure in our pain. But only as our hard things are laid in order before the Lord, does the pain they cause have any redeeming value.

Only there – as an altar – can the hard stones of difficulty be a place of worship to the Lord our God.

Let Go! **6/30 – June 30**

Roll your works upon the Lord, commit and trust them wholly to Him; He will cause your thoughts to become agreeable to His will, and so shall your plans be established and succeed.

Summing up this truth in Proverbs 16:3 (Amplified), it says simply, "Let Go!"

This can be very difficult if a person that we love has become the "work" that we must commit to the Lord. Perhaps the beginning of our problem was when they became a project to us, someone we needed to change. We've not been called to change one another, only to love one another.

Letting go is hard to do. But let's establish a few things here:

• To let go doesn't mean I stop caring – it means I can't do it all for someone.

• To let go isn't to cut myself off – it's to permit another to face reality.

• To let go isn't to care for – but to care about.

• To let go isn't to deny – but to accept.

• To let go is to allow learning – from natural consequences.

• To let go is to fear less – and love more.

• To let go is indeed – to "let God."

I've heard the expression, "I need some space!" Well, to let go of someone we love is to give them space and to trust God to fill that space with Himself. There are times when we feel that we can't trust a person enough to let them go. This is especially true of our children as they grow older and want to be free of parental restraint. I've come to know that if I can't trust a person, then I must trust God with that person. I'm never exempted from trusting.

The scripture indicates that something else is working here. Not only does letting go allow for God to work in another person's life, but some changes take place in me, too. It says, "He will cause your thoughts to become agreeable to His will."

I want that! I want to think God's thoughts after Him – to have the mind of Christ toward those that I care about.

This is promised to me if I "roll my works upon the Lord" and Let Go!

Who has despised the day of small things? (Zechariah 4:10) *And he said to him, "Well done, good servant, because you have been faithful in a very little thing, be in authority over ten cities."* (Luke 19:17)

There's a new field in science called micro-dynamics. Scientists and engineers who call themselves micro-mechanics are working hard to usher in the next machine age, featuring devices visible only under a microscope. They're learning to make ultra-small nozzles, valves, springs, levers, cantilevers and motors as small as a cell.

An example of such technology is a motor so small that it would fit inside the shaft of a human hair. Such a motor would find application in microsurgery. A Japanese micro-mechanic is attempting to build a minuscule robot surgeon that would navigate within a patient's vascular system, carrying medication or micro-tools to treat diseased tissue. This isn't science fiction; it's reality.

Benjamin Franklin wrote: "For want of a nail the shoe was lost; for want of a shoe the horse was lost; for want of a horse the rider was lost; for want of a rider the battle was lost; and all for the want of a horseshoe nail."

God values small things. We often wonder if we should bother Him with the little things in our lives. We pray about buying a house or changing jobs, but what about the tiny things? The simple fact is that, as a loving Father, if there is a matter that concerns us, then it concerns Him.

The Bible is full of admonitions for us to consider that small things are of great importance. "It's the little foxes that spoil the vines." "If you have faith the size of a grain of mustard seed…" "A little that a righteous man has is better than the riches of many wicked." "The tongue is a little member…"

It's usually the little things that cause us the greatest trouble. I've never been bitten by a lion or a tiger, but I've been troubled by many mosquitoes. A man once walked from Mexico to Canada up the Pacific Coast Trail and reported that the greatest hindrance to his trip was the little grains of sand in his shoes.

One day I spent an hour watching some birds. It was fascinating how they moved in their world to survive and flourish. I am huge to them and could do them great harm if I had a mind to. But they sing and fly effortlessly in their world of small things.

God points to birds as examples of His concern for small things. *Consider the birds of the air, they do not sow, neither do they reap, and yet your heavenly Father feeds them. Are you not worth much more than they?* (Matthew 6:26)

I can't conceive of a problem that's too big for God to handle. There's nothing bigger than Him, so everything must be small stuff in His eyes. Big and small are comparative words that only have meaning in my world, not in the domain of Jehovah God. Nothing is too big for Him – or too small.

The Paradox of Freedom — *7/2 – July 2*

There's a fable of a kite, which once said to itself, "If I could just get rid of this string that's holding me back, then I could fly above the clouds and kiss the stars." One day the string broke. Now at last, it was free to soar higher than it had ever gone before. But much to its surprise, it didn't rise above its present height. In fact, it came crashing down to the ground.

The kite hadn't realized a fact of aerodynamics: the string holding a kite down was also the string holding it up. It needed an anchor of sorts in order to rise higher and higher. That's the paradox of freedom.

This tension between release and restraint is an essential element of freedom. Eldon Trueblood said, "We have not advanced far in our spiritual lives if we have not encountered the basic paradox of freedom... that we are most free when we are bound. Discipline is the price of freedom."

That goes for governments, too. Edmund Burke said, "Men are qualified for civil liberties only to the extent that they are willing to put moral chains on their appetites."

I pray that our national leaders learn this soon. We have freedom in great abundance, but we're desperate for restraint, discipline; the string that makes the kite soar.

We acknowledge our roots by celebration. This week we celebrate two pivotal events: the signing of the Declaration of Independence and the death of Jesus, the Passover Lamb, in Communion.

I am struck by the common elements of these two events. Tyranny is one common factor – the Colonies under the tyranny of King George, and all of mankind under the tyranny of Satan. War and bloodshed are common factors. In the Revolutionary War thousands of our brethren died for national freedom. And in the Battle of the Ages at the Cross, only One was worthy to shed His blood for our eternal freedom from sin and death.

Paul prayed for those he loved, *that Christ may dwell in your hearts through faith; that you, being rooted and grounded in love, may be able to comprehend... what is the width and length and depth and height.* (Ephesians 3:17-19)

Let us celebrate the wars that bought us peace – and the death that gave us life – the paradox of our freedom.

The Lord's Supper, as it's been known for hundreds of years, is the occasion to celebrate the death and resurrection of Jesus the Christ. Everything of value to us in the family of God, hinges upon these events in Jesus' life.

It is the Lord's Supper – not man's. The Lord Jesus initiated it; it was not born in the cold, dark chambers of the councils of men. It was not conceived in the heart of man as a ritual to become bondage to those who observe it.

Jesus said some startling things about what we do here today. In John 6:51-53, 56 He said: *I am the living bread that came down out of heaven; if any one eats of this bread, he shall live forever; and the bread also which I shall give for the life of the world is my flesh. And the Jews began to argue with one another, saying, "How can this man give us His flesh to eat?"*

Jesus therefore said to them, "Truly, truly, I say to you, unless you eat the flesh of the Son of Man and drink His blood, you have no life in yourselves... He who eats My flesh and drinks My blood abides in Me, and I in Him."

That sounds like gross pagan ritual to the casual reader of the Gospels. Some of His followers left Him because of this "hard saying." But Jesus wasn't speaking of physical things. In the next few verses He clears that up. John 6:63 says, *It is the Spirit that gives life; the flesh profits nothing; the words that I have spoken to you are spirit and are life.* That's different!

When Jesus says, "He who eats my flesh and drinks my blood abides in Me and I in Him," He declares a principle that has application in the spiritual as well as the physical realm. When I eat a meal it's easy to see that the food is in me. You saw me eat it; it's in there!

What's not so clear is that I am also in the food. Today's muscle, bone, and blood cells are last week's meat, milk, and bread. My body digests the food and it becomes me. So the food is in me, and I am in the food. If I don't eat I die of starvation.

So it is in our spiritual life. By partaking of Him, so to speak, in communion, worship, the Word, prayer, and fellowship, He abides in me; He's in there!

But the person I am to become is also in what I have partaken of Him. I am in Him as surely as my flesh, bones, and blood are in the food that I eat. If I do not partake of Him, I have no life in myself. I will die of spiritual starvation.

The Lord's Supper is a living link with Him now. He attends His Supper and communes with us around the family table. The table is spread with a feast of forgiveness, comfort, and healing. Jesus is the Host of this dinner.

Pull up a chair – dinner is served!

God Wants Us To Be Free *7/4 – July 4*

A man is a slave to whatever controls him. (II Peter 2:19 Living Bible)

The idea of liberty that has kindled the fires of independence in this and many other nations is firmly rooted in the Word of God. God wants men to be free!

Jeremiah 34:8,9 says this: *The word came to Jeremiah from the Lord... that each man should set free his male servant and each his female servant... so that so that no one should keep them in bondage.*

While our nation has struggled to implement this promised liberty, it's not the only nation whose heart beats with the desire for freedom. For many years God's gracious hand has led great men everywhere in the pursuit of freedom.

Simon Bolivar accepted a gift from the people of Peru in 1824. He then asked how many slaves there were in Peru. He was told there were about 3,000. "And how much does a slave sell for," he wanted to know? "About 350 pesos for an able-bodied man," was the answer.

Then, said Bolivar, "I will add whatever is necessary to this million pesos you have given me, and I will buy all the slaves in Peru and set them free. It makes no sense to free a nation, unless all its citizens enjoy freedom as well."

It makes no sense for a nation to be free while people in it remain bound by sin, drugs, alcohol, perversion, and materialism. We're not free unless we accept the price that our Great Liberator has paid for our freedom. Each time someone receives Jesus Christ as personal Savior, freedom spreads to new territory. And whom the Son sets free is free indeed!

"This is a free country!" I hear it so often. But that's not the issue, is it? Not really. The real question is, "Am I free?"

A man is a slave to whatever controls him. Jesus Christ came to liberate those who are bound and He is available to free you now. Ask Him to set you free.

Happy Independence Day!

July 5 – 7/5 *Fire Works!*

Fire Works! Shouldn't that be one word, "fireworks" as in sparklers and bombs busting in air? Our nation has just celebrated Independence Day and everybody's been thinking about fireworks. The smoke still hangs in the air.

I'm not talking about sparklers and rockets red glare. I'm thinking literally that fire works; it really does. Fire influences every part of our lives. It can be destructive, for sure, but ever since our earliest ancestors discovered it, fire has worked for us in ways we don't often think about.

It's hard to think of any manufacturing procedure that doesn't involve fire at some stage in the process. Intense heat changes the properties of things, and makes them work together with other things to make our lives easier.

Just think about food for a moment. Without fire our daily food consumption would be dramatically different. We'd all be eating raw stuff, which may be all right for some things, but I prefer my steak well exposed to fire.

Automobiles work because of fire. An internal combustion engine means that something is "combusting" (burning) inside there. Thousands of well-timed fiery explosions work to get you on down the road. The same can be said of jet planes, or rocket engines, or locomotives, or tractors, or steam ships, or nuclear submarines, or electrical power plants, or Bunsen burners.

Fire warms us, lights our darkness, cooks our food, powers our vehicles, fuses our metals, and even helps us celebrate our freedom. Yes, fire works.

Fire works in other ways that affect our lives profoundly. *He who is coming after me is mightier than I... He will baptize you with the Holy Spirit and with fire. ...and He will thoroughly clear His threshing floor; and He will gather His wheat into the barn, but He will burn up the chaff with unquenchable fire.* (Matthew 3:11, 12)

John the Baptist, speaking of Jesus, says, "He will baptize you with the Holy Spirit and with fire." Apparently, the baptism with fire is something different from the baptism in the Holy Spirit, as we have understood it. John goes on to describe the fire baptism: "He will burn up the chaff with unquenchable fire."

Another place that describes how fire works in this way is I Corinthians 3:13, *...each man's work will become evident... because it is to be revealed with fire; and the fire itself will test the quality of each man's work*

So fire either purifies or it destroys. I Peter 1:7 says, *...That the proof of your faith, being more precious than gold which is perishable, even though tested by fire...*

The fiery trial, the painful loss, the agonizing ordeal is lovingly intended to burn away the chaff and the dross. Job 23:10 says, *When He has tried me I shall come forth as gold.* And so will we all. Let's celebrate! Fire Works!

Partial Birth *7/6 – July 6*

The Supreme Court of this great land voted 5 to 4 to strike down a state law that restricted partial birth abortion. This decision from the highest court in the land was a blow to pro-life advocates and confirmed a national set of values that allows the destruction of a baby's life at any stage in it's development.

The majority decision stated that laws restricting this gruesome procedure are unconstitutional because they interfere with a woman's right to choose.

What blindness! The sanctity of human life, with its related issues of abortion and euthanasia, promises to be a major point of contention for years to come. It's much more than a political matter; it's more than a moral issue; it reflects a deep spiritual crisis in our society.

The term "partial birth" describes a stage in the pregnancy of a woman when her baby is full-term, or nearly so, and may be perfectly capable of viability outside of the womb. But for reasons known only to the mother and her doctor (not even a father has rights here) the life of the baby is terminated in a horrible procedure that even its most liberal supporters can't bear to watch.

I don't have a lot more to say (but a lot more to pray) about this. We must deal with these issues with prayerful, intelligent, and compassionate action.

The idea of partial birth brings something else to mind. I wonder how many things God conceives in me that are almost – but not quite – brought to full term. That's how spiritual things are, too, you know. Truth, a seed of life, is planted in my heart through a song or a message or someone sharing with me. It doesn't spring into a full-grown reality overnight. It takes a while.

But every truth God plants in my heart has the potential of becoming a "child," a beautiful offspring of God's gracious at work in me. But too often, I'm left with seeds that never come to full term for lack of careful nurture which end up being partial births.

The sight of the termination of God's intended purpose in me must be as horrifying in His eyes as the partial birth abortion of a baby in my eyes today.

God deliver us from partial birth. Amen!

July 7 – 7/7 ***The Value of Time***

This I recall to my mind, therefore I have hope. The Lord's lovingkindness, indeed, never ceases, for His compassions never fail. They are new every morning; Great is Thy faithfulness. (Lamentations 3:21-23)

Imagine there is a bank that credits your account each morning with $86,400. It carries over no balance from day to day. Every evening the bank deletes whatever part of the balance you failed to use during the day. What would you do? Draw out every cent every day, of course!

Each of us has such a bank. Its name is Time. Every morning, God credits you with 86,400 seconds. Every night He writes off, as lost, whatever you have failed to invest to good purpose.

He carries over no balance in this time bank. He allows no overdraft. Each day His grace opens a new account for you. Each night the remains of the day disappear forever. If you fail to use the day's deposits, the loss is yours. And there's no drawing against the deposit of tomorrow.

I must live in the present on today's deposits; invest it so as to get from it the utmost in health, joy, and blessing. The clock is running. And now-a-days, time is measure in nano-seconds.

Speaking of nano-seconds, an instructor at the US Naval Academy was trying to find a way to explain a nano-second. This is a critical length of time when you are targeting long-range missiles and programming deep space travel.

She calculated that 17 centimeters, or about 11 inches, is the distance that light travels in 1 billionth of a second – a nano-second. Light travels at the rate of 186,000 miles per second. She cut a piece of cord 17 centimeters long and displayed it to the class of naval recruits. "This is a nano-second," she declared. They got the picture.

Time is an amazing gift. All of us have the same amount of it. All of us have choices about how we will use it. My intention is to draw attention to the value of time and not to produce a wave of frustration and self-loathing for our misuse of this gift of God's grace.

We can all do better, and we have a brand new batch of mercy every morning.

The First Stone *7/8 – July 8*

It's a doorstop – and it has evoked many a question from visitors to Pastor Roy's office. It's actually a rock, or a stone to be more precise. It's not so much that he uses this stone to keep his door in place that's the curiosity here. It's what's written on it that's the thing: "The First Stone."

He tells me that his father gave it to him as a reminder of the encounter Jesus had with a bunch of religious leaders in John 8:3-7. *And the scribes and the Pharisees brought a woman caught in adultery, and...they said to Him, "Teacher, this woman has been caught in adultery, in the very act. Now in the Law Moses commanded us to stone such women; what then do You say?"*

And they were saying this...in order that they might have grounds for accusing Him. But Jesus stooped down, and with His finger wrote on the ground, and He said to them, "He who is without sin among you, let him be the first to throw a stone at her."

There's been a lot of talk about adultery. A candidate to lead The Joint Chiefs of Staff was passed over because of an adulterous affair. The only woman in the US Air Force qualified to fly the B-52 was discharged without honor because of adultery.

It would be amusing, if it were not so tragic, to watch the media, Congress, and other "experts" deal with the matter of adultery. In a society, which is so corrupt that it blatantly promotes sexually promiscuous behavior by every means at its disposal, it's the height of hypocrisy for its spokes-persons to condemn what it endorses.

Adultery is serious sin. For those who need definitions, it's marital infidelity, sexual intercourse outside of marriage. It's called adultery – but there's not much adult about it. It's actually pretty childish, when you think about it.

President Calvin Coolidge was asked what the preacher's topic was upon leaving church one Sunday. Cal was a man of few words. His reply was, "Sin." When asked to expand upon what the preacher had to say about sin, he said, "He's against it."

That's pretty much how God feels about adultery. But that's how He feels about all sin. An action is sinful because it's harmful. God draws lines of love to keep us from destroying ourselves. He says, "Don't do it" because it hurts someone He loves.

Jesus knew the hearts of all those who had stones in their hands ready to throw them. They dropped their stones and walked away.

Pastor Roy has it right. Stones are not for throwing. They're for holding doors open. Ironically, the one qualified to cast any stones is Jesus, the Sinless Son of God – but He's no stone-thrower – He's a stone mover!

Too Much Is Not Enough

It's a matter of great consequence. It could be the ruination of our culture. The problem – we've lost our sense of enough-ness. When do we have enough?

When do we have enough money, enough pleasure, enough speed or capacity on our computers, or any other material thing? If we don't know what is enough, we'll never know when we're well off.

This is crucial to the world of technology because companies overtly play upon our desire for more. This lost sense of enough-ness is the "cash cow" of the computer industry. It's sometimes difficult to convince people they have enough because they've seen the ads and heard the hype. Everybody's got to upgrade everything.

The real concern I have, however, is the damage that's accumulating to our spirits. Materialism is the enemy of the spirit and, sadly, the stuff of this world is winning the battle in the lives of many followers of the Man of the Cross.

The Apostle Paul speaks; in his first letter to Timothy (6:5-8) about some people in the Church of a depraved mind who saw godliness as a means to great monetary gain. He says something very significant: *Godliness with contentment is great gain.*

Contentment is nothing more, nor less than a sense of enough-ness. It says, "In this moment, in this place, I have enough. And if I need more, my God will see to that or direct me in the pursuit of it."

I'm no stranger to the lure of more and better and faster. I deal with it every day in the computer world. It may be a better car, a faster computer, a bigger house, another church, or another mate that tempts – but the lure of more is a threat to all that is sacred and holy in us.

How much is enough? The prevailing secular attitude drives one to succeed and to never stop pushing the limits. If you ever become content with what you have you'll be run over by the crowd that's waiting to take your place.

There is a vast difference between being content and being complacent. The word "contentment" comes from the same one that is translated "sufficient," as in *My grace is sufficient for you.* (II Corinthians 12:9)

Complacency, on the other hand, is smugness, a desire to please, or a lack of seriousness. God hasn't called us to that. But He has summoned us to find our pleasure and our sufficiency in Him.

Not one of us has enough of Jesus. What if we were as driven to have more of Him as were are to have more stuff? What if I were drawn to Him with the same intensity with which I'm lured to things?

In Him alone, enough-ness finds its match – and its Master.

Revive Thy Work, O Lord! *7/10 – July 10*

O Lord, revive Your work in the midst of the years, in the midst of the years make Yourself known. (Habakkuk 3:2)

A little girl looked at her mother's egg timer – one of those small hourglasses with sand in it. Her mother explained, "It takes the sand exactly three minutes to run down to the bottom; then you turn it over and it runs out all over again."

That afternoon, the little girl brought a friend into the kitchen. "See," she said as she showed her the egg timer. "You run the sand through it in three minutes. Then you turn it upside down and you get your three minutes back!"

Perhaps that's how some of us view revival – a replay of a past era of grace. It's as if God, when He gets ready, turns over the hourglass of time and runs it all back and the church is revived for a while until the sand runs out again.

That's not what the prophet is talking about. Revival is not an instant replay of some former glory. It is a brand new infusion of life for the people of God. He said, *Behold I will do a new thing,* not an old thing again. God is making Himself known and there is enough of Him that He doesn't have to repeat Himself.

In a story from the Talmud, Rabbi Shem faced a difficult problem. When that happened he would go to a place in the woods and there light a fire and meditate in prayer. He would then and there find a solution to his problem.

A generation later, the Rabbi Meseritz, when he was faced with a problem, would go to the same place in the woods and say, "We no longer light the fire, but we still come here to meditate and pray."

A generation later, when Rabbi Leib was faced with a problem, he would go into the woods. He would say, "I cannot light the fire and I do not know the words of the prayer, but I do know the place. And he would go there."

Another generation passed and when Rabbi Israel was faced with a problem, he would sit on his chair in the synagogue and say, "We cannot light the fire. We cannot speak the prayer. We do not know the place. But we can tell the story of how it used to be."

The impediments to revival are in us and not in God. When we hunger for Him to reveal Himself to this generation, we will know the day of His power.

A young man who wanted to obtain knowledge came to Socrates. He waded waist-deep into the Aegean Sea and pushed the young man's head under the water. Gasping, the young man struggled to free himself from the hand of his teacher. "Why did you do that?" he asked. Socrates replied, "When you want knowledge as badly as you wanted air, you will have it."

How much do we really want revival in our time? God's active Presence is the air we breathe. We must have it or die.

The scribes and Pharisees came to Jesus, saying, "Why do Your disciples transgress the tradition of the elders? For they do not wash their hands when they eat bread." But He answered and said to them, "Why do you also transgress the commandment of God because of your tradition?" (Matthew 15:1-3)

There existed, in the time of Jesus, a system of rules and regulations passed down through the generations that became as binding upon a person as the commandments of God. These traditional standards were known as "fences".

The original idea was to build a protective barrier back far enough from the Law of God that if one observed the rule, or fence, that he would not even come close to transgressing the Law.

This tradition had its origin in the fence that was built around Mt. Sinai to protect the people from trespassing on holy ground. In time it evolved into a system of prevention carrying the same moral weight as the Law of God itself.

The Pharisees in Jesus' day, for instance, would not look in the mirror on the Sabbath lest they see something that needed fixing requiring them to do work on that holy day. And they expected everyone else to do the same.

They were referred to by the youth of their day as "tumblers" because they would often stumble down the street with hands covering their eyes lest they look at a woman and it lead to lusting after her.

The fences became a very real factor in the hatred that developed among the Pharisees and other sects toward Jesus. He disregarded their fences frequently because, to Him, they did not bear the weight of the Law of His Father.

He crossed the fences righteously, but it led to many confrontations and eventually became the grounds for the charge of blasphemy against Him. And it could be said that Jesus was crucified on a fence.

An uncomfortably similar situation exists among Christians today. Sometimes rules that we observe don't represent the Law of God. But I need some fences in my own life at points of weakness, lest I stray into transgression territory.

God's Law applies to everyone in every culture and at every time, equally, but fences should be personally established at my own points of weakness. My fences protect me, but I cannot expect another person to live within them.

If we attempt to make our fences a standard of conduct for everyone, we too, can make the Law of God have no effect by our traditions. (Matthew 15:6) May we walk in grace and mercy toward one another and not confuse the Law of God with well-intentioned man-made fences.

So, as the old cowboy song says, "Don't fence me in."

Prophecy In A Box *7/12 – July 12*

I was indignant. It just didn't seem right. I bought white Kleenex. As a matter of fact, I bought a whole case of white Kleenex, and the last few tissues in the first box were pink. Would the whole case be defective like the first box was?

Sure enough, every box we used turned out to be the same. The last few tissues were pink, or peach, or some exotic color. But I don't like pink tissue.

It took me a few boxes to realize that this incompetence on the part of a tissue stuffer in some far-away factory was a actually clever way of saying that when the pink ones show up, it's time for another box – the end is near. It was prophecy in a box.

I hasten to add that this little crisis did not rank high on my scale of pressure points, and it didn't happen yesterday. It was when this idea first found its way to the shelves of the discount house.

I've thought about this and I've concluded that there's a lesson here for me. It's a lesson about consuming and the consummation of all things. The term "consumer" has been so over used that we may miss the idea behind it. We consume things every moment of every day of our lives. All of us are consumers all of the time.

It's easy to see that with a box of Kleenex, a tube of toothpaste, a bag of potato chips, a gallon of milk, or a tank of gas. I bought a jar of 1,000 one-a-day type multiple vitamins about two years ago. The jar is only about one-third full now. I'm watching the days of my life pass – one capsule at a time.

The economy of the free world depends upon the fact that we are all consumers. It's what makes business and industry prosper. And most, if not all, of our jobs exist because someone consumes something.

But the commodity which is most precious and which we consume without much thought of its diminishing supply – is time. We only have so much of it, you know. The sands of time are running out. The tissues in the old Kleenex box of life are changing color. The end is near.

I'm not talking about our life in Jesus. It is everlasting. But this world doesn't have such a destiny. The days of planet earth are numbered. And our stay on this globe is not without end.

Jesus Christ, our Redeemer King is coming back to earth someday soon. Signs continue to point to the eminent return of the Lover of our souls.

This is not a good time to be preoccupied with wealth and fame and the material aspects of life in this terrestrial box. When Jesus comes, we open another box, so to speak, and it will not be consumed.

It keeps going, and going and going…

Recently we were honored by the presence of some of God's choicest vessels – missionaries. In a morning service, a retired couple stood to acknowledge their first time with us, and a couple from Russia stood for the same reason.

The next Wednesday evening we had a report from Brad and Sue Smeltzer, who've accepted the challenge of taking Jesus' love to Mali, West Africa.

The encounters we have with these dear people are of extreme importance to them and to us. It's been said that they not only go from us, they go for us. They go in our stead, as an extension of the life of Jesus expressed in us.

While that may be true in a general sense, it is only true in a literal sense as we personally participate in their ministries by our prayers, our giving, and our love. Their mission becomes ours only to the extent that we give them the support, emotionally, spiritually, and financially that they need to do the job.

The Mission to which we are called is not without risk. On July 2, a few years ago, in Apartado, a little town in Colombia near the border with Panama, one member of our extended family paid the ultimate price for The Mission.

Unknown assailants gunned down Pastor Jesus Argelio Martinez as he was preparing for the Sunday gathering of the Church. His young wife and family, and we, who share his vision, mourn his death.

A few years ago there was a controversy about the term "missions." For years we gave to missions, we had a Missions Department, and we talked about foreign missions with great passion. Someone pointed out, however, that there was only one mission, not many missions for the Church. So people began to talk about our world mission.

Old habits die hard, but in fact, there is only one mission for the Church. It's the same one Jesus had when He came to this mission field called Earth. He said, "The Son of Man has come to seek and to save those who are lost."

Everything else we do is corollary and secondary to that. Jesus healed people. He fed hungry people. He brought peace and joy by His gracious words and ways. But His mission was to save people from hell.

Shouldn't we focus on human need and concentrate our efforts on healing and feeding and making people happy and whole? Certainly, if we can do it as Jesus did – with an eye to the value and eternal destination of the human soul.

As important as healing is for my body, and wholeness is for my emotions, of greater significance is the condition of my soul. Everything else is temporary.

Permanent preoccupation with temporary matters is typical of the spirit of this age. The followers of the Crucified One must not make that mistake. The Mission, to seek out and save lost people, has everything to do with eternity.

Grandma's Closet ***7/14 – July 14***

God lived in Grandma's closet. At least that's what my sister and I felt at ages six and eight, respectively. Our grandmother on our mother's side, prayed a lot. And when she prayed she went into this small closet, cleared of anything unnecessary, and she stayed there sometimes for hours.

We talked about this at a family reunion on the occasion of our mother's 80th birthday. It was one of those classic moments when the elders of the tribe sit in a circle and pass on verbal history to those who never knew some very special people in our family.

As we spoke of Grandma Greene I felt we were treading on holy ground. My sister said something I will never forget: "I would never go into Grandma's closet because I knew God lived there."

This sweet, gentle, frail woman was what we came to know as a "prayer warrior." We never questioned that designation because we were witnesses to the battles she fought and won in her closet.

What a heritage! My mother and her three children share a rich relationship in the Lord today in great measure because of the closet-prayers of Grandma Greene fifty or sixty years ago. I've been committed to ministry for fifty years because of her influence. And I'm grateful.

Jesus said, "When you pray, enter into your closet…" This is a call to secret prayer, which the Father rewards openly. This practice has gone the way of horse-drawn carriages and buggy whips but it remains the command of Jesus.

Just when lots of folks in the world are "coming out of the closet," announcing secret lifestyles, Christians are called to go in there. And we are. But we're not going in there to pray – we're going in there to hide!

The news media, the courts, and many of our leaders are openly espousing the idea that religious convictions must not be injected into public debate. Judges are forced to hear cases without moral or religious considerations affecting their decisions. And scandals in the church have not helped matters at all! So we withdraw and are content to be the invisible – and silent – body of Christ.

Ironically, at a time when moral and religious considerations are not allowed to influence state matters, candidates for public office are being scrutinized much more carefully for their moral character, or lack there of.

The closet isn't a hiding place. It's where we come to know the heart of Jesus. When Grandma came out of the closet, it wasn't to announce some secret sin. She glowed with a radiance that lives in my memory today.

She had been with Jesus.

For as long as I can remember I've been a cautious person. When faced with some measure of risk, I considered it virtuous to "err on the side of caution." But as I entered my senior years I have questioned the wisdom and the virtue of a lifestyle of caution.

Don't get me wrong; I've had my foolish and painful moments when I threw caution to the winds in some fleshly pursuit. And I'm not advocating that caution be forsaken when dealing with the world, the flesh, or the devil. In these areas, the light is not cautious yellow – but blood red!

What God has been dealing with me about is my habit of caution in response to His Word. And now I get to pass this humiliating, penetrating lesson on to you. I'm too cautious in obeying the simple commands of His Word.

When it comes to the clear command of God, wisdom demands action – not caution. Such commands as: "Love one another with a pure heart fervently," "Forgive one another as I have forgiven you," and "Go into all the world and preach the Gospel to every creature," don't call for caution but immediate action, even if we stumble on the road of obedience.

At the other extreme are foolhardy souls who "err on the side of action" in matters of the Spirit. I've known some who assumed that every utterance from a charismatic leader was a word from God. They were the first to loose the bonds of earth in a flimsy flight of fancy. I took some morbid comfort in their inevitable crash landing.

So, we have two scenarios. The first is considered a virtue – to err on the side of caution. The other – to err on the side of action – is considered a vice, since there's often a trail of debris in the wake of errors of action. Those of us who err on the side of caution leave nothing at all behind us.

I know why caution seems so virtuous. It's because if you're cautious, people don't usually get hurt. But when caution rules, people don't get healed, saved, or made whole either. The avoidance of pain isn't the ministry to which God has called us.

In fact both scenarios involve erring, even sinning. We can sin by omission as well as by commission. For instance, it is just as disobedient to stay, when God says, "Go," as it is to go, when God says, "Stay." We who err with caution stay, when we should go. And the world is dying for want of go-ers.

You've heard of the proverbial boss who says, "Jump," and you say, "How high?" Well, when God, the Ultimate Boss, says, "Go," we should be saying "How far?" But for too many Christians the response is, "Why me?"

I'm beginning to think that those who err on the side of action get more done for the Kingdom than the whole bunch of us who err on the side of caution, even if they blow it big occasionally. We cautious souls don't make many mistakes – but we don't see many miracles either.

A Stirring *7/16 – July 16*

David inquired again of God, and God said to him, *You shall not go up after them; circle around them, and come upon them in front of the mulberry trees. And it shall be, when you hear a sound of marching in the tops of the mulberry trees, then you shall go out to battle, for God has gone out before you to strike the camp of the Philistines.* (I Chronicles 14:14, 15)

What's the story here? What's this about "the marching in the tops of the mulberry trees?" Well, when David was made king over Israel, one of the first things he did was set out to bring the stolen Ark of God back to the City of David. The Philistines were upset by this news. They made a raid on the Valley of Rephaim and were soundly defeated by David's mighty men.

Not willing to accept defeat, the Philistines raided the valley again. David asked God what to do about this and God gave him the winning strategy: "Circle around them and come upon them in front of the mulberry trees."

And then God said something very interesting: "When you hear a sound of marching in the tops of the mulberry trees, then you shall go to battle, for God has gone out before you." Do you get the picture? God Himself will signal the onset of the battle by causing a stirring – a marching – in the tops of the mulberry trees.

Something extraordinary is happening across Argentina, Canada, Britain, South Africa, India, and the United States. An overwhelming awareness of God's Presence characterizes these manifestations. Repentance and hundreds of conversions and healings are reported, reminding old-timers of the Day of Pentecost and more recent charismatic outpourings.

One church in a suburb of Chicago reports hundreds of baptisms and so many marriages healed that "our counseling load has virtually disappeared." In England, the "times of refreshing," as they call this phenomenon, has fallen on several hundred congregations in many denominations. One church in Surrey reported people weeping under conviction and many "overcome with a sense of the awesomeness of God."

With typical English under-statement, one man said, "People don't expect things like this to happen to us, but it is rather pleasant when they do." I say, old chap, rather pleasant, indeed!

Is this revival? Or is this the "marching in the mulberry trees?" I think it's the latter. What we're witnessing is a sovereign work of God, but it's meant to stir us to battle, not celebration. It's a call rise up against the enemy who has stolen away the glory of God, as the Philistines did.

Revival is on the other side of the battle when the Ark – The Presence of God – once again comes to His resting place in His sanctuary.

Then we will celebrate His Presence. That's revival!

The newspaper declared the news: Rangoon, Burma. April 21, 1994 “A relic, said to be Buddha’s tooth, arrived in Burma from China yesterday. It was carried by elephant-drawn carriage past thousands of chanting devotees.

“The tooth relic is one of two believed to have survived since Buddha’s death 2,500 years ago. The other one is kept in Sri Lanka. Millions are expected to visit the relic during its forty-five day stay in Burma.”

I imagined myself a tourist walking down the street in Rangoon minding my own business when a chanting crowd heads in my direction. Towering above the crowd is a huge elephant decked in ceremonial colors pulling a large carriage. I ask, “What’s going on? Who’s in the carriage?”

“No one’s in the carriage. Its Buddha’s tooth.” “Buddha’s what?” I ask. “His tooth.” The picture is a bit humorous to me but I know better than to laugh out loud at such a sacred occasion here in Rangoon. Burmese officials do not take kindly to such insults.

But all this fuss over a tooth? These people are sincere, no doubt about it. They are believers. If sincere faith alone could save, Rangoon would be the scene of great redemption this day. But, alas, Burmese continue their lives in spiritual darkness.

If sincerity saved, everyone in the world would be a saint since everyone is sincere about something. And if faith alone could justify, the world would be a sinless paradise since all men have faith in something.

But sincere faith, to be redemptive, must embrace a worthy object. It must embrace truth – not a tooth! This has been the simple motivation of missionaries for hundreds of years and continues to cause believers in Jesus to leave homes and jobs to carry the Good News everywhere.

Burma is not alone in the rage for relics. Any traveler to the Israel, Italy, Greece, or, for that matter, the USA, is struck with the obsession with religious relics by a large segment of the population. Why? What is it in the human heart that craves a piece of someone’s life?

Relics are a link with past glory. Relics are reminders that the object of our faith and love was once real. But Jesus Christ left no relics for the world to parade, or go to war over. You will not find His bones or teeth if you sift every ounce of earth. He left no manuscripts to be sold at auctions.

What did He leave us? Do we have anything of His to link us to Him? Is there any reminder that He lived and died and rose again?

Yes! Emphatically, Yes! He left us His very own Spirit, the Spirit of Truth – and nothing but the Truth – to be with us forever!

The Comforter has come!

The Secret Presence *7/18 – July 18*

This mystery... which is Christ in you, the hope of glory. (Colossians 1:27)

The Apostle Paul refers to the amazing fact that Jesus Christ lives inside of every believer as a mystery, which was hidden from generations past but revealed to us now. I suggest that the presence of Jesus within us was not only a mystery to ancient believers, but none of us, even now, understands very much about it.

The fact is – there is a dimension to the life of every redeemed child of God that is – deeper than feeling – far beyond knowledge – and more secure than the whims of will. That dimension is the realm of the Spirit of Jesus Who lives and moves within me even when I don't feel or know it. All that Jesus is, is inside of you and me always.

Our problem seems to be that we have a need to feel His presence. If we don't, we assume that He is gone, or doesn't care, or has forsaken us in our time of need. We are so sense-oriented that even our worship must feel good to us or we assume that something is wrong. But worship, by its very nature, is not for my pleasure.

Similarly, we have an insatiable need to know things. If we don't feel His presence, and don't understand what He's doing, we're in a major crisis. Actually, He is working and moving to accomplish higher purposes than we could ever understand at a level deeper than our mind or emotions.

Psalm 91:1 says, *He that dwells in the secret place of the Most High will abide under the shadow of the Almighty.* Moses probably wrote those words and was referring to the Tent of Meeting in the wilderness. Inside the tent was a special place called the Holy of Holies, and inside that place was the Ark of the Covenant upon which was the Mercy Seat – the dwelling place of God's glorious presence.

When Jesus died, the veil that separated everyone from God's presence was torn away, symbolizing that He no longer would rest on a piece of furniture inside of a room no bigger than the average bedroom. He would now live inside of anyone who would come to Jesus and accept the sacrifice of His blood for the forgiveness of sins. Amazing!

Now the body of every believer is the Secret Place of the Most High, and their heart is the Mercy Seat. From this secret place He convicts me, He comforts me, He directs me, He defends me, He heals me. And most of the time I don't even feel or know that anything is happening.

Human pride has assumed all along that man was the initiator and God the responder. Not so. From the secret place He rules and I respond.

This is my greatest comfort – and my only hope of glory.

Higher Ground

The mighty Mississippi River has seen many flood seasons but none like the one that has recently taken dozens of lives and left thousands of people homeless in six Midwestern states. We grieve for the losses and pray for an end to the creeping devastation brought by many weeks of heavy rainfall.

I grew up not far from the Mississippi River and worked on a farm on the banks of the Illinois River, one of "the Big Muddy's" tributaries, for two summers as a young man paying his way through Bible School. I've seen the devastation to homes and businesses in flood season. But I've also seen the long-range effects of the river's apparent madness.

Storms are part of the climate in the Midwest. And when you get a series of storms over a short period of time you will have floods – some worse than others. When the floods come they are a creeping, seeping menace and not a raging torrent like I have seen on the North Coast of California. But there is no way to stop the rising waters. The only defense is to go to higher ground, or better yet – build your home there.

The fact is that while the waters devastate towns and villages they bring with them the rich topsoil which makes that part of the country the nation's bread basket. Next year will bring a bumper harvest of the very crops destroyed by this year's flood. That's why there are farms and towns and villages right up to the river's edge. That's where the best soil is.

Our family lived through the "Thousand Year Flood" in 1964 in Northern California. A unique combination of a tropical storm bringing 30" of warm rain to the mountains, melting the snow in mid-December, and unusually high tides in the Pacific Ocean, which, in effect, dammed up the Eel, Klamath, and Smith Rivers, brought great devastation to three counties.

One thing that was a revelation to me was that the flood permanently affected nothing that God made. A year later, trees and foliage had grown back but man-made structures and institutions never did recover completely.

Life on planet earth sometimes includes deluges of one kind or another. Financial, physical, relational, or spiritual trouble can rise like the waters of the Mississippi and overwhelm the soul. But nothing that God has established will be destroyed.

As the hymn says,

> "Lord lift me up and let me stand, by faith on heaven's table-land.
> A higher plane than I have found, Lord plant my feet on higher ground."

Everything material is in the path of the rising waters of judgment. Find higher ground quickly – and build your life on it!

A Vicious Cycle *7/20 – July 20*

We've just been subjected to the specter of political conventions. Upon such occasions we have a chance to see both the strengths and weaknesses of our unique democratic system of government. Our strengths are many, but our weaknesses are fatal.

The most glaring weakness of America today has to do with the love of money. I Timothy 6:10 says, *For the love of money is the root of all kinds of evil.*

Alexander Fraser Tytler, (1748-1813) at the end of the 18th century, wrote, "The Decline and Fall of the Athenian Republic." Long before the American Democracy had been tested he made the following observation about the ancient Greek democracy: "The average age of the world's greatest civilizations has been 200 years. Those nations always progress through the following sequence:

"From bondage to spiritual faith; from spiritual faith to great courage.
From great courage to liberty; from liberty to abundance.
From abundance to selfishness; from selfishness to complacency.
From complacency to dependency; from dependency back into bondage."

I hasten to explain that it is not money that is the root of all evil, but the love of it. Every political issue addressed by our politicians, including the heart-rending matter of abortion, has as its bottom line the love of money. Everyone wants something from the public treasury but it is bankrupt.

In the 1930's an American Secretary of State named Roger Babson visited South America. When he arrived in Brazil, the president of Brazil asked Mr. Babson this question, "Why is it that North America is so far ahead of South America in so many ways? We have great natural resources, a fine climate, good people, and many other things conducive to growth and success. Why is it that America is so far ahead of us?"

Mr. Babson hesitated, "I'm not sure. Why do you think that North America is so far ahead?" The president replied, "I believe it is because when our forefathers settled South America they were looking for gold. The Pilgrim Fathers looking for God settled North America. We found neither gold nor God. Your country has found both God and gold."

The promise applies to nations, too – *Seek first the kingdom of God and His righteousness and all these things will be added to you.* (Matthew 6:33)

July 21 – 7/21 **Steadfastness**

My beloved brethren, be steadfast, immovable, always abounding in the work of the Lord, knowing that your toil is not in vain in the Lord. (I Corinthians 15:58)

I am the Lord, I change not. (Malachi 3:6)

These passages speak of a quality missing in the world at large but present in the Church – steadfastness.

On a moonless, stormy night 200 years ago, four men stood on a grassy knoll overlooking the Atlantic Ocean and peered seaward at a ship's light glowing in the blackness. One man paced back and forth, leading a horse with a lighted lantern tied to its nodding neck. These men were called "wreckers" because they would lure ships carrying precious cargo to run aground and be wrecked by the pounding waves off Cape Hatteras, North Carolina.

The key to their treachery was the moving light tied to the horse. A ship would assume the light was stationary and steer toward it. By following the moving light the fate of the ship, its crew, and its cargo was doomed. Eventually the sands would cover the wreckage, but not before everything of value had been taken by these men who made their living as wreckers. They say that some 2,300 ships lie buried in this sandy graveyard. Most of them found their fate through the treachery of the wreckers.

Our nation needs a steady beacon, a lighthouse, as a point of reference in a changing world. This must be the Church and its individual expression in every community, neighborhood, office, factory, school, and home.

We can and ought to be flexible in our methods but never in our message. We can't change our message about man's need of a Savior, morality, and the value of life just because the world clamors for "relevancy." The Gospel of Jesus Christ is always relevant, though our application may leave something to be desired. This is a flaw in our method, not in our message.

The steadfastness of the Church rests fully upon the nature of the Church's God. He is our immovable beacon. God is always God. He is always Himself.

Because He is Who He is always – and unchanging, we can be "steadfast, immovable, always abounding in the work of the Lord."

This Too Shall Pass *7/22 – July 22*

Two small boys walked into the dentist's office. One of them said bravely, "I want a tooth taken out and I don't want any gas, and I don't want it deadened because we're in a hurry!" The dentist said, "You're quite a brave young man. Which tooth is it?" The boy turned to his smaller friend and said, "Show him your tooth, Albert." The world is full of volunteers like that.

Well, the thing, which I feared, has come upon me. Pain! I am not fond of pain. For most of my life I've heard about people who have endured great pain and I've been exceedingly grateful that, physically, mine has been a relatively pain-free existence – until Monday night. Please forgive my reference to personal experience, but it has been my greatest teacher in the knowledge of the Holy One.

About 11 pm on the afore mentioned night, I was sitting at the computer and felt a nagging pain in the lower right side of my back. Supposing it to be bad posture, I didn't think much about it and it went away in a few minutes. I went to bed and the pain returned. No possible position provided relief. I tried them all. It hurt a lot! I became nauseated and pale and my wife urged me to call the doctor. I refused, so after about a half and hour, she called and he said that I should go to the emergency room. By the time we arrived, the pain had eased.

To make a long story short, the pain returned three times while I was there. They told me that I was passing a kidney stone. While in the throes of one such pain (on the one-to-ten scale, about an 8.5) I had a thought that made me chuckle a bit. "This, too, shall pass," referring to the stone. But it was a comfort to me in the middle of it.

It's true of all pain, isn't it? It does pass. Even if the pain is constant, it's not everlasting. Jesus has seen to that by providing the ultimate relief from pain – everlasting life in His presence. But pain here and now has some important things to teach us. (Don't you just hate people who draw spiritual lessons from physical pain?)

One thing I noticed was that when the pain stopped I felt such euphoria that it surprised me. I wasn't doped up or imagining it either. It was a real sense of wellbeing. It was confirmation of what I had already suspected, that to know real joy one must have known real pain. To appreciate God's provision, one must have known human need. To enjoy peace, one must have known conflict. It's the contrasting extremes of human experience that gives value to them. It's hard to keep that in mind when it's the pain of a broken heart.

A French writer, Paul Claudel, wrote, "Christ did not come to do away with suffering. He did not come to explain it; He came to fill it with His presence."

As kidney-stone pain goes mine certainly wasn't as bad as some that I've heard about. But it was an occasion for me to say to myself – with pun definitely intended – "This too shall pass!"

The world witnessed a breakthrough of major proportions in Eastern Europe. Television covered the political and economic implications of the crumbling of the Berlin Wall and the melting of the Iron Curtain, but we didn't hear of the most significant developments on the networks.

For instance, Luis Palau was invited to conduct meetings in Romania. Crowds of 35,000 and 50,000 packed a stadium in Oradea to hear him preach the Gospel. In the first evangelistic meeting in Romania since World War II, 32,000 people made public commitments to Jesus Christ in two meetings.

In Moscow, more than 60,000 Soviets attended evangelistic meetings at the Olympic Sports Palace. About 20,000 of them registered their response seeking to know God's love and forgiveness. The meetings were promoted in TV ads, outdoor posters and banners hung across Moscow streets.

Youth With A Mission reports 65,000 decisions for Christ last year, most of which were in Europe. YWAM is also active at the World Cup Soccer games in Italy. Working with the Italian Bible Society, they are distributing scripture portions at 12 stadiums and offering each participant in the games a New Testament in his own language. Millions of Bibles are on their way to the people of the Soviet Union.

The Colorado-based International Bible Society will print one million New Testaments on a government-controlled press near Moscow. They will be distributed through the Soviet Children's Fund. The Fund's chairman, a member of the Supreme Soviet, requested the Scriptures. An additional 1.37 million Scriptures have already been distributed through the churches.

The Slavic Gospel Association is seeking to distribute 50 million Bibles and train 50,000 lay pastors and equip 5,000 churches in the USSR. Soviet authorities have already given approval for a weekly 30 minute Bible reading program on state television to the entire nation.

Leningrad officials signed a joint-venture agreement with Paul Crouch of Trinity Broadcasting Network permitting him to join with local evangelicals to produce Christian television programs. The state also hopes to encourage travel by American Christians to the Soviet Union.

This will be old news by the time you read it, but I share these developments to report answers to prayer. The Spirit is still moving in Europe.

Psalm 66 says, *Make a joyful shout to God, all the earth! Sing out the honor of His name; make His praise glorious. Say to God, "How awesome are Your works. Through the greatness of Your power Your enemies shall submit themselves to You. All the earth shall worship You and sing praises to You.*

Trees — *7/24 – July 24*

This is about trees. I've had more than a casual relationship with trees for as long as I can remember. I've climbed them, chopped them, pruned them, picked them, photographed them, and generally admired them in beautiful places all over the world.

They are a wonder worth noting as we worship the Lord of creation. Notice, for instance, how many shades of green they display, and how their arms are lifted upward toward the sunlight. Notice the patterns created by the shade of the trees and be thankful that they provide refuge from the hot sun, not only for you, but also for countless numbers of other creatures great and small.

Notice how much easier it is to breathe deeply of the fresh air around trees. That's because they are exhaling massive quantities of oxygen, which we are inhaling. They inhale the carbon dioxide that we exhale. It's a marvelous balance that God has established. Trees are the greatest anti-pollution devices that exist. One acre of trees provides five or six tons of pure oxygen in a year.

What would this valley be without trees? A desert, that's what. Thousands of acres of trees provide much more than the obvious harvest of fruit that sustains this valley commercially. In addition to pumping tons of fresh oxygen into our atmosphere, trees are climate moderators. Winter temperatures will range as much as nine degrees warmer in areas with lots of trees than in cleared areas. In summer the effect is reversed; temperatures will be five degrees cooler where there are lots of trees.

Of all the trees in the world, the palm tree is said to be the most useful. There are eight hundred different uses for products of the palm tree. The breadfruit tree of Australia has the unique capacity to produce fruit on its branches when it is young, on its trunk when it is middle-aged, and on its roots when it is old.

A controversy rages about trees these days, mostly because trees are a great source of lumber for constructing homes and businesses. Wood is still a preferred building material in a much of the world. My appreciation of trees does not cause me to line up with the "earth-first" crowd, who almost see them as objects of worship.

I'm not suggesting that we make shrines of trees, but that we appreciate them for what they are: amazing gifts to us from the hand of Creator God. With thanksgiving, I worship the Lord of the trees.

Let the field exult, and all that is in it. Then all the trees of the forest will sing for joy. (Psalm 96:12)

Do you not know that all of us who have been baptized into Christ have been baptized into His death? Therefore, we have been buried with Him through baptism into death, in order that as Christ was raised from the dead through the glory of the Father, so we too might walk in newness of life. (Romans 6:3, 4)

Ivan the Great was Tsar of all Russia during the 15th century. As a fighting man he was courageous; as a general he was brilliant. However, Ivan was so busy waging his campaigns that he could not have a family. They reminded him that there was no heir to his throne "You must take a wife who can bear you a son," they insisted. The busy soldier told them that he did not have the time, but if they would find a suitable bride he would marry her.

And find her they did. They reported to Ivan about a beautiful dark-eyed daughter of the King of Greece. She was young, brilliant, and charming. He agreed to marry her sight unseen.

The King of Greece was delighted. It would align Greece with the emerging giant to the north. But there was a condition, "He cannot marry my daughter unless he joins the Greek Orthodox Church." Ivan's response, "No problem!"

So a priest was sent to Moscow to instruct Ivan in Orthodox doctrine. Arrangements were concluded and Ivan made his way to Athens accompanied by five hundred troops of his personal palace guard.

He was to be baptized into the Orthodox Church by immersion. His soldiers, ever loyal, asked to be baptized also. Five hundred priests were assigned to give the soldiers a one-on-one crash course in the catechism and the soldiers, all five hundred of them, were to be immersed in one mass baptism

What a sight that must have been, five hundred priests and five hundred soldiers, walking into the beautiful blue Mediterranean. Suddenly, there was a problem. The Church prohibited professional soldiers from being members; they would have to give up their commitment to bloodshed. They could not be killers and church members too.

After a hasty round of diplomacy, the problem was solved. As the words were spoken and the priests began to baptize them, each soldier reached to his side and withdrew his sword. Lifting it high over his head, every soldier was totally immersed – except for his fighting arm and his sword.

This is a true historical account. But perhaps we don't understand the total nature of baptism even today. There are many un-baptized arms, wills, talents and other parts of us that seem to survive the grave.

We don't know newness of life, until we know death to sin – totally.

Children Matter! *7/26 – July 26*

I was deeply grieved as I read of the Iraq terrorists killing children with their bombs, and even using children as suicide bombers. In the Iran-Iraq war several years ago children were sacrificed in horrible ways.

The Iraqis had laid a huge mine field to deter the advancing Iranian army. Thousands of children were recruited in the cities of Iran and bussed to the front. They were sent off, on foot, across the minefield. They were told that Paradise was just on the other side. Over five thousand children died, clearing the way for tanks to cross safely.

Such is the value of children in the twisted mind of the terrorist nations. The vast majority of Muslims, who value their families and their children very highly, however, do not share this view.

Closer to home, a U.S. legislator said, "In Washington we mouth concern for children, but in reality they don't matter because they can't vote." Could this be true? Children can't vote but their parents can and we must let their voice be heard in the halls of our government.

Children matter in the church. There's a long and strong commitment to reaching and teaching them to know Jesus and walk in His ways.

Children matter to God. Psalm 127 reveals His heart toward them. They are precious in His eyes.

Unless the LORD builds the house, they labor in vain who build it;
Unless the LORD guards the city, the watchman keeps awake in vain.
It is vain for you to rise up early, to retire late, to eat the bread of painful labors;
for He gives to His beloved even in his sleep.
Behold, children are a gift of the LORD; the fruit of the womb is a reward.
Like arrows in the hand of a warrior, so are the children of one's youth.
How blessed is the man whose quiver is full of them;
They shall not be ashamed, when they speak with their enemies in the gate.

July 27 – 7/27 **Failure**

Master, we have toiled all night and have taken nothing. (Luke 5:5) This was Peter's response when Jesus asked him to go for one more try to catch fish.

I can relate to Peter's statement. I've known failure after toiling to the point of exhaustion with nothing to show for the effort. Jesus blessed this particular occasion with an abundant catch, but this was not the first time, nor the last, that Peter would come up empty in the fishing business. The miracle Jesus performed was noteworthy because it was exceptional.

Failure, to one degree or another, is the rule. No one bats a thousand. There was the time that the Russians invented the "dog mine." The plan was to train dogs to associate food with the undersides of tanks, in the hope that they would run hungrily under advancing German tanks with bombs strapped to their backs. Unfortunately, the dogs associated food solely with Russian tanks. The "dog mines" forced an entire Soviet division to retreat.

One might determine from this account that poor innocent animals are the only ones to suffer for human failure. Not so, and I have the scars to prove it. But I've learned that one can fail without being a failure. In fact, often I must fail before I succeed.

Buckminster Fuller said, "All of my advances were made by mistakes. You uncover what is when you get rid of what isn't." Thomas Edison failed over 900 times in his attempt to make a light bulb. When asked if he was discouraged by these failures, he said, "Certainly not! I now know 900 ways not to make a light bulb."

I saw a bumper sticker that must have been written by someone who knew failure. It said, "I'm not going to smile until the world says it's sorry."

How very sad, if true. For sometimes the only thing of value to survive a failed attempt – is a smile.

An In-Board Presence *7/28 – July 28*

My experience with boats is limited to an occasional ride in a paddleboat, or a rare fishing trip on the ocean, so I may reveal my ignorance when I attempt to draw parallels on the subject.

This is about the presence and power of the Holy Spirit, and I got to thinking about boats. To be specific, the difference between "in-boards" and "out-boards" and how they relate to what I'm learning about the Holy Spirit.

From what I can gather, an out-board engine is one that can be attached to the back of a boat. It can, of course, also be detached. It's usually limited in power by its size. The out-board engine seems to me to be an afterthought for a boat with a good sturdy set of oars. They also seem noisier to me than engines contained inside the boat.

An in-board engine, on the other hand, is not detachable but is an integral part of the boat. The boat was built around it. Every aspect of the boat was designed with the in-board engine in mind. An in-board is generally quieter, and the only limit to its power is the purpose and capacity of the boat. Imagine the Queen Mary with an out-board engine, for instance.

Many see the Holy Spirit as an out-board power source, that can be put on or taken off at will; an afterthought, and it's not surprising that there is little spiritual power in their lives. They remain small people and sometimes they are noisy, and if the Spirit isn't moving there's always a good sturdy set of oars, which the arm of flesh is only too eager to use to get the job done. Imagine the Queen Mary with oars.

Jesus said, in John 14:16, 17, *I will pray the Father, and He will give you another Helper, that He may abide with you forever - the Spirit of truth, whom the world cannot receive, He dwells with you, and will be in you.*

Jesus is describing a dramatic change that was to take place in God's dealings with His people. The Holy Spirit, to that point as far as I can tell, had come upon people and been with people – "out-board." But now Jesus promises that He will come into His people – "in-board." He will be to me like the in-board power source in a boat, an integral part of me, not detachable, not an afterthought, but contained within me. And His power will be limited only by the purpose and capacity of my life.

When the Holy Spirit comes in and I am baptized with His power, He is an in-board Presence for which my "body-boat" was designed. Before the foundations of the world, the blueprint for me included Him. Designed, as I am to contain His presence in-board, if I'm not allowing Him to function freely, I'm dead in the water.

Holy Spirit come in-board – and power me! Amen!

July 29 – 7/29 *The Forbidden Word*

I once saw a spot on Christian television that approached the subject of stewardship with a humorous twist. With appropriate music, its title was, "Hello Dollar!"

The narrator posed this opening question: "Have you heard about the minister who used the (echo effect) FORBIDDEN WORD?" There was a pause and the question was repeated more emphatically, "Have you heard about the minister who used the (echo effect) FORBIDDEN WORD?"

The camera zoomed in for a close-up of a minister standing behind a pulpit. Very slowly, and with great articulation, he said, (echo effect) "MONEY." With that, a trap door opened, and he disappeared from sight.

Thankfully, no one has disappeared around here lately. The subject of money is always approached with understanding and balance. But the Scriptures give a surprising amount of space to it.

Isaiah 55:1-3: *Come, all you who are thirsty, come to the waters; and you who have no money, come, buy and eat! Come buy wine and milk without money and without cost. Why do you spend money on that which is not bread and your labor for that which does not satisfy?*

Listen, listen to Me, and your soul will delight in the richest of fare. Give ear and come to Me, and I will make an everlasting covenant with you, My unfailing kindnesses promised to David.

From this and other passages, it's clear that relationship with God does not have a monetary base. One can enjoy the goodness of His Presence without money and without cost. It's all based on grace, pure and simple grace. But the questions haunt me, "Why do you spend money on that which is not bread and labor for that which does not satisfy?" Good question!

The Bible's approach to money is that the handling of it is a test of character. Whether a man is rich or poor, observe his reaction to his possessions and you have a revealing index of his heart. As someone said, "A checkbook is a theological document; it indicates who or what you worship."

One pastor used his balding head as a point of reference. He says that, as he's lost more and more hair, he's been reminded of his financial responsibilities as a Christian. In both situations, it's not so much a matter of how much you have, as one of proper distribution. Good point!

Here is good balance: I am not everyone, but I am someone. I cannot do everything, but I can do something. What I can do, I ought to do. What I ought to do, I will do – by the grace of God! Amen!

Self-Love *7/30 – July 30*

II Timothy 3:2 describes the last days. At the top of the list is this phrase: *Men will be lovers of themselves.* It's easy to point a self-righteous finger at those who support abortion, for instance, and reason that they surely fulfill the word of the Lord by being lovers of themselves, to the degree that they are willing to terminate precious life.

The Holy Spirit would not allow such finger pointing, however. He reminded me of the many things that He has conceived in me that I've aborted because of self-love. One by one He made me look at the things that held great promise, but never came to birth because I preferred the comfort of the status quo over the pain of bringing to birth something of His life in me.

We are creatures of comfort and given a choice, will not joyfully choose the path of pain. This human trait we share with those who are often the target of our criticism. It's a matter of knowing when to say "no" to ourselves. It's a matter of choice for me to "glorify God in my body", when it's not comfortable and may even be painful.

I Corinthians 6:12-20 says, *All things are lawful for me, but not all things are profitable. All things are lawful for me, but I will not be mastered by anything. Food is for the stomach, and the stomach is for food...*

Do you not know that your bodies are members of Christ? Shall I then take away the members of Christ and make them members of a harlot? May it never be... Flee immorality. Every other sin that a man commits is outside the body, but the immoral man sins against his own body.

Or do you not know that your body is a temple of the Holy Spirit who is in you, whom you have from God, and that you are not your own? For you have been bought with a price: therefore glorify God in your body.

It's difficult to say "no" to someone you love, especially if that someone is you. Most of us love ourselves so much we want to give us all the things we ever wanted. This is the fundamental sin. But saying "no" to someone you love is often the most loving thing you can do – even if it's you.

If we really care about ourselves, we will throw ourselves at the feet of the One who loves us so much He died for us.

I can never love me as much as He does.

A parable: There was a woman once who wanted peace in the world and peace in her own heart, but she was very frustrated. The world seemed to be falling apart and her personal life wasn't that great either.

One day she decided to go shopping at the mall and walked into one of the stores. She was surprised to see Jesus behind the counter. She knew it was Jesus because he looked just like the pictures she'd seen in museums and in devotional books.

Finally she got up the nerve to ask, "Excuse me, but are you Jesus?" "I am." "Do you work here?" "In a way; I own the store." "Oh, what do you sell here?" "Just about everything," Jesus replied. "Feel free to walk up and down the aisles, make a list of what you want, and then come back and I'll see what I can do for you."

Well, she did just that. She walked up and down the aisles, writing furiously. There was peace on earth, no more war, no hunger or poverty. There was peace in families, harmony, no dissension, no more drugs.

By the time she got back to the counter, she had a long list. Jesus looked over the list, then smiled and said, "No problem." And then he bent down behind the counter and picked out some things and laid out the packets on the counter.

"What are these?" the woman asked. "Seed packets, this is a catalog store." Jesus answered. "You mean I don't get the finished product?" "No, this is a place of seeds, You come and see what it looks like, and I give you the seeds. You go home and plant the seeds. You water them and nurture them and help them to grow, and someday you, or someone else, reaps the benefits."

"Oh," she said. "And she left the store without buying anything."

This is just a made-up story from an unknown source, but there's truth here. We're all accustomed to shopping – praying – for the finished product. It may not have occurred to us that the finished product – the answer to our prayers – may come in seed form and need some cooperation from us.

If you were to browse the store in the parable, what would your list look like? What do you care about? What do you care about enough to plant and water and cultivate the seeds God gives you to make it happen?

The sad conclusion of the parable: "And she left the store without buying anything." She didn't care enough to take the seeds and plant them. Do you?

Whether the Weather ***8/1 – August 1***

It's been a hot summer. Growing up in the Midwest, Illinois to be specific, I grew to appreciate the wonder of weather. Lightning and thunderstorms often punctuated the sweltering heat and humidity of an August night. Then, in a few short months you'd find yourself raking leaves or shoveling snow. I miss that. – Yeah, right!

Did you know that lightning and thunder are the equivalent of the spark and the zap you get when you walk across a carpet and touch something metal or another person. The static electricity that builds up in your body is like what builds up in the atmosphere, and it's released as a spark of lightning, and the zap you hear is the thunder. In a thunderstorm the spark and the zap are amplified millions of times, but it's the same principle.

Weather is officially defined as the state of the atmosphere at a given time and place with respect to temperature, pressure, humidity, etc. The climate of an area is defined as the average weather conditions over a period of years.

Understanding this, I believe that our lives have a spiritual climate and certain spiritual weather patterns that bring in storms once in a while. Storms are also a normal part of the spiritual climate of life. They should not be seen as unexpected intrusions.

Some lives seem to have more of one kind of weather than others do. Some live very stormy lives; others have lots of sunshine, so to speak. Occasionally, a storm blows into our life that is severe and a bit unusual.

This doesn't trouble me anymore than I'm concerned about Seattle having more rain than San Diego, or Fairbanks being colder than Phoenix. It's just the climate of life in those places. You can move from Fairbanks to Phoenix if you want to go through the trouble of change, or you can get used to the cold of Fairbanks and learn to like it.

It's that way for our spiritual life as well. Much of what we experience is nothing more than the way it is where we are; the climate of our life. There's not a lot you can do to change the weather, but you can move to a new place in the Lord, a place that may not have the same storm patterns but will have some new challenges for you.

Many years ago I learned a little poem about a man who never missed church. A Sunday School teacher taught it to us hoping we'd get the message and earn our gold stars for attendance. It goes like this:

"Whether the weather be good, or whether the weather be hot;
Whether the weather be cold, or whether the weather be not.
Whatever the weather, he weathered the weather,
Whether he liked it or not!"

That's not a bad way to look at whatever storm front may be blowing into your life right now.

A few years ago I had occasion to stop by the home of my grandchildren unannounced. My heart melted every time they came running to greet me wherever and whenever we got together. This time was no exception.

All five of them embraced me with their usual abandon. When we finished our loving little ritual, Chelsea, who was five at the time, said something I have not been able to get out of my heart since. She looked up at me with a face full of love and said, "What are you doing here, Grandpa?"

Those were the words, but it was how she said it that impressed me. I'll use upper case to give the emphasis she did. Tell your brain to think louder on the capitalized word and you'll get the idea. This is what she said: "What are you DOING here, Grandpa?"

She didn't say, "What are YOU doing here?" as if I had no right to be there. No, our relationship had already been warmly celebrated – she was not questioning the legitimacy of my presence.

She didn't say, "What are you doing HERE?" as if to say that I should be someplace else. I've heard that before when I've forgotten an appointment or a meeting. It's embarrassing to be in the wrong place at the right time. There was no suggestion in her voice that I was supposed to be someplace else.

Her question, "What are you DOING her, Grandpa?" came from an innocent curiosity about what I was going to DO now that I had arrived. I remember her question but, in fact, I've forgotten why I was there.

The question is appropriate for all of us to think about, considering the opportunities available to serve the people of our community. The harvest is plentiful. What are you DOING here?"

No one is asking, "What are YOU doing here?" We're family, we have a relationship – you belong! Your right to be here, in the life of the family of God, is not in question.

Nor is the question, "What are you doing HERE?" This is the place, now is the time. None of us should be somewhere else. This is a good place, and this is a good time.

Now that we have the emphasis in the right place, it boils down to the simple, honest, timely question – "What are you DOING here?" There is so much to do that there is something for everyone.

Jesus said, *The harvest is plentiful, but the laborers are few;* (Luke 10:2)

Since the laborers are few and harvest is plentiful – "What ARE you doing here?" Huh?

Let us not lose heart in doing good, for in due time we shall reap if we do not grow weary. (Galatians 6:9)

You Talk Too Much! *8/3 – August 3*

"You talk too much!" Those are the words I heard God speak in my heart one day in 1978. I found the note I made about it in my old Bible the other day.

I realized it was true. Talking was my business, and it still is. Preachers talk a lot. But the point the Lord wanted to address was that I was talking about the wrong things. It wasn't a matter of the quantity but the quality of my words.

I was letting life dribble out of me through my mouth. I was doing things like confessing my weakness, claiming my sickness, expressing my fears and complaining about my lot in life.

Shortly after that word from the Lord I began to read about the power of the tongue in Scripture. It's awesome. It's a good news/bad news thing. With our words we can bless or we can curse; we can heal or we can hurt; we can live or we can die. *Death and life are in the power of the tongue...* (Proverbs 18:21)

This isn't about "name it/claim it." This is about learning to speak like a child of God; growing in the grace of God and letting it come out my mouth. It's about not giving the devil an edge, or handle with which he can control me.

Since that day there's been a change in what I confess with my mouth. I'm not real good at it yet, but I'm making progress. "The Lord is good." That's my answer and I'm sticking to it.

No one can tame the tongue; it is a restless evil and full of deadly poison. With it we bless our Lord and Father; and with it we curse men, who have been made in the likeness of God; from the same mouth come both blessing and cursing. My brethren, these things ought not to be this way. (James 3:8-10)

My tongue shall declare Thy righteousness and Thy praise all day long. (Psalm 35:28)

I said, "I will guard my ways, that I may not sin with my tongue; I will guard my mouth as with a muzzle..." (Psalm 39:1)

He who guards his mouth and his tongue, guards his soul from troubles. (Proverbs 21:23)

Let the words of my mouth and the meditation of my heart be acceptable in Thy sight, O LORD, my rock and my Redeemer. (Psalm 19:14)

August 4 – 8/4 *A Sense of Humor*

The Great Physician, Jesus Christ, declared that the result of following Him is, *...that My joy may be in you, and that your joy may be full.* (John 15:11)

He knew the truth of the Proverb; *A merry heart does good like a medicine.* While Jesus was speaking of a quality of joy deeper than happiness, part of that joy may well be a spirit of mirth – happiness.

Mark Twain hinted at what science is just now documenting. In Tom Sawyer, he tells about the old man who "laughed loud and joyously shook up the details of his anatomy from head to foot," and ended by saying that such a laugh was "money in a man's pocket, because it cut down the doctor's bills like everything."

Would you believe there's an organization called Nurses for Laughter – NFL? They've discovered that humorous nurses lend a sense of well being to patients, speed up their adjustment to the hospital setting, and drain off worry.

The degree of laughter's healing qualities must depend upon what you laugh at. With all this talk about laughter being therapeutic I remind you that there is such a thing as "sick" humor. That can't be good for you. The words "sick" and "humor" just don't go together very well and I can't imagine that God intended for them to be said in the same breath.

A sense of humor is like a sense of smell – it is discerning. It senses what is and what isn't humorous. A person who laughs at everything has no more a sense of humor than one who laughs at nothing.

I always feel better after a good laugh. My biggest laughs, however, have not been at Laurel and Hardy, they've been at Larry – me. A slip of the tongue, the unveiling of a pet peeve, or just plain stupidity has sent me and my family into uncontrollable guffaws. Space does not allow me to reveal the details of such embarrassment (ha, ha) but it is important to note that of all the things there are to laugh about the most healing occurs when you laugh at yourself.

If we could see ourselves as God sees us I think we'd be pleased, and we'd laugh at ourselves a lot more.

"Joy to the world, the Lord has come" – and He's smiling!

To your good health – Ha, Ha, Ha, Ha, Ha, Ha, Ha!

Bind Us Together *8/5 – August 5*

In a rescue that transfixed the nation, all nine miners were pulled safely from the Quecreek Mine in rural western Pennsylvania in 2002, after water from an abandoned mine flooded the shaft where they were working.

All the men praised the efforts of rescue workers, who quickly pumped air into the pocket where they were trapped. The miners said they relied on each other to stay alive. They even bound themselves together in the cold water that flooded their shaft so that none of them would drift away in the darkness.

My wife and I were praying for their safe release and we were elated when we heard the news late Saturday night. The example of these nine men under the sentence of death in that mine 240 feet below the surface of Pennsylvania was something to be celebrated – and emulated.

They made a conscious choice that they would be bound together so that all of them would survive, or none of them would. They shared food and light and even the warmth of their bodies as they huddled together, the coldest one always moving to the center of the group.

There was great joy when the news came that all of them were safe. Families were reunited, and there were hugs and kisses all around. And we all welcomed good news, for a change.

The body of Christ on planet earth is much like those nine men in the mine. We live in a dark world that has the sentence of death upon it. We're aliens whose home is "above," yet we're working and socializing in places that are flooded with evil and permeated with pressure to conform and give up our lives to the darkness.

In this environment we must make a conscious choice to share our light and our nourishment. But more than that, we must be willing to be bound together in love so that none of us are swept away by the flood of evil that is upon us.

This is not comfortable. It means limiting activities to conform to what's best for those to whom I'm bound. We don't like that very much. It cramps our style and costs us time and money and our freedom. It even requires that we give some of our "warmth" to others who are growing cold in the darkness.

What if we did what the nine miners did when we sense that one of us is growing cold? What if we grabbed him or her and moved them to the center of our attention instead of letting them drift away – even from our memory?

We don't realize that we're all in jeopardy, like those miners. This world isn't home. We only work here. We used to sing, "Bind us together, Lord, bind us together with cords that cannot be broken." We've lost that kind of commitment to each other.

The challenge now is to bind together in love, and take as many people with us as we can when Jesus, the Great Rescuer, comes to take us home.

Yesterday the focus of this space was on the miners who bound themselves together to assure that none of them would drift away in the flooded mine shaft. They were an example of the Body of Christ bound together in love.

I suggest that we are not only bound together, but we are built together with a high and holy purpose – to be a temple for the dwelling place of God.

Ephesians 2:21, 22 says this: *In Whom (Christ) the whole building, being joined together, grows into a holy temple in the Lord, in Whom you also are being built together for a habitation of God in the Spirit.*

Logging trucks are a familiar sight on the North Coast. They travel the roads loaded with timber headed for the sawmills. The logs are bound together – but they don't make anything. A long process waits to make them into a house.

The Scripture declares that we're the raw material that God is using to build a temple in which He dwells. We're also the tools He uses in the process.

Master Carpenter's tools held a conference. Brother Hammer presided, since he most resembled a gavel. Several suggested he leave the meeting because he was too noisy. Brother Hammer replied, "If I have to leave, Brother Nail must go also. I have to drive him to get him to accomplish anything."

Brother Nail spoke up. "If you wish, I will leave, but Brother Plane must leave too. His work is all on the surface. There's no depth to anything he does." To this Brother Plane said, "Brother Rule will also have to withdraw, for he's always measuring things as though he were the only one who is right."

Brother Rule complained, "Brother Sandpaper, you ought to leave too because you're so rough; you always rub people the wrong way." Brother Sandpaper responded, "If I have to go then Brother Drill must leave too. He's so boring."

Amid this confusion, in came the Carpenter of Nazareth to start His day's work. Putting on His apron, He went to work to make a house for Himself and His family. He used the hammer, nail, plane, rule, sandpaper, drill and all the other tools at His command. After the day's work was finished, Brother Saw arose and remarked, "I see that all of us are workers together with the Lord."

And so they rested a while from their labors, content that all of them were tools in the hands of the Master Builder.

Do you get the picture? We're not only the material God is using to make His temple, but we're also the tools in His hands. That's awesome! God uses me to shape you, and you to shape me, so that we finally fit together. That sounds painful. And that it is.

Build us together, Lord. Build Us Together…!

Heavenly Language — *8/7 – August 7*

Psalm 19:1 says, *The heavens declare the glory of God and the firmament shows His handiwork.* The next verse in another version says, *Each day announces it to the following day and each night repeats it to the next.*

What an interesting insight into the secret communication in God's creation speaking of His glory from day to day, night to night, for millions of years.

One of the challenges to my mind and spirit is astronomy. August is an excellent time to lift your eyes skyward at night and behold His handiwork and drink in His glory.

Every year at this time one can see large numbers of meteors or "shooting stars," as the are called, since the earth passes through a lot of space debris left over from a passing comet at this point in its annual journey around the sun.

Venus is bright and beautiful for some time after sundown in the western sky and Mars, the red planet, will soon emerge from behind the sun. Jupiter is visible before sunrise and with a pair of binoculars you can see at least three of its sixteen moons.

Away from city lights one can see a cloudy mass that seems like a floating mist in the sky – it is the Milky Way galaxy, (our own) made up of literally billions of stars, and there are billions of galaxies like it in the universe.

All of these were created with the stated purpose of declaring the glory of God! Such things are too wonder-full for me!

The last verse of Psalm 19 says, *Let the words of my mouth and the meditations of my heart be acceptable in Your sight, O LORD, my strength and my redeemer.*

While the heavens declare God's glory, apparently they do not speak of His mercy and His grace. That's where we enter the picture, because that's what we can do best. I'm no match for the universe when it comes to displaying the glory of God. But no galaxy ever experienced the grace that I've known, or the mercy I've been shown.

In an interesting twist on this theme, Moses, in no uncertain terms, shouts back to the heavens in Deuteronomy 32:1-4, *Listen, O heavens, and I will speak; hear, O earth, the words of my mouth... I will proclaim the name of the LORD. Oh, praise the greatness of our God! He is the Rock, His works are perfect, and all His ways are just. A faithful God who does no wrong, upright and just is He.*

Just as the universe speaks loudly of God's glory, my mouth will shout about His marvelous grace, and His everlasting mercy – things most acceptable in His sight.

"By the time we reach kindergarten age, we have already been exposed to all the wisdom we really need in order to live good and meaningful lives." So says Robert Fulghum in his excellent book, "All I Really Need To Know I Learned in Kindergarten." In it he lists some things that are so simple that a young child understands them, but they make sense in adult life, too.

What a difference it would make if we practiced the wisdom learned in the sand pile. Sharing everything, playing fair, saying you're sorry when you hurt somebody, not striking back, not taking things that aren't yours, holding hands and sticking together are the things that Jesus taught us in the Gospels.

But life gets so complicated, doesn't it? I wonder why that is. Is it that life gets complicated or that we complicate life? Paul was concerned about this in II Corinthians 11:3, *I fear, lest somehow, as the serpent deceived Eve by his craftiness, so your minds may be corrupted from the simplicity that is in Christ.* Apparently the tactic of Satan was to complicate God's word and will for Adam and Eve in the Garden of Eden.

The word "simplicity" is from two Latin words, "sine plica" and means, "without a fold" – unclosed. The opposite of simplicity is sophistication, which means, "removed from original simplicity." The 2005 automobile is sophisticated when compared to Henry Ford's original idea. My computer is sophisticated when compared to the early room-sized devices that began the computer revolution. "That's progress!" we're fond of saying.

Progress, however, isn't measured in the kingdom of God in terms of bigger, or faster, or better, or easier. It is measured by simplicity. The more mature we become in Jesus, the simpler our lives are. The Shaker Hymn says, "Tis a gift to be simple, tis a gift to be free." The Shakers lived by the rule of simplicity.

It's possible to have simple faith and hope and love in a very sophisticated world. As one would expect, the key is to reduce everything to its lowest common denominator – relationship with my Lord Jesus Christ. That's as simple as it gets; and that's as sophisticated as it gets, too.

In the words of a brother in Christ who lived in 1466 AD, "Sever me from myself that I may be grafted into Thee; may I perish to myself that I may be safe in Thee; may I die to myself that I may live in Thee; may I wither to myself that I may bloom in Thee; may I be emptied of myself that I may abound in Thee; may I be nothing to myself that I may be all to Thee."

Amen!

They Can't Do That! *8/9 – August 9*

Is there room in the heart of a follower of Jesus Christ for outrage? I'm not an angry man but I find myself deeply troubled by the kidnapping of Americans and the beheading of hostages. Media types delight in zooming their cameras in close upon the atrocities committed by terrorists while nothing seems to be happening to stop the flood of violence. It's outrageous!

Most troubling, to me, is the feeling of outrage that lies just beneath the surface of my own heart when innocent people are victimized or when groundless accusations are given credence. I feel anger toward the terrorists who manipulate world opinion and hold billions of people helplessly hostage by the mere threat of violence. They can't do this to us! But they can, and they are doing this to us, even in the name of God.

What's a Christian to do in the face of outrageousness? What's a nation to do? Wouldn't it be better if we got angry enough to do something? – Anything! Does outrage solve anything? Or is outrage the goal of the terrorist? Do I play into his hands by my indignation? I think it's true; the terrorist seeks to evoke a reaction from the whole world. It's a matter of who's in charge here; who's in control of me.

Outrage is itself destructive to one who embraces it, whether the injustice is in Iraq or seated across the dinner table at home. It ticks away like a bomb in the body of its host. Anger and frustration take their toll in the body, soul, and spirit of the outraged.

In the face of outrageous acts, the word of the Lord speaks to my troubled heart: *Let everyone be quick to hear, slow to speak, and slow to anger; for the wrath of man does not achieve the righteousness of God!* (James 1:19, 20)

If possible, so far as it depends on you, be at peace with all men. Never take your own revenge, beloved, but leave room for the wrath of God, for it is written, 'Vengeance is Mine, I will repay,' says the Lord. (Romans 12:18, 19)

The father of outrage is fear – terror. That's why they call them terrorists; they create terror, and terror generates outrage. So, if I can control my fear, I can control my rage.

Jesus said of these last days, *When you hear of wars and disturbances, do not be terrified... you will be hated by all on account of My name, yet not a hair of your head will perish.* (Luke 21:9, 17-19)

To accomplish the righteous purpose of God, the bottom line is that outrage and vengeance do not work – ever.

The end never justifies the meanness!

The devil's masterstroke in the destruction of the lives and homes of Christians is to tell you that you're an exception to the law of God. It may apply to everyone else but not to you. You can beat the system. No one ever has, but you will be the first.

"Whatever a man sows, that shall he also reap" – "Be sure your sin will find you out" – "The soul that sins, will die" – these are for all the others less skillful than you. You can have it all. You just have to be careful, that's all. The devil says, "You're the exception to the law of God."

The root of this deception is, of course, pride. The very thought that I could be the one person to escape the cause and effect consequences of my actions is ludicrous. The deception is fed by the fact that I want to believe that it's true.

When we finally get to the place where our sin finds us out and we're left broken and wounded, then we remember – "If we confess our sins He is faithful and just to forgive us and cleanse us from all unrighteousness" and "Where sin does abound, grace does much more abound."

We're about ready to get back on track; having learned that we are not an exception to the law of God, when the devil pulls another trick from his bag. He now says, "You've sinned and you knew better. Forgiveness is available to other people but not to you. You've gone too far. You'll be the one person who comes to the Father and asks for mercy who will be refused. You're an exception to the grace of God."

The point is simply this: Not one of us is an exception to the law of God and the consequences of transgression. We do not break God's law – we break ourselves against it. But neither is there one of us who is an exception to the grace of God. His grace is not based upon what I have or haven't done, but upon what Jesus did for me on the cross.

He has utterly wiped out the damning evidence of broken laws, which always hung over our heads and has completely annulled it by nailing it over His own head on the cross. And then, having drawn the sting of all the powers ranged against us, he exposed them, shattered, empty and defeated, in His final glorious triumphant act! (Colossians 2:14,15 JBP)

Check The Foundation *8/11 – August 11*

A multi-story building had been occupied for several years when a disturbing crack appeared in a wall on the 42nd floor. The manager of the company that owned the building immediately sent for an architect to come and investigate. When the architect arrived, the manager took the elevator to the 42nd floor to meet him at the appointed time. But the architect was nowhere to be found.

Eventually the architect was found – in the 6th basement. The manager said to him, "What are you doing down here? We have a serious crack on the 42nd floor that needs immediate attention." The architect replied, "Sir, you may have a crack on the 42nd floor, but the problem is not on the 42nd floor. Your problem is here in the basement."

As it turned out, a security guard employed in the building had wanted to build a garage onto his house, but he was short of materials and money. So every evening before leaving work, he took the elevator to the 6th basement and chiseled a brick out of the wall, placed it in his lunch box and took it home. After five or six years of this a crack appeared in the 42nd floor.

Cracks in the structure are often caused by weakness in the foundation of our lives. Where are we based? What is our foundation? What are we anchored to? The answers to these questions will reveal what our lives will be like.

A spider climbed a telephone pole to spin a web. She fastened her web to the pole and, swinging her body in a wide arc, she attached her web to another pole nearby to spin a magnificent trap for unsuspecting insects.

Unfortunately, her choice of area was poor, because a railroad track ran between the poles. She had no sooner made contact with the second pole, when a train came by, taking her first strand with it. Undaunted, the persistent spider made several hasty trips from pole to pole. Swish! Another train roared through destroying her weaving.

Instinctively she persevered. Back and forth she went, as quickly as she could, calling on all the energy within herself to make the web that would trap that extremely noisy and powerful bug that kept destroying her work. She had time on her side now. The web was almost finished. She was confident of victory. Then the next train arrived.

So it is with those who attempt to oppose God's sovereignty. Man, like the spider, makes his plans and attaches his hopes to the values of the world in an attempt to circumvent righteousness. But the train will come – it always does.

God awesome! *Now to Him who is able to keep you from stumbling (or crumbling)... to the only God our Savior, through Jesus Christ our Lord, be glory, majesty, dominion and authority, before all time and now and forever. Amen!* (Jude 24)

August 12 – 8/12 *I Hate It When That Happens!*

The word "hate" does not flow easily from my lips. I was taught that I shouldn't say it lightly so I didn't. It's related to the Scripture that says if you hate your brother you are guilty of murder (I John 3:15). So, as a child I never said it, and as an adult it's not a part of my vocabulary.

Some things happened on a recent vacation trip that brought this word into focus for me. It was not directed toward people but at things that happen while you're minding your own business. For instance, it was Thursday and I had taken my two oldest grandchildren, Tessa and Michael, and my daughter April, to Yosemite for the day. We had a grand time climbing rocks and taking pictures and drinking in the beauty of that wonderful place.

We started home about 3 pm and drove to the 6,000 foot level and started down hill toward home. Just as we began the descent, the brakes on the car went completely out!

The Lord graciously provided a turnout, which I used by gearing down and applying the hand brake. But there were no brakes at all. I hate it when that happens! It was scary. A friendly park ranger stopped and called a tow truck, which towed us into Oakhurst where the car was repaired the next day.

While we were waiting for the tow truck I was overwhelmed with gratitude that the turnout "happened" to be right there and I was able to stop safely with my precious cargo intact. There was also a deep appreciation for brakes and the ability to stop. This is a go-go world, and not much thought is given to stop-stop. But when you can't stop you're in great danger. Life must have an accelerator for when God says go, but there must also be a brake for stopping for when God says "Whoa"!

When I sail right past the stop signs and the turn-offs of life, I'm faced with another thing I dislike intensely – back-tracking. It's such a waste to go too far because I didn't stop or turn off when I should have, and then cover the same territory to get back to where I should have been in the first place.

Sometimes it takes years to get back to where I should have been. I hate it when that happens. There is grace for us back-trackers but it would be better to apply the brakes in a timely fashion in the first place.

Sometimes the best we can do is to grow through those experiences. It's a compound tragedy to experience a painful episode, and not learn from it.

I hate it when that happens!

The Weakness of God? *8/13 – August 13*

I had a new thought the other day, and I was a little shocked by it. It started while I was reading I Corinthians chapter one. Verse twenty-five says, *The foolishness of God is wiser than men, and the weakness of God is stronger than men.* The thought that shook me was the possibility that God could be weak.

The Apostle Paul, under the inspiration of the Holy Spirit, says that in the view of the Greeks and the Jews, God is first foolish, and then weak. The Greeks valued wisdom and the Jews went for power. The message of the cross, where Jesus Christ subjected Himself to shame and humiliation, was to them utter stupidity and ultimate weakness. No god would ever assume such a role – not Jehovah of the Jews, or any of the myriad gods of the Greeks.

I've read this portion before and took it to mean that what looked like foolishness and weakness to men was really God's strength. This time I wondered if God was really ever weak. We've gotten carried away with thoughts of God's power because that's how He takes care of the world and us in particular. I like a strong God. He does things I can't do; He gives me things I can't get; He defends me when I am helpless. I need a strong God.

But if we look at the way in which God reveals Himself in Jesus Christ we have to acknowledge weakness. He did not come into our world with a great display of superior power; He came as a baby. In fact, one of the temptations, which Jesus had to resist as inconsistent with His mission, was to use His power to prove Who He was. The devil wanted Him to dazzle the world with His superior might by turning stones to bread and calling forth legions of angels. He didn't.

Sometimes He doesn't come into my circumstance with an irresistible display of power. Sometimes He comes in weakness, and He chooses the foolish and weak and unimportant things, things that are nothing at all, to overthrow the strength and strongholds of the world. His is a "willed weakness" to be sure; He controls the power that rules the universe by an act of His own will. No one is His equal in power or wisdom but He made Himself my equal and reduced Himself to my condition so that I could know Him.

I was six-years-old when my uncle went into the army. Our family visited him while he was in training and he gave me a book about Judo. I was fascinated by the idea of hand-to-hand combat. In that kind of combat you learn to use the strength of your opponent to bring him to the ground. You actually yield, at times, and in so doing you cause your opponent to be off balance and fall by the force of his own power.

God's like that. He comes in apparent weakness, and uses the very might of the enemy to destroy him. Sometimes He chooses weakness and foolishness and the things that are nothing at all to accomplish His purpose.

The fact is – God has nothing to give except Himself. And that's enough.

August 14 – 8/14 — *Called To Be Losers*

Everybody loves a winner. We like to be associated with winning causes. The term "loser" has massive negative implications. This presents a problem for serious followers of the One Who said, "He that finds his life shall lose it and he that loses his life for My sake shall find it." We are called to be losers!

Even as I say those words, part of my brain is saying, "that can't be right, can it? Isn't life all about winning?" It depends on what you mean by winning. The fact is, we come from a long line of losers – people who considered it winning to lose everything – even their lives – for the sake of convictions stronger than the fear of losing.

In God's system of values you win if you do your best – and finish. It's a secular set of values that requires the winner to be first. The Captain of our team says, "The first shall be last, and the last shall be first," and "he that would be greatest among you must be your servant." The phrase, "We're Number One!" is not in His vocabulary.

Why is it that no team that comes in second shouts with rabid enthusiasm, "We're Number Two"? They may be better than a thousand other teams and have lost by one point but they plunge into the depths of self-depreciation because they are not Number One, – only number two. So sad! If winning is defined as beating everyone else at any cost, we have the set up for our present moral dilemma.

It's how you play the game – whatever "game" you play – and not whether you win or lose that counts. Unfortunately, winning has become the thing with Christians, too. Some teaching in the Church at large about prosperity, wealth, and health would go over very well in corporate board rooms, but is sadly misplaced in the Kingdom of the Crucified One.

The world was watching "The Dream Team" in the recent Olympics. It was expected that they would crush every opponent and be the winners of the gold medal in men's basketball. They didn't win the gold; they won the bronze, instead. But, from what I could see, they conducted themselves as winners, even in losing.

God has a dream team, too. It's not made up of super stars but of servants with scars who carry around inside them the heart, mind and Spirit of Jesus. They are winners because they do battle with fleshly impulses and overcome them.

They may not be first but they will be there at the finish line. They're invincible – because they will outlast the universe!

A Balm In Gilead *8/15 – August 15*

Jeremiah is known as the weeping prophet, and nowhere is that characteristic more evident than in the 22nd chapter of the book that bears his name. The cause of his grief 2,600 years ago is of concern to us now.

My sorrow is beyond healing. My heart is faint within me. For the brokenness of the daughter of my people I am broken; I mourn, dismay has taken hold of me. Is there no balm in Gilead? Is there no physician there? Why then has not the health of the daughter of my people been restored? (Jeremiah 8:18-22)

Jeremiah's tears were not only for the brokenness of people he loved, but that there didn't seem to be any restoration of their health. His phrase "Is there no balm in Gilead?" describes the frustration he felt that there was no healing for the physical and spiritual condition of those afflicted.

Gilead is an interesting place. It's a region of ancient Palestine, which lies east of the Jordan River in what is now the Hashemite Kingdom of Jordan. It's the birthplace of Elijah and here, at the River Jabbok, Jacob wrestled with the Angel of the Lord.

Mizpah is in Gilead where Jacob and Laban made their famous covenant, "May the Lord watch between me and you when we are absent from each other." The region is lush with fields and forests and was famous for its healing ointments and balms.

Genesis 37:25 reveals that the caravan which picked up Joseph from the pit his brothers had put him into was coming from Gilead "bearing aromatic gum and balm and myrrh, on their way to bring them down to Egypt."

This background explains Jeremiah's frustration. There should have been a balm in Gilead. For centuries Gilead had been know as the source of healing medicines. And now, nothing seemed to be available to make a difference.

Like Gilead, the Body of Christ has been marked by its healing ministry to the spirit, soul, and body of people who believe on the Lord Jesus Christ. But we experience seasons when we grieve, like Jeremiah, for the brokenness of people we love and the legitimate question arises, "Is there no balm in Gilead?"

There's an old spiritual that I heard sung by Mahalia Jackson, from the early days of our history, that I've played often. The first verse of the song echoes the sentiments of Jeremiah – and the rest of us. It goes like this:

"Sometimes I feel discouraged, and think my work's in vain.
But then the Holy Spirit revives my soul again."

Then the chorus:

"There IS a balm in Gilead, to make the wounded whole.
There IS a balm in Gilead, to heal the sin-sick soul."

August 16 – 8/16 *Don't Let There Be Lite*

Have you noticed how words have changed meaning these days? Words like freedom, choice, gay, tolerance, etc. don't mean what they used to. Why, even taxes don't go by that name anymore; they're revenue enhancements.

But equally bothersome is the strange way that words are spelled these days. Love is "luv," night is "nite," and light is "lite." I wish my sixth-grade English teacher could see what's happened to her beloved language. I'd have gotten an "F" in spelling if I'd spelled like that.

It's this word "lite" that's got me stirred up. There's "lite beer," "lite bread," and a host of other products with the "lite" prefix or suffix. I know that it's meant to convey the idea of a few less calories, but the idea of creating a new word merely for advertising purposes bothers me a bit.

I don't have any quarrel with foods that are better for you, or any of the other "lite" things out there. It's when the "lite" philosophy filters into the life of the Kingdom of God that I become concerned. In the last three decades, there are places where the light of the Gospel has changed to a "lite" gospel, which not surprisingly, has produced a "lite" version of disciples of Jesus Christ.

The words of Jesus were not a "lite" edition of the real thing. When He said, *"Whoever of you does not forsake all that he has, cannot be my disciple,"* (Luke 14:33); and, *You shall love the Lord your God with all your heart, and with all your soul, and with all your strength, and with all your mind; and your neighbor as yourself,* (Luke 10:27) it wasn't edited to make it easier.

A "lite" version of the Gospel of Jesus Christ is like what's described in an ad for a "lite" product – "more taste but less filling." The attempt to make the Gospel more palatable to the taste buds of the un-churched is called being "seeker sensitive." It has resulted in attracting thousands to churches that preach a "lite" message, and require a "lite" commitment to Jesus. It may taste sweeter – but it's less filling – less fulfilling.

This is a time to be all we can be, and give all we can give to the task of reaching the world with the light of the gospel. When God said, "Let there be light," the universe was emblazoned with the full blast of His white-hot glory. He still seeks to drive back darkness with the same illuminating power. But a "lite" light will never do.

When it comes to being a disciple of Jesus Christ – don't let there be "lite!"

His Ways, Or His Acts? *8/17 – August 17*

Psalm 103:7 says, *He made known His ways to Moses, His acts to the sons of Israel.* Today let's consider His ways.

What's the difference between God's acts and His ways? There's a lot of difference. The acts of God are simply what He does. His ways are His "whys" – the purposes behind His acts.

Psalm 18:30 declares, *As for God, His way is blameless.*

No one can begin to know Him as He is by observing His acts alone. Nor will the Church know a resurgence of life in the Spirit if we seek His acts, His works, or His blessings alone.

Perhaps the Church has been preoccupied with His acts in recent years. While we all desire to see acts of healing and miracles of provision, the path of eternal benefit lies in seeking to know His ways. David knew this when he said, *Show me thy ways, O LORD; teach me thy paths.* (Psalm 25:4)

His ways can't be studied in a theological laboratory by the merely curious. His ways are "made known," – revealed, and are not subject to research. Romans 11:33 says, *O the depth of the riches both of the wisdom and knowledge of God! How unsearchable are His judgments, and His ways past finding out!*

One of the reasons I've been thinking about this has to do with the current political situation in America. I don't wish to choose up sides in the political arena. The Church must take a longer, deeper look at politics than any political party or the media is capable of. When I'm asked, "What's your position on political issues?" I say, "My position is – on my knees."

Does God really ordain presidents and kings? Romans 13:1 declares He does. *For there is no power but of God: the powers that be are ordained of God.* That's pretty clear. But for what purpose – why?

Establishing leadership in a democracy involves the expressed will of the people. But God doesn't stuff ballot boxes to ordain the one He's chosen. He uses elections. And here's where His "ways" come into the equation.

Ordaining one to office is an act of God. But His way – His why – is greater than the election of any candidate, and greater than the democratic process. He often ordains leadership to bless a nation and lead them to prosperity. But He has also ordained leadership to lead a nation to well-deserved judgment.

God's ways are perfect. His ways – His whys – can be trusted.

Everybody's got a health-care plan – Democrats, Republicans, The Good-Hands people, The American Medical Association, Rush Limbaugh and Larry King. And they all want the same things: universal coverage (or there-about), portability, (you CAN take it with you) and irrevocability (no cancellation).

The provisions and restrictions of the various health-care proposals fill thousands of pages, printed at taxpayer's expense, and the chances of passage of any legislation any time soon seems extremely remote.

In typical cut-to-the-chase wisdom, God offers a plan that meets the needs of universal coverage, portability, and irrevocability in nineteen words: *Beloved, I pray that you may prosper in all things and be in health, just as your soul prospers.* (III John 1:2)

It's that simple. I know we need insurance for lots of things, and I appreciate the coverage I've had over the years. I'm not against medication or doctors or hospitals. These are extensions of God's gracious hand. But the simple formula stated here in III John 1:2 works wonders in the health-care business. God's plan is both preventative and therapeutic.

Everybody wants to succeed in reaching his or her goals, and that's what the word "prosper" means. Everybody wants to be sound in body, and that's what the word "health" means. God ties these two things that everybody wants, to something that very few give any attention to – soul wellness.

If, in the words of a favorite hymn, "It is well with my soul," my prosperity and physical health are enhanced. If I spend time, energy and resources cultivating the health and prosperity of my soul, all other areas of my life will be positively affected.

What is my soul, anyhow? Where is it and how can my soul prosper? Well, as I understand it, my soul is part of the eternal me, along with my spirit. It's made up of my intellect, my emotions, and my will. These elements define my personality. Only God, Whose powerful word penetrates to the dividing point of the soul and the spirit, knows its exact location.

The word of God is living and active and sharper than any two-edged sword, and piercing as far as the division of soul and spirit... (Hebrews 4:12)

God's health-care plan is addressed in the first and last verses of Psalm 91. The first verse: *He that dwells in the secret place of the Most High shall abide under the shadow of the Almighty.* - That's soul prosperity. The last verse: *With long life will I satisfy him and show him My salvation.*

God's health-care plan is universal – for everyone; it's portable – you can take it with you, even to heaven; and it's irrevocable – God won't cancel it.

God's Health-Care-2 — *8/19 – August 19*

Beloved, I pray that you may prosper in all things and be in health, just as your soul prospers. (III John 1:2)

Here's more about God's health-care plan. God's health-care plan calls for an intellectual commitment to walk in His ways, an emotional commitment to love Him with all my heart, and a volitional commitment to make my decisions on the basis of His word. That's soul prosperity.

What might be called a prescription from God for good health as well as soul prosperity is a sense of humor. *A joyful heart is good medicine, but a broken spirit dries up the bones,* says Proverbs 17:22.

The King James Version says "a merry heart." There's a difference between a merry heart and a merry mouth. Your mouth can be laughing, but your heart may be broken. It's not a merry mouth that is good medicine. It's a merry heart – a joyful heart.

A joyful heart is a condition, not an event. It is a way of life, not a response to a joke. It's a way of seeing things – even one's self – that eases pressure, cultivates peace, and prolongs life.

I'm not talking about a frivolous heart, just a joyful heart – a sense of humor. One who frivolously laughs at everything has neither a sense of humor nor a joyful heart. One who takes everything as serious as death itself has no sense of humor either, but there may be a joyful heart inside just waiting to break through the gloom.

A sense of humor is like all the other senses with which we are blessed. A sense of smell not only detects good smells but it is quick to recognize bad smells, too. A sense of humor not only tells me what is funny but what isn't. It discerns between the sacred and the profane.

Once, during a theatrical performance, a fire broke out backstage. One of the actors, dressed as a clown, came out on stage to warn everyone of the danger. The audience, thinking it was part of the performance, laughed at the clown.

The louder he tried to persuade them of the danger, the more the crowd laughed. By the time the crowd realized that the danger was real, it was too late, and in the panic many were injured and killed.

There is a time to weep and a time to laugh, a time to mourn and a time to dance... (Ecclesiastes 3:4)

God's health-care plan – knows when to do what, and for how long.

August 20 – 8/20 *Do The Math*

I consider that our present sufferings are not worth comparing with the glory that will be revealed in us. (Romans 8:18)

Politicians argue the size and effect of the national debt. At the height of one Presidential debate one party said to the other, "Do the math!" A corporate accountant lobbies the board of directors for cost-cutting measures in light of diminishing profits, and says to the assembled millionaires, "Do the math!"

A wife explains why the family budget will not accommodate the purchase of yet another off-road vehicle, and says to her eager spouse, "Do the math!"

I've always liked math. Adding numbers was one of the few things you could count on, so to speak. 2+2=4 was the same on rainy or sunny days. And the amount of food on the dinner table had no effect on the multiplication table.

When Paul wrote to the Roman Christians, it was at a time of great peril for the followers of Jesus. Many were dying for their allegiance to Him. Families of believers were fleeing together to underground catacombs for safety.

Into this context, Paul writes these words: *I consider that our present sufferings are not worth comparing with the glory that will be revealed in us.*

The Greek word for "consider" is "logizomai", to take an inventory, to count, and to reckon. In other words – do the math! In one column is present suffering; in the other column is future glory. And when the adding is done, future glory totals so much more than present suffering, that the two sums are "not worth comparing."

If this was true in the first century when the heat was on and the persecution real, what about its veracity in the twentieth century when it's cool to be Christian and persecution is, for most of us, imagined?

If you could do the math for your life, what would the totals be? Add up the sufferings you've experienced for the sake of following Jesus, the emotional stress of living in a world hostile to your holiness.

Add to that the monetary losses you've suffered for being a faithful steward, uncompensated by the blessing of the Lord. Add the wear and tear to your body and mind for years of dutiful ministry to children and elderly folks. Add physical suffering from tragedy, sickness, disability, and aging. And put death itself in this column.

In the other column put Jesus, the joy of serving Him, and eternity in His presence. He is the Sum of all things. Now – do the math. It is all about Him.

Paul tells us, *The Spirit Himself bears witness with our spirit that we are children of God, and if children, heirs also, heirs of God and fellow heirs with Christ, if indeed we suffer with Him in order that we may also be glorified with Him.* (Romans 8:16, 17)

The Straight And Narrow *8/21 – August 21*

Narrow is the gate and straight is the way, which leads to life, and there are few who find it. (Matthew 7:14)

The term "straight and narrow" has become a code word for the Christian life, mostly for those who don't walk the road with Jesus. It's a road less traveled.

To some this refers to a legalistic lifestyle that could hardly be mistaken for the abundant life that Jesus promised. Visions of straight-lace and straight face with matching narrow options and narrow minds are suggested by this phrase Jesus used in His Sermon on the Mount. That's not what He meant.

The term "narrow" means "compressed by pressure" and I can see that. There is pressure and the options are few for the obedient child of God. It is, indeed, a narrow road – and it should be. But straight? You've got to be kidding.

The path I've taken hasn't been straight. It's had lots of switchbacks and curves in it and more than a few detours. Narrow? Certainly. But it seems to me that it's been more like a zigzag path.

Why did Jesus call it a straight way? I think that my problem here may be more one of perception than reality. That is, the road only seems full of curves and detours from my point of view.

I was taught in high school geometry that a straight line is the shortest distance between two points. And as I look back upon my life, perhaps those turns in the road were not detours at all. Maybe they were, in fact, the shortest possible way to get me to where God wanted me to be.

I had a nice straight path marked out for myself in my own mind, that was really as crooked as a dog's hind leg. But God took me, and is still taking me, the straightest way – His way, and I called it crooked. I called it a detour.

Another problem with our understanding of this concept of straight and narrow is that the words don't mean the same to us as they did when Jesus spoke them. The New King James Bible sheds some light on this:

Narrow is the gate and difficult is the way, which leads to life, and there are few who find it. (Matthew 7:13, 14) So, narrow means pressured, and straight means difficult. No wonder few people find this path. They're looking for Broadway and Jesus calls us to the back alley.

As a society, we're addicted to ease and comfort and these may be our worst enemies. They will not be found in abundance on the straight and narrow.

If the road you're walking with Jesus is lonely, difficult and pressure-filled, take heart. It's the right road. It leads to life. But it's the road less traveled.

The easy road is crowded – and deadly.

August 22 – 8/22 *Is There Life On Mars?*

But will God indeed dwell with mankind on the earth? Behold, heaven and the highest heaven cannot contain Thee; how much less this house which I have built. (II Chronicles 6:18)

They say that thirteen million years ago, or so, a comet, or something, collided with the fourth planet from the sun, Mars. They say that the impact caused debris to escape the Martian confines and go into orbit around the sun. They say that a few million years ago, or so, some of that debris landed on the third planet from the sun, Earth. It fell in Antarctica.

A few years ago, some earthling scientific types were rummaging around down there and came upon the strange debris. After years of examination, they concluded that the rocks were from Mars, and they contained evidence of life that once existed outside of the friendly confines of Planet Earth.

That's what they're saying. It's all the rage in the halls of science, the talk shows and the tabloid press. The prospect of life on Mars has caused a frenzy of speculation regarding some things important to us all.

Some say that evidence of out-of-this-world life would be a challenge to our faith. They say that if life exists elsewhere it means that we're not alone. They say that life on earth may have indeed sprung from planet-hopping life forms originating somewhere out there.

Words like poppycock, hogwash, and balderdash spring to mind. But level heads must prevail, so I'll just say that the scenario just described lacks the slightest degree of empirical evidence and is based upon the most faulty premise in the annals of human history. It's bad science.

By empirical evidence I mean clear proof of the theory, such as a clearly described structure, traces of cell division, and other widely accepted criteria for defining life.

The faulty premise is the assumption with which all pseudo-science begins – that there is no God – no ultimate cause. Therefore, men must scramble to imagine other causes for all that is.

Don't get me wrong. My faith would not be threatened in the least if there were actual evidence of life somewhere else. If your faith would be threatened by such a prospect I humbly suggest that your God – the God of your experience – is too small.

Is there life on Mars? Of course there is – God is there! As Solomon declared upon the dedication of the Temple, *...will God indeed dwell with mankind on the earth? Behold, heaven and the highest heaven cannot contain Thee.*

But what if there were actually life forms somewhere else in the universe? What would that mean to our faith? To me it would mean that my God is more creative that I ever imagined.

The Father's Faithfulness — *8/23 – August 23*

I've found a few phrases on the Father's faithfulness:

Know therefore that the Lord your God, He is God, the faithful God, Who keeps His covenant and His lovingkindness to a thousandth generation... (Deuteronomy 7:9)

The Rock! His work is perfect, for all His ways are just; a God of faithfulness and without injustice... (Deuteronomy 32:4)

For the word of the Lord is upright, all His work is done in faithfulness. (Psalm 33:4)

I will sing of the lovingkindness of the Lord forever; to all generations I will make known Thy faithfulness with my mouth. The heavens will praise Thy wonders, O Lord, Thy faithfulness also in the assembly of the holy ones. (Psalm 89:1, 5)

For the Lord is good. His lovingkindness is everlasting, and His faithfulness to all generations. (Psalm 100:5)

Thy faithfulness continues throughout all generations... (Psalm 119:90)

O Lord, Thou art my God; I will exalt Thee, I will give thanks to Thy name; for Thou hast worked wonders, plans formed long ago, with perfect faithfulness. (Isaiah 25:1)

It is of the Lord's mercies that we are not consumed, because His compassions fail not. They are new every morning; great is Thy faithfulness. (Lamentations 3:23)

What then? If some did not believe, their unbelief will not nullify the faithfulness of God, will it? (Romans 3:3)

God is faithful, who will not allow you to be tempted beyond what you are able, but with the temptation will provide the way of escape also, that you may be able to endure it. (I Corinthians 10:13)

Faithful is He who calls you, and He also will bring it to pass.
(I Thessalonians 5:24)

If we are faithless, He remains faithful, for He cannot deny Himself.
(II Timothy 2:13)

Let us hold fast the confession of our hope without wavering, for He who promised is faithful... (Hebrews 10:23)

And I saw heaven opened; and behold, a white horse, and He who sat upon it is called Faithful and True; and in righteousness He judges and wages war.
(Revelation 19:11)

The Lord our God is absolutely trustworthy in all His ways, absolutely true to His Word. No promise of His can ever fail. He can neither lie nor deceive.

He is faithful!

Truth is foundational to society. Its financial, educational, governmental, and personal relationships depend upon trust and the integrity of one's words.

It's hard to imagine a sin the does not involve lying. Whatever the original act of disobedience may be lying will inevitably compound the matter into a chain reaction of many transgressions.

It's most disconcerting to hear accusations of lying being reported in a recent Presidential campaign. In these troubled times the quality that is of critical importance in our leadership is truth; what the Bible calls "truth in the inward parts." That's truth at the core of one's being.

When there's an accusation of sin, a pattern emerges that's all too familiar to me. A pattern I call "the anatomy of a lie." I've seen it in me. I've seen it in people I love. Here's the pattern we follow with fleshly consistency when confronted with sin:

• Deny it. It never happened. I wasn't there, I didn't do it, "I never had sexual relations with that woman." We're all very good at that. Denial is much more than a river in Egypt. It's the first shot in a vast human arsenal of lies.

• Call it something else. When confronted with evidence that can't be refuted we change the names of things to make it seem like we didn't really do the dastardly deed. "It wasn't really stealing. The company owed me that money."

• Blame somebody else. The vast right wing conspiracy is to blame. My childhood was dysfunctional. My wife/husband doesn't appreciate me. The devil made me do it. Or as Adam eloquently said, "The woman You gave me…" It's God's fault.

• Everybody does it. That's one excuse that Adam and Eve couldn't make. "I'm no worse than anyone else." That's such an old song. The escapades of past leaders are often used to justify current indiscretions. Such things make my heart sick.

• It's nobody's business but mine. It's a private matter. If anyone could have claimed the private matter excuse it was Adam and Eve. But God was there, He was watching, and He was not silent. All sin has consequences. You cannot plant a private seed. It will grow into a public harvest.

If we confess our sins, He is faithful and righteous to forgive us our sins and to cleanse us from all unrighteousness. (I John 1:9)

For Mature Audiences? *8/25 – August 25*

It's time for our society to give itself a whack on the side of its collective head and say, "We've been duped, horn-swoggled, hoodwinked, humbugged, and otherwise deceived." Why? They've changed the meaning of words on us. Who are "they?" They're the ones who want to sell us something.

There are no greater examples of this "bait and switch" with our language than the words "mature" and "adult." "For Mature Audiences." "Adults Only." These are code words for pornography, violence, obscenity, profanity and all kinds of debauchery.

Read the reviews of movies and TV shows and you will find phrases like, "adult language," "adult situations," and "mature themes." What a tragic twist of language.

What's so mature about pornography? What's so sophisticated about obscenity? What's so adult about violence? What's so grown-up about the free expression of lust and rage and the vilest of human impulses? Nothing! It's all actually quite childish.

It's just crazy to equate these things with maturity when the time-honored, Biblical view of maturity is just the opposite – controlling ones childish, fleshly impulses.

The new meaning of "mature" and "adult" is that one can do and say whatever one wants to without parental disapproval. I'm my own person now. No one has a right to tell "consenting adults" how they ought to act in the privacy of their motel room. This applies, of course, to running with scissors, putting your feet on the couch – and watching pornographic movies.

Here's a flash for the followers of Jesus Christ: *Your body is a temple of the Holy Spirit who is in you...and you are not your own? You have been bought with a price: therefore glorify God in your body.* (I Corinthians. 6:19-20)

It's been said that every man has his price. I suppose that means that for the right price you can get a man to do anything. Not me. Not my fellow disciples of the Crucified One. Our price has already been paid. The bidding is over.

Age does not make one wise. Age does nothing but make one old. Maturity is a series of choices to do the right thing over time.

He has showed you, O man, what is good. And what does the Lord require of you? To act justly and to love mercy and to walk humbly with your God. (Micah 6:8)

That's a lifestyle for mature audiences.

Now that's more like it.

August 26 – 8/26   *A Breath Test*

I'm going to ask you to take the following breath test. Find a white sheet of paper. Then hold the paper near your face and blow on it. If it turns:

Green… call your doctor or have the elders pray for you.
Brown… visit your friendly dentist.
Red… call your financial advisor.
Purple… consult with your local psychiatrist.
Yellow… make an appointment with a lawyer to prepare your will.

If it remains the same color, you're in good health and there's no reason on earth why you shouldn't sign up to serve in the first available ministry.

A minister told the organist that after his message he was going to ask people to stand and commit themselves to serve in some capacity. He asked her if she would be thinking of some appropriate music that she could play while they were considering their choice.

After the minister made his appeal to the congregation, the crafty organist played at full-volume – The Star Spangled Banner.

Merry-go-rounds. I rode them when I was a kid and took my children on them in their growing up years. Almost everyone has had the experience.

The thing about the carousel is that you climb aboard a painted wooden horse and off you go. There's a lot of rattling, vibration, and loud music, and the sense of movement with the world moving past as you ride round and round.

Finally, the ride slows down and comes to rest, and when it does, you find that you have arrived at the same place you started from. In spite of all the dizzying movement, noise and excitement, you have not advanced at all. You're exactly where you were when you decided to board the carousel.

Life is like that with lots of movement, some of it up and down. There's exciting activity, accompanied by the music of a busy world. But it's never true of serving.

When you get on board you'll be going somewhere. You'll never get off at the same place you got on. You will have grown. It's just the nature of serving; we end up serving ourselves, too, in the process of serving others.

That's the genius of the call to follow Jesus in discipleship. He could have angels do what we do. But He has plans for our growth, and fellowship with Him, that involve our serving faithfully and drawing upon His power and presence in the process.

So, no breath tests are required – just the opportunity to serve and grow – and love in Jesus' name.

I Don't Know *8/27 – August 27*

There are three little words that are very hard to say. We'd rather make up an answer that sounds good than say, "I don't know."

There is, it seems to me, an unspoken law that a Christian ought to know just about everything, especially when it comes to spiritual things. So we find it difficult to say "I don't know."

I overheard a conversation among some seminary students some time ago that took me back fifty years. They were discussing, or rather arguing, the same question we used to argue when I was in training for ministry.

The question was, "If nothing is impossible with God, can He make a rock so big that He can't lift it?" We used to debate this for hours and I suppose that it was a harmless intellectual exercise, but no one, then or now, ever said those three little words, "I don't know." You're supposed to know these things, I guess, to qualify for ministry.

Another popular question that has much more practical implications is, "Why do bad things happen to good people?" Its corollary is, "Why do good things happen to bad people?" Those are good questions and most of us have some helpful suggestions.

Probably the best answer that I know is to these two questions is – "Why not!" But what is it about us that we must have an answer? It's as if our lives would instantly be blissful if we had answers to these questions.

There are a lot of questions about healing, or rather non-healing. "We prayed for my mother, we anointed her with oil, we called for the elders, we took her to healing services and she died anyhow. Why, Pastor, why?"

Or, "Why do some people seem to get healed and I don't. I live for the Lord as well as I know how but I'm still in constant pain. Why, Pastor, why?"

Or, "My son was just sixteen with his whole life ahead of him. We never dreamed he would do something like this. Why, Pastor, why did he take his life?" Pastors are supposed to know these things.

I once had some stock answers that had to do with God's will or man's will or something. But my answers just raised more questions. That's how it is with human answers to spiritual questions.

I'm comfortable now saying, "I don't know." There are many things about God that I don't know; yet the Accuser tells me that I ought to know. His scheme is to reduce God to completely knowable, manageable proportions, and that's impossible. There is a universe of things that are unknowable in my present state.

It's enough that I know Him – and He knows all things.

August 28 – 8/28 *If*

It's the biggest little word in any language. It suggests a condition, a proviso, and a disclaimer to a contract or a promise. Here are just a few of the 232 examples in the Gospels alone of the use of the word IF:

Jesus said to him, "If you can believe, all things are possible to him that believes." (Mark 9:23)

Jesus therefore was saying to those Jews who had believed Him, "If you abide in My word, then you are truly disciples of Mine." (John 8:31)

"If you ask Me anything in My name, I will do it." (John 14:14)

"If you abide in Me, and My words abide in you, ask whatever you wish, and it shall be done for you." (John 15:7)

The clear implication in each of these cases is that when we don't do the IF part, the promise is not fulfilled; the contract is invalid. In other words: "If you do not believe, nothing is going to change." Or: "If you do not abide in Me and My words don't live in you, don't bother asking. It's not going to happen."

This brings into focus the age-old debate about God's part and man's part in the whole scheme of things. God's part is clear. He does the impossible stuff. My part is the IF part. And that's always the possible part. It's do-able but sometimes difficult.

There are some major IFs regarding the healing of our land. They're found in a verse we've heard dozens of times. It's II Chronicles 7:14:

IF My people who are called by My name humble themselves and pray, and seek My face and turn from their wicked ways, then I will hear from heaven, will forgive their sin, and will heal their land.

Four IFs make up this "covenant promise": humble ourselves, pray, seek His face, and turn from our wicked ways. Then He will heal our land. And if we don't, He won't.

It isn't so much that He won't, it's that He has committed Himself to work through His people and He can't do that if we aren't a humble, praying, seeking, pure people.

David, a man after God's own heart, cried out and said, *Search me and try me and see if there is any wicked way in me.* (Psalm 139:23)

Do we have any wicked ways? It's time to open our hearts to a serious search by the Spirit of God.

I think He will find some.

Do You Have Gravitas? *8/29 – August 29*

The newest nifty word is "gravitas." Media pundits have picked up the word and throw it around as if they actually know what they're talking about.

"So-and-so has gravitas", they say. And in the next breath they say, "What's-his-name does not have gravitas." By it they mean credibility and charisma, I suppose. But this is an absurd demonstration of pseudo intellectual verbiage that has little meaning to average Joe Voter.

But it has meaning to me. Gravitas, and its related adjectives have profound meaning in God's order of things eternal. "Gravitas" is Latin for gravity, that ever-present force that keeps us all from flying off into outer space. The Greek equivalent is "axios" – weighty, scales, by comparison heavier.

Romans 8:18 says this, *For I consider that the sufferings of this present time are not worthy to be compared with the glory which shall be revealed in us.*

The word used here for "worthy" is axios, "weighed on the scales." The picture is this: the sufferings of this present time are placed on one side of the balance scales. On the other side is the glory and blessing we shall know in the age to come. And future glory tips the scales.

Another illustration of gravitas is my favorite. The scene is the throne room of heaven in Revelation 5:11, 12: *And I looked, and I heard the voice of many angels around the throne and the living creatures and the elders; and the number of them was myriads of myriads, and thousands of thousands, saying with a loud voice, "Worthy is the Lamb that was slain to receive power and riches and wisdom and might and honor and glory and blessing."*

Jesus alone is worthy. Lend me your imagination, please. Visualize a gigantic balance scale, arms stretching 100 million light years into space. Its base is resting on the Rock of Ages. Its balance beam reaches beyond the Andromeda Galaxy to the farthest edge of the known universe.

Now take all that's on the earth, all of its riches, mountains and valleys, cities and farmland, oceans and rivers. Put them on the one side of the scale. Add all of the planets in the Solar system, all of the stars in the Milky Way, (billions) and all of the billions of galaxies in the universe. Then add all of the animals and the human beings who've ever lived. Put all of the mass of created energy and matter and life on one side of the scale.

And on the other side, all by Himself – put Jesus – The Lamb that was slain.

And watch as the scales creak and begin to pivot to the side of the Lamb. He weighs more than the universe and everything and everyone in it.

He is worthy. He has gravitas!

A new phrase has crept into our national vocabulary and has been added to the latest editions of dictionaries. It's funny how language evolves. Anyhow, the phrase I'm referring to is "no-brainer."

It's come to mean anything that you don't have to use your brain to figure out. The concept is implied in the words of our Declaration of Independence when it speaks of self-evident truth. That all men are created equal is a no-brainer.

I'm amazed that there is such great division and controversy in our society over things that are in fact no-brainers. For instance, that life begins at conception – a no-brainer. How could a living egg combine with a living sperm and produce anything but life?

That marriage is supposed to be between and man and a woman is a no-brainer. How else has civilization survived but by children being conceived in the committed union of male and female to form the most basic of human relationships – the family.

The apostle Paul wrote to the Corinthians and included some rhetorical questions, the answers to which he knew were obvious to the Corinthians. They were no-brainers.

Do not be bound together with unbelievers; for what partnership have righteousness and lawlessness, or what fellowship has light with darkness? Or what harmony has Christ with Belial, or what has a believer in common with an unbeliever? Or what agreement has the temple of God with idols? For we are the temple of the living God. Therefore, "come out from their midst and be separate," says the Lord. (II Corinthians 6:14-17)

These were the no-brainers of Paul's 1st century world. Righteousness and evil cannot find agreement. Light and darkness cannot coexist. Christ and His people, and the devil and his crowd have no common ground. And in the temple of the living God there's no room for idols.

Unfortunately, these have become the 21st century's "brainers." What was once self-evident truth is now self-gratifying relativism. The lines between Paul's incompatible extremes are not fuzzy – they've disappeared altogether.

The Holy Spirit concludes His list of rhetorical questions with this: *Therefore, "come out from their midst and be separate," says the Lord.*

The problem in a relativistic world is this: how can we "come out from among them and be separate" if we don't know where the line is? If there's no difference between good and evil, where's the separation to begin?

This phrase haunts me: "Unless there is within us that which is above us, we shall soon yield to that which is about us."

Let us yield and be filled with that which is above us – the Spirit of Jesus.

WYSIWYG *8/31 – August 31*

Hebrews 11:1 in the Amplified Version beautifully expands a familiar passage about faith: *Now faith is the assurance (the confirmation, the title-deed) of the things we hope for, being the proof of things we do not see and the conviction of their reality - faith perceiving as real fact what is not revealed to the senses.*

WYSIWYG, pronounced "wiz-e-wig," is an acronym from the world of computers. Unfolding the acronym we learn that it translates to, "What You See Is What You Get." In other words, what you see on your computer screen is exactly what will be printed out on your printer.

A book was written a few years ago that restates this phrase to suggest a spiritual principle with great following in some areas. The paraphrase says: "What You Say Is What You Get!" This idea has great appeal and has given birth to the concept of "positive confession" which certainly has some validity, as do all single-focus truths.

But the idea of speaking something I want into existence must be balanced with everything that the Scripture says about faith. And the process begins with seeing, not saying. Faith sees the invisible, believes the incredible, and receives the impossible.

It's also true, however, that fear sees what isn't there and believes incredible things. I've known painful things I never thought possible; all because of fear. So it's not that we believe, but what we believe.

Believing is seeing. Faith embraces what God says; fear embraces what Satan says. And whether it's faith or fear, "WYSIWYG!" – "What You See Is What You Get!"

There's a flip side to a positive faith, which embraces what God has said. Fear is a kind of negative faith that also sees the invisible and embraces what it sees. Fear responds to what the world, the flesh and the devil project upon the screen of our soul. And what you see is what you get.

Many live in bondage created by what fear leads them to believe, expressed with their lips. In this context, it's what God says, not what I say, that matters.

But when faith embraces what God has said, a kind of seeing occurs; the sight of the spirit that envisions what God has said in a way not definable in material terms. The Bible does not propose that the people of God develop a kind of blind faith. While we do walk by faith and not by sight, faith is not blind. It sees! It sees what God sees and reaches to receive it.

Therefore, we ought to major in the utterances of God; become expert in the majesty of His Word, and speak what our faith sees with confidence. In this sense, indeed, what you see is what you get – WYSIWYG!

I have good news and bad news. *Whatever a man sows, that will he also reap.* (Galatians 6:7) That's how the whole universe operates. If that were not true there'd be no structure, no framework for agriculture, the physical sciences, or human relationships. But hidden in this simple axiom are three important truths, and not just one.

First, you always reap what you sow. We think this is bad news, but it's good news as well. Sowing seeds of kindness brings a harvest of kindness, just as surely as sowing seeds of bitterness brings a bitter harvest. If one sows quality one reaps quality. When God created the universe, He commanded that living things bring forth after their kind. They've been doing it ever since.

Second, you always reap later than you sow. There's a growing season for every kind of seed you plant. And that's a problem. When we sin we don't see immediate harm coming from our action, so we're deceived into thinking that we've beaten the system. This leads to more sin, which brings more harvest of pain eventually. In the same way, when we sow good seeds we don't see immediate blessing, so we're deceived into thinking that it doesn't pay to do good. This often discourages us from planting more good seed.

Third, you always reap more than you sow. There's an exponential increase over the amount of seed planted. The increase is staggering. As someone has said, "Anyone can count the number of apples on a tree, but only God knows the number of trees in an apple." When we sow evil seeds we will reap a harvest of grief many times larger than what we sowed, and we say that it's just not fair. But that's the way it is when you plant something. It works that way for good seed, too, and we don't deserve that increase either.

Early missionaries to China found a community where the main crop was the potato. They had good climate and good soil, but their harvest was potatoes about the size of marbles. The missionaries asked if any big potatoes ever grew there. "O yes, we do get a few big ones now and then," they admitted. "What do you do with them?" the missionaries asked. "We eat them, they're the best," the farmers said. They were planting the ones that had the genes for small potatoes. They were reducing the size of their crop as they took the biggest and best for themselves. The missionaries showed them that only when you plant the best, would you get the best in return.

We may smile at these simple farmers, but we do the same thing. We keep the best for ourselves, and whatever's left we give to God. Then we wonder why our lives become smaller and smaller.

It's amazing how universal this principle is – "Whatever a man sows, that will he also reap." There's no way around it so why not use it to our advantage?

A Wake Up Call — *9/2 – September 2*

A chorus has found it's way into my heart. It expresses the desire of so many of us these days to be awakened to new life in Him. The song "Awaken My Heart," has its basis in several places in Scripture. There is a universal tendency for the human heart to doze off when it comes to spiritual priorities, so God periodically issues a wake-up call His people.

In Ephesians 5:14 Paul quotes the Old Testament admonition in regard to the unfruitful works of darkness. He says, *Awake, sleeper, and arise from the dead, and Christ will shine on you.* It's easy to fall asleep in the dark. And when we do we become part of the darkness by becoming spiritually unconscious.

In Psalm 57:8, 9, David uses the wake-up analogy on himself when he says, *Awake, my glory; awake the harp and lyre, I will awaken the dawn! I will give thanks to Thee, O Lord, among the peoples...* He's talking about praise and his tendency to become unconscious to the glory of God and His praise-worthiness.

In Romans 13:11, Paul issues a wake-up call about the last days: *And this do, knowing the time, that it is already the hour for you to awaken from sleep; for now salvation is nearer to us than when we believed. The night is almost gone and the day is at hand.* Salvation here refers to the coming of the Lord and it is, indeed, nearer than when we first believed.

When we sing, "Awaken my heart, to love and adore You, O, my God; Awaken my heart to pour out before you, O my God," I wonder if we really know what we're asking. We're not naturally inclined to do either of those things and we're pretty sound sleepers, when it comes to things spiritual.

If you're like me, when the alarm goes off at 5:45 am, I reach over and hit the snooze button and get another ten minutes of sleep. I've been know to do that four or five times before I have to wake up and get going. Chances are, we've been hitting the old snooze alarm already where God is concerned, and it just may take something pretty drastic to wake us up.

"Awaken My Heart" is a very easy song to sing. It's melodic and the words fit nicely with the notes, but to take the words seriously is to invite disruption of our routine. We may be in the middle of a beautiful dream of material wealth and fleshly pleasure when the Lord gives us His wake-up call. Do we really want to be awakened to His reality? Do we really want to come alive to the things that He values, and die to the things the world holds dear?

I pray that we do. To stay asleep is to die.

September 3 – 9/3 ***Morning Has Broken***

I will awaken the dawn. I will praise You, O Lord! (Psalm 57:8, 9)

I found myself singing an old song in the car the other morning as I headed up the highway for San Mateo. The sun was just spreading its light over the mountains in the east and the words of an old hymn came fresh to my lips.

This tune goes back a couple of hundred years to the early days of our nation:

"Morning has broken, like the first morning,
Blackbird has spoken like the first bird.
Praise for the singing! Praise for the morning!
Praise for them springing, fresh from the Word!
Mine is the sunlight! Mine is the morning,
Born of the one light Eden saw play.
Praise with elation! Praise ev'ry morning,
God's re-creation of the new day!"

Driving northward I saw vineyards heavy with wine grapes nearly ready for harvest. Whatever your views on wine, (I prefer the juice of the young grape before its old enough to have a mind of its own) you have to appreciate the beauty of the vine and the wonder of its fruit. Jesus was well acquainted with the process we see in grand profusion all around us this time of year.

It shouldn't have surprised anyone when Jesus turned water into wine the day of the wedding in Cana of Galilee, considering that it was God Who did it. Jesus had the servants of the house fill six large pots with water, and He proceeded to turn it into wine before their eyes.

We shouldn't be surprised either, when He does the same thing every year in the thousands of acres of vineyards surrounding us. He distills water from the clouds and deposits it on the earth – and water is turned to wine. We channel the water all over the fruited plain, but we can't produce it – it must come from above. And if it doesn't come, we can do absolutely nothing about it.

Perhaps I had it backwards when I said that no one should be surprised at the water to wine miracle. Actually, we should be as much surprised, or at least awestruck, by the every day miracles of His grace, as those first century guests were by water jugs full of wine. We take it all for granted, but the earth keeps spinning and seasons keep changing, while beneath our feet and within our reach – miracles abound!

A pseudo-scientist would say that it's all a quite natural process. How sad to see and yet be blind to the wonder. Lord, help us rediscover and cherish a sense of wonder each time morning breaks.

If nothing else surprises you try this – "His mercies are new every morning!"

Mind Your Own Business *9/4 – September 4*

I Thessalonians 4:11 says, *...aspire to lead a quiet life, to mind your own business, and to work with your own hands...* There's a connection between these three phrases. Literally it could read, "in order to lead a quiet life – mind your own business – by working diligently with your hands."

A well-known speaker asked an audience recently, "What do you think God is using to build His church in this generation?" We all expected him to say something like worship, or miracles, or the gifts of the Spirit. But what he said was "work," – consistent, directed, hard, physical work.

We tend to think of work as being unrelated to revival and God restoring His church, and perhaps some of us even think of work as man's effort, out of which no good thing can emerge. Two points can be made here.

First, there's a spiritual dimension to physical labor. When you're working at something God wants done, spiritual life and benefits are produced. If God wants it done – and that covers a wide spectrum of jobs and professions from abbot to zoologist – then there's a spiritual dimension to that work. When Paul said, "mind your own business", he wasn't saying it sarcastically. He was saying, "do what you do best; do what you're trained to do."

Second, there's a physical dimension to spiritual labor. It's hard work to intercede and wrestle with Satan for the souls of men. It's hard work to care for the souls of children and be there week after week to lay a foundation for their lives in Jesus. It's hard work to carry a daily burden for young people and become a part of their lives, while you have your own life and family to care for. We honor these spiritual "blue collar workers" who have joyfully accepted the challenge of working in the kingdom, and take it as seriously as any labor the world offers.

Another aspect of work that's worth mentioning is rest. Work and rest are companions in the creative process. God worked for six days, and then He rested. People who don't work have a problem – they can never stop and rest.

Jesus said, *Come unto me all you who labor and are loaded down, and I will give you rest.* (Matthew 11:28) He knows how to rest. He is not driven for more things, or stars, or planets, nor does He drive His people to work without rest.

Minding your own business involves rest as well as work.

September 5 – 9/5 *AMDG*

I've visited Gothic Cathedrals in England and St. Peter's Basilica in Rome. The sights and sounds of these great churches are magnificent. Many people, however, feel that time, effort, and expense were wasted on these stone-cold edifices. I don't think so.

If you crawl under a choir stall in any one of these cathedrals, you'll find, carved in the wood, four letters: AMDG. The same four small letters are etched into the cathedral's stained glass, stitched on its vestments and altar cloths, and chiseled into the stone of its majestic walls.

You won't find the names of the artists there; only four letters: AMDG, which stand for "Ad Majorem Dei Gloriam" – To the Honor and Glory of God.

A man could spend his entire life carving the decorations for one tower of the cathedral, or joining the woodwork of a chapel. Yet the artist received no recognition. His workmanship went unsung and unsigned, except for AMDG.

These grand creations, which took as long as 150 years to complete, stand in awesome testimony that Someone was, and still is, worthy of such devotion. Every chisel stroke, every pass of the plane, every stitch of the cloth was offered wholly to the honor and glory of God alone.

I've been deeply moved, on more than one occasion, while walking though these grand cathedrals. I've wondered why I was so moved. I believe it was the workmanship. The Scripture says an amazing thing about workmanship in Ephesians: *For by grace you have been saved through faith, and that not of yourselves; it is the gift of God, not of works, lest anyone should boast. For we are His workmanship, created in Christ Jesus for good works....* (2:8-10)

Workmanship is the Greek word "poiema," meaning, a thing that is fashioned, created; workmanship. We get our word "poem" from poiema.

It's not a stretch at all to say that I am – you are – God's poem. A poem is a special creation. There is rhyme, rhythm and reason about a poem. You have to think ahead about a poem. If you're writing a letter you can ramble and write as you think. But a poem is something else. You've got to plan a poem.

And God did. He planed that my life should have a kind of rhyme to it so that my days, like the lines of a sonnet, end with amazing grace and beauty. He planned that a rhythm of change should bring me from glory to glory toward His likeness. And He planned that my life should have a reason and make sense at the end – like a poem.

The reason? Good works. It's as if God is saying, "you are My workmanship, now you go create something good through your work." That's godliness – God-likeness. And when the day's work is done, like the artisans of cathedral fame, let us inscribe our work with these four letters, AMDG:

"Ad Majorem Dei Gloriam" – For the Honor and Glory of God!

Love's Labor — *9/6 – September 6*

"Love's Labor's Lost" is a play by William Shakespeare in which he pokes fun at the frivolous, fruitless courtship antics of 16th century England. With apologies to Will Shakespeare, love's labor is never lost – agape love, I mean.

This Labor Day weekend, to those who have labored lovingly in ministry to touch tender lives with grace and love, the Lord says. *My beloved brethren... your labor is not in vain in the Lord.* (I Corinthians 15:58)

There's power in love, the kind of love the Bible talks about. God's love, agape, isn't just the reason we labor; it's the power by which we labor. It energizes us to do what we would not think to do, or be able to do otherwise.

I am doing a great work, and I cannot come down. So said Nehemiah when his enemies requested that he stop his work and compromise his purpose. (see Nehemiah 6:2, 3) What was this "great work"? Was it preaching, or prophesying, or praying? No, it was manual labor, building a wall around Jerusalem. It was hard work, but it was great work. It was a labor of love.

Any work that has purpose and meaning is great work. Any work requiring the investment of a day of one's life is great work. Any work that can be done without compromise, with all of your might, is great work. Any work done in the name of Jesus is great work, and a labor of love.

Perhaps you're standing on the brink of a challenge and don't know where the strength will come from to do what you've committed yourself to do. Love has already motivated you to make the commitment, now you'll know the power of God that works through love. Your love's labor will not be lost.

Work will be with us always, so we might as well see it as God sees it, embrace it and enjoy it. So, to all who labor lovingly any place on earth – this is for you:

We give thanks to God always for all of you, making mention of you in our prayers; constantly bearing in mind your work of faith and labor of love and steadfastness of hope in our Lord Jesus Christ in the presence of our God and Father, knowing, brethren beloved by God, His choice of you. (I Thessalonians 1:3,4)

Let us pause briefly for a few words in praise of work. Without work, nothing would ever get done. It will always be there – it's a friend for life. By work I mean the entire range of human activity directed toward the doing of some task. Scientifically, work is defined as the expenditure and application of energy along a certain line of action.

This includes the farm worker and the factory worker, of course, but it also includes the secretary, the salesman, the doctor, the lawyer, the waitress, the accountant, the truck driver, the computer programmer, the janitor, the butcher, the baker, the candlestick maker, etc., and the housewife.

The phrase, "you work too hard" could apply to any endeavor, including being a housewife, for that matter. Let me explain what I mean by this statement. A young man went to Canada in search of a job as an axe-man for a lumber company. He approached the foreman, asking if there was an opening. The foreman replied, "That depends. Let's see you fell that tree over there."

The young man set his feet and deftly felled the tree. The foreman was impressed. "You start Monday." Monday, Tuesday, Wednesday, Thursday rolled by, and Thursday afternoon the foreman said, "Pick up your paycheck on your way out." The man replied, "But I thought you paid on Friday." "Normally we do," said the foreman, "but we're letting you go today because you're too lazy. We keep a chart on the number of trees each man cuts and you've dropped from first place on Monday to eighth place on Wednesday."

"I'm not lazy!" the young man responded. "I arrive first, leave last and often work through my coffee break." The foreman, sensing his honest response, asked a very important question: "Do you sharpen your axe daily?" "I work too hard, I don't have time to sharpen my axe," was his reply.

Moral: you're working too hard if your axe isn't sharp. Abe Lincoln said, "If I had eight hours to chop down a tree, I'd spend six sharpening my axe."

Spiritually, we sharpen our axe with prayer, God's word, and obedience. But in every part of life there's a way to sharpen your axe to accomplish more with less wear and tear on body and soul. Whatever your particular vocation, you won't have to work so hard if you use a sharp axe, so to speak.

The Scripture has a lot to say about work. One of my favorite passages is in Psalm 90:14,17: *Satisfy us in the morning with Your unfailing love, that we may sing for joy and be glad all our days. May the favor of the Lord our God rest upon us; establish the work of our hands for us - yes, establish the work of our hands.*

And Lord, in all of our labors, help us keep a sharp axe. Amen!

Gold-Collar Workers *9/8 – September 8*

We've had blue-collar workers and white-collar workers, but a new term has been coined by management experts – gold-collar worker. This defines an employee who is worth his or her weight in gold by today's business leaders.

What's a blue-collar worker? These hard-working people are generally seen as laborers in construction, manufacturing, farming and other get-down-and-get-your-hands-dirty kinds of jobs. Our nation was built by such as these and they do indeed earn their living by the sweat of their brows. Jesus attracted such people to follow Him. He was at home with carpenters and fishermen. Jesus Himself was a blue-collar worker – a carpenter.

White-collar workers are generally seen as office-type people; secretaries, salesmen, managers, clerks and all kinds of other people who serve with their time and talents in banks, offices, and stores. They serve us daily in ways we will never know about, processing information and keeping the wheels of our economy well oiled with their skills. Jesus attracted white-collar people, too – tax collectors, merchants, physicians, and a host of others who found that following Him gave new meaning to their lives.

Gold-collar workers are not another class of employees. They're found within the groups just mentioned. Typical gold-collar workers are creative, highly skilled and knowledgeable. They're independent to the point of being stubborn at times. They consistently meet and exceed standards that are expected of them, and they occasionally give their managers grey hair. But they constantly enhance the organization's production and profits.

A Christian should be a gold-collar worker in any field. We have resources available to us that others don't. We have the Holy Spirit, Who will teach us all things. We have godly standards of honesty and integrity that are valued qualities in any occupation. And drugs or a preoccupation with lust does not impede Christians, because of a commitment to holiness. A boss will never have to deal with a hung-over Christian employee. Creativity, faithfulness, and consistency – are Christ-like traits grow in us as we become more like Him.

Actually, Jesus has something a bit higher in mind for those who are found faithful. Is it a gold collar? Not really. A gold crown is what He has in mind.

And when we see Him, we'll cast our crowns, the symbols of our faithfulness, at His feet in worship and adoration to the One Who is our ultimate employer.

I confess that it's blatantly self-serving for me to write this today. You see, September 9 is Grandparent's Day, and I, happily, am one. President Jimmy Carter proclaimed it such on September 9, 1979. He ordained that the first Sunday following Labor Day would be Grandparent's Day in our nation. This may not be the exact day this year, but who's counting?

There's evidence, based on interviews with children and grandparents, is that children need their grandparents, and vice-versa. The study shows that the bond between grandparents and grandchildren is second in emotional power and influence only to the relationship between parents and children.

Grandparents affect the lives of their grandchildren, for good or ill, simply because they exist. But sadly, of the children studied, only 5% reported close, regular contact with at least one grandparent.

The majority of children see their grandparents infrequently, not because they live too far away, but because the grandparents have chosen to remain emotionally distant. These children appear to be very perceptive about their grandparents. One of them said, "I'm just a charm on grandma's bracelet."

The positive roles that grandparents play in children's lives are many, such as caretaker, storyteller, family historian, mentor, confidant, negotiator between child and parent, and model for the child's own old age. The love of grandparents comes with no behavioral strings attached.

I was blessed to know both sets of my grandparents in my growing-up years. They positively influenced my life. I'm grateful, beyond my capacity to express, that I was touched by their love and their lives.

I say both sets of grandparents, and I'm reminded that many children have more than two sets of grandparent because of the proliferation of divorce in recent years. That must, at the very least, dilute the influence of grandparents in children's lives. At the very worst, the animosity generated by painful divorces may place children in the center of the conflict, and they may become pawns in the extended family's warfare.

If you're a grandparent, you have promises from the Lord:

But the lovingkindness of the Lord is from everlasting to everlasting on those who fear Him, and His righteousness to children's children. (Psalm 103:17)

The righteous will flourish like a palm tree... They will still bear fruit in old age, they will stay fresh and green, proclaiming, "The Lord is upright; he is my Rock. (Psalm 92:12-15)

Atonement *9/10 – September 10*

Jewish people all over the world will celebrate Yom Kippur, the Day of Atonement, sometime soon. This day is the last of the Ten Days of Penitence, which began with Rosh Hashanah – the Jewish New Year's Day.

The Day of Atonement is the most solemn holy day in the Hebrew calendar. In ancient times, all work was forbidden and a strict fast was commanded for all the people from sundown to sundown. Modern observances include fasting and blowing the Shofar, the ram's horn.

I'm reminded of a church in a predominantly Jewish section of a certain city that wanted to reach out to their Jewish friends. They decided that Yom Kippur was the day that they would make the effort. They would have a dinner and send invitations to the neighbors. They prepared a feast, but no one came. Yom Kippur is a day of fasting. I think there's a lesson there.

This annual holy day served as a reminder that sin is a deadly thing and it hinders access to God. The blood of animals was shed to atone for the sins of the people and thus give them access, through the high priest, into the Holy of Holies, the dwelling place of God.

In the New Testament there are 290 times that God declares His love for man. In the same pages, there are more than 1,300 references to the atonement – 1,300 assurances that salvation can be had through the blood of Christ.

Now every day is a Day of Atonement. The blood of the Lamb – Jesus Christ – guarantees forgiveness and entrance into God's presence anytime, anyplace.

One of my favorite people from the past, the great English preacher Charles H. Spurgeon, said that he was so sure of his salvation through the atonement that he could grab on to a cornstalk and swing out over the fires of hell, look into the face of the devil, and sing, "Blessed assurance, Jesus is mine!"

The key element in Atonement is blood. Romans 5:11 says, *And not only this, but we also exult in God through our Lord Jesus Christ, through whom we have now received the reconciliation.* The word "reconciliation" is the Old Testament equivalent of the word "atonement." Jesus' death was "at-one-ment." God and man – once enemies – are friends by the blood of the atonement.

George Bernard Shaw once observed this about Jesus, "We crucified Him on a stick, but we have always had a curious feeling that He somehow managed to get hold of the right end of it."

Jesus did just that – and He built a bridge to God with it.

September 11 – 9/11 *The Bottom Line*

On Tuesday Morning, September 11, 2001, the United States of America, this blessed land, was recipient of the worst terrorist attack in the world's history, forever altering our way of thinking and our way of life.

America will never, and should not ever, be the same. Many questions still abound, not the least of which is, "Why?"

There's a principle of problem solving involving asking a series of five "why" questions to get to the root of any matter. We could begin by asking the first question, which is, "Why did this happen to us on 9/11?" Because some people hate us.

Then we ask "why" question #2, "Why do some people hate us?" Because of America's support for Israel.

Question #3, "Why do we support Israel?" Because we are "people of the Book" and share a common spiritual heritage.

Question #4, "Why do we share a common spiritual heritage?" Because Jesus Christ, Who died for our sins on the cross, was a Jew.

Question #5, "Why does that enrage radical Islamists like Osama bin Laden?" Because they are enemies of the cross who believe they must destroy us to establish Islam by any means possible.

That's the bottom "why" line.

Another question that comes to mind when there's a time of remembrance on the anniversary of 9/11/01: "Why are we doing this?" "Because it's important to remember the thousands who died, and honor the hundreds of firemen and policemen who acted heroically."

Question #2, "Why do we remember those who died and honor those who acted heroically?" Because those innocent victims of terrorists, and those who put their own lives in jeopardy to save them, did so for a just cause.

Question #3, "What is the just cause for which so many sacrificed their lives to preserve?" Freedom.

Question #4, "Why is freedom that important?" Because freedom gives us the ability to chose to do what is right, not simply what we want.

Question #5, "What is right?" *He has showed you, O man, what is good... to act justly, and to love mercy, and to walk humbly with your God.* (Micah 6:8)

And that's the bottom line.

Even So, Come — *9/12 – September 12*

He who testifies these things says, "Surely I come quickly." Amen! Even so, come, Lord Jesus! The grace of our Lord Jesus Christ be with you all. (Revelation 22:20)

Several years ago about this time of year, a book was making the rounds in the Christian community that caused quite a stir. It was a book that gave 88 reasons why Jesus would return to the earth in 1988. He didn't.

The author admitted an error in his calculations and another book, perhaps, will be forthcoming projecting yet another date for the Lord's return. I've lived through dozens of such panic-generating predictions. It's like yelling, "fire" when there isn't any. You don't pay much attention to the warnings after so many false alarms.

You'd think that God would put a stop to such things in the interest of credibility, but the Lord of the church is apparently less concerned about His reputation than we are. His kingdom still stands, His promise is still valid, and His return is nearer today than it was yesterday.

He even finds a way to turn the foolishness of man to His own glory. I heard the testimony of a young man who plays baseball for the Minnesota Twins, who read that book about the imminent return of Jesus and was so struck by the fact that he was not ready to meet the Lord, that he surrendered his life to the Lord on the spot.

It didn't seem to matter that the date predicted came and went. He's still living for Jesus years later and gives testimony of his faith whenever and wherever he can. God used a prediction about the return of Jesus to get his attention.

Does the coming of Jesus have your attention? I don't know when He will return; I only know that He will return. He said He would and I believe Him. The message of His return dominates the pages of Scripture, and should find a priority place in our plans and goals.

On the Isle of Patmos, John wrote down the revelation that Jesus opened to him. At the close of it, Jesus said to him, "Surely I come quickly." John's response seems spontaneous and animated, – "Even so, come, Lord Jesus!"

His reply suggests that the return of Jesus had a priority place in John's life. It could be said this way: "Lord, there are a lot of things I want to see happen, - even so, come." Or, "I haven't reached my financial goals – even so, come." "My kids are not raised yet – even so come." "We just bought a new house – even so, come." In other words, "There is nothing in my life that takes precedent over Your return, Lord."

Even so – Come Lord Jesus. What a great way to live!

September 13 – 9/13 — *This Same Jesus*

After He had said these things, He was lifted up while they were looking on, and a cloud received Him out of their sight. And as they were gazing intently into the sky while He was departing, behold, two men in white clothing stood beside them; and they also said, "Men of Galilee, why do you stand looking into the sky? This Jesus, who has been taken up from you into heaven, will come in just the same way as you have watched Him go into heaven." (Acts 1:9-11)

"This same Jesus," says the King James Version, is coming back to planet earth. The hope of the return of Jesus Christ puts each day in the perspective of eternity. It puts material things in their place. It makes a major crisis into a minor matter when the gaze of the soul is upon His return.

I'm not suggesting a "pie-in-the-sky-bye-and-bye" approach to life. What I do suggest is that to be ready for His return is to be ready for anything that life may bring. Many of us would like to know when He's coming back just so that we could get ready in time. It's so much better to live ready.

For you yourselves know full well that the day of the Lord will come just like a thief in the night. (I Thessalonians 5:2)

A prayer by an unknown saint touched a place in me that longs for His return.

"O Blessed Lord Jesus, give us thankful hearts for You, our greatest gift. Let not our souls be busy inns that have no room for You and Yours, but quiet homes of prayer and praise, where You will find good company; where holy thoughts pass among us as we fervently watch and await Your coming.

"So, when You come again, O, Blessed One, may You find all things ready, and Your servants waiting for no new master, but for One long known and loved. Even so, come, Lord Jesus!"

I Thessalonians 4:16-18 says, *For the Lord Himself will descend from heaven with a shout, with the voice of the archangel, and with the trumpet of God; and the dead in Christ shall rise first. Then we who are alive and remain shall be caught up together with them in the clouds to meet the Lord in the air, and thus we shall always be with the Lord. Therefore comfort one another with these words.*

The Grace of the Lord Jesus be with you all. Even So – Come.

The Many-Splendored Name *9/14 – September 14*

"In Jesus' Name." As of Monday, September 9, 2001, those words can't be spoken legally in a state institution. The California State Court of Appeals upheld a federal court's ruling that this phrase violates the principle of the separation of church and state.

Monday's ruling was "an answer to my prayers," said Roger Diamond, lawyer for the two men who sued the City of Burbank over the issue. "Religion doesn't belong in City Hall," Diamond declared. "It belongs in the churches, mosques, and synagogues." What's wrong with that picture?

It's still all right to have invocations, the ruling added, but you can't use the name of Jesus Christ in your prayer because it constitutes the establishment of sectarian religion and is an offense to nonbelievers.

The prayer that touched off the controversy was given at a 1999 Burbank City Council meeting and ended with these words: (dare I put them in print, they're so offensive)

"We are grateful, heavenly Father, for all that you have poured out upon us, and we express our gratitude and our love in the name of Jesus Christ, Amen."
(O, the scandal of it.)

Judge Kathryn Todd ruled that, "the expression of gratitude and love 'in the name of Jesus Christ' was an explicit invocation of a particular religious belief. It could be inferred that the council was advancing a religious belief."

It's still OK to use the name of Jesus Christ to swear, anywhere, anytime; as many times as your blasphemous anger rages. But don't you dare use the name of Jesus in love and gratitude at the end, or anywhere in a prayer in any state institution – or your name is Mudd.

It doesn't matter that millions of us are offended when we hear that precious name spoken in anger. This should make me angry, but it doesn't. It makes me hurt and it makes me weep.

But it is testimony of the power in the name of Jesus Christ. The devil hates it; the world is offended by it; but in that name sick people are healed, bound people are freed, and darkness is driven back at its mere mention.

In fact, the awful mess we're in, government-wise, is because Jesus and His gentle ways are not part of any government agency's mode of operation or standards of practice. Indeed, the government is not yet "upon His shoulders."

There are 256 names given in the Bible for the Lord Jesus Christ. That's because He is infinitely beyond what one name can express. Wouldn't it drive our legal system crazy if we used all 256 of them – one at a time?

Sue that!

September 15 – 9/15 **God is Still God!**

He who has an ear, let him hear what the Spirit says to the churches. This phrase appears seven times in the Book of Revelation.

It most certainly says that we must listen to the Spirit, but a word is used here that can be easily overlooked in a casual reading. The word is "churches."

The Holy Spirit doesn't say "the Church" here – that is the great invisible entity composed of all those who have trusted Jesus. That entity exists in the eyes of God worldwide. He says "the churches," the local expressions of the universal church. Not universality, but locality is implied here.

John, Peter, and Paul were the "media superstars" of their day. Their medium was not television or radio, of course, but they were no less influential than the media giants of our day. John, Peter, and Paul were masters of the print medium of their day by their letters – epistles – which they wrote to local fellowships, encouraging them, correcting them, and instructing them in the ways of the Lord.

With the love and respect that these men had in the churches, it would have been easy to turn such high esteem into personal gain. They did not. As a matter of fact they gave themselves to the building up of the community of believers in every city.

When the New Testament speaks of the church, the word "ekklesia" is the Greek word most often used. This word means "a calling out." But it also implies a gathering together. The assembly of the called out ones – that's the church, and the finest expression of it on earth is in the local assembly. What the church does best, it does here – where we live!

Everyday the world turns over upon someone who has just been sitting on top of it. This happens to many in the body of Christ at large. We hear of great controversy and heresy in certain expressions of the church. Righteousness and sound doctrine are being cast aside in favor of that which is "politically correct" but morally corrupt.

This entire world system is corrupt to the core and ripe for God's judgment. It's an increasingly difficult challenge for us to maintain our distinctive identity as God's representatives. But we must be pure in a filthy world.

During the Communist takeover in China some sixty years ago, Gladys Aylward sought to escape war-torn Yang Chen. There was no apparent hope of reaching safety.

A 13 year-old girl tried to comfort her by saying, "Don't forget what you told us about Moses in the wilderness." To which Gladys replied, "Yes, but I'm not Moses." The young girl replied, "But God is still God!"

These are perilous times for the Church – but God is still God!

Gone To Seed *9/16 – September 16*

"A lament of the seventies", is what they called it. Joan Baez sang it with her crystal-clear voice saturated with emotion. "Where have all the flowers gone? Long time passing." The song lamented the lost innocence of the Viet Nam War era. It was a protest song that stirred deep feelings in those caught up in the political storm of those painful years.

Flowers are emotional things. They're things of beauty; they smell good; they're symbols of love. But life in the kingdom of plants isn't only about flowers. It's about seeds. Where have all the flowers gone? They've gone to seed – that's where. And the seed goes into the ground, it hides for a while, and then another generation of geraniums is born.

Recently, it was said in my hearing, "I wonder what ever happened to the renewal of the seventies?" It sounded like, "Where have all the flowers gone?" You see, the war wasn't the only thing happening in the seventies. God was doing something powerful, too. He was renewing His people.

Can I suggest that what we consider renewal is really a flower? It's beautiful; it has about it the fragrance of heaven; it stirs emotions and it promises the long-awaited manifestation of God's glory in our time and place.

But life in the Kingdom of Jesus isn't just about flowers; it's about seeds. Renewal or revival or refreshing – whatever we call it, is but a flower and flowers fade and they go to seed – and seed's the thing.

To lament the fading of the flower is to misunderstand renewal in God's entire created universe. It's about life conceived in a seed and bought to fruit. It's no different in the Kingdom of His dear Son – the Church.

What can abort the life of a new seed-thing in the Church? One thing and only one thing – SIN. Sin in the life of God's people is as deadly as it is in the life of an unbeliever. It deadens my spirit to the presence of God.

Everything God does begins in the hidden place in us, and that's where sin lives, too. And that's where abortion takes place. Only repentance and the blood of Jesus can kill the sin and insure that the seed of life will grow. Then when the blossoming seed becomes evident, we take heart because we know His life is still in us.

The flower is the promise of fruit and not fruit. It's the substance of things hoped for – evidence of things not seen. In fact, the flower must fade for the seed to emerge.

God has set Himself to do mighty things in His people. But when renewal takes longer than we think it should and we wonder, "where have all the flowers gone," take heart, they've gone to seed.

And that's good news

September 17 – 9/17 *This I Believe*

I was struck with the amazing depth of a song the other day as we sang it in worship. It is simple yet very profound. Here are the words:

"I believe in Jesus.
I believe He is the Son of God;
I believe He died and rose again,
I believe He paid for us all.
And I believe He is here now,
Standing in our midst;
Here with the power to heal now,
And the grace to forgive."

This sounds a bit like the Apostle's Creed or the Confessions of Saint Augustine. But it mostly reminds me of a truth in Romans chapter 10:8-10. Here's what it says:

The word is near you, in your mouth and in your heart...that if you confess with your mouth Jesus as Lord, and believe in your heart that God raised Him from the dead, you shall be saved. For with the heart man believes, resulting in righteousness, and with the mouth he confesses, resulting in salvation.

That's precisely what we do every time we sing that song. We make confession that Jesus is Lord, the Son of God, and that He died and rose again from the dead to pay the debt for our sins. That's awesome!

The power of truth uttered in faith is, indeed, awesome. Whether I say it or sing it, truth has power to change everything. Sometimes I find myself singing such songs without recognizing the power of the truth upon my lips and without claiming its impact in my life.

It's not just speaking or singing things; it's believing them and speaking them. When the heart and the mouth match in the confession that Jesus Christ is Lord and risen from the dead – "you shall be saved."

The same principle applies to any thing that God has promised. This is not a name-it-claim-it kind of thing. It's simply believing in my heart what God says, and then confessing what my heart believes.

Further in Romans 10 it says: *Whosoever shall call upon the name of the Lord shall be saved.* The term "saved" is used frequently in Scripture to describe what happens when someone receives Jesus Christ as their Lord and Savior.

A Savior saves people that need to be rescued. It's that's simple.

A Crisis Crisis — *9/18 – September 18*

Here's The American Heritage Dictionary definition of the word, "crisis", "cri-sis, noun; plural, cri-ses; a crucial or decisive point or situation; a turning point; an unstable condition, as in political, social, or economic affairs, involving an impending abrupt change."

I've had those, and so have you. We can handle a crisis pretty well if it's a critical, single point in time. But an observation of our current national and global condition leads me to believe that we are in a crisis of crises.

In other words, there are several areas that appear to be headed for that crisis point all at the same time – at any time. And that's a "crisis crisis."

Let me name a few, any one of which should drive Christians to their knees in fervent prayer. But when these critical areas appear to be headed for a common crisis point, that's reason to prepare for a total collapse of our society and/or the coming of Jesus Christ to planet earth.

A Leadership Crisis: There's no one who can step forward and command the ship of state through the stormy waters ahead. Partisanship and all-out hatred have crippled any hope of bi-partisan agreement on crucial issues.

A Terrorism Crisis: Tensions have escalated to the point that travel abroad is more challenging than at any time in my memory. The threat of biological, chemical, and nuclear weapons give small men big voices. The war in Iraq and the threat of militant Islam makes the next year or so critical in the arena of international terrorism.

A Genetic Crisis: Recent predictions project that the human DNA mystery will be unlocked and cataloged in the near future. Human cloning is just over the horizon, and I have no doubt that such genetic experimentation is going on covertly at this time. The implications of genetic engineering are ominous, leading to the further devaluation of human life.

An Economic Crisis: We've been floating along for some time in the economy department, but the last few years have revealed a fatal flaw: we are now a global economy. The world's economic systems are falling like dominos and we can do nothing to stop it. The crash point is near for many nations.

A Moral Crisis: This is the most troubling of all. While we should take prudent action in the face of all the other crises upon us, the one that concerns me most isn't the economy, or even the terrorists. It's moral depravity that has precipitated these many crises and leaves us powerless to change things.

Is there any good news? *In all these things we overwhelmingly conquer through Him who loved us.* (Romans 8:37-39)

He who overcomes, I will make him a pillar in the temple of My God... and I will write upon him the name of My God, and the name of the city of My God... and My new name. (Revelation 3:12)

I've read many opinions about this passage, and I still don't know what it means. I know a little bit about overcoming, and I desperately want to be one of those kinds of people. But, "a pillar in God's temple", and that business about His name being written upon me, I can only speculate about what it means. One thing I'm sure of – I can hardly wait to find out.

Several years ago I made a decision to sign up for e-mail on the Internet. I had to choose a name that would identify me to the World Wide Web. I decided to choose a name that would say something about who I am and what I stand for. I'm fond of idea of "wonder", so I checked various combinations of that idea, but they were all taken.

I picked one that has deep meaning for me. It's the central theme of the Gospel and the only reason I'm alive today. I choose larryb@resurrection.com as my new name. There's a story behind this.

My personal experience with resurrection is linked to a time in Jerusalem, Israel, on Easter Sunday morning in 1986. I took a cab to The Garden Tomb at 5 a.m. to attend the English Sunrise Service there.

When I arrived, the gate was closed, so I knocked, and the keeper came to open it. I asked about the service and he informed me that it had been canceled due to terrorist threats. I asked if I could go in by myself, and he granted me permission. I was not in a good place emotionally or spiritually. I was going through traumatic change. But that's another story.

There I was, in the Garden Tomb in Jerusalem, alone at sunrise on Easter morning. I should have felt something, but I didn't. My emotions were shot. But while I was in the tomb, at someplace deeper that my emotions, I knew that I was to memorize I Peter 1:3. Three months later, in Fresno, California – I did. It changed my life.

It says: *Blessed be the God and Father of our Lord Jesus Christ, Who according to His great mercy, has caused us to be born again to a living hope through the resurrection of Jesus Christ from the dead.*

My e-mail address is different now since the church has its own identity and web site. Now it's larryb@vccfresno.org, although I still own the resurrection one. The Lord has healed me at the deepest level of my being as a direct result of that moment in Jerusalem and the living hope of the resurrection.

Are You Sincere? **9/20 – September 20**

Paul wrote, in his second letter to the Corinthians, *Just as you excel in everything - see that you also excel in this grace of living - I am not commanding you, but I want to test the sincerity of your love...* (2:7, 8)

There was a love song, which asked the plaintive question "Are you sincere?" Evidently someone wasn't quite sure about the matter. It became a popular song on the charts of the day. It's a good question, and one that seems appropriate in an age where style is more important than substance.

We close our letters with the words "Sincerely Yours," but most of us don't know what it means. The word "sincere" has its roots in the marble quarries of ancient Rome. When quarry workers found a flaw in a piece of marble, they would sometimes attempt to hide the flaw by rubbing wax into the crack.

The cover-up became widespread and many accidents occurred because of faulty marble being used in buildings. The wax would melt and the hidden cracks would reappear. The Roman Senate outlawed the practice of covering a flaw with wax.

They decreed that all marble must be "sine cera," or "without wax." A piece of marble, from that time on, had great value if it was marked with the official stamp of Rome – "sine cera."

Every Christian should wear that stamp. In our culture, it's standard procedure to cover one's flaws with make-up, clothing, and an air of sophistication, so that hardly anyone really knows what or who is underneath the cover-up.

I'm not against make-up, nice clothing or sophistication, but there just ought to be a place where one can be accepted "as is."

Sincerity is a two-way street. Not only must I be sincere – without wax – but there must also be people who allow me to be that way, who will accept me "without wax." Such a place is the Church. "Just as I am, without one plea."

Many have discovered that they really couldn't change until they found someone who would love them whether they changed or not.

God sincerely does! And there is power to change in that!

September 21 – 9/21 *Consistent Change*

As long as the earth remains, there will be springtime and harvest, cold and heat, winter and summer, day and night. (Genesis 8:22)

It's here! The official start of Fall is sometime today. In the old days the season that we call autumn or fall was simply called "harvest" because that was the major preoccupation for everyone. Families were mainly concerned with surviving the winter ahead, so they had to make sure there was enough food to eat, and fiber for clothing to last until Spring.

We don't have the same approach to the Fall season as our ancestors did. We are pretty sure that when the rains and fog and cold of winter come, we will still be able to make it to the supermarket and the mall. We don't have to stock up for the winter, so the change of seasons is mostly an adventure in nostalgia for most of us. And I love it!

Some of my favorite memories are framed in the sights and sounds of autumn: football games, homecoming celebrations, the first frost, and the brilliant colors of the leaves. In Illinois I grew up with the smell of those leaves burning, which I had to rake, by the way. Nowadays you'd have to get special permission from the Environmental Protection Agency to burn your leaves.

The changing of the seasons demonstrates an apparant contradiction: consistent change. How can anything be consistent and change? How can anything change and still be consistent? That is the wonder of God's creation. While there are seasonal changes around the world, there is a consistency to those changes from year to year.

Every year we have four seasons. The hot sun and dry months of summer, the cool nights and gentle rains of autumn, the cold days and fog of winter, the warm sun and drenching rains of spring, all contribute to the abundance we enjoy in the Valley. If any one of those changes didn't occur in a given year the damage would be enormous.

Only God doesn't change. He doesn't have to; He's already perfect. Theologians call that attribute of God immutability – changelessness. When I change, He doesn't. When the world changes politically, He doesn't. When the stock market changes, He doesn't. When the seasons change, He doesn't. *"I am the LORD, I change not!"* says He. (Malachi 3:6)

There's security in the immutability of my Father's love. There are seasons of the soul; times of dryness, times of storm, and times of fruitfulness, times of coldness, but through them all there's the same God.

We don't like change. But, change is the natural order for all living things, and until we're perfect, as God is, we must change.

The largest room in the world is the room for improvement. God loves us too much – to leave us this way!

September Song — *9/22 – September 22*

"It's a long, long time from May to December; but the days grow short when you reach September." These words are from a popular song of some forty years ago – "September Song." I heard a story, that I can't confirm, that said that the words of this song were written to describe the agony of a man who was informed in May that he was probably going to die in December.

By the time September came, he realized that he hadn't much longer to be with the one he loved. The love song closes with the touching words, "these precious days, I'll spend with you."

September has long been one of my favorite months. That special something about September that feels so familiar is the feeling of renewal. From our childhood when we were in school, a new term began every September.

"The years we date from January, but it's in September that we routinely open another file on our lives," wrote a columnist. I always started September with a new pencil, new books, a new lunch box, new gym shoes, and at least some new clothes. The smell of new things dominates my memory of September.

Another thing about September is that it often meant spiritual renewal to me. This was the time of year when revival services were planned, vacations were over, new Sunday School programs were launched, and everything took on increased levels of energy and excitement. By the end of August, summer had become quite boring but it was fun to live my Septembers.

Autumn begins in late September. We usually associate this season with dead leaves and brown things. Springtime has flowers and green things, so it's natural to celebrate life and resurrection in April.

There's something about God's renewal process that's demonstrated even in the dead leaves and brown things of September. The death and release of old things is as much a part of renewal as the birth and emergence of new things.

Psalm 104:24-30 says, *O Lord, how manifold are Your works! In wisdom You have made them all. The earth is full of Your possessions... living things both small and great.... You take away their breath; they die and return to their dust. You send forth Your Spirit, they are created; and You renew the face of the earth.*

I'm aware that this process is going on in me – death and renewal. Some things in me must die that other, better things, may live. And what's more, decaying, rotten smelly, dead things are the best fertilizer for new things. Indeed, Lord, "In wisdom You have made them all!"

"I worship You, my God-of-all-Seasons. You send forth Your Spirit, and I am made new. These precious September days – I'll spend with You!"

And come December, I will praise you then, too.

September 23 – 9/23 *700 Left Handed Men*

Out of all these people seven hundred choice men were left-handed; each one could sling a stone at a hair and not miss. (Judges 20:16)

This chapter describes a great atrocity that had been committed in the area controlled by the tribe of Benjamin, and Israel was preparing to avenge the awful deed. The enemy they faced was formidable with a special force of 700 left-handed sharp shooters from Gibeah.

The term "left-handed" is interesting because it means more than that they were better with their left hand than their right. It literally means, "Shut, as to the right hand." Or to put it another way, the left hand was all they had "left".

The idea is that they were once like all their comrades who went to battle, holding a shield with their left hand and a sword with their right hand. This meant that the right hand was exposed to attack. The right hand and arm were often injured, making it impossible to hold a weapon with that hand.

So, rather than give up, or retire, or spend their life in self-pity, they practiced throwing rocks with a sling, until they became so skilled with their left hand, that they could sling a stone at a hair and not miss.

These guys were enemies of the Lord's people, but I admire their dedication. When they couldn't get the job done one way they'd get it done another way. Such a tactic made them a serious threat and awarded them special mention in the Scriptures.

These 700 left-handed men of Gibeah both shame me and inspire me with their dedication. This is the kind of ingenuity to which God is calling us. One way or another, we must get it done!

Can we be less committed to victory than the enemy? A battle is raging for the souls of men, women, and children. The enemy is committed to use any means he can to steal, kill and destroy. If we succeed against him on one front he devises some other scheme for his evil work. He is relentless.

We must not retreat from the battlefield just because we are tired, or sick, or wounded, or we've run out of ideas. A relentless onslaught from the enemy must be met by an even more relentless, innovative, well-conceived offensive by the people of God.

We must teach our kids the ways of God's kingdom. The Word of God, the Presence of the Holy Spirit, and the love of their family in Christ must protect them from within their own hearts and minds. They won't survive otherwise.

If we can't get the job done one way, we'll do it another way – but we'll get it done in His Name! Faithfulness is long obedience in the same direction.

That will get it done – big time!

A Beautiful Mind — *9/24 – September 24*

Finally, brethren, whatever is true, whatever is honorable, whatever is right, whatever is pure, whatever is lovely, whatever is of good repute, if there is any excellence and if anything worthy of praise, let your mind dwell on these things. (Philippians 4:8)

Finding something honorable, something excellent, something lovely to think about isn't all that difficult. It's a mind-set.

Proverbs 23:7 says, *As a man thinks in his heart–so is he.* That means to me that if I want to be honorable, of good repute, lovely, excellent, and worthy of any honor at all, I must begin with letting my mind dwell on these things.

Before we dismiss this concept as weird new age type stuff, which is just so much psychobabble to me, let's not forget that this is the Holy Spirit speaking here. This is not psychobabble – it is Spirit Truth.

What you think about does make a difference. *Thou wilt keep him in perfect peace whose mind is stayed on Thee, because he trusts in Thee,* God said in Isaiah 26:3

One cannot seek beauty for very long without ending up in the Presence of God. David knew this about the Lord God – He is beautiful. From Psalm 27:4:

One thing I have asked from the Lord, that I shall seek: that I may dwell in the house of the Lord All the days of my life, to behold the beauty of the Lord, and to meditate in His temple.

I've been meditating today on something beautiful and the subject of my musings warms my heart. I learned this morning that a dear friend went to be with Jesus today. He made several trips taking the Gospel to Kashmir, a beautiful country in the Himalayas. As God sees things, he has beautiful feet.

How lovely on the mountains are the feet of him who brings good news, who announces peace, and brings good news of happiness, who announces salvation, saying, "Our God reigns!" (Isaiah 52:7)

The LORD is the portion of my inheritance and my cup; Thou dost support my lot. The lines have fallen to me in pleasant places; indeed, my heritage is beautiful to me. (Psalm 16:5, 6)

Something Beautiful? – Think about it!

September 25 – 9/25 *The Right Hand of Fellowship*

Paul said, in Galatians 2:9, *When James, Cephas, and John perceived the grace that had been given to me, they gave me and Barnabas the right hand of fellowship.*

This simple action carried with it a wealth of meaning then, and still does to this day. It meant that the hostility between Paul and the elders in Jerusalem was over. It was a new beginning for their relationship.

The handshake is an ancient sign of peace. The extended, weaponless right hand said, "I will not harm you, I gladly take your hand, heedless of any danger, for I trust you. I give my strongest defense – my right hand – to you."

This is essentially what we do when we greet each other. We've checked our weapons at the door, so to speak. My hand is extended without threat to you. It is, indeed, a hand of fellowship.

God has hands, too. A little girl came home from Sunday School one day and told her mother what she had learned about God. She said, "Mommy, did you know that God created everything with His left hand."

Her Mom said, "Where did you ever hear a thing like that?" Her little girl responded, "He must have, Mommy, because teacher said that Jesus is sitting on His right hand!"

The Bible encourages other uses for our hands. For instance, I Thessalonians 4:11 says, *and make it your ambition to lead a quiet life and attend to your own business and work with your hands...*

The early church knew yet another use for their hands. In Mark 16:18 Jesus said, *they shall lay hands on the sick and they shall recover.* They acted on the command of Jesus, and thousands then and millions since have been healed by the touch of a hand extended in His name.

Hands that labor faithfully through the week, now reach out to heal in His Name. Hands reaching to heal are lifted in praise to His Name. *Therefore I want the men in every place to pray, lifting up holy hands, without wrath and dissension.* (I Timothy 2:8)

Laboring hands, lifted hands, and healing hands, are the same hands that we extend to one another in love. As our hands touch, let us by this act, say, "I am free of any weapon to harm you, I trust you."

As I reach out to you in Jesus' Name, be healed!

We lift up hands, made holy by His blood, and we praise Him for the marvelous gift of our hands.

A Sure Thing — *9/26 – September 26*

I rode the Boomerang at Knott's Berry Farm on vacation. It's a roller-coaster-like ride that takes you through a series of loops and inclines at break-neck speed. Then it takes you through the same course just as fast – backwards.

I debated with my wife about my choice to take the plunge, so to speak. She was concerned for the risk "at my age." But I won. I told her I was doing research for this article. She bought it. I stood in line with kids the age of my grandchildren. I hung on for dear life, but I enjoyed it.

I play a little game with myself when I face risk. I think of all the people who have done what I'm about to do, and factor in any fatalities I know about. I figured the risk was in the millions to one.

We all do something like that. We assume some risk, but we're willing to do so hoping that the unlikely thing will not happen to us. On the other hand, we do other things, like playing the lottery or other forms of gambling, with astronomical risks hoping that an extremely unlikely thing will happen to us.

Millions of people buy lottery tickets, even though they are 3 times more likely to be struck by lightning than to strike it rich. When it comes to taking risks, most of us are curiously – very irrational.

Many people fear dying in a plane crash, yet the odds against that are over 100,000 to 1. Statistically, a person is more likely to be kicked to death by a donkey than to die in a plane crash. Fear of being murdered is also extremely high, yet a person is eight times more likely to die while playing a sport than to be murdered.

We spend money on things with extremely improbable odds, and completely ignore the certainty of things that concern our health and well-being. For instance, smoking causes 1 of every 6 preventable deaths in the U.S.

The point is that we spend our time and resources, not to mention emotional energy in the form of fear, on things that are only remotely possible, yet we're reluctant to put our full weight upon the Word of the Living God.

Consider this: *Bring all the tithes into the storehouse; if you do, I will open the windows of heaven for you and pour out a blessing so great you won't have room enough to take it in! Try it! Let Me prove it to you, says the Lord.* (Malachi 3:10)

To many of us, obeying this command seems like something of a risk. Call it that if you like, but to my mind, it's no risk at all to put my hand in His and let Him take me where He will.

It's no risk to surrender the security of sameness for the exciting adventure of active faith. His Word is a sure thing. The greatest risk of all to my life and health is in not trusting Him.

September 27 – 9/27 *So What!*

I run the risk of being misunderstood by what I am about to write, but it's important that I take the risk. I became aware recently that a fruitful ministry is under attack by the forces of darkness. A group of witches have taken exception to some aggressive moves by this ministry and have met in counsel with darkness to frustrate the efforts of these dedicated servants of the Lord.

Isaiah 54:17 says, *No weapon that is formed against you shall prosper; and every tongue that accuses you in judgment you will condemn. This is the heritage of the servants of the Lord, and their vindication is from Me, says the Lord.*

While I was praying for this matter, the Lord spoke to my heart. I wasn't sure it was the Lord because it sounded out of character for Him. What I heard was, "So what!" I had just heard of an overt attack upon physical bodies and relationships of people who are serving on the front line of the battle against sin in our community. To hear the report was enough to make your skin crawl.

Then I read what God said about the attempts of the enemy to come against His people. And the answer I heard was kind of an "in your face, devil", – So what! It didn't matter which witches were witching, how many covens were convening, or how many demons were demonstrating – God still said, "no weapon that is formed against you shall prosper!"

I flipped to Ephesians 6:16 which says that with the shield of faith we can, "extinguish all the flaming missiles of the evil one." I wondered what it must be like to raise my faith shield and see the flashy, flaming missiles of the devil just fizzle out like they had plunged into a barrel of water. They threatened so much havoc as they approached but they sputtered to an ignominious end when faith rose to meet them head-on.

We are soldiers at war with darkness and evil, wherever it looms its ugly head. While a soldier must have a healthy respect for the firepower of the enemy, he can also have an "in your face" contempt, dare I say, a holy arrogance, toward the enemy in light of the overwhelming power at his disposal.

Jesus said, *I give you power over all the power of the enemy and nothing shall by any means hurt you.* (Luke 10:19) To believe that is to possess the power it promises. To disbelieve it is to be a soldier disarmed in the face of his enemy.

Do not be overcome by evil, but overcome evil with good. (Romans 12:21)

Character Counts *9/28 – September 28*

"What specifically will determine who you'll vote for?" A reporter of a local newspaper posed this question to me recently. I told him that character is the determining factor for me. Here are some thoughts on character.

A member of the President's cabinet was introduced to a group recently by his grandson with these words; "My grandfather is a great public serpent." The difference between a public servant and a public serpent is a matter of character. The essential quality, the moral strength – the character – of a man or a woman who aspires to public office should be the deciding factor for us when we enter the voting booth.

Everybody has one, a character, that is, but not every one's character qualifies him for leadership in these troubled times. One's choices are determined by the quality of one's character – for good or bad.

There is entirely too much poll-taking these days. The fragile nature of public opinion is not a sure compass by which to guide the ship of state. True, ours is a government of, by, and for the people but the people are not always given truth enough to make snap decisions in the presence of a poll taker.

Winston Churchill said, "The nation will find it very hard to look up to leaders who keep their ears to the ground." Leaders must lead, and the one who leads the orchestra must turn his back to the crowd.

I want a man who tells the truth when it may not be in his best interest to do so. I want a man who keeps his word to his wife and children. I want a man who says, not, "read my lips," but "read my heart," and whose heart makes good, clear, interesting reading.

Many Christians believe that somehow God will work it all out and the right person will be elected. How does He do that? Does He cause the computers to turn out numbers different than the actual count? Perhaps He multiplies the good votes like Jesus multiplied the loaves and fishes. "It's a miracle. The right man won and I didn't even have to vote!" How absurd! God is not a cheat – He does not stuff ballot boxes.

He rules in an election the same was He does every day – by good people making good choices – prayerful choices, and trusting Him to make their choices right. If our founding fathers were inspired by the Heavenly Father, as I believe they were, then our form of government has the distinctive touch of God's holy purpose upon it.

The voting booth and not the White House or the Congress, then, is the central core of the Republic. That flimsy booth becomes a kind of sanctuary in which I meet and participate with the God of the universe in His righteous rule in the affairs of men.

The power of the Holy Spirit promised in the first chapter of Acts is not given that the Christian may enjoy an unusual religious experience. It is given that we may take the gospel to the world.

A missionary, lost at sea, was by chance washed up out of the sea on the edge of a remote native village. Half dead from starvation, exposure and seawater, he was found by the people of the village and was nursed back to full health. He lived among these people for twenty years.

During the whole of that time he sang no songs. He preached no sermons. He recited no Scripture. But rather, when people were sick, he attended them, sitting long into the night. When people were hungry, he – without exception – gave them food.

After twenty years of this, missionaries came to the village and began talking to the people about a man called Jesus. After hearing of Jesus, the natives insisted that this man, Jesus, had lived among them for the past 20 years. "Come, we will introduce you to the man about whom you have been speaking." There, in his hut, they found the long-lost fellow missionary who they thought was dead.

It will be the Word in flesh, walking the streets of Amsterdam and Athens, Katmandu and Kinshasa, Ulan Bator and Ulster, Frankfurt and Fresno that will offer hope to millions who live in darkness. I'm not talking about preaching on the streets or passing out tracts, or any of the snappy things that come to mind when we think of witnessing. I'm talking about living the radiant life of the risen Lord under the tremendous pressure of life in any culture, anywhere. It's not the gospel in black and white, but the gospel in flesh and blood that will make the difference.

A ship in harbor is safe, but that is not what ships are for. We want to be safe and happy, but safe and happy are not what we're for.

Go into all the world and preach the Gospel to every creature. (Mark 16:15)

It Will Come *9/30 – September 30*

A significant feast marks the beginning of a new year of the Hebrew calendar. It's a two-day celebration called Rosh Hashana. It's been celebrated around the world for centuries and is the beginning of "Ten Days of Awe," ending with Yom Kippur, The Day of Atonement. The very first event in Rosh Hashana is The Feast of Trumpets when the priest blows the shofar, the ram's horn, to open the New Year.

Some have speculated that it will be at the time of the Feast of Trumpets that Jesus Christ will return to the earth. We're not given such detailed information in the Scriptures, but it seems that God does expect us to know the general if not the specific time of His coming.

I Thessalonians 5:1, 4 says, *Now as to the times and the seasons, brethren, you have no need of anything to be written to you... For you, brethren, are not in darkness that the day should overtake you as a thief.*

All my life I've heard that Jesus is coming soon. For much of that time I've had a deep personal love for Jesus and a longing to see Him, Whom my faith has embraced. But He hasn't come yet. Sometimes I feel like those described in II Peter 3:4 who said, *Where is the promise of His coming? For, all continues just as it was from the creation.*

Peter answers that honest question a few verses later by saying, *The Lord is not slow about His promise, but is patient toward you, not wishing for any to perish but for all to come to repentance. But the day of the Lord will come...* (II Peter 3:9)

"The day of the Lord will come!" The trumpet will sound, and we will see Jesus! Hallelujah! It's very important to our wholeness as Christians that we look forward to the Lord's return. The bride is described in the Song of Solomon 6:10 KJV, as "looking forth to the morning." That's a vital quality.

It's possible to get caught up with getting "caught up," so to speak, instead of being caught up – enraptured with Jesus, Who lives in us now. As I walk with Him now, I am assured of my place in His kingdom now and forever.

October 1 – 10/1 *Keep Swinging*

The baseball season is winding down for this year. The playoffs are just around the corner and the World Series isn't far behind.

I've been a baseball fan nearly all of my life. My grandfather and my mother are responsible for this strange quirk in my nature. They were both avid baseball fans.

I recently came upon a list of baseball's lifetime achievement statistics. The list had some rather impressive names on it. At the top of the list was Reggie Jackson, followed by Willie Stargell. Also on the list, near the top, were Jose Canseco, Tony Perez, Mickey Mantle, Sammy Sosa, and Willie Mays.

Do you know what lifetime achievement this list represented? It was for the most strikeouts. Can you believe it? Reggie Jackson, Mickey Mantle, Willie Mays. These three men combined struck out almost 6,000 times.

One ballplayer set the major league record in his era for strikeouts with 1,316. The same guy set a record for five consecutive strikeouts in a World Series game. The holder of both records was Babe Ruth.

The greatness of these men is in the fact that they kept stepping up to the plate. Even when the strikeouts were piling up, even when their slumps extended game after game, even when their failure caused their team to lose, even when disgruntled fans called them overpaid bums – they kept swinging.

Failure, to one degree or another, is the rule – not the exception. "No one bats 1.000." In fact, the greatest hitters in the game fail two-thirds of the time. I've known failure, but I've learned that one can fail without being a failure. Failure is an event, even a series of events, but failure is never a person.

You may have a string of strikeouts behind you, and you may feel as though you're on the verge of setting the world's record for failure. Keep stepping up to the plate. No matter how many times you miss, if you keep swinging – you will eventually make contact.

Solomon the Wise wrote these words: *Though a righteous man falls seven times, he rises again, but the wicked are brought down by calamity.* (Proverbs 24:16)

Bring It On! **_10/2 – October 2_**

For I can do everything through Him who gives me strength. (Philippians 4:13)

Yesterday's topic was baseball and the fact that even the best players fail most of the time. That doesn't compute in our success-oriented world. But often, I must fail before I succeed.

Buckminster Fuller said, "All of my advances were made by mistakes. You uncover what is, when you get rid of what isn't."

Thomas Edison failed over 900 times in his attempt to make a light bulb. When asked if he was discouraged by these failures, he said, "Certainly not! I now know 900 ways not to make a light bulb."

Many of us have entered that phase of our lives where we feel that the game is no longer fun for us. "Let the younger 'players' step up to the plate. It's their game to win or lose. Our playing days are over." Nonsense!

This one of the hazards of growing older, but there's room on the field of play for some veterans who may know a thing or two about the game of life. To that I say, "Bring it on!" By the grace and power of God, it's never too late to be what you might have been. Instead of a "has-been," you're a "will-be."

To a world that values youth and scorns the aging process, I say – "bring it on!" In the face of new technology that daily challenges my mind – "bring it on." With the prospect of failing health and diminished strength – "bring it on!" And to the devil and all the hoards of hell that steal, kill, and destroy, in Jesus' ageless, almighty name I say – "bring it on!"

For I can – even now – do everything He asks me to do, through Him Who gives me strength. (Philippians 4:13)

Life has been seriously disrupted lately. I've experienced delays, detours, and major distractions. What's the cause of this havoc? Cal-Trans is building a highway that cuts across my twice-daily access between my office and home.

I'm only kidding about the seriousness of this situation. As a matter of fact, I've watched with great fascination the process of making a road where there was none before. It's a major project. It will be great when it's finished. Those of us who live in Southeast Fresno will have faster access to Northeast Fresno and all points in between. It is – after all is said and done – about access.

Nearly every day, while I'm waiting for trucks and bulldozers at the construction site, I think about a passage of Scripture in Isaiah 40:3-5 that talks about making a highway for God. Here's what it says:

Clear the way for the LORD in the wilderness; make smooth in the desert a highway for our God. Let every valley be lifted up, and every mountain and hill be made low; and let the rough ground become a plain, and the rugged terrain a broad valley; then the glory of the LORD will be revealed, and all flesh will see it together.

I have a new appreciation for the major project that highway is. Like the one that Cal Trans is building, the highway for God's full access into my life is no instant miracle.

Our society, unlike any in history, has grown accustomed to instant answers. Microwaves, cell phones, and computers have conditioned us to expect solutions to our problems and answers to our prayers in microseconds, not months or years. Sitcoms can solve life's most troubling issues in 30 minutes, or at the most, an hour.

It takes time to build a highway where none was before. There are some things that must change for a new road to be built. Lots of dirt, rocks, and old pathways must be removed. Delays, detours, and disruptions are inevitable.

When Isaiah talked about moving mountains, lifting valleys, and smoothing rough places to build a highway for God, with the tools they had in his day, he must have known it would take a while. Then road building took lifetimes – not merely years.

Is it too much of a stretch to say that making a way in the wilderness of our lives for the glory of God to be fully realized, takes time, and that means delays and detours and major disruption of things as they are. It means removing lots of dirt. But it is – after all is said and done – about access.

It's about the access God desires into every area of our lives. It's also about our access to His glory, "then the glory of the LORD will be revealed." We get to see His glory!

To see His glory – even if it takes a lifetime – is worth it!

"You've got to face the music!" This little maxim, which most of us have heard all our lives, makes absolutely no sense at all... unless you know the story behind it. It's from something that happened many years ago in China.

Once there was a man who was chosen to play the flute in the emperor's royal orchestra. The pay and the privileges were excellent, so the man hid the fact that he couldn't play the flute. He had never seen the instrument before.

Instead of confessing his lack of skill he spent many months going through the motions. Whenever the orchestra performed, he would hold the flute to his lips pretending to play. But he never dared blow, even softly, into the instrument lest he reveal himself as a fraud.

One day the emperor announced that there would be a special banquet and told the orchestra that to demonstrate each musician's virtuosity, each one would be required to play a solo for the dignitaries. The fake flutist flew into frenzy.

For a few weeks he secretly took lessons from a professional, but to no avail. He had no musical ear and couldn't read a note of music. A few days before the banquet, he pretended to be ill. The emperor sent his personal physician, who pronounced him perfectly well, and the emperor was relieved.

All was set for the banquet. But on the morning of the great event the emperor was dismayed, for the flute player was found dead on the floor of his home. He had taken poison. He just couldn't face the music.

Except for the tragic conclusion, something like that happens when we gather for worship. Each of us is asked, in a sense, to stand before the King and offer our song of worship. It's true that as we sing together we form a symphony of praise to the Lord, but we're also performing a solo for His ears alone.

The acceptance of our worship has nothing to do with the quality of our singing voice and absolutely everything to do with the condition of our heart. If my heart is in tune with His, my worship will be music to the ears of my King. If not, I will someday have to "face the music."

Martin Luther said, "I wish to see all arts, principally music, in the service of Him Who gave and created them. Music is a fair and glorious gift of God. Music makes people kinder, gentler, more peaceful and reasonable. I am strongly persuaded that, after theology, music is the only art capable of affording peace and joy in the heart."

Sing to the Lord, for He has done excellent things! (Isaiah 12:5)

There's been lots of talk about Attention Deficit Disorder, ADD. Apparently it's a serious matter that affects millions. I heard of another one that's not a disease that can be treated with drugs, but is a commentary on the moral and social climate of our day. It's called Integrity Deficit Disorder.

What are some of the symptoms of this condition (IDD)? A person with this disorder knows what's right but doesn't do what's right. He or she makes a promise or commitment, and then fails to keep it. So when you meet a person with IDD you're never quite sure if you can trust that person.

A second symptom: people who have IDD live from the outside in rather than from the inside out. They let feelings and emotions govern their behavior more than doing what's right, regardless of their feelings of the moment.

To put it another way, people with Integrity Deficit Disorder are reactive rather than proactive. They base their decisions and actions on what's going on around them. If someone is rude to them, they're rude in return. If someone is nice, they're nice, too.

In addition, the physical environment often affects reactive people. If the weather is good, they feel good. If it isn't, it affects their attitude and their performance. Worse still, reactive people blame whatever happens to them on someone or something outside of themselves. It's always the fault of someone or something else. This is Integrity Deficit Disorder.

On the other hand, people with no integrity deficit carry their own weather with them. Integrity is about behaving the way you promised, even though the mood or the environment has changed. Integrity protects you from your own changing moods, desires and feelings. It even protects you from the changing moods of other people.

According to the dictionary, integrity is "the state of being whole or entire." The root of the word "integrity" is "integer," a whole number.

The United States Navy uses this word to describe the reliability of its submarines. They speak of the integrity of a vessel. That is, are there flaws in the structure of the vessel that will cause failure under the pressure of deep-sea dives; is it whole?

As followers of Jesus Christ we are called to a life of integrity under pressure. We live in a world of great social and moral pressure. But greater than that, there is an internal – eternal Presence that rules our lives.

Jesus Christ is Lord and we need not be crushed any external force. Because – *Greater is He that is in you than he that is in the world.* (I John 4:4)

The Power of Choice *10/6 – October 6*

So much can come from our simple choices. I recently read of a very real example of the impact that choices make on our future.

This is a story of two close friends who were teammates on a football team, friends who shared a promising future in professional sports and also looked forward to continued success in their collegiate career.

These two friends made separate choices one November night. One chose to stay at home while the other decided to go hunting with two other friends. But hunting wasn't all that was on the list of activities. These three decided to drink into the early morning hours, and then they also decided to go driving.

The center of the southern university football team was the friend that chose to drink and drive. He lost control of his truck and a horrible accident occurred. He and the other two friends were thrown from the truck. Only the driver survived. The other two, also legally drunk, lay dead on the ground.

He went before a judge to face the inevitable consequences of his actions. He was remorseful. He wished it had never happened, but it did, all because of his choice. He plead guilty to two counts of manslaughter, and was sentenced to ten years in jail. His life was changed forever because of the impact of his choice that November night.

The other teammate decided not to join his friends that weekend. And in 1999 he was picked as the number one draft pick in the National Football League. He signed a seven-year contract for a reported 48 million dollars, including a 12.5 million dollar signing bonus with an NFL team. His life was also changed forever by his choice that November night.

The future for these two teammates was determined and changed forever because of their simple choices. So much can come from our choices. When we choose the beginning of a road, we also choose the place to which it leads.

Our values are not best expressed in words; they're best expressed in the choices we make. In the long run, we shape our lives and ourselves by our choices. The process never ends until we die.

At a crossroad in the wilderness, Joshua issued an ultimatum to Israel: *...choose for yourselves this day whom you will serve, whether the gods your forefathers served... or the gods of the Amorites, in whose land you are living. But as for me and my household, we will serve the Lord.* (Joshua 24:15)

Joshua draws a line in the sand and demands a choice as to the god they will serve. The god-options abound in the world around us. Each god demands our allegiance; the god we choose is the god we will serve.

Only the Lord God – Who loves us and gives us the awesome power of choice – is worthy to be served, and worshiped, and adored.

October 7 – 10/7 *Fear and Terror*

He who dwells in the shelter of the Most High will abide in the shadow of the Almighty. I will say to the LORD, "My refuge and my fortress, my God, in whom I trust!" (Psalm 91:1, 2)

Planet earth is not the only one in the solar system to have a moon. Jupiter has at least sixteen, and five others have at least one.

Mars has two moons that are in constant orbit around this planet, which is most like earth in many ways. The two moons of Mars are named Phobos and Deimos – Greek words for fear and terror.

These massive celestial bodies exert a strong influence upon the surface of the cold, dry planet of Mars, much as our own moon's effect upon the tides of our oceans. Phobos and Deimos actually alter the motion of the planet around which they move.

Since 9/11/2001, fear and terror have been "in orbit" over our nation. The tides generated by terrorism are at an all-time high. Our mobility is being affected and many of us live in a state of constant anxiety. What are we to do about it? More importantly, what is God doing about it? And where was He when all of this horror was being planned and executed?

I don't have answers for these questions and I never will, but my faith and knowledge of the God Whom I love and serve tells me that He was involved, just as He is deeply involved in our national grief. He is good!

I only know that, for me, it's vital that I abide in the shadow of the Almighty. When I live there the rest of the Psalm comes alive for me.

You will not be afraid of the terror by night, or of the arrow that flies by day; of the pestilence that stalks in darkness, or of the destruction that lays waste at noon. (Psalm 91:5, 6)

Nightly terror; daily arrows; stalking pestilence, and high-noon destruction – that sounds like terrorism to me. God says I needn't fear any of it, if I live in His shadow. From that place of intimacy I can listen for His voice and hear Him say, "Go this way, or that way."

When fear and terror reign, it's imperative that I "stay tuned" – for further instructions from The Almighty.

Many preachers and teachers are prone these days to talk about contemporary subjects and psychological issues, and often forsake the message of the Bible.

"The Bible says..." That phrase, repeated many thousands of times in Billy Graham's 60+ years of preaching, is the key to everything we have witnessed in his amazing, anointed, always up-to-date, fruitful ministry.

When the missionary, Dr. David Livingstone, started his trek across Africa in 1852, he had 73 books in 3 packs, weighing 180 pounds. After the party had gone 300 miles, Livingstone was obliged to throw away some books because of the fatigue of those carrying his baggage. As he continued on his journey his library grew less and less, until he had but one book left – his Bible.

As we move through the hazards and jungles of the 21st century, we might well cast aside all other wisdom and cling tenaciously to God's Word for wisdom and power.

Many years ago in a Moscow theater, matinee idol Alexander Rostovzev was playing the role of Jesus in a sacrilegious play entitled "Christ in a Tuxedo." He was to read two verses from the Sermon on the Mount, remove his gown, and cry out, "Give me my tuxedo and top hat!"

But as he read, "Blessed are the poor in spirit, for theirs is the kingdom of heaven. Blessed are they that mourn, for they shall be comforted," he began to tremble. Instead of following the script, he kept reading from Matthew 5, ignoring the calls, and foot stamping of his fellow actors.

Finally, recalling a verse he had learned as a child in a Russian Orthodox Church, he cried, "Lord, remember me when You come into Your kingdom!" Before the curtain could be lowered, Rostovzev had trusted Jesus Christ as his personal Savior.

Such is the power of the Word of God.

God said it. I believe it – that settles it for me. The Bible Says...

October 9 – 10/9 *A Strange Language*

The heavens declare the glory of God; the skies proclaim the work of his hands... There is no language where their voice is not heard. (Psalm 19:1, 2)

I've decided to write to you today in English. The reason I decided to do that is that it's the only language I know. I often wish I had learned another one but this one will have to do for now. Besides, it's very difficult to write in a spiritual language.

Did you know that English is the youngest language in the world? It's less than 500 years old, yet it's spoken by more people that any other language. It also contains more words than any other language.

Our language has grown from 70,000 words in 1828 to more than 600,000 today. English contains more separate sounds – 46 different ones – than any other tongue. To express all those sounds and all those words we have an alphabet of just 26 letters.

Our language consists of words and phrases derived from many other languages. English is: 35% French, 25% German, 16% Latin, and 14% Greek. Whole words from other languages make up about 10% of our "native tongue" as we speak it today.

We have the most incredible spelling in the world, and the way we pronounce our words is a nightmare for those who are trying to learn to speak and write in English.

Below are some examples of why English is very hard to learn. You'll have to read carefully to get the gist of it, even if English is your only language. Just imagine how hard it is for our Hispanic and Asian friends.

"The bandage was wound around the wound."
"The farm was used to produce produce."
"We must polish the Polish furniture."
"He could lead if he would get the lead out."
"The soldier decided to desert his dessert in the desert."
"There's no time like the present, so it's a good time to present the present."

And so it goes... And God uses the English language, as crazy as it is, and all others languages as well, to convey His marvelous grace to the world.

Here is the amazing scene at the end of days when Jesus Christ, the Lamb of God, appears: *And they sang a new song: "You are worthy to take the scroll and to open its seals, because you were slain, and with your blood you purchased men for God from every tribe and language and people and nation."* (Revelation 5:9)

There will be no language barriers then. What a day that will be. Hallelujah!

Knowing Him — *10/10 – October 10*

I count all things to be loss in view of the surpassing value of knowing Christ Jesus my Lord, for whom I have suffered the loss of all things, and count them but rubbish in order that I may gain Christ... that I may know Him, and the power of His resurrection and the fellowship of His sufferings, being conformed to His death; (Philippians 3:8, 10)

William Saroyan told of an old man that sat in his garden playing the cello. All day long, from morning to night, he played the same note. Hour after hour, he played the same single note.

Finally, his wife could stand it no longer; timidly she said that other cello players moved their fingers up and down the strings playing various notes. "I might have expected that from you," he replied, "Of course others play different notes. They are trying to find the right place, but I have found it!"

The Apostle Paul had reduced the expenditure of his energies to one thing: the prize! What was the prize? It may get lost in all the words of this scripture but it's very clear for all to hear and emulate in verse 10 of the third chapter – "That I may know Him!"

That's the prize; that's the one note worth playing; that's what Paul found that others were searching for.

There's stability in that. "A double-minded man is unstable in all his ways," says the Lord. In the light of that truth then, a this-one-thing man would be stable in all his ways. There's power in that.

Like the laser beam that focuses light waves along a narrow path and cuts through steel, a this-one-thing focus cuts through the darkness of hell. There's victory in that.

What if the "one thing" for each of us was to know Him? What a difference it would make when we worship together or even when we struggle with life's challenges together. Our lives would be a whole lot simpler if we could reduce all of our hours and days, months and years, joys and sorrows, achievements and failures, to this one thing – knowing Him.

If all things the things that happen to us, good and bad, were seen in the light of how each thing helps us know Him more, we could grow a whole lot more.

"That I may know Him" – He is one-note worthy.

George Matheson was a Scottish minister in the year 1890. George was blind but had an amazing gift of expressing himself in the English language. His sermons and poems are legendary.

George was engaged to be married to the love of his life – a beautiful Scottish lass. When the day of the wedding came she told him that she could not spend the rest of her life with a blind man; so she left him at the altar.

Shortly after this painful rejection George Matheson wrote a hymn, "out of the most severe mental suffering," he said. That hymn is "O, Love That Will Not Let Me Go." It took him only five minutes to write it.

"O, love that will not let me go, I rest my weary soul in Thee;
I give Thee back the life I owe, that in Thine ocean depths its flow
May richer, fuller be."

George Matheson knew that his life belonged to God and that even in his deepest pain the ocean depth of God's unfailing love was a safe refuge. In his journal he wrote these words some time later:

"My God, I have never thanked Thee for my thorns. I have thanked Thee for my roses, but not once for my thorns. I have looked forward to a world where I shall be rewarded for my cross, but I have never thought of my cross as itself a present glory.

"Teach me the glory of my cross. Teach me the value of my thorns. Show me that I have climbed with Thee to Golgotha by the pathway of pain. Show me that my tears have made a rainbow in the brightness of Your glory."

A love that will not let me go… that's the love of God for His people.

The LORD declares, I will be the God of all the families of Israel, and they shall be My people... I have loved you with an everlasting love; therefore I have drawn you with lovingkindness. (Jeremiah 31:1, 3)

6 Billion Souls *10/12 – October 12*

October 12, 1999, the United Nations declared that the world population had reached the astounding level of 6,000,000,000. That's 6 billion, for those of us who are numerically challenged.

Actually, this event probably occurred on July 18th, at about 5:24pm Pacific Daylight Time. (I wonder how they know that. Were they watching the birth of that new baby?)

They decided to mark October 12 as the day of "celebration." To many people this isn't a thing to celebrate; it's sign of impending doom because of the dangers of over-population. The jury is still out on that particular matter.

To me, this revelation means that there are a whole lot more people who need Jesus, Who died for the sins of all the people on the earth.

Of the 6,000,000,000 people on planet earth, half of them – 3,000,000,000 – live in what is called the 10/40 Window. The 10/40 Window refers to degrees of latitude from 10° to 40° north of the equator.

The geographic area of the 10/40 Window has been the target of prayer for several years. Most of the world's Muslims live here, and most of the world's poverty is here, too. Terrorism is also rampant in this part of our world.

Less than 5% of the 6,000,000,000 live in the United States; 25% of the total live in China, 17% live in India, and 2% live in Japan.

Each one of the 6,000,000,000 of them have an eternal soul and need to hear the Good News that God loves them – they need Jesus. All of them!

Jesus said an amazing thing in light of how many people are on the earth today. He said, *" Indeed, the very hairs of your head are all numbered. Do not fear; you are of more value than many sparrows.* (Luke 12:7) That's a lot of hair!

Apparently, big numbers are no problem for the God of the universe, Who numbers the stars and call them all by name. Check out Isaiah 40:26:

Lift up your eyes on high and see who has created these stars, the One who leads forth their host by number, He calls them all by name; because of the greatness of His might and the strength of His power not one of them is missing.

I need a God Who isn't intimidated by huge quantities. I can trust the One that Job was talking about in Job 5:8, 9. In the middle of his trouble, Job said this, *But as for me, I would seek God, and to God I would commit my cause, Who does great things and unsearchable, marvelous things without number!*

A new television season is upon us. I was shocked by the title of the latest "reality" show that aired just last night. It's called, "Wife Swap" or something like that. I didn't watch it, but I gather from the promos, that it's about families that switch wives and mothers for a time. I haven't seen it so I can't make a judgment on the content of it. But the idea of wife swapping has a less than honorable connotation.

Such things were unthinkable, or at least unmentionable in public, in the past. Francis Schaeffer said in his book, *How Shall We Then Live:* "One generation's unthinkable, becomes the next generation's thinkable, and the next generation's do-able."

I've lived long enough to see the truth of that statement. The process has accelerated to the extent that it doesn't even take a generation, but a season of television and movies to see this escalation.

Studies by the Parent's Television Council report that sex, profanity, violence, and other kinds of immorality have invaded what was supposed to be a safe haven for children's viewing – the family hour, between 8:00pm and 9:00pm.

"The Fall-en TV Season" is not an original phrase. I got it from the September 18, issue of World Magazine, back in 1999.

In a survey of the new TV fare it was reported then, that two-thirds of programs during the family hour contain explicit sexual references. The rating system, designed to give parents some clue about content, was inconsistent and meaningless.

Profanity is up 58%. Language once regarded taboo is now common in the TV world. Producers of the new fall programs pride themselves in "pushing the envelope." Shows that rely on titillation rather than creativity will ratchet up the sleaze.

There's clearly a spirit, and evil one, behind the degradation of this medium. It defies logic to see the recent Emmy Awards, where the television industry tells us what it thinks is quality fare. The awards consistently go to shows with the most profanity, violence, and sexual innuendo, while family friendly shows are completely ignored.

As with most of the moral issues facing us, the answer is not found in external factors alone. These are heart matters, and Jesus died to change the hearts of us all. His command to His people is clear: *Be not conformed to this world but be transformed by the renewing of your mind that you may prove what is that good and acceptable and perfect will of God.* (Romans 12:2)

Mis-Belief *10/14 – October 14*

What you believe can kill you. Some time back, six men, thought to be illegal immigrants from Mexico, were killed while sleeping on the railroad tracks.

A 94-car train traveling at 45 MPH was unable to stop, even though the engineer saw the men lying between the tracks several hundred yards away. We learned that the men were sleeping on the tracks because they believed that snakes would not cross the tracks to get to them. They believed a lie.

Do not cast away your confidence, which has great reward. For you have need of endurance, so that after you have done the will of God, you may receive the promise.

These words from Hebrews 10:35 have been great strength in recent years. There's indication that this has reference to trust that is misplaced, cast away to someone or something other than God.

Misplaced confidence can have disastrous effects. I call it mis-belief. It's not exactly unbelief, because we do believe something. But we can believe the wrong thing, and mis-belief can kill you. We've all had the sad experience of trusting someone only to find that there was no basis for our trust.

Confidence, trust, or faith, has value only as it embraces that which is worthy. We can stand confidently upon the promise of God because the God of the promise is faithful. What God has promised has stood the test of millions of saints before us. What God has promised has borne the weight of kingdoms.

What God has promised He will do! Believing His word is not mis-belief; it's the essence of our faith.

What you believe can kill you, if it's mis-belief; but what you believe, if it's the right thing, can save you. Romans 10:9-11 says this:

If you confess with your mouth Jesus as Lord, and believe in your heart that God raised Him from the dead, you shall be saved; for with the heart man believes, resulting in righteousness, and with the mouth he confesses, resulting in salvation. For the Scripture says, "Whoever believes in Him will not be disappointed."

Lord, I believe; help my unbelief – and my mis-belief.

God has given each of us the ability to do certain things well... If your gift is that of serving others, serve them well... When God's children are in need, you be the one to help them out. (Romans 12:6, 13, The Living Bible)

Today there are a myriad of opportunities to serve in the name of the Lord Jesus. It seems right to establish some Scriptural foundation for this most essential part of our life in Jesus.

The Church is composed of many different people with different gifts and different ministries. We're from different ethnic and cultural backgrounds. Some would say that the Church is a melting pot where we all come together as one. But the manner in which these diversities come together in ministry is not so much like a melting pot, where individual ingredients melt with other ingredients, as it is like a salad bowl. Think about it.

There is no loss of individual identity when we serve one another, as there would be in a melting pot. Rather it's the combining of elements that maintain their distinctiveness, as in a salad bowl, that creates a new, and delicious offering to the world in Jesus Name.

God has three sorts of servants in the world. Some are slaves. They serve Him from fear. Others are hirelings. They serve Him for wages. The last are sons, who serve Him because they love Him.

Robert Chapman, a friend of the George Muller of Bristol, England, whose ministry among children is legendary, was once asked, "Would you advise young Christians to do something for the Lord?" "No," was his reply, "I should advise them to do everything for the Lord."

And whatever you do in word or deed, do all in the name of the Lord Jesus, giving thanks through Him to God the Father. (Colossians 3:17)

Football coach Bud Wilkinson was asked, "What contribution does football make to the physical fitness of Americans?" He said, "Very little. A football game is an event where 50,000 spectators, desperately in need of exercise, sit in the stands watching 22 men on the field, desperately in need of rest."

Being a Christian is not a spectator sport. God did not put us in the stands to watch the work getting done by a few. When we were born again by the Spirit of God we emerged immediately onto the field of action.

To borrow a term from another sport, I suggest, "It's your serve." I'm, of course, using a tennis term, which means that it's your turn to put the ball in play, to make a difference in the outcome.

Your service is unique – no one else can serve like you.

The Third World? ***10/16 – October 16***

Take me to Miami," hijacker Woody Edouard told the pilot of a DC-3 owned by MFI, Missionary Flights International.

The twenty-four year old Edouard had grabbed a female missionary and held her hostage at gunpoint, commanding the pilot to take him and the ten missionaries aboard to Miami International airport.

Upon arrival, the hijacker surrendered to FBI agents, being charged with one count of air piracy. But his life would be eternally changed by his encounter with the missionaries. "The Lord took over," said Bob Johnson, who spent most of the flight preaching to the hijacker.

Johnson, a missionary to Haiti, shared the gospel with Edouard, who grew calmer as they discussed spiritual things in Creole. Johnson led the hijacker to Jesus Christ, and before the plane landed he gave him his gun saying he would rather be in prison alive in America, than stay in Haiti.

This isn't an isolated incident. Millions of people from what are called "third world" nations look to America as a refuge from poverty and anarchy. But America is not their Savior – Jesus is.

The world needs to know this, but the ones who can't seem to get it are not Haitian, or Mong, or Serb, or Hispanic. It's the Church that doesn't quite understand that half the world is desperate for the good news that Jesus is the Savior of all men everywhere.

People don't need to come to America – they need to come to Jesus! So we must go to them with Jesus' love.

The term "third world" is divisive. Who ever came up with that phrase anyhow? And where's the second world, and the first world? This artificial segregation of the souls of humanity does not exist in the heart of God. *For there is no distinction between Jew and Greek; for the same Lord is Lord of all, abounding in riches for all who call upon Him; for Whoever will call upon the name of the Lord will be saved.* (Romans 10:12-13)

"For God so loved the (whole) world that He gave His only Son that whosoever believes in Him should not perish but have everlasting life." (John 3:16)

God didn't create three worlds – He only made one – and He loves it.

The annual list of the world's richest people has just been published. To no one's surprise, Bill Gates of Microsoft fame is near the top the list with nearly 50 billion dollars. It's probably more than that now since he earns a cool $100 million a week.

There were others on the list. One notable inclusion was Ted Turner, who has recently decided to make a public display of his benevolence by announcing a gift of one billion dollars to the United Nations. An admirable gesture, no doubt one designed to shame his billionaire peers into doing the same.

It's just possible that this gigantic gift is less than a tithe on all of his assets. And furthermore, those of us in a somewhat lower tax bracket may actually be giving more than him, percentage-wise, if we faithfully tithe on that which God has graciously entrusted to us.

It not only matters what you give, it matters where you give it. Historically, the Kingdom of God has been a much more effective place to give resources to than any government agency, national or international.

Giving is a powerful way to affect the future. Someone has said that giving has more economic power than spending. When I spend, I trade this for that. I get something back for my own use. But when I give, I actually transfer power to another place without diminishing it by asking something in return.

The dollar is a miraculous thing. It's our personal energy, our labor, reduced to a portable form. It is endowed with power we do not ourselves possess. It can go where we cannot go; speak languages we cannot speak; lift burdens we cannot lift; save lives we cannot touch directly. It's an extension of our heart.

Our money, given to God's work, buys more to relieve human suffering and meet the eternal needs of children and adults than any other place we may choose to give it. It does matter where you give.

When we speak of the world's richest people we must mention the Sultan of Brunei. He makes Bill Gates look like a pauper with his extravagant life-style.

I have one question to ask the world's richest people – which world? Jesus said that His kingdom is not of this world. To be rich in the commodities of this world, doesn't count for much in the Kingdom of God's dear Son.

Do not lay up for yourselves treasures upon earth, where moth and rust destroy, and where thieves break in and steal. But lay up for yourselves treasures in heaven, where neither moth nor rust destroys, and where thieves do not break in or steal. (Matthew 6:19, 20)

Stay Warm and Pure *10/18 – October 18*

See that ye love one another with a pure heart fervently. (I Peter 1:22)

A pure heart and warm love – what a combination. If we could really love each other with a pure heart that would really be something. There are plenty of influences in this world to make our love anything but pure and warm.

Pure love gets contaminated in many ways. The most obvious pollutant is sensuality. Sensual love is advertised in nearly every song, movie, and magazine that comes from the studios and publishing houses of this society.

But that's not the only threat to love's purity. There's pride and selfishness, anger and rage, jealousy and fear, possessiveness and greed. These too, are environmental pollutants to pure love.

The Lord asks us to take our love for one another to a new dimension and stay warm in the process. Pure, warm love, this is the way Lord of the Church has called us to walk together. There's healing and wholeness in such love.

But just as there are influences that contaminate love so that it's hard to stay pure, it's also hard to stay warm. Years ago there was a movie with the strange title; "It's a Mad, Mad, Mad, Mad World." Well, to paraphrase – it's also a cold, cold, cold, cold world. And it's hard to stay warm in a cold, cold, world.

Our love is cooled by misunderstanding, rejection, and self-interest. And by the time one reaches adulthood, there've been enough painful experiences to make one's heart cold, hard and closed forever. It's a challenge worth accepting to stay warm in a cold world. This means I will be kind and gentle, open and accepting, in the face of pain and rejection.

We can learn something from NASA and their space shuttle missions. They approached the challenge of the -200° cold of space in two ways – insulation and internal warmth. They found new ways to insulate the space suit to keep the cold out, and heat the suit from within to counteract the creeping cold.

If we are to stay warm in a cold, cold world need have both of these things. We must have insulation against the cold. Sadly, many Christians attempt to solve the creeping cold problem with isolation. Jesus didn't call us to isolate ourselves. He said we're in, but not of this world. That requires insulation.

As to the inner source of heat, we have the ever-dwelling presence of the Holy Spirit, Who warms us from within. The love of brothers and sisters, worship and praise also help keep the fire burning within.

Staying warm, kind, gentle, open and loving in a cold world isn't an easy matter. But we must. The world needs a warm reminder of the Savior's love.

Stay warm – and stay pure.

October 19 – 10/19 **A Heart Transplant**

I will give you a new heart and put a new spirit in you; I will remove from you your heart of stone and give you a heart of flesh. (Ezekiel 36:26)

The Hebrew word used here is "lebab," lay-bawb'; the heart, the most interior organ; the center of anything.

Early in my ministry I was impacted greatly by Dr. Bob Pierce, the founder of World Vision, who said, "Let my heart be broken with the things that break the heart of God." Bob Pierce had a heart like God's for the world.

I often asked the Lord to give me a heart like His. I was brought up short recently when He said to me, in a way I've come to know, "When you ask for a heart like Mine, you don't know what you're asking."

I explained to Him that what I wanted was to feel like He feels about the people in Calcutta, Karachi, Beijing and Cairo. I was open to letting my heart be broken like His for the poverty and idolatry of the people in these places.

Then I understood Him to say, "You can't have a heart like Mine as long as you have one like yours." Then He began to probe the deep recesses of the core of my being to expose the things that grieve Him.

I was ashamed of what I saw. Some of what He exposed is too personal to write about. Most of it, however, is probably true of the Church in general, a fact in which I take no personal comfort.

The Lord said His heart was broken for my preoccupation with material things. If I had a heart like His I would see cars, computers, houses and bank accounts like He sees them. I don't yet, but I want to.

If I had a heart like His I wouldn't be committed to comfort and convenience. I would not be so concerned about the future or the past. I wouldn't care so much about appearance or acceptance – if I had a heart like His. I don't yet, but I want to.

The point He made was this: I will never care as He does about people in India or China until I stop caring so much about myself in this place. And that would take a new heart – a transplant.

Couldn't He just give me a piece of His heart, that part that cares about lost people, and add it to my mine? No – it's incompatible with my heart. It's genetically different. It will be rejected, in time.

A heart transplant began in a communion service. As I took the bread and the cup I was aware that what I held in my hand, a small piece of bread and a taste of grape juice, for millions of people was all they would eat or drink that day.

I asked the Lord to link me with them in the Spirit. My center – my heart – is changing. Do I have a heart like His? I don't yet, but I'm going to.

Greener Grass *10/20 – October 20*

Where were you in October, 1961? If you're younger than 43, you were only a twinkle in the eye of God. For our young family '61 was a time of recovery.

My first experience with burn-out was at the age of 25 as the assisting pastor of a large church in Illinois. On January 2, '61 we packed all our worldly goods and our four-year old daughter into a Volkswagen Bug and headed for California. There was a job waiting for us at Old Oak Ranch.

As we pulled into the camp near Sonora, we wondered what the year held in this beautiful, green haven of recovery. I was to be in charge of the grounds and the crew of this very busy youth camp.

We survived the summer as thousands of kids inflicted radical wear and tear on the grounds and buildings. By October, it was time to get ready for winter. Before the first snow, the lawn above the swimming pool must be fertilized.

I'd never done anything like that before, but it seemed easy enough. Just put the nitrogen-rich compound in the spreader and push it back and forth over the lawn, and be done with it. I made quick work of it.

The snows came and then in January of '62, we accepted the pastorate of a church. Pastoral duties required a return to Old Oak Ranch in March of that same year. I was embarrassed by what I saw as I drove into the camp.

The lawn I had fertilized five months earlier was green all right – at least two shades of green. The darkest green stripes were exactly the width of the spreader I had used. In my haste in October, I had missed a few patches of grass. I had no idea it would make that much difference. But there it was for the world to see.

The fertilizer had worked wonders – where it was applied. Dark, lush green grass had survived the harsh winter and was flourishing in the Springtime sun. The places I had missed were several shades lighter green and shorter than the treated areas. The difference was dramatic.

I learned much through this shameful episode. Not only did I add a new dimension to my work ethic, but I learned a lot about the care and feeding of grass, as well. You've just got to take fertilizing seriously.

Contrary to the popular idea that the grass is always greener on the other side of the fence, it isn't. It's greener – much greener – were you fertilize it.

The Bible draws a connection here: *All men are like grass, and all their glory is like the flowers of the field; the grass withers and the flowers fall, but the word of the Lord stands forever.* (I Peter 1:24, 25)

Carelessness in October will show up in March. It's inevitable. And some care-starved living things may not survive the cold, dark winter of crisis.

"What's the one verse in the Bible that you'd pick as your favorite?" This was asked of a Bible scholar who had reached his eighty-seventh year.

He was well qualified to answer such a question. Ever since childhood he had read at least one chapter of the Bible every day. He had read the Bible through many times and had intimate knowledge of the Hebrew and Greek languages.

His answer was extraordinary. He said, "You will find my favorite verse 434 times in the King James version of the Bible. It is, 'it came to pass.'" He added, "There is no verse in the Bible that can help you more than this. And I have lived long enough to know the truth of that phrase."

It's an Old English expression used as a connecting or an introductory phrase. It's taken to mean that something happened that was worthy of mention. For example: *And it came to pass in process of time, that the king of Egypt died: and the children of Israel sighed by reason of the bondage, and their cry came up to God...* (Exodus 2:23)

And it came to pass in those days, that there went out a decree from Caesar Augustus, that all the world should be taxed. (Luke 2:1)

Perhaps taking these words "it came to pass" literally is reading more into them than is intended, but I see a gem of truth here that has helped me. The words literally mean, "it came to pass on." It did not come to stay.

Events in our lives are transitory – moving along the road of time. All the miseries of life come to pass. Even the joys of life come to pass. All the heartaches, troubles, wars, crime – all come to pass.

The most important things in a Christian's life, however, have come to stay; they did not come to pass; for instance, the presence of Jesus. He said, *I will never leave you nor forsake you.* (Hebrews 13:5) His comforting, healing, forgiving, delivering presence will never pass from me. He's here to stay.

I John 2:17 says, *the world passes away and the lust of it; but he that does the will of God abides forever,* or as J.B. Phillips puts it, "He who does God's will is part of the permanent and cannot die."

Heaven and earth will pass away, but My words will by no means pass away. (Mark 13:31) Stars and galaxies, rocks and mountains, rivers and valleys "came to pass." God's powerful, prophetic, promising, precious Word is here to stay.

You won't find the phrase, "it came to pass" in the NIV or the NASB versions of the Bible. The phrase is changed to words appropriate for today's language.

But I rather like – it came to pass.

Treasures In Heaven — *10/22 – October 22*

Lay up for yourselves treasures in heaven, where moth and rust do not destroy, and where thieves do not break in and steal. For where your treasure is, there will your heart be also. (Matthew 6:20)

Most of us don't think about heaven much. The church, throughout history, has talked about heaven mostly in times of war, famine, and calamity, but not much when things were going well. Jesus calls us to think about heaven. The grave is not a period at the end of the sentence of life, but a conjunction, connecting us with the life to come.

Jesus invites us to lay up treasures where there's no corruption or deterioration and then follow that treasure with our hearts. For many, the treasure is people; loved ones and friends who have that have preceded them into the glory of His presence. Our heart is there with them.

One eight-year-old named Eric said, "Heaven is a place where there is a lot of money laying around. You could just pick it up, play with it, and buy things. I think I am going to buy a basketball and I am going to play basketball with my great-great grandmother. I miss her a lot."

A prominent citizen was dying. As he laid in his lovely home, the best doctors surrounding him, he whispered, with a note of despair, "I'm leaving home, I'm leaving home."

Across town lay a solitary figure in surroundings bare. Her modest home contained only the most threadbare of life's essentials. In her eye was a gleam. Before she died she was heard to say, "I'm going home, I'm going home!"

The question often arises, "Will we know each other when we get to heaven?" Given the limitations of our understanding, and our capacity to love down here, the truth is that we won't really know each other until we get to heaven.

For many of us the treasure we send ahead is made of righteous deeds and unselfish acts which no one but God sees. They do count for something.

For many of us the treasure, which will lead our hearts to heaven, is Jesus Himself. Though we have never seen Jesus, it will be an incredible moment when we behold with our eyes, Him Whom our faith has embraced.

We shall see Him as He is! (I John 3:2)

October 23 – 10/23 *Omnipresence*

My people will be strong with power from Me. They will go wherever they wish and wherever they go they will be under My personal care. This is how the Living Bible paraphrases Zechariah 10:12.

A fact that may get lost in the all that power and personal attention is that our mighty, caring God will be wherever you go. You cannot be where God is not.

The omnipresence – the everywhere-everytime-presence – of God is one of the most frequently mentioned and wonderful facets of His nature. *"Am I a God who is near," declares the Lord, "And not a God far off? Can a man hide himself so I do not see him?" declares the Lord. "Do I not fill the heavens and the earth?" declares the Lord.* (Jeremiah 23:23, 24)

Even the most skeptical or scientifically demanding person is likely to accept that there is a fundamental, sustaining force in all of reality. There is That which holds reality together in unity and order; That which sustains spontaneity within a framework of regularity. I capitalize "That" because that force is God.

Many see Him as merely the source of truth, beauty, goodness, and love; a kind of passive, yet benevolent, force. It's nice to have Him around. This "passive force" (how's that for an oxymoron?) requires little from man and gives little to him. This caricatured god bears little resemblance to the omnipotent, omnipresent, sovereign Lord of the universe.

All that He is, He is here now, and everywhere, always. We cannot remove ourselves from His presence. He is close to everything, next to everyone. There is no place in the universe where He is not. *He is not far from each one of us; for in Him we live and move and have our being.* (Acts 17:28)

Now this is good news and bad news. To those who live their lives in the rebellion of sin, the Omnipresence assures that painful reaping will surely follow sinful sowing. *Though they dig into Sheol, from there shall My hand take them; and though they ascend to the heavens, from there will I bring them down. And though they hide on the summit of Carmel, I will search them out and take them from there.* (Amos 9:2, 3)

But those who have yielded to His presence and trusted His grace will find that the Omnipresence is good news indeed. He is closer than the air we breathe. Jesus, God in flesh, said, *I am with you all the days, perpetually, uniformly, everywhere, and on every occasion, to the very close and consummation of the age.* (Matthew 28:20, Amplified Bible)

His everywhere-presence makes the whole universe full of majestic wonder. Prayer is but a whisper of faith, and abiding in Him is no struggle at all, since He fills all that is. You cannot be where God is not.

The Fountain *10/24 – October 24*

A new song we've been singing recently has stirred my heart. It starts out slowly with the words, "Who can satisfy my soul like You, Jesus? I will trust in You, I will trust in You, my God!"

Then the words and music rise to the inspiring declaration, "There is a Fountain Who is a King…" The music inspired me but the words puzzled me. A fountain who is a king – what's that about?

I found two references that clearly declare that the Sovereign Lord is Himself the "fountain of living waters." The King does not merely have the living water. He does not lead us to the fountain. He is the fountain!

Jeremiah 2:13 says, *For My people have committed two evils; they have forsaken Me the Fountain of living waters, and hewed them out cisterns, broken cisterns, that can hold no water.*

Jeremiah 17:13 adds, *O LORD, the hope of Israel, all that forsake Thee shall be ashamed, ...because they have forsaken the LORD, the fountain of living waters.*

The word "fountain" here is the Hebrew word, "maqowr," maw-kore'; meaning source: fountain, spring, wellspring. The other key word is "LORD". This is the Hebrew word "JAH," or the sacred name JEHOVAH, the Self-existent, Sovereign Lord, – the KING!

The Amazon River is the largest river in the world. The mouth is 90 miles across. There is enough water in it to exceed the combined flow of the Yangtze, Mississippi and Nile Rivers. So much water comes from the Amazon that they can detect its currents 200 miles out in the Atlantic Ocean.

Sailors in ancient times died for lack of water in the South Atlantic. They were dying of thirst. Sometimes other ships from South America who knew the area would come alongside and call out, "What is your problem?"

They would exclaim, "Can you spare us some water? We're dying of thirst!" And from the other ship would come the cry, "Just lower your buckets. You're in the mouth of the mighty Amazon."

The tragic irony of ancient Israel and America today is that the fountain of living water is right here, and we don't recognize Him!

In His last message, Jesus said, *I am Alpha and Omega, the beginning and the end. I will give unto him that is athirst of the fountain of the water of life freely.* (Revelation 21:6)

"There is a fountain – Who is a King!"

October 25 – 10/25 **_I Love You, Lord!_**

Because he has loved Me... says the Lord in Psalm 91 of the one who dwells in His presence, *I will deliver him and honor him..., I will be with him in trouble..., and with long life I will satisfy him and let him behold my redemption.* The door to all that benevolence hinges upon one thing – "because he has loved Me!"

Much is said, in these years between refreshings for the Church, of "hanging in there," and the disciplines of the Christian life. Worship often becomes a determined act of will and praise, a labored repetition of words we know and mean but do not feel.

That's not a bad thing; it's just not the best thing. At the same time, for many, there's an aversion to the expression of too much passion, and those who speak over-much of their devotion to Jesus are seen as being without depth.

Of course, there are those who take what they call love for God and people, to ridiculous extremes ignoring discipline and holiness. The some go too far has kept many from going far enough. Perhaps the masterstroke of genius in our adversary's plot to deceive a few – is to paralyze many.

It's impossible to define love without including an element of passionate devotion. We talk about love being a choice, not a feeling – an act, not an emotion. However we define love for God in theological, psychological, or philosophical terms it boils down to four simple, passionate words – "I love You, Lord!" And my Father, Who loved me first, responds with an outpouring of love from His infinite well of devotion.

He loves His children passionately – the cross proves that, and when I come into His presence with my battered, wounded heart tight-sealed, I've entered the only truly safe place for holy passion to find pure expression.

There is holiness here – in my devotion to my Lord. Only by stronger passion can evil passion be expelled. Emotions do not often bow to reason. There is hardly a sin known to the flesh that does not feed upon feelings. Temptation to sin begins with temptation to feel, and when my heart is occupied with Him, there is no room for lesser loves.

The ancient writers knew this. When Ulysses passed the Isle of Sirens, he had himself tied to the mast of the ship and had his ears stopped with wax, that he might not hear the sirens singing, and be entranced by their beauty. But when Orpheus passed the Isle of Sirens, he sat on the deck unmoved, for he was a musician and could make melody so much more beautiful than the sirens, that their alluring songs were to him discords.

Orpheus conquered the siren's song by surpassing it with a more beautiful song of his own. When I say, from a full heart being healed by His grace, "I love You, Lord," it's a love song that cancels all other melodies.

And it's music to His ears.

The Father's Special Treasure *10/26 – October 26*

In Colossians, Paul the Apostle prays for people for whom he cares and says, *that their hearts may be encouraged, having been knit together in love, and attaining to all the wealth that comes from the full assurance of understanding, resulting in a true knowledge of God's mystery, that is, Christ Himself, in whom are hidden all the treasures of wisdom and knowledge.... For in Him all the fullness of Deity dwells in bodily form, and in Him you have been made complete...* (Colossians 2:2, 3, 9, 10)

Our modern minds have a hard time with this truth. We're so accustomed to thinking of wealth and treasure in terms of gold and silver and cars and houses, that the treasure is Christ Himself just doesn't compute.

But if we miss the point here we'll never begin to understand the Father heart of God, for this is a statement, first and foremost, about God and the love He has for His Son.

That's important. Jesus said, *as the Father has loved Me, so have I loved you.* (John 15:9) If we can grasp a bit of how the Father loves His Son then we have some idea of the depth of Jesus' love for us. The Father treasures His Son.

Jesus – God's only begotten Son, loved of the Father – is God's special treasure, His gift to broken people. And in Him are hidden all the treasures of wisdom and knowledge. You are complete, whole, fulfilled – in Him.

To see things as God sees them – to see Jesus as God sees Him – and to value what He treasures, is evidence of our separation from the world's system of values. A prayer of Thomas à Kempis (1379-1471) in "Imitation of Christ," expresses this very well.

"Grant me, O Lord, to know what I ought to know, to love what I ought to love, to praise what delights Thee most, to value what is precious in Thy sight, to hate what is offensive to Thee.

"Do not suffer me to judge according to the sight of my eyes, nor pass sentence according to the hearing of the ears of ignorant men; but to discern with a true judgment between things visible and spiritual, and above all, always to inquire what is the good pleasure of Thy will."

Amen!

October 27 – 10/27 *I'm Looking Forward*

I'm looking forward to Thanksgiving. I'm looking forward to Christmas. I'm looking forward to 2006. I find myself using that expression a lot and I hear other people use it a lot, too. It's a good expression; it says something about the person who uses it. It says he or she is not looking backward, but forward, and that's good!

There are always temptations for us to look backward over our shoulder at something that we could have done different, or better, or something we shouldn't have done at all, but it's really tough to walk a straight line here and now if you're always looking backward. God had purpose in the fact He made our eyes and ears and all of our senses, for that matter, to be forward oriented.

A clear example of the balance we need to have between yesterday and tomorrow happens every time you drive your car. You have a rear-view mirror and perhaps a couple of mirrors on the side, but the car was designed for you to face forward. You can imagine the difficulty you would have driving your car if all you did was stare into the rear-view mirror.

The mirror is there for an occasional glance in order to avoid danger but not for a steady gaze. So we glance backward occasionally, in our spiritual walk, but we are created for tomorrow, not yesterday.

If we're wise, we will not gaze backward into another's life any more than is healthy in our own. There's something about our fleshly nature that "needs" to know about the dark places in another's past. The flesh often disguises itself as an angel of light to expose another's sin but "love covers a multitude of sins." There's a time for light to shine into the dark corners of our lives, but the hand that holds the light and the pruning knife must be a loving hand.

If we are children of God, and our Heavenly Father has responded to our repentance with forgiveness, (and He always does) then the least important thing about us is our past. It is covered with the blood of Jesus. It is "crossed" out! We may have some consequences to work out but He is there to help us with grace enough.

Psalm 130:2,3 says, *If Thou, Lord, shouldst mark iniquities, O Lord, who could stand? But there is forgiveness with Thee, that Thou mayest be feared.* If I were God (that's a scary thought!) and I wanted people to fear me I would not offer them forgiveness. I would have said something like, "there is wrath with me, that you may fear me."

It's a curious fact of church history that when the church has been at it's best, despite persecution and pressure from the world and the devil, she has looked forward to the day when her Bridegroom would come.

When He went away He said He would return for us. Things past and things present can distract our gaze, but I'm looking forward to His return!

Right about now seems like a good time.

In Praise of Teachers *10/28 – October 28*

In the office of Alex Haley, the author of "Roots" hangs a picture of a turtle sitting on a fence post. When Haley looks at the picture he is reminded of a lesson taught to him by a friend: "If you ever see a turtle on top of a fence post, you know he had some help getting there."

Whatever fence post we may be sitting on, whatever success any of us may enjoy, one thing is sure – we had some help getting where we are. Much of that help has come from teachers, all the way from pre-school to graduate school to Sunday School. Their influence upon our lives is incalculable.

I began to reminisce a bit about teachers in my life. My first recollection of the face and name of a teacher was Mrs. Fairweather, my third grade teacher in 1943. She was as pleasant and bright as her name, and made me feel O.K. Mrs. Sullivan, my fourth grade teacher, was stern and gray haired and I was a little afraid of her, but she has a warm place in my heart now.

Then there was Mr. Settle, a junior high school science teacher who opened my mind to the wonders of weather and rocks and stars and plants and animals in 1948. Mrs. Hebron made me love geometry in high school. I wrote a poem for her, though I don't remember a single word of it now.

In 1952, Mrs. McMillan, my English Lit. teacher, made the coronation of Queen Elizabeth II come alive. We didn't have TV then, only radio, so we were left to imagine the splendor of this historic event in my senior year of high school. She was English with a quick wit and contagious enthusiasm for her homeland.

There was Mr. Garber, and Mr. Kintner, who challenged me to excel in athletic endeavors. You won't find my name on any trophy, but I learned a lot about life from these men in my high school days.

Tiny Mrs. McNabb at Milliken University, while lecturing on the intricacies of broadcasting, would all of a sudden yell at the top of her lungs, "Principle, principle, principle!" She was about to inform us of a very important matter and wanted to make sure we were awake for it. We listened.

These teachers introduced me to science, history, mathematics, music, athletics, and words. Their labor is constantly manifested in my work and my leisure. I'm grateful to them that I can read and write and think and wonder.

The names and faces are different for each of us. Those I mentioned are symbolic of the teachers in all of our lives who have helped climb to the top of our little fence post.

And the view from there is wonderful!

October 29 – 10/29 *Easter In October*

Let's move Easter to October. Ghosts and goblins, witches and warlocks, death and darkness – Yuk! We go through this song and dirge every year at this time and I'm getting a little impatient with it all. By what authority and for what possible purpose do we annually glorify the inglorious and celebrate the dark side of the spirit world?

One explanation is that the god of this world has so thoroughly blinded the powers that be, that this orgy of awfulness is dismissed as harmless fun. On top of the doom and gloom of Halloween this year (2004) we have the doom and gloom of a presidential politics. Everyone's vision of reality is so distorted by self-interest that the average Joe Voter is confused, and not a little discouraged by the whole process.

I think we ought to move Easter to October, and celebrate resurrection right in the face of such darkness. The resurrection of Jesus Christ from the grave is the ultimate "in your face", to gloom and doom wherever it's found, in the graveyard, the halls of Congress, the campaign trail, or the nightly news.

If God can take crucifixion (it doesn't get any worse) and make resurrection (it doesn't get any better) out of it in three days He can do anything. The empty tomb speaks hope to every man's desperation.

Just listen to this! *Blessed be the God and Father of our Lord Jesus Christ Who, according to His great mercy, has caused us to be born again to a living hope through the resurrection of Jesus Christ from the dead!* (I Peter 1:3)

The resurrection factor gives a living hope to shattered dreams and broken homes, to recessions and depressions, to poverty and disease. The heavy, ponderous Roman-sealed stone that would have kept Jesus in the confines of that rock-walled tomb was no match for the Rock of Ages!

Because He lives, I shall live also! Because He lives, I shall live as He lives – victoriously, abundantly, fearlessly – eternally! To leave the resurrection factor out of my personal or our national equation is to succumb to the death that lingers in the darkness of every tomorrow.

The resurrection factor is the antidote to the perverseness of Halloween and the gloom and doom of the politicians. We must look this present darkness square in the face and declare with holy gusto, "He is Risen!"

And a choir of voices, which no man can number, responds with one grand unfettered shout – "He is Risen Indeed!"

Why Are We Doing This? *10/30 – October 30*

I've never had a scary Halloween. Some people are really traumatized by the whole thing with witches and skeletons, ghouls and vampires. For me, as a kid growing up, it was just plain uncomfortable.

For many, Halloween is a time of innocent fun, and I don't want to be a spoilsport for them. But the phrase that comes to mind when I think of putting on a mask and a weird costume is, "Why am I doing this?"

I hated Halloween masks. After an hour or two of heavy breathing, they smelled funny and tasted even worse. At Halloween, I would not have been the life of your party. And that would be equally true for any other season, too, I must confess.

Where I came from, they played a game with the costumes. Everyone would parade in front of the crowd and people would try to guess who was behind the mask. A prize was always given to the person who most successfully concealed his or her true identity. I was always the tallest kid so it was hard for me to hide behind mask. And the prize never seemed worth all the hassle.

If I sound cynical of Halloween and masks and costumes – I am. To this day, when I see kids and grown-ups dressing like hideous creatures or infamous people, I wonder, "Why are they doing this?"

The idea of masks and costumes centuries ago was to fool evil spirits into thinking you were someone else so they would leave you alone. Come on now, evil spirits may be stupid but they're not that stupid.

Concealing one's true identity runs counter to life in the family of God. Sadly, many Christians have never felt safe enough to unmask. We wear smiley masks to hide our pain, pretty masks to hide our faults, and spiritual masks to hide our flesh. And some of us wear scary masks to hide our fear, and ugly don't-touch-me masks to hide our need. I've known good people to have several layers of masks of one kind or another.

After so many years of pretending, it gets pretty smelly inside the mask. And the prize the world gives for concealing your real face isn't worth all the trouble it takes to maintain the mask. Those who live behind a mask must often say to themselves, "Why am I doing this?"

Why do we wear masks? Perhaps because we've never tasted the sheer joy of being accepted – even loved – as we are. Historically, the Church has either been the great merchant of masks, or the dispenser of the love of Jesus, to know and be known.

Therefore, laying aside all malice, all deceit, hypocrisy... if indeed you have tasted that the Lord is gracious. (I Peter 1:25-2:3)

It's time to unmask.

October 31 – 10/31 *Trick Or Treat?*

A huge trick is being played on unsuspecting Americans, and it's no treat at all. I have very few pleasant memories of Halloween from my childhood. It was a bit confusing for our church back then to play to the darker side of the spiritual world with parties where witches and goblins were featured openly

Halloween goes back to the ancient British Celts. Their Druid priests practiced a religious observance at the end of their harvest season, marking the end of their year and the beginning of a new one. So this night was the equivalent of many modern New Year's Eve celebrations 2,500 years ago.

On that day they held a festival to honor Samhain, the Celtic lord of death. It was believed that the souls of the dead were allowed to wander the earth on this evening. The Celts did whatever they could to either drive these spirits away or appease them so as to invoke their blessing.

Great bonfires were built on hilltops to honor their sun god and frighten away the evil spirits who had been released that night. In an effort to fool these spirits, the Celts wore heads and skins of dead animals while dancing and singing around the fires. Many would jump over or dash through the flames, supposedly escaping the evil spirits who were chasing them.

Animals and human beings were sacrificed to appease evil spirits. They tried to determine their future by examining the entrails of sacrificial victims. Along with this witchcraft came the superstitious concepts of ghosts, goblins, fairies, witches, etc. The cat was considered sacred and they believed that it had once been a human being and had been changed into a cat as punishment.

When the Romans invaded England in 55 B.C. they incorporated their gods into the festival, and in 800 A.D., the Roman Church incorporated these pagan rites into it's celebrations, moving "All Saints Day" to November 1, honoring the dead saints of the church and calling October 31 "All Hallows Eve."

This annual festival of fright poses a problem for the followers of Jesus Christ. As you read this, thousands, if not millions of people around the world are preparing for their biggest celebration of the year. It will occur tonight. It's a dark sabbath, the spiritual antithesis of Resurrection Day, where the god of the underworld, Satan, is worshipped.

Blood will be shed; sacrifices made. Somewhere the hoards of hell giggle with fiendish glee on this, their night of unbridled expression. Cities are preparing for the mayhem this night of darkness fosters. Lives will be lost, businesses will be burned, and destruction will be rampant.

Doesn't it make you wonder why these things don't happen on Easter or Christmas?

This is the day that the Lord has made! And He didn't make it for witches, ghosts, and goblins.

Says Who? *11/1 – November 1*

"Says who?" This two-word phrase sums up the plot of an amazing movie titled "Time Changer." The scene involves a seminary professor who has been transported from his native environment in the 1890's to the 21st century to see first hand the end result of the premise of a book he has written.

The premise in question is whether or not one can teach morality apart from Jesus Christ and His teachings. The professor has just ordered his first ever hot dog and sits down to sample it when a little girl sneaks up behind him and steals it. A chase ensues.

Upon confronting the girl he says to her, "Young lady don't you know that it's wrong to steal." And she says, "Says who?" To which he replies, "God says," which means nothing to a child who has been brought up with no moral authority upon which to base moral activity.

Today, many believe there are no moral absolutes – (and they're absolutely sure about that.) They hold to a philosophy of moral relativism, which says, "What's right for you may not be right for me." "If it feels good do it." "Nothing is intrinsically right or wrong, there are just different opinions?"

All of this is the result of the feeling that there's no absolute truth, there's no one who has the moral authority to say what's right or wrong, good or bad. You're entitled to your truth, and I'm entitled to mine!

A recent poll found that 67% of Americans don't believe in moral absolutes. Among "Baby Busters", born between 1965 and 1983, the percentage was higher at 78%. Even 62% of professing Christians said there was no absolute standard of morality.

Our nation was built upon the moral authority of God's word. James Madison, the fourth President of the United States said, "We stake the future of this country on our ability to govern ourselves under the principles of the Ten Commandments." But that won't mean anything to moral relativists.

In Miami, a 15-year-old and his 17-year-old brother, decided to celebrate their parent's absence over a weekend by cruising the streets in the family Mercedes shooting spear darts into the backs of elderly pedestrians.

The boys' parents wept before TV cameras, apologizing for the boys' behavior and insisting, "They're really good kids." Good kids? Give me a break? They are bad kids who did bad, evil things.

The little girl's question, "Says who?" is a valid one. But it's not enough for me to flippantly say, "God says, that's Who!" It's not enough because of decades of Godless schools and powerless churches.

It's not enough because God's people have not, for the most part, themselves been examples of the authority of God's gracious word and His loving ways.

America is at war. Iraq's Sadaam Hussein may object to being compared with Hitler, but comparisons are unavoidable. As a young boy, I remember the fear that the name Adolph Hitler brought to my heart and the joy I felt when he was finally defeated. The same fear once lived in the hearts of Iraqis, and now the same joy is expressed in his defeat and capture.

The church is often referred to as an army. But some years ago, major denominations had "Onward Christian Soldiers" deleted from their hymnals because the song just didn't fit the peace-loving, docile community that the church had become. But there's a real and present danger facing the church and it's time to adopt a wartime stance against the menace of the Prince of Darkness who rules this world.

Every thinking person hopes and prays that the physical warfare will not last much longer. However, just as there are enemies that threaten us and other nations, so the church must be engaged in battle against the forces that would destroy homes and children and the lives of millions destined for bondage.

The strategy of Satan may be somewhat different than we assume. Contrary to the movie version of war, the object of battle is not always to kill enemy soldiers. The object of battle is often to wound them. When a soldier dies the army, in principle, has completed its duty toward him. However, when a soldier is wounded, an average of three other soldiers must care for him.

Satan knows that he can't kill those who belong to Christ, so his tactic is often to inflict injury. Could it be that the reason the church doesn't do more to attack the enemies of this age is that it spends its time, resources, and personnel caring for its own wounded ones. Perhaps.

I'm fascinated by the way an army handles it's wounded. Each casualty goes through a process known as "triage", which, with the prefix "tri", suggests three options:

1. Requires immediate attention; get the patient in right now. 2. Does not require immediate attention; the patient can wait. 3. No amount of treatment will help; leave the patient alone. This is a hopeless case. A tag is placed on each patient in triage and they're treated in accordance with the color of the tag they've received.

I remember hearing of a Christian nurse in the Korean War who would go to the hopeless section of triage and prayerfully change the tags of some from "hopeless" to "immediate attention." As the story goes, she saved many lives and, in fact, ended up married to one of the men whose tag she had changed.

One of the things the church does best is to go all over this broken world, changing people's tags from "hopeless" to "requires immediate attention."

This is love, and it's the most powerful weapon in the arsenal of a Christian.

Tear Down This Wall! *11/3 – November 3*

Godless democracy isn't much better than Godless communism. That's why I wasn't too excited about the dismantling of the Berlin Wall. I watched people streaming from the east to the west in Europe and my enthusiasm was tempered with concern.

It's clear that they were driven by a desire for western style democracy, but it's just possible they have exchanged one kind of bondage for another. Western Europe has been bound up to its eyeballs by materialism, and has very little time for God.

The church in Western Europe was mobilizing to move into territory that was forbidden years ago. New freedoms made it possible not only to preach the gospel, but also to hear about what was happening behind the wall.

They heard reports of a thriving church in eastern bloc countries in spite of (or is it because of?) oppression and bondage. The church behind the wall was in better shape than the one in West Germany, France, The Netherlands or the U.S.A., for that matter.

At another time and in another place some walls stood in defiance of the people of God. Joshua commanded the people to march around those walls for seven days. Hebrews 11:30 says, *By faith the walls of Jericho fell down.*

But while everyone was having a grand time celebrating free access to the city, Achan was helping himself to its treasures – ancient materialism. This led to the defeat at Ai. It would have been better for Achan and his family if the walls of Jericho had never fallen. He couldn't handle freedom.

Some people need walls. Walls offer security, and freedom is a frightening responsibility. The East Germans erected the wall years ago, ostensibly to keep democracy out, but made prisoners of their own people. Since the walls were broken down and they saw what life was like on the other side, many chose to return to the security of their homes on the east side. Some said things like, "now that I'm free to go it makes me want to stay."

The good news about the fall of the wall was that families and friendships were restored. Tears of joy flowed freely as lovers are reunited and parents saw their children for the first time in years. The personal implications of the changes in Eastern Europe were more significant than the politics of it all.

Ephesians 2 speaks of another barrier that once existed. *But now in Christ Jesus you who once were far off have been made near by the blood of Christ. For He is our peace, Who has made both one, and has broken down the middle wall of division between us, having abolished in His flesh the enmity... thus making peace.* (2:13-15)

Jesus tore down the wall between God and man – and made peace. Now we have free access to His presence. We are free to live and move in Him.

But can we handle such freedom – and stay pure?

November 4 – 11/4 *Animal Rights?*

I love animals as much as anyone, I suppose. My choice of weapons, however, for hunting creatures of field and forest is a camera with a long lens and a tripod. But there's a movement in our land, which in the name of compassion, raises some concern. It's the animal rights movement.

The extreme arm of this movement, demands that no animal be killed for any reason whatsoever including for food, medical research, or sport. Some of the same people who risk their lives to save whales or snowy owls are strong advocates of aborting human babies. What's wrong with this picture?

My concerns are not political but spiritual. First, the trend toward the sanctity of animal life reflects the influence of Eastern religion upon our culture. I'm reminded of the Hindus. There are 330 million gods and goddesses in the Hindu religion, many of which are animals. Hindu religion teaches that animal life is sacred. And so, while most of India's Hindus live in great poverty, 240 million cows are worshiped.

And then there are the rats. There are nearly 3 billion of them in India; six rats for every human. All rats are considered holy because Hindu mythology holds that they are "divine mounts" upon which the gods ride to bring prosperity. In fact, the rats are eating India out of house and home, consuming 1.5 billion tons of grain costing 800 million dollars annually.

My second concern has to do with the place of animals in God's order of things. We all could tell touching stories about how much our favorite pets are like members of the family, but animals were created for man's use and benefit and are not equal to man in God's eyes. There's no evidence that Jesus Christ died for the animal kingdom.

The attempt to elevate animal life to the level of man results only in the lowering of man to the level of the animals. This idea is the fruit of many years of indoctrination in evolutionary theory which links man with the animals, as if all of us – man and beast alike – came from the same primeval slime. The elevation of animals to the status of having "rights" is an inevitable effect of the evolutionary cause. If the textbooks are right, the whale is my brother and the cow is my sister in the mysterious world of natural selection, and they "deserve" the same rights that I enjoy. Nonsense!

I'm certainly not advocating the abuse of animals. I am concerned, however, that we may be seeing Romans 1:22-25 being lived out in our culture.

Professing themselves to be wise, they became fools, and changed the glory of the incorruptible God into an image made like corruptible man - and bird and four-footed beasts and creeping things. Therefore God also gave them up to uncleanness, in the lusts of their hearts, to dishonor their bodies among themselves, who exchanged the truth of God for a lie, and worshipped and served the creature rather than the Creator.

God, help us keep our balance!

The Back Roads *11/5 – November 5*

I like to take the back roads when we travel. There's a whole network of well-maintained county roads that are rich in beauty and history. These roads less traveled take a little longer but most of them are worth the extra time.

Because of my many experiences with back roads and country lanes, the story I read the other day made sense. It made things a little clearer for me in my spiritual journey, which also has taken me through some unfamiliar territory.

It seems there was a traveler who took one of the country lanes in the state of Vermont. He was convinced he was on the wrong road, so he stopped his car at a house in a village and knocked on the door. When the man of the house came to the door the traveler said, "Friend, I need help. I'm lost."

The villager looked at him for a moment and said, "Do you know where you are?" "Yes," said the traveler. "I saw the name of this village when I entered."

The man nodded his head. "Do you know where you want to be?" "Yes," the traveler replied, and named his destination. The villager looked away for a moment and said, "You ain't lost. You just need directions!"

Frequently, when overwhelmed with a crisis we become disoriented and feel lonely, powerless, and lost. We feel cut off from the past and fearful of the future. Like the traveler we feel that we're on the wrong road and can't get back on track.

At such times it is good to listen to the advice of the villager and get a fix on where we are and affirm where we want to be. Then all we need is directions. A thousand minor details don't seem to matter much any more when I can clearly see those two things. But they're not always easy to define.

Where am I? This basic question is the heart of the matter. What makes a soul lost, in the spiritual sense, is that he doesn't know or doesn't acknowledge where he is – that he is a sinner in need of Jesus Christ. But a sense of lostness can invade us when we are in a crisis even if have accepted Jesus as Lord and Savior. We lose sight of the fact that we're IN CHRIST – that's where we are. And He's in us! That's where He is.

"But where am I in Jesus?" I hear some say. I can't answer that specifically for you, but I am sure of one thing – you're near His heart. He understands and cares. He is touched by your crisis; it's His crisis, too. And *He that has begun a good work in you will perfect it...* (Philippians 1:6)

The next question is also important: "Where do you want to be?" I'm not a goal-oriented person; I wish I were. But I do have a very clear sense of where and what I want to be when I grow up. It may sound a little corny and the obvious thing to say, but I really do want to be like Jesus. I know where I am now – and I'm not there yet.

I'm not lost; all I need is a few directions – and the time to get there.

What we do today is called receiving communion. We understand those terms to mean that, once a month at least, we will be offered bread and grape juice and will sing songs about the cross and think about the death of Jesus. But communion isn't something you take or receive, it is something in which you engage, in which you participate, which involves fellowship and interaction with other people – and God.

Although what we do today is about death, this is not a funeral. I have childhood memories of a lady, Clara was her name, who always dressed in black and wore a black veil on Communion Sunday. As she took the bread and the juice she began to sob and morn for the death of her beloved Lord. She really did love Jesus, but I wondered what all the crying was about, since I had read the rest of the story.

Maybe a bit more sorrow for our sins is in order, but communion is a time to joyfully receive the forgiveness that the blood of Jesus offers to all who come in faith. That's good news! This is a celebration of life – not death alone.

Communion is about remembering, but it's not a memorial service. Memorial services are traditionally held when the body of the deceased is not present and members and friends of the family gather to reminisce about good times past. That's not what we are doing here. The deceased is no longer deceased. He lives! And His body is here – we're it! And as far as remembering the good old days, the Best (Jesus) is yet to come; "we ain't seen nothin' yet!"

Although what we do today we do frequently, it's not a ritual. Anything we do with regularity is liable to become mindless repetition. That's the way human beings are. But that's not the way our spiritual being is. It has been *rescued from the tyranny of change and decay,* (Romans 8:21, JBP) so that when I worship, or pray, or read God's Word, or participate in communion, my spirit delights in the experience, even though my flesh may be weary of the routine.

What we do today is personal, but it's not exclusive. It's not just a time for me to examine my own life and receive cleansing for my sins; it's a time of corporate cleansing, as well. Our lives are so intimately tied to each other that I can't live unto myself, and I can't sin unto myself; what I do does affect you and what you do does affect me.

The Lord Jesus has wisely called us together around His table periodically to deal with our sins and our wounds by bringing them to the cross – the finishing place.

Whenever you eat this bread or drink this cup, you are proclaiming that the Lord has died for you, and you will do that until He comes again.... a man should thoroughly examine himself, and only then should he eat the bread and drink the cup. (I Corinthians 11:26, 28, JBP)

WOW Is Me! *11/7 – November 7*

What's wrong with this picture? A world famous basketball player of such ability that they call him "Magic," announces that because of "un-safe sex" he is infected with HIV, the condition that leads almost inevitably to Acquired Immune Deficiency Syndrome, (AIDS). He's immediately acclaimed as a hero for his openness and invited to tell of his sexual exploits on all the talk shows and tabloids in the land while praising the value of "safe sex."

What's wrong with this picture? The Vice President of the United States tells a national audience that the only safe sex is abstinence, except within the monogamous union of marriage, and he is ridiculed and caricatured as being totally out of touch with reality for daring to suggest that consenting adults should not engage in sexual activities as much as they please if they take "proper precautions."

What's wrong with these pictures is that they are expressions from a society that has whole-heartedly adopted an up-side-down set of values that lead to total destruction. The athlete mentioned is a nice man, a great basketball player, and a whiz at selling anything from shoes to sodas, but he sinned against God, himself, his wife, and society. His sin against society is that he gives credence to the lie that you can have it all – if you're careful.

In his eyes, and the eyes of the great majority, the problem is not sin but a disease. No matter how compassionate we are and how one tries to separate the sin from the disease, they are inseparably linked. Even if one is completely innocent, like a baby in the womb, or one who is infected through a blood transfusion, or through a health practitioner, somewhere in the equation that led to that conclusion – is sin.

I guess what troubles me most is that there is no "woe is me" in the disclosures. There's no sense of remorse. And where there is no remorse, there can be no repentance; where there is no repentance, there can be no forgiveness. And where there is no forgiveness, there can be no healing.

It's the difference between saying, "WOE is me" or, "WOW is me!" We have embraced the "WOW" and forsaken the "WOE." We make heroes of those who could have contributed so much more for so much longer, if sin had not ruined their lives. When the response to the devastation which sin brings is "WOW is me!" instead of "WOE is me," I worry about what message we send to our children.

By the heroes we enshrine, we define the values we esteem.

Sodom and Gomorrah and the adjacent cities who, in the same way as these men today, gave themselves up to sexual immorality and perversion, stand in their punishment as a permanent warning of the fire of judgment. (Jude 7 JBP)

November 8 – 11/8 *Random Acts*

Random acts of violence, senseless destruction, indiscriminate vandalism; these are symptoms of a deep moral sickness that continues to go undiagnosed and untreated in our once-great nation. Random, unreasoned acts of violence mark the spirit of the age.

Last weekend there were drive-by shootings, a car jacking, hit-and-run incidents and dozens of other painful, destructive activities in our city, and many times more in the nation and the world. Most of these acts are random.

Since Cain and Abel there have been acts of violence that reflect conflict within a relationship. But it's a quantum leap from that kind of violence, as abhorrent as it is, to random violence, where there is no relation between the victim and the victimizer.

Rage is a part of the equation of random acts of violence. But lots of us are outraged, and we don't do what we see being done in the name of outrage. No, there's more than rage at work here.

There's arrogance. I can't imagine the level of arrogance it must require to rob someone at gun-point at a local mall and then, after full cooperation by the victims, point the gun at a young man about to be married, and shoot him dead before the eyes of those who loved him.

There's also fear in this equation, perhaps paranoia that everyone is an enemy and to survive in this world, it's kill, or be killed. Those who carry the weapons that randomly wound and kill, must be filled with irrational fear. When mingled with anger and arrogance, it becomes a deadly combination destined to find expression in random acts of violence.

But there's another side to this equation, as there always is. And the other side of the equation is the answer. An equation should have a solution. And the solution is that in-but-not-of-the-world followers of Jesus, not only survive, but also affect change despite the spirit of the age.

A good starting place is II Timothy 1:7, *For God hath not given us the spirit of fear; but of power, and of love, and of a sound mind.*

Empowered by His fearless Spirit we answer random acts of violence with random acts of kindness, in His name. Anger can be met with compassion – put the passion back in compassion. Indiscriminate vandalism can be met with undiscriminating grace. Arrogance is countered with humility, and the love of Jesus drives out all fear.

Practice random acts of kindness. It'll drive the devil crazy!

Life-style – now there's a phrase for our time, for sure, Dude. Everyone talks about life-style and everyone's got one, and wishes they had a better one. A generation or so ago, however, in harder times, the term was unknown and unnecessary. Affluence has given us the option of a life-style.

A popular television program allows us commoners to peer into the life-styles of the rich and famous. Such things captivate Americans. People who have all that stuff and do all those things have become heroes – the idols of our time.

A newspaper reported the emergence of a new syndrome, as if we needed another one. The counselors to the rich and famous say that people who have everything they want, have developed an inordinate number of ailments and physical complaints not found so frequently among the poor and fame-less.

They've given this syndrome a name. They call it "affluenza." It turns out that riches and fame are not all they are cracked up to be, and they don't satisfy the aching need of the human spirit. The frustration of the emptiness of affluence without God, produces a long list of physical and emotional effects that are making therapists and physicians as rich as their unhappy patients.

Jesus recognized the futility of Godless affluence. He said, *The ground of a certain rich man yielded plentifully. And he thought within himself, saying, 'What shall I do, since I have no room to store my crops?' So he said, 'I will do this: I will pull down my barns and build greater, and I will say to my soul, "Soul, you have many goods laid up for many years; take your ease; eat, drink, and be merry."'*

But God said to him, 'Fool! This night your soul will be required of you; then whose will those things be which you have provided?' So is he who lays up treasure for himself, and is not rich toward God. (Luke 12:16-21)

What are the symptoms of affluenza? What's its cause? Both questions have the same answer: ingratitude. Ingratitude is symptomatic of the diseases of our affluent society, but it's the root cause, as well. An ungrateful heart is fertile ground for trouble.

The life-style of the poor and fame-less, on the other hand, is marked by gratitude for all things great and small. As it turns out, those who hold title to the kingdom of heaven are the really rich ones, and their riches don't make them sick. They heal.

I've known many who are wealthy and their lives are full and satisfying. They consider their abundance to be a blessing from God, and not merely the result of their shrewdness and ingenuity. They are grateful. They are poor in spirit.

What Is A Veteran?

Tomorrow is Veteran's Day. I share this from an unknown source:

"What is a Veteran? Some veterans bear visible signs of their service: a missing limb, a jagged scar, a certain look in the eye. Others may carry the evidence inside them: a pin holding a bone together, a piece of shrapnel in the leg – or perhaps another sort of inner steel: the soul's alloy forged in the refinery of adversity.

"Except in parades, the men and women who have kept America safe wear no badge or emblem. You can't tell a vet just by looking. Just what is a vet?

"He's the cop on the beat who spent six months in Saudi Arabia sweating two gallons a day making sure the armored personnel carriers didn't run out of fuel. He's the loudmouth, whose overgrown-boy behavior is outweighed a hundred times by four hours of exquisite bravery near the 38th parallel.

"She, or he, is the nurse who fought against futility and went to sleep sobbing every night for two solid years in Da Nang. He's the POW who went away one person and came back another – or didn't come back at all.

"He's the Quantico drill instructor that has never seen combat – but has saved countless lives by turning slouchy, no-account rednecks and gang members into Marines, and teaching them to watch each other's backs.

"He's the parade-riding Legionnaire who pins on his ribbons and medals with a prosthetic hand. He's the career quartermaster who watches the ribbons and medals pass him by.

"He's three anonymous heroes resting in The Tomb Of The Unknowns, whose presence at the Arlington National Cemetery forever preserves the memory of all the anonymous heroes on the battlefield, or in the ocean's sunless deep.

"He's an ordinary, yet extraordinary human being, a person who offered some of his life's most vital years in the service of his country, and who sacrificed his ambitions so others would not have to sacrifice theirs. He's a soldier and a savior, and a sword against the darkness.

"So remember, each time you see someone who has served our country, just lean over and say, "Thank you." That's all most people need, and in most cases, it will mean more than you can imagine."

Two little words that mean a lot: "THANK YOU."

Veteran's Day *11/11 – November 11*

Today at precisely 11am, a combined color guard representing all military services will execute "Present Arms" at the Tomb of the Unknowns in Arlington National Cemetery. The laying of a presidential wreath and a bugler playing "Taps" marks our nation's tribute to its war dead.

This ceremony takes place every year in three countries at the 11th hour of the 11th day of the 11th month to honor those who have given the last full measure of devotion in the service of their respective countries. In London, England, the ceremony takes place at Westminster Abbey; in Paris, France, it's at the Arc de Triomphe.

It's been this way since November 11, 1926, when Armistice Day was made a National holiday to commemorate the end of World War I, on the 11th hour of the 11th day, of the 11th month in the year 1918. In 1954, the name of the holiday was changed to Veteran's Day to honor the dead of all the wars since the Armistice of World War I.

Our nation is even now engaged in a war against terrorism in a far way place with many strange sounding names. Our cause is just, our mission is honorable, but the real cost in lives and property of this war is staggering.

A group of academics and historians has compiled this startling information: Since 3,600 B.C., the world has known only 292 years of peace. During this period there have been 14,351 wars large and small, in which 3.64 billion people have been killed.

The value of the property destroyed is equal to a golden belt around the world 97.2 miles wide and 33 feet thick. Since 650 B.C., there have also been 1,656 arms races, only 16 of which have not ended in war.

A few years ago, a Dutch professor took time to calculate the cost of an enemy soldier's death at different epochs in history. He estimated that during the reign of Julius Caesar, to kill an enemy soldier cost less than one dollar. At the time of Napoleon, it had considerably inflated – to more than $2,000. In Vietnam, in 1970, to kill an enemy soldier cost the United States $200,000.

At another time and another place, another war was ended at the cost of blood. The war was between sin, sickness, and death, and the God of creation. The blood was not ours – it was His. Here's a glimpse of the grand celebration yet to be when our Well-Known Soldier, Jesus Christ, appears.

And they sang a new song: "You are worthy to take the scroll and to open its seals, because you were slain, and with your blood you purchased men for God from every tribe and language and people and nation. You have made them to be a kingdom and priests to serve our God, and they will reign on the earth." (Revelation 5:9, 10)

Hallelujah!

November 12 – 11/12 — *Lovingkindness*

How precious is Thy lovingkindness, O God! (Psalm 36:7) *The Lord appeared to him saying, "I have loved you with an everlasting love; therefore I have drawn you with lovingkindness."* (Jeremiah 31:3)

Every time I use the word "lovingkindness" in this writing, the spell-checker flags it. It's an old fashioned word with a meaning as fresh as today. The newer translations of Scripture have chosen less archaic expressions. They say things like, "unfailing love," "grace," or "compassion." But lovingkindness says something that others words don't quite communicate.

It's not just love; it's love in tangible, touchable form – kindness. And it's not just kindness, (which could be given grudgingly, with a frown) – but no! It's given with a smile and motivated by genuine selfless love. And it's not just any lovingkindness – it's God's lovingkindness. What a concept!

A child was asked to define lovingkindness and he came up with my favorite explanation. He said, "If you're hungry and someone gives you a piece of bread that's kindness. But if they put lots of your favorite jam on it – that's lovingkindness!"

I think this describes the ministry of Steve and Linda Tavani and their "WOW Jam" ministry. Can I suggest that an appropriate expression, with the child's definition of lovingkindness in mind, would be – "Wow! Jam!"

What Steve and Linda bring to the inner cities of America is an unmistakable demonstration of God's lovingkindness. It's more than a piece of bread given to hungry souls, it's bread smothered with delicious sweetness.

When grocery bags and houseplants, bicycles and footballs, family portraits and haircuts are given without strings attached – that's lovingkindness. When babies are rocked and faces are painted, bicycles repaired and games are enjoyed, and love is extended without reservation – that's lovingkindness.

When Steve and Linda sing their songs and pour out their hearts to people they've only just met – that's lovingkindness. And when the message of God's offer of forgiveness is announced – that's lovingkindness.

I love the phrase in the Scripture above, *I have loved you with an everlasting love; therefore I have drawn you with lovingkindness.* It makes you think that you're very special to God. This is true, but it says more about our Heavenly Father.

God doesn't extend His lovingkindness to us because we're so special. We're all sinners – every last one of us. He draws us to Himself because He's so special – unique in all the universe. He calls us to follow Him in a lifetime adventure that sees His lovingkindness in every day that we live.

And His lovingkindness is new every morning.

What Have You Learned? *11/13 – November 13*

The heart of a prudent man acquires knowledge, and the ear of the wise man seeks knowledge... The fear of the Lord is the beginning of wisdom and the knowledge of the Holy one is understanding. (Proverbs 18:15, 9:10)

We live in a world of way too much information. It's everywhere – coming at us from all sides – trying to convince us to buy this or that, vote for him or her, or manipulate us in hundreds of other ways.

"Knowledge is power," they say, and there's no shortage of people gaining and using knowledge to control the market place of our minds for personal profit. This is not what Solomon had in mind when he wrote about the priority of knowledge.

Wisdom and knowledge – learning – must begin with reverent awe (fear) of the Lord. If we don't begin here, the stream of data flowing to and through us can be contaminated with fatal self-interest. The fear of the Lord, for me, is a filter insuring that the information I ingest is tested for contamination.

I embrace the learning process. I love to learn new things. A day in which I don't gain some bit of new knowledge is pretty much a wasted day. But with so much information from which to choose, I must constantly discern between what is good and what is evil, what to keep and what to throw away. The grid that helps me discern the difference is the "fear of the Lord" – an awesome reverence for His presence and power in my life.

True knowledge isn't power – it's humility. The more I know, the more I know that I don't know. Every time I learn something – anything – it becomes an exercise in wonder; a reverent peek into the heart of the Holy One Who made all things, and already knows everything about everything.

Have you learned anything lately? What have you learned? How has what you have learned changed you? We not only live and learn, but when we stop learning – we stop living as God intended living to be.

Aunt Lucy had become somewhat deaf in her advanced years and a specialist suggested an operation to improve her hearing. But she promptly vetoed the idea, saying: "I'm 94 years old, and I've heard enough"

God help us if we ever come to the place where we say, "I've learned enough." There is strong evidence that we will continue to learn new things for all the ages of eternity.

I wondered how I would respond to the question, "What have you learned?" It's hard to reduce a lifetime of learning to one sentence, but if pressed to do so I would say, "I've learned that God is good!"

I don't expect that gem of knowledge of the Holy One will ever change.

A honeycomb – that's what it looks like; a cellular telephone network looks like a honeycomb. It's a wonderful innovation. You can drive anywhere in the nation and be in touch with anyone with a telephone through your cell-phone. Move from one area to another and your call is "handed off" to another cell in the network. Amazing.

The Church in this area is a cellular thing. Geographically, our various and sundry congregations have the Valley covered. Doctrinally, we've got all the bases covered, too. Together, we cover the range of racial, cultural and ethnic spectrums, as well.

Like the cellular telephone, we carry the same message – Jesus is Lord – handing it off from neighborhood to neighborhood, creed to creed, and nationality to nationality. Come to think of it, that's how the human body functions – living cell to living cell.

The various expressions of the Church in the Valley are a lot more alike than they are different. But there's a lot more talk about the differences than the one-ness. In these lines I invite you to join me in celebrating our alike-ness – our "cellular-one-ness," if you please.

I'm so aware of the limitations of my own experience. I only know what I've been taught. My experience is confined to what has actually happened to me. I am not better or worse than my brothers and sisters in another "cell" for my knowledge or experience – just different.

We need all the other "cells" so we can be His whole body on the earth. Whatever the Holy Spirit is up to in the earth, will touch every cell of the Body of Christ.

A song on Christian radio captured my attention. The grammar leaves a bit to be desired but the message of the song is the core of this page. I don't remember the artist or the verse. I only remember the chorus:

> "No one of us has got it all together, but all of us together, got it all."

We can learn a lot from each other, if we give ourselves a chance. And we can learn a lot from those who have trod this path before us. Our cellular-one-ness not only links us to our contemporaries, it spans the centuries to link us with the historic church.

The Church has its critics and naysayers. They say we're out of touch with reality. They say we have no place in the public arena. They say we're too divided to be effective. Wrong, wrong, wrong.

We touch eternal reality. We're in the public arena but not of it. And our diversity is not division – it's the genius of our cellular-oneness. Send the message from living cell to living cell – around the world: JESUS LIVES!

Watch Yourself! — *11/15- November 15*

Be on the alert, stand firm in the faith, act like men, be strong. (I Corinthians 16:13)

The King James Version of "be on the alert" is "watch ye", which literally means, "watch yourself."

We're quite good at watching the weather, watching television, watching the stock market, and watching our friends and neighbors, but when it comes to watching ourselves we don't do much of that. Certainly, some of us are too introspective, and that can lead to a condition I call "in-grown eyeballs."

Fix your eyes on Jesus, says the Hebrew writer. Yet Jesus Himself delivers this admonition to those who would follow Him, *And what I say unto you I say unto all, Watch.* (Mark 13:37)

Watch your thoughts; they become words. What we think is important, but quality thinking is becoming a lost art. Our culture is obsessed with amusement. We have TV, movies, sports, electronic games, the Internet, etc. all designed to amuse us.

I wondered about the origin of the word "amuse" so I looked it up and found something revealing. "Muse" means to think. A museum is where one goes to think about amazing things.

The prefix "a" in the ancient Greek means "not." An a-theist is one who is not a theist, a God-believer. So "a-muse" means not thinking. Amusement is a diversion from thinking, and it has its place, in balance, but we're being amused to death. And the first casualty is wholesome, meditative, creative thought.

Watch your words; they become actions. Shallow thoughts produce empty words, and empty words lead to superficial, ineffective action. Our mouth often leads they way, either into trouble or triumph. We say things we don't mean because we haven't thought about their meaning.

Watch your actions; they become habits. When weeds are young, they can be easily pulled up by the roots. But the longer they grow, the deeper they're rooted. And at some point they can't be uprooted, except by a hand stronger than our own.

Watch your habits; they become character. Over time, actions repeated shape our lives more deeply that we can imagine. And character counts.

Watch your character; it becomes your destiny. It all begins with thoughts.

Let the words of my mouth and the meditation of my heart be acceptable in Thy sight, O Lord, my rock and my Redeemer. (Psalm 19:1)

"And I say unto you – watch!"

November 16 – 11/16 ***The Preparations of The Heart***

The preparations of the heart belong to man, but the answer of the tongue is from the Lord. (Proverbs 16:1) Ready or not the holiday season is upon us. Some preparation of our hearts is in order.

To this day in many rural areas in our country unpaved roads outnumber paved ones. Over time deep grooves are formed by the wheels of traffic in the earth of the road's surface. Once an automobile has steered into one of these tracks in the road, a driver will find it very difficult to steer out of it.

On one such dirt road in Iowa, there's a warning sign posted that reads: "Choose your rut well – you'll be in it for the next twenty miles."

We have, at this early date, a chance to choose the track we will take into the Holiday Season. Choose well, because whichever rut you choose, you'll be in for the next month or so.

Our city, our nation, and your family, are about to be caught up in the mad rush toward Thanksgiving and Christmas. Many respond to this annual orgy of spending, commercialization, and hectic activity by simply refusing to participate in any way, shape, or form.

But there's something of great value in giving thanks and the celebration of God with us, that a little preparation of the heart will preserve for our families and for the church.

I've been thinking about that verse in Proverbs that says, *The preparations of the heart belong to man.* My part is the preparation of my heart; and this means time to pray and think about the wonder of God's unspeakable gifts to me.

To my part God adds His, which is the answer of the tongue – to give life to the words I hear and speak, and the songs I sing.

What can I do to prepare the heart of my family? That will be up to you and your family but it begins with taking time to think about it, and talk about it.

Modern Christians don't take time to think very long or very deeply. So we don't talk to each other very much either. Our thinking is, for the most part, done for us by pastors and teachers, whose job it is to think and talk.

But your heart will never be prepared for worship or celebration by someone else's meditation. Indeed, the preparations of your heart belong to you!

So do your holiday thinking early – and avoid the rush!

I've Had It! *11/17 – November 17*

Usually, when someone says, "I've had it!" they're in a state of utter frustration. "I just can't take any more," is soon to follow. Sometimes the frustrated one will say, for emphasis, "I've had it – up to here," and point to the head and neck area.

What is "it?" The pronoun "it" generally refers to some tangible, usually inanimate, object whose name we choose to substitute for "it." Well, I'd like to define "it," from one man's perspective.

"I've had it!" for me, is not an expression of frustration but of gratitude. And when I say, "I've had it up to here," I point, not to my head but my heart; and from the abundance of my heart I speak of the "its" I've had.

"It" is forgiveness – I've had it! I weep as I write of the grace of the Lord extended to me that enables me to minister in His name, and live to the praise of His glory. My heart overflows with gratitude that I am forgiven.

"It" is a Godly heritage – I've had it! My parents and my grandparents on both sides were men and women of God. They introduced me Jesus. My wife's parents gave her a Godly heritage also. And when I speak of a Godly heritage I refer, not only to the one I got, but also to the one I give to my children and grandchildren. I'm grateful.

"It" is opportunity – I've had it! I've been graciously given the opportunity to write words like these for over eighteen years. That was a gift to me – I didn't earn it. I've had the opportunity to grow and develop skills that are useful in the Kingdom of God. I'm grateful.

"It" is freedom – I've had it! America is a great place to live. The freedom we enjoy is unique in the world. But I speak of a more personal, intimate freedom – freedom from bondage to sin, substance, and Satan that could have destroyed my life by this time. It is the grace of God, not my strength that has kept me free. I'm grateful.

"It" is wonder – I've had it! God has granted me a wonder-full heart, an awe-filled mind, and the emotional capacity to appreciate grandeur and glory, and the awesome majesty of His presence. And, wonder of wonders, I get to pass the wonder on to my grandchildren and anyone else who cares. I'm grateful.

"It" is family – I've had it with my family! They are precious to me – my wife, Beth; my son, Lincoln; my daughter, April; my daughter, Cathy, her husband, Mike and their children, Tessa, Michael, Chelsea, Justin and Ryan. These people are the joy of my life – and I'm grateful!

"It" is life – I've had it! Abundantly! Eternally! It is great to be alive! Thank You Jesus! I'm grateful.

I hope you can identify with some of my "its" and fill in some of your own. When it comes to blessing of the Lord – I've had it!

November 18 – 11/18 *Deeper Thanks*

Do you expect to be thankful? Thanksgiving is coming up next week and it's worth a little effort to plan to be grateful. Expectations go a long way toward shaping reality.

This year I expect to reach down a little deeper for my thanksgiving. Let me explain. We generally can come up with some material things for which to be thankful, like our home and our health and our tangible blessings. There's nothing wrong with that.

But when I say I'm going to reach a little deeper this year I'm reminded of a prayer that I read recently in a sermon entitled "Washed," by Stephen Shoemaker. I don't normally read prayers but this one was originally written on the inner wall of a Nazi concentration camp in Germany.

It said, "O Lord, when I shall come into the glory of Your kingdom, do not remember only the men of good will; remember also the men of evil.

"May they be remembered not only for their acts of cruelty in this camp, the evil they have done to us prisoners, but balance against their cruelty the fruits which we have reaped under the stress and in the pain; the comradeship, the courage, the greatness of heart, the humility and patience which have become part of our lives, because we have suffered at their hands.

"May the memory of us not be a nightmare to them, O Lord, when they stand in judgment. May all that we have suffered be acceptable to you as a ransom for them."

I was deeply moved by the thought of those so cruelly treated reaching down to find gratitude for their captors because of what the pain had produced in them. I realize it's not possible for any one but Jesus to be a ransom for sinners but, the point is that they bore their suffering the way Jesus bore His, so it's not surprising that they would feel as He felt toward His enemies.

I've known pain; not like those in concentration camps, but pain nonetheless. And you have, too. I also can define some qualities in me that would not be there if it hadn't been for the pain. God has caused me to be shaped by the stress, and I am grateful!

Rejoice always; pray without ceasing; in everything give thanks; for this is God's will for you in Christ Jesus. (I Thessalonians 5:16-18)

In Everything Give Thanks *11/19 – November 19*

Martin Rinkart wrote one of the best-loved Thanksgiving hymns – "Now Thank We All Our God." He wrote it in 1637 in the middle of the Thirty Year's War. He was pastor of a church in Saxony, in northern Germany.

Saxony was severely attacked three times during the war but survived. The city became a haven for refugees and wounded soldiers. As the population doubled, and then doubled again, food and water supplies were depleted, and what little food they had was contaminated with rats and insects.

Plague swept the city and for a time, Rinkart was the only pastor in the city. Due to the plague and the war he conducted as many as fifty funerals a day. In the midst of these circumstances he wrote these words:

"Now thank we all our God, with heart and hands and voices,
Who wondrous things hath done, in Whom the world rejoices.
Who, from our mother's arms hath blest us on our way,
With countless gifts of love, and still is ours today."

Only the hardest heart is ungrateful for the blessings of life. It's human nature to be thankful for good things. But those with hearts made new by the Spirit of God can joyfully obey the admonition of I Thessalonians 5:18, *In everything give thanks for this is the will of God in Christ Jesus for you.*

Giving thanks in difficult times should not be confused with giving thanks for difficult times. While I'm grateful for God's grace revealed to me in some very dark times, I've not yet been able to muster sincere thanksgiving for those times of desperate loneliness and grief.

It's a distortion of truth to say that we should thank God for everything, even the tragedies and havoc caused by sin, the disobedience of fallen man and the treachery of Satan. But in the middle of all that, I can be grateful that God's grace is enough.

Pastor Rinkart knew this. The second verse of his hymn reflects the difficult times in which he lived and his grateful spirit, despite the pain and death all around him.

"O may this bounteous God through all our lives be near us;
With ever joyful hearts, and blessed peace to cheer us.
And keep us in His grace, and guide us when perplexed;
And free us from all ills, in this world and the next."

The voice of joy and the voice of gladness, the voice of those who say, "Give thanks to the LORD of hosts, for the LORD is good, for His lovingkindness is everlasting"; and of those who bring a thank offering into the house of the LORD. For I will restore the fortunes of the land as they were at first,' says the LORD. (Jeremiah 33:11)

Give thanks unto the Lord, call upon his name, make known his deeds among the people... O give thanks unto the Lord; for he is good; for his mercy endures forever. (I Chronicles 16:8, 34)

When he was released from prison after being convicted of conspiracy in the Watergate affair, G. Gordon Liddy said, "I have found within myself all I need and all I ever shall need. I am a man of great faith, but my faith is in George Gordon Liddy. I have never failed me."

This macho mind-set is just so much hot air, but if he really believes this, it reveals a brain the size of a pea and a heart as hard as a rock. But sadly, it's an attitude shared by an increasing number of people who worship at the altar of a god made in the likeness of them.

How absurd to think that any of us could exist without air, water, food, faith, hope, and love, all of which were here when we arrived, and are not the product of human effort or ingenuity.

There's a revival of "spirituality" in our culture, but the word has a strange new meaning. To be "spiritual," by the new definition, means to be self-aware, self-actualized and self-absorbed. True spirituality isn't self-anything. It's all about God, and it begins with a grateful heart.

A Gallop Poll survey of 1,000 people last Thanksgiving revealed American's gratitude levels. 61% percent were most thankful for their family. 50% named health; 21% their occupation; 20% were most grateful for children. Just being alive accounted for 12%. Only 8% included God as the thing for which they were most thankful.

Maybe they forgot or just assumed their gratitude for God. But perhaps we've become so thankful for the blessings, that we have forgotten the Blesser.

George Washington made Thanksgiving his first proclamation for the new nation. The occupant of the oval office has renewed it every year since then. This is much more than mere ceremony. It's a reminder of our roots and testimony of God's grace so bountifully poured out upon us.

Thanksgiving has been the audible expression of grateful hearts since the angels sang creation's accompaniment. (see Job 38:7) And according to Revelation 7:12, it will continue throughout eternity.

Blessing, and glory, and wisdom, and thanksgiving, and honor, and power, and might, be unto our God forever and ever. Amen.

You Can't Just Be Grateful *11/21 – November 21*

I don't usually begin by quoting William Shakespeare, but he did have a way with words. "Ingratitude, thou marble-hearted fiend, more hideous, when showest thou in a child, than a sea monster." That's from "King Lear."

And here's another gem from the bard: "I hate ingratitude more in man than lying, vainness, babbling, drunkenness, or any taint of vice whose strong corruption inhabits our frail blood. How sharper than a serpent's tooth it is to have a thankless child." You get the idea that Shakespeare didn't much like ingratitude. And neither does God.

This week we celebrate Thanksgiving. A group declared an "International Year of Thanksgiving" a few years ago. We didn't hear much about it from our politically preoccupied media, but people around the world were encouraged to give thanks.

But I wonder about such a general and nebulous move toward encouraging gratitude. It was good on the surface, but gratitude, like love and faith, must embrace a worthy object. You can't just be grateful.

In the material I read from the International Thanksgiving movement, there was not hint of a suggestion that we direct our thanks toward God. "Just be thankful." But we have the opportunity to set that matter straight in our circle of influence.

Calvin Coolidge, known for brevity of words, said this: "We have been a most favored people. We ought to be a most grateful people. We have been a most blessed people. We ought to be a most thankful people."

Favored and blessed by whom? By Almighty God – that's "Whom." You can't just be grateful – you've got to be grateful to someone for something. It's good to be thankful, but for what – and to whom?

When Shakespeare said, "thou marble-hearted fiend" he pictured a heart so hard that even gratitude couldn't escape it. Well, nothing can get into a marble heart, either.

May the Lord soften our hearts to allow His grace to enter and our praise to find expression this week and always.

It is good to give thanks to the Lord, and to sing praises to Thy name, O most high; to declare Thy lovingkindness in the morning and Thy faithfulness at night. (Psalm 92:1, 2)

And He took the seven loaves and the fish; and giving thanks, He broke them and gave them to His disciples... (Matthew 15:36)

What Jesus did before He and His disciples ate the bread and the fish has given rise to the uniquely Christian custom of giving thanks at mealtime. We call it "saying grace." That's an interesting phrase, when you think about it. It's actually about remembering God's grace and giving thanks for all of the blessings His gracious hand supplies.

We live in an increasingly secular world where fewer and fewer children are being taught gratitude. In this environment of thoughtless indulgence, don't ever under estimate the value of giving thanks at the table for teaching gratitude. This practice has been a factor in my life for sixty-nine years and has greatly helped in the shaping of my grateful heart.

Giving thanks for God's provision may be a ritual that seems to have little meaning, but the measure of its value can be seen over time. Consider the affect of not giving thanks. That amounts to a ritual, too. Anything one does, or doesn't do for that matter, with regularity becomes a ritual or a habit. And, sadly, most people who walk the earth practice the ritual of ingratitude.

The author Fulton Ousler tells of his nurse who was born a slave in Maryland. She had been with the family for many years, tending to the birth of his mother and his own birth. She taught him a lesson in giving thanks.

"I remember her as she sat at the kitchen table; the hard, old, brown hands folded across her starched apron, the glistening eyes, and the husky old whispering voice, saying, 'Much obliged, Lord, for my vittles.'

"'Anna,' I asked, 'What's a vittle?' 'It's what I've got to eat and drink, that's vittles.' 'But you'd get your vittles whether you thanked the Lord or not,' I said. 'Sure,' she replied, 'but it makes everything taste better to be thankful.'"

Some years ago a popular TV program took viewers into the "life styles of the rich and famous." Interestingly, many of those who were "stars" of the show are now neither rich nor famous; they're destitute and infamous. Their wealth and fame were fleeting fancies.

Well, thanksgiving is the life-style of the poor and fame-less, for theirs is the kingdom of heaven! Some call things like saying grace, or uttering a spontaneous "praise the Lord!" a mindless ritual, but I'd rather call it a life-style – a life-style of thanksgiving.

Have a blessed and happy Thanksgiving!

The Gift Of A Grateful Heart *11/23 – November 23*

And in that day you will say, "Give thanks to the LORD, call on His name. Make known His deeds among the peoples; make them remember that His name is exalted." Praise the LORD in song, for He has done excellent things; let this be known throughout the earth. Cry aloud and shout for joy, O inhabitant of Zion, for great in your midst is the Holy One of Israel. (Isaiah 12:4-6)

He wants us to have a grateful heart and tell everyone about it. In just such a simple way God's people can dramatically affect life in their world. Imagine it – thousands of people all over this city who are grateful, and say so. How unlike the world – but isn't that what it's all about?

In southern Alabama is the town of Enterprise. There they have erected a monument to an insect, honoring the boll weevil. In 1895 the boll weevil began to destroy the major crop of the county, cotton. In desperation the farmers had to diversify, and by 1919 the county's peanut crop was many times what cotton had been at its height. In that year of prosperity a fountain and a monument was built.

The inscription reads: "In profound appreciation of the boll weevil and what it has done as the herald of prosperity, this monument was erected by the citizens of Enterprise, Alabama. Out of a time of struggle and crisis came new growth and success. Out of adversity came blessing."

Leo Tolstoy, tells the story of a rich peasant who was never grateful for what he had. He always wanted more and heard of a chance to get more land. For 1000 rubles he could have all that he could walk around in a day. But he had to make it back to the starting point by sundown or he would lose it all.

He arose early and set out. He walked on and on, thinking that he could get just a little more land if he kept going. But he went so far that he realized he must walk very fast if he was to get back in time to claim the land. As the sun got lower in the sky, he quickened his pace. He began to run.

As he came within sight of the starting place, he exerted his last energies, plunged over the finish line, fell to the ground, and collapsed. A stream of blood poured out of his mouth and he lay dead. His servant took a spade, dug a grave, and buried him there.

This is the sad plight of those who aren't grateful for today – whatever it brings. They wear themselves out in the pursuit of more.

What a blessed gift is a grateful heart!

November 24 – 11/24 *Squanto Thanks*

Today Americans will consume 75 million pounds of turkey. When one young man was asked what he was thankful for he replied, "I'm thankful that I'm not a turkey." Amen! I'm thankful I'm not a cranberry, too.

Our national observance of a day set aside to give thanks traces its origins to the Pilgrim's thanksgiving feast in November, 1621. But there is more to this story than we may have been taught in school.

Incredibly, when the Pilgrims stepped ashore in 1620, a Native American who spoke perfect English met them. One of the most amazing characters in early American history was this man, Squanto.

He was a member of the Pawtuxet tribe of Cape Cod. In 1605 he was kidnapped and taken to England. He was treated well and lived in London until 1614 when he was able to return to America.

Unfortunately, he was kidnapped again and taken to Spain. There he was sold to a group of Christian friars. He was treated kindly, and under their influence, was baptized upon his profession of faith in Jesus Christ.

In 1617, Squanto left the monastery and made his way to England again where a ship captain, in 1619, agreed to take him back to America. The year after he returned, the Pilgrims landed at Plymouth Rock, and Squanto was there to greet them.

In the Spring of 1621, Squanto taught the Pilgrims native methods of planting and fertilizing corn and squash. He showed them how to hunt and fish. Had it not been for Squanto, the Pilgrims might well have all perished.

It was Squanto who was sent to invite Chief Massasoit and his tribe to the thanksgiving feast in 1621. More than anyone else, Squanto was responsible for the peaceful relationship between the Pilgrims and most of the Native American tribes in New England. In 1622, Squanto, also called Tisquantum, died while leading the Pilgrims around Cape Cod.

The Pilgrims, while still on board the Mayflower in 1620, asked God for help in their venture, but none of them would have dared to ask for anything like a friendly native who spoke English and would help them because of a common faith in Jesus Christ.

God had prepared Squanto for sixteen years to speak English, to find faith in Jesus, and to be there to meet those whom He would send in to establish a new nation in His name. Amazing!

I wonder how many things in our lives that are painful for us now and disastrous, as Squanto's kidnappings, must have been for him, are part of a greater plan than we can possibly understand now. I'm grateful for Squanto.

Happy Thanksgiving!

Not All Of This Is Me — *11/25 – November 25*

A professor at the University of Chicago tells of his three-year-old granddaughter who liked to visit him late in the afternoon so she could walk home with him.

One day she asked him if she could ride on his shoulders across the campus. That day, another professor walked by, and with a twinkle in his eye he said, "My goodness, how you've grown! You're much taller than you were last week." The little girl replied with a grin, "Not all of this is me."

No matter how great our accomplishments, we're all riding one the shoulders of people who have loved us, helped us, encouraged us, and gone before us. It's through the mercy and grace of Jesus that we are who we are. "Not all of this is me," ends up being "without Him I can do nothing."

A ninety-year-old woman gave this piece of advice to her son. "I want to tell you something and I want you to remember it and pass it on to your children. Here it is: Every material possession you acquire becomes a stick to beat you with – unless you're grateful."

There is some truth in that statement. Too much is not enough, to an ungrateful heart. And the things we possess begin to possess us and rule us with a big, expensive stick.

We will have many opportunities to voice our gratitude. It would be wise if we didn't neglect a single one of those. Our Father is a good listener. Our songs and words of thanksgiving are music to His ears. Redeemed voices sing His favorite song of all.

The day after Thanksgiving may be a good time to talk about dieting, so I thought this was a cute little story, which might lighten the season a bit.

A certain Mrs. Watson was overweight so her doctor put her on a diet. "I want you to eat regularly for two days, then skip a day, and repeat this procedure for two weeks. The next time I see you, you'll have lost at least five pounds.

When Mrs. Watson returned to the doctor in two weeks, she shocked him by losing nearly twenty pounds. "Did you follow my instructions?" Mrs. Watson nodded. "I'll tell you what, though, I thought I was going to drop dead that third day," she responded.

"You mean from hunger?" asked the doctor. "No, from skipping."

Open to me the gates of righteousness; I shall enter through them, I shall give thanks to the LORD. This is the gate of the LORD; the righteous will enter through it. I shall give thanks to Thee, for Thou hast answered me; and Thou hast become my salvation. (Psalm 118:19-21)

November 26 – 11/26 *Long Chains*

I find cartoons to be a source of inspiration sometimes. Such was the case once in the San Francisco Chronicle. The man in the cartoon thinks he's free, but he's still attached to a chain, the other end of which is firmly anchored in a prison cell. He's "yahooing" it up, but he just hasn't gotten to the end of his chain yet. The caption was, "Long chains and how they create a false sense of security."

It got me thinking how it's possible to feel free at times and yet still have the chains of bondage attached – chains so long that we haven't gotten to the end of them yet.

I'm not talking about the freedom that Jesus gives those who come to Him repenting and confessing their sin and weakness. That freedom is absolute and those whom the Son sets free are, indeed, free!

I'm talking about other kinds of bondage, bondage to debt, for instance. Or take bondage to habits that linger beyond one's entrance into the Kingdom of God's dear Son. It may be an attachment to a relationship that's gone beyond the bounds of discretion. In these cases, there are times when one feels free only to discover that the chain is still there – you just haven't gotten to the end of it yet.

I had an Irish Setter once. We kept him in a rather small back yard with a six-foot high fence. That was fine until he grew up. Then with one grand leap he could clear the fence and be off roaming the neighborhood.

I finally had to chain him with enough length to let him roam the yard but not enough to reach the fence. At first he would run toward the fence with memories of past freedom in his dog brain. Then, when he reached the end of his chain, he was jerked back to reality. He thought he was free but he wasn't.

But consider the falconer with falcon on his leather-girded arm. He ties a long cord to the bird's leg and his own arm. He throws raw meat and the bird flies after it. The falcon takes the meat and flies to freedom. Then, at the moment that the bird reaches the end of the cord the falconer blows a whistle.

After hundreds of such experiences the cord can be removed and only the whistle used. The bird hears the whistle and believes he's still bound and returns dutifully to his perch. He is free and doesn't know it.

So we have a picture of people who are really bound but feel free, and people who feel bound but are really free. Do you fit in this scenario? Are there areas where you just haven't reached the end of your chain yet? Jesus will be there at the end of your chain – to set you free.

Or perhaps you are indeed free because Jesus redeemed you, but the devil keeps blowing that crazy whistle of condemnation, and you feel so bound.

Well, you can ignore the whistle and just keep on flying!

What's a Christian Marriage? *11/27 – November 27*

I've had it "up to here" with statistics that are fashioned to prove one point or another which, after closer examination, don't prove anything at all.

The old adage – figures don't lie, but liars do figure – is descriptive of our political and social climate today. It's getting so bad that I actually tune out anyone who attempts to prove a point by citing statistics.

One such statistic that troubles me deeply is the one that suggests that the failure rate for marriages is essentially the same for Christians as it is for non-Christians. Well, to follow the example of one famous user of statistics, "That depends on what you mean by 'Christian.'"

I refuse to believe that any serious disciple of Jesus Christ, striving to walk in His ways, in private and in public, takes marriage as lightly as one who has no knowledge at all of what it means to be a Christian – but calls himself one.

If by Christian they mean anyone who just clams to be one, then we have an entirely different database, and the results would be radically different. It's true that the institution of marriage is under severe attack, and even more so among the followers of Jesus Christ. Marriages are failing at record rates.

But it's also true that many of use have weathered storms that would have sunk our marital ship, had it not been for the healing grace of Jesus ministered by brothers and sisters who cared for us with genuine understanding and love.

The world doesn't know such power to heal broken marriages. It can't know it apart from relationship with God through Christ. And if one's commitment to marriage is no different than Donald Trump's or Jennifer Lopez's, then I have reason to question one's walk with Jesus.

As the church is subject to Christ, so also the wives ought to be to their husbands in everything. Husbands, love your wives, just as Christ also loved the church and gave Himself up for her; that He might sanctify her, having cleansed her by the washing of water with the word, that He might present to Himself the church in all her glory, having no spot or wrinkle or any such thing; but that she should be holy and blameless. (Ephesians 5:24-26)

I challenge any wife who calls herself a Christian to honor her husband in everything as the church does Christ. I challenge any husband who calls himself a Christian to love his wife as Christ loves the church and gave Himself for her to present her holy and blameless before God.

If that doesn't happen, then how can we be called followers of Jesus Christ – Christian? And if get the form to fill out that the surveys are based upon, and you come to the box that says "Christian" don't check it – leave it blank!

We begin our family's Advent Celebration soon. I guess I've reached the stage in my life where I'm sort of the patriarch of my family. I once didn't even know how to spell patriarch and now "I are one." As such, I sense the need to begin early to reinforce the spiritual essence of Christmas, before the materialistic deluge takes over completely.

In trying to stem the flood of secular values, I feel like the Dutch boy with his finger in the dike holding back the ocean. You might say I'm doing my Christmas "stopping" early. But it's worth the effort when I see wonder in my grandchildren's eyes.

I read something the other day that relates to the need to constantly renew the values that make for godliness. G.K. Chesterton wrote it. He said:

"It would seem that if you leave things alone you leave them as they are. But you do not. If you leave a thing alone you leave it to a torrent of change. If you leave a white post alone, it will soon be a black post. If you want it to be white you must always be painting it white again."

Christmas is like that white post. If we would know the deep, eternal meaning of Advent, the Savior's birth, we must be "painting the post" constantly with fresh insights and new inspiration. This isn't easy, but to fail is to allow creeping secular decay to win the battle for the hearts and minds of our children.

Think, for a moment, about the shepherds that came to the Christ Child at the urging of angels. They were simple people that suddenly found themselves in the presence of God. And they worshiped Him.

What must it have been like to be the first ones on earth to worship Jesus? I'd like to capture that freshness for my family this year.

I invite you to consider how you can give the old Christmas post a fresh coat of paint – red and green, of course.

Renew us, O Lord.

Recipe For A Miserable Marinade *11/29 – November 29*

Our family is beginning to focus on the amazing events surrounding the miracle of the virgin birth of Jesus – the Incarnation. We do this, not as ritual, but as an attempt to combat the inescapable exposure to the spirit of this age, and the commercial emphasis so prevalent during the Christmas season.

I've been thinking about a recipe for marinade? What's that got to do with Christmas? Well, I'm about to tell you.

I happened across a definition of "marinate. It's a verb meaning "to soak, steep, or saturate." And the noun, the substance with which something is soaked, steeped, or saturated, is called "marinade."

It's drawn from the French and Italian languages and, not surprisingly, applies mostly to foods, like steak or chicken or salad. But the marinating principle applies to our minds and hearts as well. We're exposed 24/7 to the values of a culture driven by greed, pride, and lust. We've become soaked, steeped, and saturated with a marinade of a godless culture.

The recipe for this "miserable marinade" is simple: take four to six hours of television daily, stir in CDs, MP3s, and radio's top-twenty hits – to taste. Add generous amounts of newspapers and magazines advertising the latest must-have styles and stuff. Season with unsupervised Internet surfing, chat rooms, and violent video games.

Simmer until blended into a smooth, enticing mixture. So, to have yourself a marinated Christmas, select a young tender mind, an old tough one, or for that matter, any mind will do. Soak, steep, and saturate it for a long season in the miserable marinade just described.

When finished you will have a mind and heart that resists truth, rebels against correction, and scoffs at the good news of God becoming flesh and living among us. You will have a heart and mind thoroughly steeped in the values of a godless culture.

Perhaps all this sounds a bit radical. After all, isn't TV just an innocent way to pass the time of day? And what's wrong with the Internet? Well, it's not so much what's wrong with it; it's what's right with it. I do find a lot that's right with much of what's in my recipe for a miserable marinade.

But we must always make choices in the use of any of the world's resources. The numbing influence of constant exposure to the world's values has already had a devastating effect upon generations of Christians.

Romans 12:2 says, *Don't copy the behavior and customs of this world, but let God transform you into a new person by changing the way you think. Then you will know what God wants you to do, and you will know how good and pleasing and perfect His will really is.*

These are days when it is cool to be half-hearted. This is the don't-let-them-see-you-sweat period of American life. But if this attitude invades the Church it certainly will not stand the light of Scriptural scrutiny.

Cornell University researchers wanted to know what people most regret. They surveyed university employees, students, retired professors and nursing home residents. They found that twice as many people were bothered more by what they did not do rather than what they had done.

Missed opportunities were the most common of all regrets, mostly from those who were unwilling to take chances and suffer the short-term consequences.

Years ago a missionary was traveling into the mountains of Mexico on a narrow gauge train. He noticed that the train took a sharp curve slowly and then started to ascend a steep grade. The engine was working as hard as it could to get them up the mountain.

Halfway up the engine began to slow down. The fireman poured on the coal as fast as he could but it continued to slow. Finally, with one last burst of steam, they made it to the top and coasted down the other side.

They stopped to fill up with water and coal and everyone got out to see what had happened. The firemen and brakemen gathered and talked about their close call. If they had lost power on the way up the hill and had begun to slide down, they never would have made the curve at the bottom of the grade.

Then one of the brakemen spoke up and said, "Yes, I was afraid of that. That's why I applied the brakes half-way up."

What's wrong with that picture? The train going up hill needs all the power it can muster, and a fearful brakeman applies the brakes on the way up.

There's a lot wrong with that picture, and sometimes it's like that in the life of the Church. Just when we need full steam ahead, somebody throws out the anchor, drags their feet, or applies the brakes at a critical moment.

These are such days. The harvest is white; the time is now for us to love the Lord our God with ALL our heart, ALL our mind, ALL our strength, and with ALL our soul.

The prince of this world cannot stand against a church united in its dedication to Jesus and obedience to His commands. It's an up hill battle, to be sure, which is even more reason to take the brakes off of our mission to "God into all the world and preach the Gospel to every creature."

Jesus is worthy of our whole-hearted devotion.

Do Your Christmas Thinking Early *12/1 – December 1*

I'm doing my Christmas thinking early. Commercialism gets such a head start on us that by the time we get around to thinking seriously about Christmas we're already sucked into the vortex of a secular, unholy spending binge.

My heart breaks when the Christmas binge begins before Halloween. I'm grieved by the full-court press our culture attempts in the name of a "healthy business year-end." Buying gifts is good, but there's got to be more to it than the sound of cash registers and credit-card machines measuring the success of the year for our local economy.

John the Baptist and Isaiah speak words appropriate for this season: *Prepare the way; make straight the path.* I offer these thoughts in the spirit of preparation for Advent. Incidentally, advent simply means, "the appearing."

Christian faith rests entirely upon the conviction that God has fully revealed Himself in Jesus Christ. *He is the image of the invisible God... in Him the fullness of God was pleased to dwell.* (Colossians 1:15, 19)

Think with me for a while about fullness. Imagine how you felt after your Thanksgiving dinner when you had eaten everything in sight. That's fullness. But that's discomfort, too.

Now imagine how full a little baby named Jesus might have felt. He was, the Bible declares, filled of all of God in His human body. And He appeared to be very comfortable with that kind of fullness.

Jesus is not only full of God, He is equal to God (Philippians 2:6), He is God, (John 10:30, 38; 12:45; 14:1-11); and as the image of the invisible God, He is the exact representation of God in human flesh.

He came from heaven, not from the dust of the earth (I Corinthians 15:47), and He is Lord of all (Romans 9:5). He is completely holy (Hebrews 7:26-28), and He has authority to judge the world (Romans 2:16; II Corinthians 5:10).

Therefore, Jesus Christ is supreme over all creation, including the spirit world. We, like our Colossian brothers, must believe that Jesus, the Babe in the manger, is God in flesh or our Christian faith is hollow, misdirected, and meaningless. This is a core value of Christianity and the essence of Christmas.

This amazing truth casts a wholly, (holy) different light upon our celebration the birth of the God-Man, Jesus. One writer declares, "The hinge of history was on the door of a Bethlehem stable."

Spiced cider and spicy living isn't what the Christmas season is about. Abundant life – fullness – that's what it's about.

God's fullness in Jesus, and His fullness in me.

In Cambridge, Mass. there's a stone, marking the grave of John Pierpont. The words in granite read: "Poet, Preacher, Philosopher, Philanthropist. He accomplished nothing he set out to do or be." Yet in one important sense, John Pierpont was not a failure. Every year in December, we celebrate his success.

It's a song. It's not a song about Santa Claus or angels or even Jesus. It's a terribly simple song about the simple joy of whizzing through the cold white dark of winter's gloom in a sleigh pulled by one horse; and with a company of friends, laughing and singing all the way, "Jingle Bells."

John Pierpont wrote "Jingle Bells." One snowy afternoon in deep winter, he penned the lines as a small gift for his family and congregation. In doing so he left behind a gift for all of us at Christmas.

The song "Jingle Bells" has absolutely no spiritual implications. It's just a simple little ditty that millions of people know but very few have any first-hand knowledge about. I wouldn't mention this song at all, except for a thought I had some time ago as I was reading in Exodus, of all places.

I've never dashed through the snow in a one horse open sleigh with bells jingling have you? But when I read Exodus 28:33-35 the song took on new meaning for me. It's talking about the garments (the ephod) of the high priest. Here's what it says:

The bottom edge of the ephod shall be embroidered with blue, purple, and scarlet pomegranates, alternated with gold bells. Aaron shall wear the ephod whenever he goes in to minister to the Lord; the bells will tinkle as he goes in and out of the presence of the Lord in the Holy Place, so that he will not die. (TLB)

The last phrase, "so he will not die," is understood to mean, "so that the people will know that he did not die." The picture is this: Aaron would go into the Holy of Holies, to do the work of the high priest. As he moved around, the people could hear the "bells of the ephod" jingling on the hem of his robe.

He offered the blood of the lamb for atonement for the sins of the people, he would sprinkle the blood on the walls and on the Mercy Seat, and as he moved the bells would jingle. If the sacrifice were accepted, he would live. As long as the bells jingled, the High Priest was alive, and the sacrifice was accepted.

Why do I get excited about "Jingle Bells?" Jesus was born, lived and died to offer sacrifice for my sins. His sacrifice was accepted when He rose from the dead as my High Priest, and He "ever lives to make intercession for us."

I'm going to sing "Jingle Bells" this year to celebrate my ever-living High Priest. "He's alive and I'm forgiven, heaven's gates are open wide!"

"Jingle Bells! Jingle Bells! Jingle all the way!"

The Irrational Season *12/3 – December 3*

"Christmas is the irrational season," someone has said. The word "irrational" isn't a pleasing word to our ears. There's something about it that makes us hold back and shrink from the idea that Christmas could be irrational.

Irrational behavior, for instance, usually describes the bizarre actions we see on the nightly news. We hear of a man who takes a rifle and shoots into a crowd; then kills himself. That's irrational behavior. It's unreasonable, out of control. We need lots of rational controls. We need order and reason.

There's something about the season of Christmas that brings out the irrational beast in us. It comes to the surface at the checkout counter of a busy store when someone tries to elbow his or her way ahead of the 18 people in line. Anyone willing to do such a thing may be savagely attacked, verbally, if not physically. The law of the jungle prevails here.

This is not about this kind of madness. A far different kind of irrationality is at issue here, a kind of irrationality that would challenge my deepest thoughts, and draw me to itself – and into deep wonder.

If life is always and only rational, it's a poor and colorless thing. Faith goes a step further than rationality; it declares that reason alone cannot save us. My personal faith in my living, risen Lord leads me to be open to a kind of irrationality that's not against reason – but that's beyond it.

That's what I mean when I say, "This is the irrational season." Any deeply thinking person must conclude that there is much about the Enfleshment of God in the form of a little child that is irrational – beyond reason.

Here reason gives way to wonder, and rationality surrenders to reverence. The astounding truth that we celebrate at Christmas is that at a particular time and place God came to be with us – Himself.

When Quirinius was governor of Syria, in a town called Bethlehem, a Child was born who, beyond the power of anyone to account for, was the high and lofty One made low and helpless. The One who inhabits eternity came to dwell in time. The One Whom none can look upon and live is delivered in a stable under the soft, indifferent gaze of cattle. The Father of all mercies puts Himself at our mercy.

This is the incarnation – the enfleshment. This is most profound thought that could occupy the intellect of any man. The human mind cannot contain the immensity of this event, but it's of great importance that we try.

This is the irrational season. To make room for Jesus this season, we must be willing to go beyond reason – to faith, and wonder, and joy!

There they go again. Every year it's the same old thing, only someplace else. They're banning Christmas Carols again in public.

Why do you suppose anyone would object to "Joy To The World" and not "Jingle Bells?" Why would a massive protest arise at the singing of "Silent Night" and none for "Santa Claus Is Coming To Town?"

Why, pray tell, are city councils and boards of education concerned with "Hark The Herald Angels Sing" and have no problem with "Rudolph The Red-Nosed Reindeer?"

Why all this fuss? I think it's the Name. When you consider that at the mention of the Name of Jesus, devils flee, kingdoms tremble, and gates of hell are shattered – it's no wonder there's such a fuss about it

If I were the prince of this world I'd protest, too. It's O.K. to sing, "Joy to the world," just don't sing, "the Lord is come!" "Silent Night's" no problem until you get to, "Christ the Savior is born!"

"Hark! The herald angels sing," is no threat until that marvelous line, "God and sinners reconciled." It's no wonder there's a howl of protest. It's evidence of the power of the Name!

This is the stuff of praise, not pouting! Of rejoicing, not recrimination! Rejoice that the mere mention of His Name evokes a reaction that no other name even comes close to!

Rudolf, Santa Claus, and good king Wenceslas don't stir the ire of the enemy. It's no wonder – they're dead; but Jesus is a living threat to very real powers that feed on greed, lust, and pride.

No one can remain neutral about The Name. Jesus Himself said, "you're either for me or against me. You cannot serve two masters." It's no wonder some don't like it.

God has given Jesus a name above every name to which every knee will bow, and there are lesser names that don't like being low in the pecking order of eternity. (It's the bowing part that gets them.) Jesus had this transcendent, "bow-able" name while He was lying in the manger in Bethlehem.

It must infuriate the prince of darkness that a Baby has a bigger name than he does. Nobody sings about his birth. No wonder Christmas carols cause such havoc. And when the Baby grew up, despite all of the devil's attempts to destroy Him, the war was on – the battle for the souls of men.

Then when the Man-child died, he thought he had won. But people began to sing about that, too – Hallelujah! Music everywhere, about His birth, His life, His death, His resurrection; we even sing about His return to earth.

No wonder the prince of this world is mad.

Merry Rest *12/5 – December 5*

A popular Christmas carol begins with this often-misunderstood line: "God rest you merry, gentlemen, let nothing you dismay." It's another old English expression that we don't use today.

It may seem a small thing, but this song isn't about merry gentlemen. It's about merry rest. Literally, the English expression is, "May God give you happy rest, gentlemen."

That is my prayer for you as you read these lines today – some happy rest from the business and the busy-ness of the Christmas season.

• Eight-year-old Melissa was showing her younger sister, Chelsea, a picture of Mary and the baby Jesus. Chelsea examined the picture closely, and then she asked, "Where's Joseph?"

Melissa thought for a moment and then replied, "O, he's taking the picture."

• A woman purchased a vacuum cleaner just before Christmas. The demonstration in the store had convinced her that this was indeed the vacuum cleaner for her. It was a wonder. It did everything one could imagine a vacuum cleaner could do – and more.

When she got it home she was not impressed. There must have been a short in it or something. The crazy thing kept going off and on. The woman was mad. "I just bought a brand new vacuum cleaner, and it's already on the fritz."

She called the salesperson that sold it to her and complained about this piece of junk he had sold her. The man was unable to explain what the problem was so he finally agreed to come to her home and look at the vacuum cleaner.

Within a few seconds after arriving at her home, the problem with the vacuum cleaner was solved. The woman, in her holiday haste, had plugged the vacuum cleaner cord into the Christmas tree light blinker outlet. Vacuum cleaners don't work well that way.

"God rest you merry, gentlemen, let nothing you dismay.
Remember Christ our Savior was born on Christmas Day,
To save us all from Satan's pow'r when we were gone astray,
O tidings of comfort and joy, comfort and joy.
O tidings of comfort and joy!"

May God give you and your family merry rest – in this amazing season.

December 6 – 12/6 *Why Bother?*

Christmas is lots of work! Lots of people spend lots of hours doing lots of things to make the celebration of Christmas meaningful this year.

For some it has meant months of planning and preparation; for others it means a flurry of activity over a two or three week period of decorating, rehearsal, choreography, staging, sound, lights, and music. Why bother?

That's a good question considering the cost in time, energy, and resources. The number of collective hours is staggering, well into the hundreds of hours for a Christmas program, and the decorating, etc. After it's all over every one breathes a sigh of relief.

Is it worth it? Well after almost seventy years of involvement in pageants, cantatas, children's programs and various and sundry celebrations of the birth of God in human flesh, I say YES!

I say yes, first of all because He is worth it. We who live in the sophisticated 21st century have lost the sacred art of celebration, largely because, in a world full of confusion, pain, and conflict, we see little worth celebrating.

The occasion of the invisible, untouchable, unknowable God becoming visible, touchable, and knowable flesh is indeed worth celebrating. Come! Celebrate Jesus! – is the message musicians and singers, the children and youth, and those who work behind the scenes, bring to us.

Why bother? Because of what Christmas would be without the bother of programs, music, lights and sounds. It just wouldn't be the same. There's a principle here about giving and receiving. When you give time, energy, or resources in the name of Jesus there's a harvest that exceeds the expenditure. You always reap more than you sow.

It has worked that way as long as I can remember. The ones most affected by the joy of Christmas are those who've worked the hardest and longest bringing joy to others.

Another reason we bother is that we are faced with a flood of materialism, and the darkness of this world, that requires constant effort by dedicated people to keep the light of truth glowing brightly.

I shudder to think of what Christmas would be like if there were no children's voices raised in simple songs of joy and choirs united in anthems of praise. We'd be left with Santa, and Rudolph, and Frosty the Snowman – Yuk!

So, to all who toil now to enhance our celebration, we say, "Thank You!"

Our Christmas would not be the same without your labor of love.

Read It And Weep *12/7 - December 7*

Can anyone credibly argue that our world is not in terrible shape? I read a newspaper every day and I'm sort of a news junkie. I find myself weeping often. There is no peace on earth – anywhere. Today is the anniversary of the attack on Pearl Harbor, which thrust America into World War II.

The Middle East conflict tears at my soul. Israel and the Palestinians are dear to me and I grieve over the hundreds of men, women, and children that have been killed in the last few years. And there's no end in sight.

The massacre of thousands of my brothers and sister in the Sudan and Indonesia causes me to pour my heart out before the Lord on their behalf. And similar atrocities are taking place daily in China and other parts of the world.

I waver between great empathy for those whose lives are not valued, and "compassion fatigue." It's easy to be exposed to so much crisis that one's heart is weary of the load. After all, what can one person do about any of this, anyhow?

I learned a new word the other day that describes the spirit of this present age. The word is "solipsism," (sol-ip-sism.) Mr. Webster defines solipsism as the attitude that nothing exists or is real but that which affects the self.

A solipsist is one who lives his or her life as though nothing is real unless it touches his or her life. Therefore, the above-mentioned situations may be sad, but have no effect upon them directly. They never read it and weep.

"'Tis the season to be jolly." So, solipsists can't be bothered by what happens to all those Muslims, Jews, and others who seek to disturb the peace in their hearts at this joyous, happy season.

In the face of all the blood shed and chaos in the world, "Merry Christmas" doesn't have the same happy ring, does it? Something must change! To change the world there must be a way to change the heart of man. Unless this can be found, all other change is cosmetic. Science and technology have only given us more ways to sin and kill each other. They bring no peace.

God found a way to change the world. He had it in mind all along, and in the fullness of time – He sent His Son.

I've decided to take a different approach this season. I'll continue to weep for the suffering in the world, but I will also rejoice that God has sent His Son to redeem us. Christmas is about changing the world and ending the killing.

For a child will be born to us, a son will be given to us; and the government will rest on His shoulders; and His name will be called Wonderful Counselor, Mighty God, Eternal Father, Prince of Peace. And the government will be upon His shoulders. (Isaiah 9:6)

Read it and weep — for joy!

There is much talk these days of the "rule of law." Even the Supreme Court cannot seem to decide what the law means, and just how it should be applied. We are desperate for final authority.

Apparently, the law is only as good as the lawyers. And justice and judges aren't blind, as the statue of "Justice" depicts, which the scales and blindfold would indicate; they see the world through multi-colored political glasses.

One of the more obscure prophecies of the coming of Messiah, and one of the oldest, is in Genesis 49:10. Jacob is about to die so he calls his sons together for his final blessing. He speaks these prophetic words to his son, Judah:

The scepter shall not depart from Judah, nor the ruler's staff from between his feet, until Shiloh comes, and to Him shall the gathering of the people be.

The word Shiloh means - "Him to whom we belong," and it carries the idea of tranquility that results from orderly rule. I have peace – I belong to Him.

Many such prophecies of His coming speak of His rule, and the peace that follows. *And of His government and peace, there shall be no end.* (Isaiah 9:7)

We don't equate peace with Lordship, but they're inseparable. Peace is the product of the benevolent, gracious rule of the Lord Jesus Christ in nations, homes and lives.

He was born with a scepter in His hand. He was born to rule, and we were born to be ruled by Him. Life works best that way – that is peace.

The Babe in the manger grew up and is Lord on the throne, a fact not thrilling to the people of the world. They eagerly celebrate the birth of the Child but passionately reject His rule in their lives.

"Give us a god like Aristotle's god, they say." Poor Aristotelian god – he is a do-nothing king; the king reigns, but he does not rule.

This is not true of the Lord Jesus; He reigns and rules. There's a crown on His head, and beneath the crown, is a mind that calls the signals for His body.

"Joy to the world! The LORD is come!"

Shiloh has come! And to Him shall the gathering of the people be.

This Bulb's For You *12/9 – December 9*

When Pope Julius I authorized December 25 to be celebrated as the birthday of Jesus in A.D. 353, who would've thought it would become what it is today?

When Charles Follen lit candles on America's first Christmas tree in 1832, who knew that decorations would become as elaborate as they are today?

It's a long time since 1832, longer still from A.D. 353, longer still from that dark night brightened by a special star, in which Jesus the King was born. Yet, as we approach December 25, it gives us yet another opportunity to pause in the midst of the elaborate decorations and commercialization of Christmas, to honor Emmanuel – the Person whose birth we celebrate.

We've come a long way from the flaming candle on the first American Christmas tree in 1832. In fact, the fire department would have a conniption (whatever that is) if millions of homes decided to light candles on their tinder-dry trees this year.

We've gotten safer, if not saner, in the festival we call Christmas, by adorning our trees, houses, stores, and almost anything within range of an electrical outlet with lights of various colors and designs.

A trip down Christmas Tree Lane will expose one to the wonder of electrons flowing freely through wires and bulbs, in bright celebration of Christmas. The power company is de-lighted, I'm sure.

I wonder why we don't have lights at other holidays. We do have fireworks on the 4th of July and jack-o-lanterns on Halloween, but only Christmas is aglow with such an amazing display of light. Hmmm... I wonder if this isn't God's not-so-secret way of honoring His Son, the Light that lights every man.

Several years ago our family was driving along as saw an immense display of lights that one homeowner had assembled to honor the Christ-child. I was deeply moved by the extravagance of it all, and said something that has stuck in our family tradition. I said, "Jesus, this bulb's for You!"

Some would say it's sacrilegious to paraphrase a beer commercial and make it about Jesus. I think otherwise. It forever spoils the beer commercial for us, and declares the purpose (intended or not) for all these beautiful lights – Jesus, the Light of the world.

His birth is unique in all of history. This is John's testimony of Jesus: *All creation took place through Him and none took place without Him. In Him was life and this life was the light of all mankind. The light still shines and the darkness cannot extinguish it.* (John 1:3-5)

Jesus, all these beautiful bulbs – are for You!

A few years ago, a 33-year-old man, decided he wanted to see his town from a new perspective. He went down to the local army surplus store one morning and bought forty-five weather balloons.

That afternoon he strapped himself into a lawn chair, to which several of his friends tied the helium-filled balloons. He took along some water, a peanut-butter-and-jelly sandwich, and a BB gun, figuring he could shoot the balloons one at a time when he was ready to land.

He assumed the balloons would lift him about 100 feet. He was caught off guard when the chair soared more than 11,000 feet into the sky – smack into the middle of the air traffic pattern at Los Angeles International Airport.

Too frightened to shoot any of the balloons, he stayed airborne for more than two hours, forcing the airport to shut down its runways for much of the afternoon, causing long delays in flights from across the country.

When he was safely on the ground and cited by the police, reporters asked him three questions: "Where you scared?" "Yes." "Would you do it again?" "No." "Why did you do it?" "Because," he said, "you can't just sit there."

This is the season of Advent, and when it comes to celebrating the most significant event in the history of the universe – you can't just sit there. That event – the advent – is the "enfleshment" of Almighty God. And every time we celebrate Christmas, it should be an "advent(ure)".

Today we worship the god of technology. They tell us that this god has changed the world. We have cell phones and web sites, super computers and smart bombs, DVDs and weapons of mass destruction, genetic engineering and satellite TV. But how has the world changed?

We still have wars, but now we use computers to fight them. We still have hunger; now we use technology to count the hungry people, but we still aren't able to keep pace with famine. We still have disease and sin and hatred and terrorism and broken homes, in this kingdom of the god "Technology."

To change the world there must be a way to change the heart of man. A computer is amoral – it has no intrinsic morality. It can be used for good or evil; people are sinning every second with their computers. Without a change at the core of man's being, science and technology only give us more ways to sin and kill each other.

Our family will celebrate Advent by lighting candles and worshipping Jesus. It may seem old fashioned to many but it helps counteract the materialism and commercialization of the season. And just as surely as God entered the body of a child, Jesus can enter the heart of a child.

And that's how the world is changed. What an Advent(ure)!

Joy Suckers *12/11 – December 11*

"Joy to the world, the Lord has come!" These words inspire us every Christmas, and we sing them with great gusto. But a close look at the world today reveals that there's not a lot of joy on planet earth. Here's an interesting glance at our joyless world.

If you live in a good home, have plenty to eat and can read, you are a member of a very select group. And if you have a good house, and food, can read and have a computer, you are among the very most elite.

If you woke up this morning with more health than illness, you're more blessed than a million people who won't survive this week. If you've never known the horror of war, the loneliness of imprisonment, the agony of torture, or the angst of starvation, you're ahead of 500 million people in the world.

If you attend a church without fear of harassment, arrest, torture, or death, you're blessed. More than three billion people in the world can't do that. If you have food in the refrigerator, clothes on your back, a roof overhead and a place to sleep, you are richer than 75% of this world. If you have money in the bank, in your wallet, and spare change in a dish someplace, you are among the top 8% of the worlds wealthy.

So that's what our world looks like, but why is there so little joy there? Joy suckers – that's why. The world is full of joy suckers. What's a joy sucker? Glad you asked.

Some say it's poverty; that's a joy sucker, for sure. So much of the world is poor, and America has so much of the world's wealth. If we could just even things out, there would be joy to the world.

Yeh, right! According to that theory, America should be the joy capitol of the world. The fact is, some of the poorest people are the most joyful, and some of the richest are the most joyless. Wealth isn't the source of joy, and poverty isn't the great joy sucker.

Maybe the great joy sucker is a genetic factor – the race you happen to be born into. Or maybe it's where you were born, or your religion or your level of education. Wrong again. The great joy sucker is none of the above.

It's sin! Sin sucks the joy right out of life. It's the cause of all the other conditions that affect humans, like war and poverty, and grief and disease – and death. And that's what Jesus came to deal with. He brings joy to the world because He takes away the big joy sucker – sin.

Behold the Lamb of God that takes away the joy suckers of the world! Rejoice!

December 12 – 12/12 — *A Story, A Star and A Stirring*

A line from a recent children's drama says, "Wise men still seek Him." This is true! But I wonder if these so-called wise men, Magi, as they were known then, were considered all that smart by their countrymen.

I can imagine the questions: "Well, why do you want to take this foolish and dangerous trip? Why are you going to all this trouble?" The wise men must have replied, "Because we have heard a story from the ancient Scripture; we have seen the star in the sky; and we have felt a stirring in our souls."

A story, a star and a stirring, eh? Like Abraham of old, the wise men went out, not knowing whither they went. And wise men of every generation have done the same. May I introduce you to some of them?

William Carey, an English shoemaker, read the Great Commission, *"Go into all the world and preach the gospel to every creature."* He stood at a minister's conference and asked whether or not these words were binding upon us today. An older minister rebuked him saying, "Sit down, young man. When God wants to convert the heathen, He'll do it without your aid or mine!"

He didn't sit. Carey traveled to India and labored seven years before he saw even one soul won to Christ. He worked relentlessly and translated the Bible into several languages. He became known as the "father of modern missions."

David Livingstone took the Gospel message to Africa. In 1896 he spoke to a group in Scotland and said, "What supported me through 50 years among people whose language I could not understand, and whose attitude toward me was often hostile? It was this: *'Lo, I am with you always, even to the end of the world.'* On these words I staked everything, and they never failed.'"

Auca Indians murdered five men, Jim Elliot, Nate Saint, Ed MacCully, Roger Youderian and Peter Fleming in 1958. Some were critical of their attempts to reach those savage people with the Gospel. "What a waste. How foolish to throw your life away for nothing," it was said. To their critics who called them fools, Jim Elliot said, "He is no fool who gives what he cannot keep, to gain what he cannot loose."

When the book of God is finally opened, these and many more, though foolish in the eyes of the world, will be listed as wise men and women who ventured forth in faith.

They heard the story of God's redeeming love. They "saw" the star of hope that led them to believe they could make a difference. And they yielded to the stirring of the Holy Spirit to go into the unknown with the Gospel.

The story, the star, and the stirring – all center on the Child in the manger whose birth we celebrate.

Wise men seek Him, and when they find Him – they want to tell everyone!

The X Factor *12/13 – December 13*

Folks have often complained about that "XMAS" abbreviation for Christmas. They shout, "Keep Christ in Christmas," decrying the commercialization of the whole season as much as the use of "X."

Half of the complaint is valid. No one would deny that the season has been taken over by the wizards of mass marketing in their quest to be the first-est with the most-est. There is, in fact, a conscious effort to remove Christ from every arena of public life.

Most of us remember the not-too-distant past, when Christmas advertising began the day after Thanksgiving. Now we get it in late September. Buyers for the major retail chains begin their search for Christmas merchandise in February and March. There's no question that Christ has been replaced by the over-commercialization of Christmas.

As to the other part of the complaint – the X – there's less validity. To the English-speaking world, X is simply the twenty-fourth letter of the alphabet. But to the Greeks, the ones in whose language the New Testament was written, those diagonally crossed lines are the letter "Chi," the first letter in the name "Christos," the Messiah. Through the years it has been an acceptable symbol for Christ.

I'm less than accurate when I say that "X" to us is only a letter of the alphabet. Any math student would happily correct me. In algebra, it represents an unknown factor: 2+3 = X, or 3x = 12. But in Christianity "X" represents someone I can know in increasing degrees of intimacy.

The symbol "X" is also the sign for multiplication. It reminds me of the truth in John 10:10, *The thief comes only to steal and kill and destroy; I came that they may have life, and have it abundantly.*

In other words, the devil, the thief, comes with a mega minus sign - but Jesus comes with a mega multiplication sign; life abundant – life multiplied by His life in me! And this X Factor makes a mighty big difference.

The X symbol is also used to cross something out that needs to be deleted. That's what Jesus did when He died for our sins – He "crossed" them out, deleted them from the record of heaven, never to be seen again.

People are especially aware of the X Factor at Christmas, or Xmas, if you prefer. But let's not forget that "The X Factor" is Jesus Christ.

Don't "X" Him out of your Christmas.

Laurie, five-years old, upon seeing the plastic bells, which decorated the streets of her town, asked, "Mommy, why don't those bells ring?" Good question, Laurie.

The theme of Christmas is genuine, jubilant, holy Joy! The Joy of which the angel speaks is not a contrived, superficial joy, but a heart's response to the central theme of Christmas: Emmanuel – God with us!

All around us are fake-bearded Santas, plastic bells and baubles, toys and tinsels. The scene is well symbolized by bells that do not, and cannot ring, and by lifeless trees cut from their source in a futile attempt to capture brief moments of yuletide nostalgia.

I saw a bumper sticker, which seems appropriate at Christmas. It said, "God is coming! LOOK BUSY!" Well, we've certainly mastered that part. Busyness is the environmental hazard of a modern celebration of our Savior's birth.

In the center of my being is a sense of wonder at angelic hosts proclaiming this amazing event to unsuspecting, terrified, shepherds tending their flocks by night. Heaven and earth have mingled. Time and eternity have merged.

Perhaps we can think of the Christmas saga as a musical score. Picture it – the lower clef is composed of the notes of earthly events: a stable, a humble peasant woman, a village carpenter, shepherds tending sheep, and some obscure eastern magi.

Then, in the upper clef the heavens are opened, a guiding star appears, and angelic messengers suddenly announce tidings of great joy – and God stoops down to take the form of an earth creature – a baby.

Together, the lower clef and the upper clef make beautiful music! Listen to the most magnificent symphony ever composed telling of Great Joy! It's the world's greatest love song, the story of our Lover-Redeemer. Hear it again – for the first time!

The wise men knew Great Joy. As a matter of fact – read it for yourself in Matthew 2:9, 10: *...The star, which they had seen in the east, went before them, until it came and stood over where the Child was. And when they saw the star, they rejoiced with exceeding great joy.*

"Exceeding great joy!" Wow! That must have really been something. I don't think I've ever experienced exceeding great joy. Joy – yes, even great joy – I've known that. But exceeding great joy? That's a once-in-a-lifetime, or a once-in-all-history event.

May your hope be rekindled in this splendid hour to trust Him for all things good. May your home be aglow with His peace.

And may your heart catch the warm glimmer of Great Joy!

A Rebel Without A Claus *12/15 - December 15*

Although I'd like to take credit for it, this play on words is not original; it was on a sign I saw on the highway years ago. It's sad that most people younger than thirty-years-old, have never seen the series of salient sayings selling Burma Shave along the highway. This one went like this:

"Dickens' Christmas Carol should really give one pause,
For Scrooge is obviously a rebel without a Claus! Burma Shave"

I fit the category of a rebel without a Claus this holiday season. I'm absolutely rebellious when it comes to sharing the glory of Christmas with any man, especially this Claus fellow.

The original Nicholas may have been a kind, giving man, but the world has made a graven image of him. It's idolatry to make this man the centerpiece of God's masterstroke of redemption. It's a diversionary tactic.

Our celebration of this event, the Incarnation, must not be diluted with attention to any other being. There's no room in the stable for another god! And if you doubt that Santa Claus is a god, consider that he has taken on god-like attributes.

He's supposed to be omnipresent, visiting every home in the world on the same night. Yeh, right!

It's claimed that he's omniscient, "he sees you when you're sleeping, he knows when you're awake, he knows if you've been bad or good," etc.

He answers prayer – sort of – when you tell him what you want, and you're supposed to get it.

Yes, Virginia, there is a Santa god!

I stand in rebellion to the chaos and confusion, the greed and grasping, the pressure and the panic, that accompany the Santa Claus spirit.

I embrace the peace, joy, love and redemption that the Spirit of Jesus brings.

This Christmas I am, most certainly – a rebel without a Claus.

I attend trade shows and seminars that center on the computer, especially the Macintosh computer. I went to such a gathering in San Francisco where several thousand people listened to the big boss of Apple Computer, John Scully, sing the praises of his product. It was rather like being at an old fashioned evangelistic meeting. It was even a little scary.

He told how he got involved with the company. Steve Jobs is the whiz kid, with Steve Wozniak, who created computers in a garage and founded Apple Computer. He was certain that his data processors could compete with Big Blue, IBM, but his expertise was in electronics not marketing. So Jobs set his sights on John Scully, of Pepsi Cola.

Scully, at age 38, had driven Coke, for the first time in history, from its number one market position. Scully was the brains behind the "Pepsi Generation" strategy. He was secure at Pepsi, and enjoyed one of the most lucrative positions in America. To leave Pepsi to join an insignificant computer geek didn't hold much enticement for Scully.

Jobs tried every way he could think of to get Scully to join him at Apple. Jobs wined and dined him and made many generous offers. Each time he was turned down. Finally in exasperation, Steve Jobs challenged Scully, "Do you want to spend the rest of your life selling sugared water, or do you want to change the world?" That did it.

It's questionable whether any computer has really changed the world. It's certainly changed the way the world does things but – change the world? I don't think so. It takes more that technology to change the world.

We often hear, "Jesus Christ came into the world to learn what it means to be human; it was His experience on earth that let Him understand our situation."

Nothing is further from the truth. Jesus Christ is God, and He is omniscient, He already knows everything. So He didn't need to come to earth to know what it was like to be human. He came so that we would know that He knew. He didn't come to reveal man to God, He came to reveal God to man! *The Word (the expression of God) became flesh and dwelt among us!* (John 1:14)

The world has a head start in the wrong direction in to celebrating Christmas, so our family will celebrate Advent. Advent means the coming, or the appearing of Jesus on earth. We take a theme for each Sunday and gather with all the kids and grandkids to celebrate the birth of Jesus with candles and praise and songs of joy.

In just such a simple way, our world is changed – and
Christmas is about changing the world!

I'm Dreaming Of A Light Christmas *12/17 – December 17*

Mary rejoiced! The shepherds rejoiced! The wise men rejoiced with exceeding great joy! Even John the Baptist leaped for joy in his mother's womb. All this joy was because God came in flesh so we could know what He's like. And by the evidence of the joy His appearance ignited, He likes joy a lot!

Henry Ward Beecher said, "The test of Christian character should be that one is a joy-bearing agent to the world." With that in mind, I'd like to take a look at the lighter side of Christmas.

Profound events often carry with them a lightness that makes one smile. I'm dreaming of a light Christmas, so laugh with me and celebrate His joy!

* A husband asked his wife what she wanted for Christmas. She said, "O, just surprise me." So, at three o'clock Christmas morning, he leaned over and said, "BOO!"

* And then there was the wife who said to her husband, "This year let's get each other more practical gifts, like socks and fur coats."

* Two weeks before Christmas another husband asked his wife what she would like for a gift. She said she wanted something impractical and romantic. Christmas morning he presented her with a lovely golden bracelet. "A little four letter word made me get this for you, honey," he said softly. "Oh, how sweet, she whispered. "L-o-v-e?" "No," he replied. "S-a-l-e."

* Five-year-old Billy was showing his Christmas presents to grandma when she asked, "Did you get everything you wanted for Christmas?" Billy thought for a moment before he answered, "No, I didn't, Grandma. But that's O.K. It wasn't my birthday."

I'm dreaming of a light Christmas. Merry, Merry, Merry, Merry Christmas!

December 18 – 12/18 *Prince of Peace*

The prophet boldly declared that He would be known as "Prince of Peace," a military term meaning "Captain-in-charge-of Peace."

The angels announced His birth to shepherds saying, "Glory to God in the highest, and on earth peace among men of good will." He was, indeed, the "Peace Child," Whose coming brought hope to all men everywhere that wrath and war, discord and dissension, would come to an end.

Jesus Christ is the Prince of Peace! But often our picture of that peace is limited to the Babe in the manger and the quiet still of the holy night in which He was born. And that was a peaceful and tranquil scene. But the peace that Jesus Christ came to bring was not the fruit of the stable – it was the fruit of His ugly, cruel death upon the cross.

As Captain-in-charge-of-peace, He commands the forces that disturb my peace to flee. He establishes peace in my mind in the midst of confusing distractions. Isaiah 26:3 says, *Thou wilt keep in perfect peace, whose mind is staid on Thee, because he trusts in Thee.*

But the peace, of which He is Prince, doesn't primarily have to do with peace of mind, or peace among nations. It has directly to do with peace with God, with Whom hundreds of generations of mankind had been at war. When the Prince of Peace came, He made peace on this front, and that glorious truce is the beginning place of peace of mind and peace among men on the earth.

It's the distance between God and man, which is at the core of human discord. Jesus bridged this gap and dealt with the dreaded thing that kept us apart – sin. And He rose from the dead as Captain-in-charge-of the peace He made by His death. He was then, He is now, and He will forever be – Prince of Peace!

For unto us a child is born, to us a Son is given; and the government will rest upon His shoulders; and His name shall be called Wonderful Counselor, Mighty God, Everlasting Father, Prince of Peace. There will be no end to the increase of His government or of peace, on the throne of David and over his kingdom, to establish it and to uphold it with justice and righteousness from then on and forevermore.

The zeal of the LORD of hosts will accomplish this. (Isaiah 9:6,7)

He is the Prince of Peace. That's His official title, given to Him by the Father. I can trust Him completely to be my personal Captain-in-charge-of-Peace.

Home For Christmas *12/19 – December 19*

I invite you, if you haven't done it yet, to do your Christmas thinking early. The astounding truth that we celebrate at Christmas is that at a particular time and place God came to be with us Himself. When Quirinius was governor of Syria, in a town called Bethlehem, a child was born who, beyond the power of anyone to account for, was the high and lofty One made low and helpless. The One who inhabits eternity came to dwell in time.

"Twas much, that man was made like God before. But, that God should be made like man, much more!" This is called the incarnation, or literally, the enfleshment. The word "incarnation" has at its root, "carne", meaning meat or flesh. "Chili con carne" is chili with meat in it. A carnivore is an animal that eats meat – flesh. The term "enfleshment," is another word for "Incarnation." I continue to believe that this is most profound thought that could occupy the intellect of any man.

But this miracle didn't happen to Jesus alone; it happened to all flesh. The first ones to be effected by it were Mary and Joseph. We identify with Mary because she, like we, became the dwelling place of God. But I like Joseph. He, too, was a chosen vessel.

Orville and Wilbur Wright tried repeatedly to fly a heavier-than-air craft. Finally one December day, off the sand dunes of Kitty Hawk, North Carolina, they did what man had never done before. They actually flew! Elated, they wired their sister, "We have actually flown 120 feet. Will be home for Christmas." Hastily she ran down the street, shoved the telegram – the news scoop of the century – at the editor of the local paper. He read it and smiled, "Well, well! How nice the boys will be home for Christmas."

The idea of being home for Christmas has great sentimental appeal to us. But may I suggest that home, for us, is not a geographic location, but home is the magnificent revelation that God came in human flesh.

The enfleshment of God is a repeatable miracle – it happens every time someone is born again by the same Spirit that overshadowed Mary. He has become flesh – our flesh! This truth is home base for us.

Let's make plans to be "home for Christmas."

December 20 – 12/20 ***The Reason For The Season***

In a few days we will celebrate Christmas – which has become a secular holiday and an important time for the commercial interests of millions of people across the land. We see bumper stickers that announce: "Jesus is the reason for the season."

This is certainly true. But for those of us who have, by grace, come to walk in personal relationship with the God of the Universe it is, of course, much more. Christmas marks the beginning of a long chain of events that culminate in a grand celebration that no earthly venue could possibly contain.

It's important to keep the big picture in mind as we celebrate that which is known as The Enfleshment. Standing alone, the birth of Jesus was an obscure event involving a peasant couple, a few shepherds, an angelic host, and some wise men from somewhere to the east of Bethlehem. But it was much more.

When God came to earth, His Word became flesh, His nature became human, and His glory became approachable. And what's more, something was set in motion that won't find complete fulfillment until this same Jesus comes to earth again.

There couldn't be a second coming if there weren't a first one. From the beginning, Father God had the second coming of Jesus in mind as a done deal. It's in fact, the ultimate "reason for the season." God's plan is a continuum; it didn't end at the cross, or the resurrection, or Pentecost. It keeps going, and going, and going.

It doesn't end until Satan is defeated and Jesus Christ is enthroned as King of kings, and Lord of lords. Then He will take a bride, who will rule by His side for all eternity. The bride? That's us!

Let us rejoice and be glad and give him glory! For the wedding of the Lamb has come, and his bride has made herself ready. Fine linen, bright and clean, was given her to wear. (Fine linen stands for the righteous acts of the saints) Blessed are those who are invited to the wedding supper of the Lamb! (Revelation 19:7-9)

There was an identifying and encouraging word shared by Christians in the catacombs and arenas of 1st century Rome – Maranatha, "the Lord is coming."

That's the reason for the season!

Have yourself a Maranatha Christmas!

This year in the USA alone, 21 million pounds of candy canes will be produced in every size and color. This holiday season 13.4 billion (that's billion with a "B") toys will be given away. You'd think that with all the candy and gifts changing hands we'd have the kind of joy the song talks about. But "Joy to the world" is tied to the next phrase: "The Lord is come!"

I was in one of those discount food stores the other day to get a few things. I learned that it's not a good idea to go there to "get a few things" this time of year. The lines at all twelve checkouts were incredible, and all the shopping carts were loaded. As I waited I studied the faces of the scores of people who were waiting with me. Most were sad; many were expressionless; only a few were smiling.

I started smiling at people and got smiles in return. A man with a crutch ahead of me caught my smile and it led to a warm exchange between us. It was noisy in that warehouse-like building, but if you listened carefully you could detect the faint sound of music coming from the hopelessly inadequate sound system. It was playing "O Come, O Come Emmanuel."

For many centuries the season of Advent has been a time to celebrate the "comings" of the Lord. The whole idea of Advent, though lost in ritual, has been to look upon the first coming of Jesus to earth, as the promise of His second coming. I'm stirred to think that as surely as He came – He will come again! My heart sings its prayer, "O Come, O Come Emmanuel" – again!

Without His second coming, the first one would be just a nice story. He was born to live and die and be raised from the dead. He is alive now and waiting again for "the fullness of time" to come back and finish what He started at the cross. Without His return as King of kings and Lord of lords, what we have is a tale half told, and unfinished symphony, a touching story without an ending.

The first time He came veiled in the form of a child. The next time, He will come unveiled, and immediately the entire world will know Who He is.

The first time He came, a star marked His arrival. The next time He comes, the whole heavens will roll up like a scroll and all the stars will "fall out of the sky" to bow before Him. The first time He came, wise men and shepherds brought Him gifts. The next time He comes, He will come bearing gifts – rewards for His faithful followers.

The first time He came, there was no room for Him. The next time He comes the world will not be able to contain His glory. The first time He came, only a few attended His arrival.

The next time He comes, every eye shall see Him, every knee shall bow, and every tongue will confess that Jesus Christ is Lord!

Christmas is celebrated nearly everywhere in the world today. Even in pagan countries there is some sort of festivity. The birth of Jesus Christ was first celebrated in the year 98 AD, but it was forty years later that it was adopted as a Christian festival.

A look back into history reveals that no great battles were ever fought on Christmas Day, but some remarkable things did happen on this day. Clovis, the first Christian king of France, was baptized on Christmas Day, 496. Charlemagne was crowned Emperor of the Holy Roman Empire on this day in 800, and William the Conqueror was made King of England, Christmas Day, 1066. The pilgrims started building their first house in the New World on Christmas Day, 1620.

The world changed when God became flesh here. The prospect of "Joy to the World" is more than an empty promise. But it must be alive in each heart. To add to the merriment of the season I include here a few lines designed to bring joy to your world.

A pastor was sitting in his office on the first Saturday of December. Outside in the courtyard of the church, men were in the process of building the stage for a live nativity scene. Since his door was open, he heard two children discussing the process. Asked one of the other, "What is this going to be?" Answered the other, "Oh, they're building a live fertility scene."

The pastor of a small town church sent one of his parishioners to the big city to order a Christmas sign to be hung outside on the door of the Church. The parishioner lost the note, which the pastor gave him, which gave the dimension of the sign and the inscription that was to be printed on it. So he wired the pastor: "Rush copy of motto and dimensions." A new lady clerk in the Western Union office got the reply and almost fainted. It read: "Unto us a child is born. Eight feet long, three feet wide."

A young wife, wishing to announce the birth of her first child to a friend in a distant city, telegraphed: "Isaiah 9:6," which begins, "For unto us a child is born, unto us a child is given." Her friend, not familiar with the Scriptures, said to her husband: "Margaret evidently has a boy who weighs nine pounds and six ounces – but why on earth did they name him Isaiah?"

Christmas Eve was hectic. Father was worried with bundles and burdens. Mother's nerves reached the breaking point more than once. The little girl was hustled up to bed. As she knelt to pray, the feverish excitement mixed her up. When she prayed "The Lord's Prayer," she said, "Forgive us our Christmases, as we forgive those who Christmas against us."

Bashing Through The Snow *12/23 – December 23*

"Your Honor, I object!" "On what grounds, Counselor?" "Your Honor, the testimony of the distinguished Mr. Claus is misleading and irrelevant to the issue in this season."

And in the Supreme Court of Public Opinion the judgment is a resounding, "Objection overruled!" And we who hold dear the worship of God-in-flesh quietly take our seats and watch the proceedings. And so it goes as we arrive at another Christmas season with Santa Claus in the driver's seat. What's wrong with this picture?

I have nothing personally against this Claus fellow. As a matter of fact, Nicholas probably loved Jesus the same way I do. He was a good man and would be appalled at how his name has been glorified.

Some suggest that the promotion of Santa Claus is a harmless exercise in childish fantasy. What possible damage could jolly old St. Nick do? They would say that to deny his place in the holiday festivities is "Santa bashing."

Well, here we go, "bashing through the snow." I do have some concerns about his influence. This Claus fellow is not without his effects.

First, the effect of materialism. It's Santa, not Jesus, who fosters the orgy of spending that goes on unabated as we speak. "What do you want Santa to bring you for Christmas?" is perhaps the most frequently asked question.

The gifts related to the birth of the Son of God were gifts given to Him, not from Him. Gold, frankincense and myrrh were presented to the Baby King. Wise men still know the difference between giving and getting.

Second, the effect of myth. Everyone knows that Santa can't make it down the chimney of every house in the world with his bag of toys. We all know that reindeer can't fly, and that he doesn't really know if you've been bad or good.

We accept these anomalies as good-natured fun. But the effect is to introduce mythology into a season where the greatest Truth ever told is declared: that at a certain time and place, eternity intersected time and the God of all creation – the God of all men everywhere – became a man like us.

Third, is the effect of displacement. Two objects cannot occupy the same space. Schoolteachers aren't allowed to mention Jesus. But Santa Claus is no problem. Many must substitute "Yuletide Season," or some such drivel for "Christmas" because the word contains a reference to Christ.

The ancient agenda of the god of this world is to draw attention and worship away from Jehovah, and to ultimately be like Him. Well, for a lame duck, defeated, tinhorn dictator, he's doing a pretty good job in the world at large.

The energy, time, and attention of Christmas belong, not to Santa, but to the Savior. He's coming back to claim His throne. Even so, come, Lord Jesus!

A mother told her four-year-old daughter, Emily, that they were going to their relative's house to exchange names for Christmas. This brought a loud protest from Emily who said, "But I don't want to. I like being Emily!"

Then there was the six-year-old who was asked, "Who was the first one to know that Jesus was born?" Her reply, "Mary!" Then when asked who Mary's husband was she said, "Virg – you know, Virg and Mary."

We chuckle when kids don't quite get the words right, and they have that trouble partly because our adult vocabulary is very strange sometimes. This is especially true of this time of year in some of the Christmas Carols we sing. They're full of strange words and phrases that don't turn up in everyday conversation. It seems morally significant that we don't say "virgin" much anymore. And incidentally, when was the last time you used "Hark!" in a sentence (as in Hark! the herald…)?

The title of this page, "The Way in a Manger," could've been one of those childish goofs, but it wasn't. I made it up. I started to turn the phrase "away in a manger" around in my brain and thought about how strange it must sound to 21st century kids.

What does it really mean? I have a notion that the writer of the song, which is over 100 years old, was referring to the fact that the birth of Jesus was "away" from the eye of the general public; that "away in a manger" spoke of the rejection of Mary, Joseph and Jesus when there was no room in the inn.

The words of the carol continue this idea of rejection, "no crib for a bed," etc. I suppose this is designed to make us feel sympathy for the Baby in the manger, seeing as how His family was so poor that they couldn't afford anything better. But God isn't looking for sympathy.

The "away-ness" of Messiah's birth was by grand design. God does His best work in obscurity; the manger in Bethlehem is proof of it. Away from the religious establishment of Israel, away from the political machinery of Rome, away from the red-hot zeal of the revolutionaries, away from the gaze of the merely curious – God clothed Himself in flesh and came to live among us.

The proper response is not pity for the poor Baby forced to be born in a manger, but reverent worship to the God Who is so sure of Himself that He could become a Baby, and not be less than God.

The idea of Christmas is that God has made a way for us to know Him. Jesus is the Way, and no one knows the Father except by Him. Like the little girl lost in the fog of London who asked a bobby, "Which way is it to my house?" He asked her the address and, sensing that she did not know which way to go in the fog, he said, "I'll take you there, I'll be your way home."

Jesus is, indeed – The Way in a manger.

Twas Not A Silent Night *12/25 - December 25*

With apologies to Joseph Mohr and Franz Grüber, the lyricist and composer of "Silent Night," the occasion of the appearance of God's Son on planet earth was not a quiet experience. Holy, yes; silent – No.

The idea was a good one – that The Almighty would slip silently into human flesh, but the method He chose has not been known for its serenity. Incredibly, God came to earth by natural childbirth.

My first eyewitness experience of the birth process was several years ago. It was December 20, 1986 in Vancouver, Washington. It was a home birth, and the living room floor was the scene of the action. The midwife was late. I suggested that we were having a "midwife crisis." But she arrived in time for Chelsea's marvelous birth.

I have an audiotape of Chelsea's journey from the womb to the room, and I can tell you that it's definitely audible. But the sounds are not limited to obvious expressions of the anguish of labor. There's a lot of laughter, between contractions, of course, and words of encouragement, and expressions of warm love between a husband and his very pregnant wife.

The birth moment was a riot of noise – healthy noise – even holy noise. "It's a girl!" the midwife announced. "Hallelujah," shouted Dad. "Thank You, Jesus," breathed a weary mother. My son summed up everyone's feelings when Chelsea emerged, with a loud, exuberant, "All right!"

Why do we assume that the birth of Mary's Boy-child was any different? His conception was miraculous, but His birth was quite natural. Mary knew pain, and reacted to it. Joseph loved Mary, and expressed it. The Baby cried – and the angels sang. It was not a silent night.

I like "Silent Night," but "Joy To The World," captures the moment best for me. And "Hark! The Herald Angels Sing," and "Angels We Have Heard On High," with its resounding "G-l-o-r-i-a," isn't bad either.

No indeed, it was not a silent night. But it was a holy one – holy in the sense of virgin purity and sacred purpose. And when He comes again, it will be the holiest of all – but it will not be silent then, either. There'll be shouting and a trumpet blaring, and the unmistakable sound of the chains that have bound us to earth, snapping and falling to noisily the ground.

Even so, come Lord Jesus – again! With loud sounds of joyful praise!

All is well – Merry Christmas!

December 26 – 12/26 **Pondering**

Mary kept all these things, and pondered them in her heart. And the shepherds returned, glorifying and praising God for all the things that they had heard and seen. (Luke 2:19, 20)

There's not a lot of pondering these days. People are content to let someone else do their pondering for them. Newsmen ponder, and tell us what to think about the news. Politicians ponder, and tell us what to think about the issues. Preachers ponder, and tell us what to think about God.

Mary had no one to tell her what to think about what had happened. She treasured and pondered the events of the last few days of her life in her own heart, and her heart was a deep well of living truth.

It was the morning after God stepped down from heaven. The herald angels have delivered their message and resumed whatever it is that angels do between announcements. The shepherds have gone back to work, and it will be some time before the wise men show up.

Joseph is off taking care of the registration business that brought them to Bethlehem in the first place. The innkeeper wonders what all the commotion was about last night, and by the way, and there's still no room in the inn.

Now Mary is alone with her baby for the first time. The cattle (if there were any) are still lowing, but that line that says, "but little Lord Jesus, no crying He makes," don't you believe it; He's crying this morning.

Even good babies cry. He's hungry and needs attention as all babies do. This morning He needs changing and bathing. To do this Mary must un-swaddle the Son of God.

The morning after such times of such great emotional experiences often leave one with emptiness and frustration. So I wonder if Mary had thoughts like, "Is that all there is?" or, "Now what?"

She must have pondered the memories of angels and shepherds and gentle Joseph – but now what? And no mother could forget the moment of the first sight of her baby, but this Baby, she knew more than anyone else, was the very Son of God. But now, what do I do with Him – how do I handle Him?

There, with His mother the morning after, in all His un-swaddled nakedness, lays Almighty God. And Deity He was, and is! With the shepherds back in their fields, the angel's song ended, the colored lights darkened, the candles blown out, the Christmas tree taken down – He is still God.

His glory isn't a fragile thing or a fleeting fancy. It has endured the test of time and the challenge of tyrants.

His glory and majesty survive and thrive to this very day. Hallelujah!

Nobody Knows *12/27 – December 27*

"Nobody knows the trouble I've seen." These are the words of an old spiritual from the days of slavery. This is not about me; it's about all of us, and the human tendency to want everyone to understand the troubles we've seen.

As we end one year and move into another it's often a time of assessment. Last year was not a good year for many, and for some there's been a string of bad years. All of us can look back and find injustice, and maltreatment. And if we could look into the future we would see more of the same, because life on planet earth is not fair – God never promised it would be.

There was a time in our Nation's history when men, women, and children were enslaved, and many were sinfully abused. From that era came a song, usually sung in a deep bass voice and soulful tones singing, "Nobody knows the trouble I've seen." That's true. And perhaps that's the way it ought to be.

Everybody's a victim these days. Our society is extremely conscious of abuse and victimization, and the political landscape is littered with programs to help people recover from the troubles they've seen.

I'm not taking lightly the very serious and sinful problems of spousal abuse, child abuse, and sexual abuse, which needs to be talked about and healed. Those who perpetrate such abuse need to repent before God and those whom they have harmed.

What I'm talking about is a victim mentality. It's everywhere, in politics, economics, music and the arts, and sadly – in the church. A victim mentality causes one to whine at the first hint of trouble, perceives hardship as a personal insult, and refuses to take responsibility for sinful responses to the troubles they've seen. It's our response to trouble that troubles us most.

Injustice happens! There is no such thing as victimless sin. That's why God says, "Don't sin!" Somebody always gets hurt – even if it's only the sinner. So with all that sin out there in the world there's bound to be a lot of victims who lament the pain caused by someone else.

But why must one feel compelled to whine about his trouble in the ears of another who also has reason to whine? The old Negro Spiritual, in its original version, continues, "Nobody know the trouble I've seen. Nobody knows but Jesus." And that's as far as it really needs to go!

Victims get stuck in a kind of time warp that prevents their happy emergence into the future that God has promised. He said, *I know the plans I have for you... plans to prosper you and not to harm you, plans to give you hope and a future."* (Jeremiah 29:11 NIV)

I respectfully suggest that we declare next year a "No Whining Zone." It's impossible to whine and worship, to pout and praise at the same time. Incidentally, the last line of the old song is, "Nobody knows the trouble I've seen – GLORY, HALLELUJAH!"

Our nation is still reeling over the devastation of 9/11/01. Osama bin Laden and his kind have threatened further destruction any time, and in any place where "the infidels" live and work and play.

The videos we have seen are well seasoned with praises to Allah for the killing of innocent people and the impending destruction of America.

We've been praying for our brothers and sisters in Indonesia, on the island of Sulawesi who've have been fleeing their homes under threats by Islamic jihad warriors who are followers of Osama bin Laden.

What's this all about? Is the religion of Islam the motivation for all of this devastation? Then here's the question every one's asking: Is the god of Islam the same as the God of the Christians?

Part of the confusion is that the only word for god in the Arabic language is Allah. But just because you call whatever it is you worship by that name, doesn't mean that it's the true God.

We've all heard statements inferring that we're serving the same God, so why can't we just get along. The talking heads of government and the media don't want to offend "the vast Islamic religion" so they lump all people who believe in some form of "higher power" into the same religious wad.

Here are some actual quotes from Mohammed directly from the Koran. Not all Muslims would say that they believe these statements should be taken seriously, but see for yourself the roots of the madness of many.

Islam is to be imposed by force. Mohammed said, "I have been ordered to fight with the people till they say, 'None has the right to be worshiped but Allah,'" (Vol. 4:196)

Apostasy is punishable by death. Mohammed said, "Whoever changes his Islamic religion, kill him." (Vol. 9:57) Mohammed said, "A Muslim must not be killed, if he kills a non-Muslim. No Muslim should be killed for killing a Kafir." (infidel) (Vol. 9:50)

The destruction of Israel is encouraged. Mohammed said to the Jews, "You should know that the earth belongs to Allah, and His Apostle Mohammed, and I want to expel you from this land (Arabian Peninsula)." (Vol. 4:392)

Mohammed's last words at his deathbed were: "Turn the pagans (non-Muslims) out of the Arabian Peninsula." (Vol. 5:716)

As we close one year and enter another, we will surely be faced with Islamic militant threats. I'm reminded that God said, "No weapon formed against you shall prosper."

That's the good word for today.

Not Willing That Any Should Perish *12/29 – December 29*

The Lord is not slow about His promise...but is patient toward you, not wishing for any to perish but for all to come to repentance. (II Peter 3:9)

I've traveled in the Middle East, and have known many dear people in Egypt, Jordan, Lebanon, and Israel. But in recent years, we've been greatly affected by terrorist acts that spring from Arab countries like these in the Middle East.

First of all, not all Middle Easterners are Arabs. The Egyptian people and their culture predate the Arab race, which is descendant from Ishmael, Abraham's son by Hagar, who was an Egyptian.

Second, not all Arabs are Muslims. There is a strong contingent of Arab Christians in the countries I mentioned. They worship God as we do and sing the same songs, in a language that is strange to the ears of Westerners.

Third, not all Muslims are terrorists. Islam has grown in recent years, not because of fear or radical Islamist teaching, but because of strong family ties and a desire to be insulated from the negative influence of Western culture. And America has exported some pretty bad stuff over the years.

A young Muslim student beamed, "We seek the same God. You call Him God; we call him Allah. You know his prophet Jesus; we follow his prophet Mohammed. Does it not all come to the same thing?"

The Christian professor said, "Abou, you have misunderstood. We do not follow Jesus simply as a prophet. We believe Allah Himself came down! We believe God Himself came to earth as a man to live among us."

Abou responded: "Allah came down. What sacrilege." Later, after Abou had asked around, he returned, "Yes, I have checked on you. Christians do believe that Allah came down. What a most wonderful thought, if only it could be true."

It IS true, Abou. There is, indeed, a stark contrast between Islam and the God Who came down in Jesus Christ. He said, *Come to Me, all who are weary and heavy-laden, and I will give you rest.* (Matthew 11:28)

The Lord is not slow about His promise...but is patient toward you, not wishing for any to perish (including Muslims) *but for all to come to repentance.* (II Peter 3:9)

What an amazing opportunity we have, against the dark background of terror, to declare the grace, mercy and love of God!

December 30 – 12/30 *Crutches In The Sanctuary*

The eternal God is a dwelling place, and underneath are the everlasting arms... (Deuteronomy 33:27)

When I was a young teenager, my family took a trip from our home in Central Illinois to the big city of Los Angeles, California. We saw all the sights along the way and many wondrous things in the L.A. area.

The day that stood out most in my impressionable mind was the day we visited Angelus Temple. In the entry way of the church was a huge glass case full of braces, casts and crutches, left there by people who didn't need them anymore, because God had healed them in the sanctuary of Angelus Temple.

These devices were visible evidence of a great wave of healing that swept this land 75 years ago. There's evidence that many such waves have moved upon the shores of human history, not by the will of man, but by the sovereign bidding of Jehovah-Raphe – the Lord Who heals.

I've seen crutches in the sanctuary. I'm not talking about the physical crutches we need occasionally when we have an injury of some kind. I'm talking about the ones we don't need any more, because the Lord Jesus has healed us. Our preoccupation with the physical has blinded us to very real crutches in our emotions, our minds, and our spirits – our inner being.

When we're healed in our inner being, the evidence may not be as spectacular as what I saw in the trophy case at Angelus Temple, but the healings are no less miraculous. In the light of eternity the discarding of these invisible crutches may be of more value than any physical deliverance.

I've left some crutches in the sanctuary, and I walk in greater freedom because the Lord has healed me of my dependence upon them. The sanctuary isn't a place – it's a Presence – "the secret place of the Most High."

The "everlasting arms" are not just for falling upon in desperation with our last gasping breath, they are there to lean upon every day in our walk with Jesus. "The Eternal God is a dwelling place," – not only an emergency room.

If you haven't cast away your crutches yet, today might be a good day to let the Lord Jesus heal your brokenness, deliver you from dependence on anything but Him, and free you to walk, where once you could not.

We're about to cross over into the New Year. You don't need to hobble into it on your old crutches.

Leave them here, and please don't trip over mine as you walk on in victory.

Arrival or Survival? *12/31 – December 31*

Forgetting what is behind and straining toward what is ahead, I press on toward the goal to win the prize for which God has called me heavenward in Christ Jesus. (Philippians 3:13, 14)

On this last day of the year, many of us will celebrate, with great anticipation, the arrival of the New Year. Some of us, however, will celebrate, with equal enthusiasm, our survival in the old year.

Which will it be for you – arrival or survival? For me and my house, it's a little of both, perhaps a lot of both. But praise and thanksgiving, glory and honor will pour from our grateful hearts to the Lord, for our having survived this year, and for the arrival of a never-yet-lived New Year.

The Greeks had a god named Kronos, the god of time. We get our words chronology and chronograph from his name. His stature depicted him on his tiptoes, running.

Kronos' statue had long hair that hung down in front of his face, so that one could grasp him from the front. But the back of his head was completely bald, so that once he had raced by, no one could take hold of him from behind.

That's how time is. I can lay hold of time before it passes, if I plan ahead, but once it is gone, I cannot capture the moment again. For many, time is a master. The wise man makes time his servant.

I saw a profile of the Masai tribe of Africa on PBS the other night. When the Masai leave a village, they set fire to it. They walk away and never look back. They carry no pictures or reminders of their former village, and they don't name their children after their ancestors.

Could this be what the Lord had in mind when He said, *Forget the former things. Do not dwell on the past. See, I am doing a new thing... I am making a way in the desert and streams in the wasteland... for the people I formed for Myself, that they may proclaim My praise.* (Isaiah 43:18, 19, 21)

The Lord isn't advocating amnesia. God asks us to remember His goodness and His mercy. But our God is Lord of this moment; He is God NOW. He doesn't need a temple built only of memories in which to dwell. "Behold, I am doing a new thing," He says. There's enough of His grace and mercy and love that He doesn't have to repeat Himself.

Here's a thought to carry into the New Year. It's a gift that can keep on giving all year long. It has changed my life. Make it your own. Here it is:

***"I'm not a human being – having a spiritual experience.
I'm a spiritual being – having a human experience."***

May you have a hope-filled, spirit-conscious – Happy New Year!

Index of Scripture References – Old Testament

Genesis: ***1:1*** (1/30); ***1:3*** (2/25); ***2:7-14*** (2/5); ***2:15*** (5/11); ***8:22*** (4/18); ***17:7*** (3/18).

Exodus: ***2:23*** (10/21); ***3:14*** (4/24); ***15:2*** (6/17); ***15:11*** (4/24); ***23:26*** (6/1); ***28:33-35*** (12/2); ***32:29*** (2/9); ***34:6*** (3/19).

Deuteronomy: ***6:5*** (1/11); ***7:9*** (3/18, 4/24, 8/23); ***11:10-15*** (1/14); ***11:26-28*** (6/18); ***18:9-13*** (1/29); ***27:5, 6*** (6/29); ***28:3-6*** (6/27); ***32:1-4*** (8/7, 8/23); ***33:26, 27*** (3/12, 12/30).

Joshua: ***24:15*** (10/6).

Judges: ***4:14*** (5/7); ***5:7*** (5/7); ***ch. 14-16*** (6/25); ***20:16*** (9/23); ***24:15*** (10/6).

I Samuel: ***7:12*** (1/19, 5/1).

II Samuel: ***24:24*** (2/9).

I Kings: ***8:56*** (3/31).

II Kings: ***6:14-17*** (5/26); ***21:7*** (2/15).

I Chronicles: ***14:14, 15*** (7/16); ***16:8, 34*** (11/20).

II Chronicles: ***6:6*** (3/20); ***6:18*** (8/22); ***7:14*** (2/26, 8/28).

Nehemiah: ***4:10*** (1/29); ***6:2, 3*** (9/6).

Job: ***5:8, 9*** (6/2, 10/12); ***23:16*** (7/5); ***26:7*** (1/30); ***38:7*** (2/25, 11/20).

Psalm: ***1:1-6*** (6/21); ***3:1-3*** (5/18); ***4:1*** (1/10); ***8:9*** (2/3); ***16:5, 6*** (2/6, 9/24); ***16:11*** (6/5); ***18:30*** (8/17); ***19:1*** (11/5); ***19:14*** (1/17, 8/3); ***23:1-6*** (1/31); ***24:2*** (2/2); ***25:4*** (8/17); ***25:21*** (1/4); ***27:4*** (9/24); ***32:10*** (3/19); ***32:11*** (3/19); ***33:4*** (8/23); ***33:5*** (4/24); ***33:12*** (2/21); ***35:28*** (8/3); ***36:5*** (4/24); ***39:1*** (8/3); ***46:7, 8*** (5/18); ***47:1*** (1/28); ***48:14*** (4/24); ***54:3, 4*** (5/19); ***57:1-11*** (9/3); ***57:8, 9*** (9/2); ***66:1-20*** (7/23); ***86:12*** (6/5); ***89:1-5*** (8/23); ***89:26*** (6/18); ***90:14, 17*** (9/7); ***91:1-18*** (5/26, 6/1, 7/18, 8/7, 8/18, 10/7, 10/9, 10/25); ***92:1, 2*** (11/21); ***92:12-15*** (9/9); ***92:13, 14*** (6/1); ***93:2*** (4/24); ***95:6, 7*** (4/22); ***96:12*** (7/24); ***99:5*** (4/22); ***100:5*** (8/23); ***102:24-27*** (4/24); ***102:27*** (4/24); ***103:1-7*** (3/19, 8/17); ***103:17*** (9/9); ***104:24-30*** (9/23); ***118:19-21***(11/25); ***119:68*** (4/24); ***119:90*** (4/24, 8/23); ***119:137*** (4/24); ***122:6*** (2/15); ***125:2*** (2/15); ***127:1-5*** (7/26); ***128:1-6*** (6/27); ***130:2, 3*** (10/27); ***137:5, 6*** (2/15); ***139:1-10*** (4/24); ***139:13, 14*** (1/22); ***139:23, 24*** (1/2, 8/28); ***145:9*** (4/24).

Proverbs: ***3:1, 2*** (6/1); ***6:23-27*** (6/28); ***6:32*** (6/28); ***9:10*** (1/31, 6/1, 11/13); ***10:5*** (6/22, 6/23); ***11:3*** (1/11); ***16:1*** (11/16); ***16:3*** (6/30); ***17:22*** (8/19); ***18:15*** (11/13); ***18:21*** (8/3); ***21:23*** (8/3); ***23:7*** (9/24); ***24:16*** (10/1).

Ecclesiastes: ***1:9*** (1/3); ***3:4*** (8/19); ***12:1*** (1/30); ***12:7*** (4/18).

Song of Solomon: ***2:11-13*** (3/28, 6/21); ***6:10*** (9/30).

Isaiah: ***1:18*** (4/16, 4/27); ***2:3*** (2/15); ***6:3*** (4/24); ***6:5*** (3/9); ***9:6*** (12/7, 12/22); ***9:7*** (12/8, 12/18); ***12:4-6*** (11/23); ***12:5*** (10/4); ***25:1*** (8/23); ***26:3*** (9/24, 12/18); ***40:3-5*** (10/2); ***40:22*** (1/30); ***40:26*** (10/12); ***43:18-21*** (1/3, 12/31); ***45:3*** (3/10); ***45:21*** (4/24); ***46:4*** (6/1); ***46:10*** (4/24); ***50:10*** (1/4); ***52:17*** (9/24); ***53:6*** (3/6, 3/21); ***54:13*** (1/31); ***54:17*** (9/27); ***55:1-3*** (5/2, 7/29); ***65:19*** (2/15).

Jeremiah: ***1:5*** (1/21); ***2:13*** (10/24); ***8:11, 12*** (6/15); ***8:18-22*** (8/15); ***9:23, 24*** (1/31); ***17:13*** (10/24); ***23:23, 24*** (4/24, 10/23); ***29:11*** (12/27); ***31:1, 3*** (10/11); ***31:3*** (11/12) ***32:17*** (4/24); ***33:11*** (11/19); ***34:8, 9*** (7/4).

Lamentations: ***3:21-23*** (1/3, 4/24, 7/7, 8/23).

Ezekiel: ***11:19*** (1/3); ***22:29, 30*** (6/3); ***36:26*** (10/19).

Daniel: ***4:34, 35*** (4/24); ***9:7, 14*** (4/24).

Amos: ***9:2, 3*** (10/23).

Micah: ***6:8*** (8/25, 9/11).

Habakkuk: ***1:12, 13*** (4/24); ***3:2*** (2/26, 7/10).

Haggai: ***1:6*** (4/15).

Zechariah: ***4:10*** (7/1); ***8:3*** (2/15); ***8:8*** (2/15); ***8:22*** (2/15); ***9:9*** (4/9); ***10:12*** (10/28); ***12:10*** (2/15).

Malachi: ***3:6*** (4/24, 7/19, 9/21); ***3:10*** (9/26); ***4:6*** (6/19).

Index of Scripture References – New Testament

Matthew: ***2:9, 10*** (12/14); ***3:11, 12*** (7/7); ***5:1-10*** (5/4); ***5:2*** (5/4); ***5:6, 7*** (5/4); ***5:13*** (4/8); ***5:27, 28*** (6/28); ***6:19, 20*** (10/17, 10/22); ***6:26*** (7/1); ***6:28*** (5/25); ***6:33*** (5/22, 7/20); ***7:13, 14*** (8/21); ***11:28*** (4/16, 9/4, 12/29); ***15:1-3*** (7/11); ***15:6*** (7/11); ***15:36*** (11/22); ***17:20*** (5/10); ***18:3*** (4/26); ***18:10*** (5/26); ***18:20*** (4/24); ***23:37*** (2/15); ***24:6-13*** (1/8); ***25:42-45*** (3/13); ***26:39*** (3/24); ***28:1-7*** (4/16); ***28:19, 20*** (2/8, 10/23).

Mark: ***6:56*** (2/8); ***8:18*** (4/2); ***9:23*** (8/28); ***11:24*** (3/31); ***13:31*** (10/21); ***13:37*** (11/15); ***16:15*** (9/29); ***16:18*** (9/27).

Luke: ***1:31, 32*** (3/25); ***1:37*** (4/24); ***2:1*** (10/21); ***2:19, 20*** (12/26); ***2:49*** (5/24); ***5:5*** (7/27); ***6:22, 23*** (2/29); ***6:38*** (4/4, 4/15); ***6:45*** (2/22); ***7:32*** (2/8); ***10:2*** (8/2); ***10:19*** (9/27); ***10:27*** (8/16); ***10:34-37*** (4/6, 4/7); ***12:7*** (10/12); ***12:16-21*** (4/9); ***12:32*** (3/15); ***13:30*** (2/18); ***14:33*** (8/16); ***19:10*** (2/20, 4/28); ***19:17*** (7/1); ***19:41, 42*** (3/20); ***21:9, 17-19*** (8/9); ***23:34*** (1/23, 2/22); ***24:1-6*** (4/11); ***24:17*** (6/16).

John: ***1:3-5*** (2/25, 12/9); ***1:14*** (1/12, 2/22, 12/16); ***3:7*** (1/9); ***3:16*** (2/5, 2/21, 3/25, 10/16); ***3:17*** (1/17); ***3:30*** (2/22); ***4:19*** (6/7); ***5:26*** (4/24); ***6:37*** (4/27); ***6:51-53*** (7/3); ***6:63*** (7/3); ***7:37-39*** (5/31); ***7:38*** (3/2); ***8:3-7*** (7/8); ***8:31*** (8/28); ***10:4*** (1/1); ***10:10*** (12/13); ***10:30, 38*** (12/1); ***11:25, 26*** (4/30); ***12:32*** (6/14); ***12:45*** (12/1); ***14:1-11*** (12/1); ***14:14*** (8/28); ***14:16*** (7/28); ***14:18-20, 26*** (4/17); ***14:27*** (3/20); ***15:5*** (5/3); ***15:7*** (8/28); ***15:9*** (10/26); ***15:11*** (8/4); ***16:32*** (6/18); ***19:28-30*** (5/24); ***20:26-28*** (4/20).

Acts: ***1:8*** (9/29); ***1:9-11*** (9/13); ***2:3, 4*** (4/25); ***2:40*** (6/5); ***3:16*** (2/3); ***16:19*** (2/8); ***17:17*** (2/8); ***17:25-28*** (3/11, 4/24, 10/23); ***28:1, 2*** (2/1).

Romans: ***1:22-25*** (11/4); ***2:16*** (12/1); ***3:3*** (8/23); ***5:11*** (9/10); ***5:20, 21*** (1/13); ***6:3, 4*** (7/25); ***8:16, 17*** (8/20); ***8:18*** (8/20, 8/29); ***8:21*** (11/6); ***8:37-39*** (9/18); ***9:5*** (12/1); ***10:8-10*** (9/17, 10/14); ***10:12, 13*** (10/16); 11:2-5 (2/23); ***11:33*** (8/17); ***11:33-36*** (4/24); ***12:1*** (6/29); ***12:2*** (4/3, 10/13, 11/29); ***12:6, 33*** (10/15); ***12:17-21*** (4/29); ***12:18, 19*** (8/9); ***12:19-21*** (6/26); ***13:1*** (8/17); ***13:7*** (5/8); ***13:11-13*** (2/1, 9/2); ***14:19*** (6/7); ***15:13*** (5/23).

I Corinthians: ***1:18*** (4/5); ***1:23-27*** (4/1); ***1:25*** (8/13); ***3:13*** (7/5); ***4:10*** (4/1); ***6:12-20*** (7/30, 8/25); ***6:19, 20*** (4/13, 5/16); ***9:25-27*** (2/13); ***10:13*** (1/6, 8/23); ***11:24-26*** (2/7); ***11:26-28*** (11/6); ***11:28*** (1/2); ***12:18*** (5/12); ***12:22, 23*** (5/12); ***12:24-27*** (5/13); ***14:8*** (3/14); ***15:47*** (12/1); ***15:58*** (7/21, 9/8); ***16:13*** (11/15).

II Corinthians: ***2:7, 8*** (9/20); ***2:11*** (4/23); ***5:16*** (12/2); ***5:19*** (4/14, 5/24); ***6:14-17*** (8/30); ***7:1*** (3/3); ***7:10*** (3/9); ***11:3*** (8/8); ***12:9*** (3/7, 5/13, 7/19).

Galatians: ***4:1-7*** (1/9); ***4:6, 7*** (1/9); ***6:3*** (5/3); ***6:7*** (9/1); ***6:9*** (8/2).

Ephesians: ***1:3, 4*** (6/10); ***1:11*** (4/24); ***1:12*** (3/5); ***2:8-10*** (9/5); ***2:12*** (5/23); ***2:13, 14*** (1/7); ***2:13-15*** (11/3); ***2:21, 22*** (8/6); ***3:14-19*** (6/27); ***3:16*** (3/2); ***3:17-19*** (7/2); ***4:14*** (2/28); ***5:14*** (9/2); ***5:15*** (4/1); ***5:24-26*** (11/27); ***6:12*** (4/2); ***6:16*** (2/19, 9/27).

Philippians: ***1:6*** (1/18, 11/5); ***1:21*** (4/19); ***2:6*** (12/1); ***3:8, 10*** (10/10); ***3:13, 14*** (12/31); ***3:18-20*** (5/14); ***4:8*** (9/24); ***4:13*** (10/2).

Colossians: ***1:15, 19*** (12/1); ***1:17-19*** (1/15); ***1:27*** (7/18); ***2:2-10*** (10/26); ***2:13-15*** (3/23); ***2:14, 15*** (8/10); ***3:17*** (10/15); ***4:6*** (4/8).

I Thessalonians: ***1:3, 4*** (9/6); ***4:3-5*** (6/28); ***4:4*** (8/28); ***4:11*** (9/4, 9/25); ***4:16-18*** (9/13); ***5:2*** (9/13, 9/30); ***5:16-18*** (11/18, 11/19); ***5:23-28*** (6/27, 8/23).

I Timothy: ***2:1-4*** (1/20); ***2:8*** (9/25); ***6:5-8*** (7/9); ***6:10*** (4/5, 7/20); ***6:13-16*** (1/20).

II Timothy: ***1:7*** (11/8); ***2:13*** (8/23); ***3:2*** (7/30); ***4:6-8*** (5/27).

Hebrews: ***2:15*** (6/1); ***4:12*** (8/18); ***4:16*** (1/12); ***6:17-19*** (5/23); ***7:26-28*** (12/1); ***9:11-14, 22*** (3/16); ***10:19*** (3/4); ***10:23*** (8/23); ***10:35*** (6/6, 10/14); ***11:1*** (8/31);
11:1-40 (5/29, 5/30); ***11:30*** (11/3); ***11:34*** (5/30); ***12:1*** (5/28); ***12:2*** (4/19); ***12:26, 27*** (1/26); ***13:4*** (2/14, 3/4, 6/24, 9/22); ***13:5*** 10/21); ***13:8*** (4/24); ***13:12*** (3/16); ***13:20-22*** (6/27).

James: ***1:17*** (4/24); ***1:19, 20*** (4/29, 6/15, 8/9); ***2:13*** (3/19); ***2:17*** (1/27); ***3:5, 6*** (4/25); ***3:8-10*** (8/3); ***5:16*** (3/31); ***5:20*** (4/28).

I Peter: ***1:3*** (3/27, 5/23, 9/19, 10/29); ***1:7*** (7/6); ***1:18-20*** (6/10); ***1:22*** (10/18); ***1:23*** (1/25); ***1:24, 25*** (10/20, 10/30); ***2:9*** (1/9); ***3:4*** (3/2).

II Peter: ***1:4*** (6/28); ***2:19*** (7/4); ***3:4*** (9/30); ***3:9*** (9/30, 12/29).

I John: ***1:5, 6*** (2/17, 4/24); ***1:7*** (3/3, 3/4); ***1:9*** (8/24); ***1:9-2:2*** (2/17, 3/6); ***2:17*** (10/21); ***3:2*** (10/22); ***3:15*** (8/12); ***3:18-20*** (2/16, 3/8, 4/24); ***4:4*** (10/5); ***4:10*** (3/6); ***5:14*** (6/6).

III John: ***1:2*** (5/4, 8/18, 8/19).

Jude: ***1:7*** (11/7); ***1:24, 25*** (6/28, 8/11).

Revelation: ***1:8*** (2/18); ***1:17*** (2/18); ***1:18*** (6/5); ***3:7, 8*** (1/1); ***3:12*** (9/19); ***4:9, 10*** (4/24); ***5:9, 10*** (10/9, 11/11); ***5:11, 12*** (8/29); ***7:12*** (11/20); ***13:8*** (4/9, 6/10); ***19:6*** (4/24); ***19:7-9*** (12/20); ***19:11*** (8/23); ***21:6*** (10/24); ***22:20*** (9/12).

Index of Topics

Abortion: 1/21, 1/22, 1/23, 1/27, 4/29, 7/6, 7/20, 7/30, 9/16.

Aging: 1/23, 3/18, 6/1, 6/3, 8/4, 8/20, 8/25, 9/9, 10/2, 11/25.

Astronomy: 1/27, 1/29, 1/30, 2/10, 2/25, 6/2, 6/23, 8/7, 8/22, 8/23, 8/29, 10/7, 10/9, 10/12, 10/21, 10/23, 10/28, 12/21.

Atonement: 2/1, 3/26, 5/20, 6/9, 9/10, 9/30, 12/2.

Bible/God's Word: 1/29, 2/3, 5/9, 5/27, 6/5, 10/8, 10/21.

Children: 1/5, 1/28, 1/31, 3/18, 4/21, 6/17, 6/18, 6/19, 7/14, 7/26, 8/2, 9/9, 10/13, 10/15, 11/7, 11/17, 11/28, 12/6.

Church: 1/15, 1/16, 1/25, 1/27, 1/28, 2/1, 2/20, 4/9, 4/15, 4/19, 4/22, 4/25, 5/12, 5/22, 6/4, 6/9, 6/24, 7/10, 7/13, 7/21, 8/1, 8/15, 8/17, 9/4, 9/14, 9/15, 9/16, 9/20, 9/25, 10/15, 10/25, 10/30, 11/2, 11/14, 11/27, 11/30, 12/30.

Commitment: 1/10, 5/17, 8/16, 8/19, 9/8, 10/5, 11/27.

Conversion/Salvation: 1/4, 2/15, 3/10, 3/17, 3/22, 3/26, 4/26, 6/1, 6/17, 7/4, 8/18, 9/2, 9/10, 9/17, 10/8, 10/16, 11/5.

Cross: 1/12, 1/24, 2/5, 2/7, 2/22, 3/6, 3/22, 3/23, 3/25, 3/26, 4/1, 4/5, 4/12, 4/14, 4/27, 5/24, 7/2, 7.9, 8/10, 8/13, 9/11, 10/11, 11/6, 12/13, 12/18, 12/20.

Death: 1/10, 1/12, 1/13, 1/21, 1/24, 1/27, 2/3, 2/7, 3/6, 3/17, 3/23, 3/28, 3/30, 4/9, 4/11, 4/13, 4/30, 5/24, 6/1, 6/3, 7/2, 7/17, 7/25, 8/3, 8/5, 9/22, 10/29, 10/31, 11/6, 11/11, 11/19, 12/28.

Faith/Trust: 1/2, 1/27, 1/30, 2/19, 2/20, 3/1, 3/10, 3/11, 3/12, 3/15, 3/18, 3/22, 3/26, 5/9, 5/10, 5/25, 5/29, 6/6, 6/10, 6/27, 6/30, 7/1, 7/17, 8/22, 8/31, 9/17, 9/25, 9/27, 10/5, 10/7, 10/14, 11/20, 12/1, 12/3.

Faithfulness: 1/3, 3/18, 4/24, 5/29, 6/6, 8/23, 9/8, 9/23, 10/14, 11/21.

Family: 1/1, 1/5, 1/8, 1/9, 1/15, 1/16, 1/17, 1/18, 1/21, 1/25, 2/2, 2/12, 3/2, 3/12, 3/18, 3/25, 3/29, 4/19, 4/27, 5/8, 5/24, 5/28, 6/16, 6/20, 6/30, 7/3, 7/14, 7/25, 8/2, 8/4, 8/13, 8/25, 8/30, 9/4, 9/9, 10/13, 10/30, 11/1, 11/3, 11/6, 11/16, 11/17, 11/20, 11/22, 11/28, 11/29, 12/5, 12/9, 12/10, 12/16, 12/24, 12/25.

Fear: 2/8, 2/16, 2.25, 3/1, 3/15, 5/11, 5/20, 5/26, 5/31, 6/1, 6/6, 6/30, 8/3, 8/9, 8/31, 9/26, 10/7, 10/30, 11/8, 11/30.

Fellowship: 1/16, 2/7, 2/17, 3/4, 7/3, 8/30, 9/25, 11/6.

Forgiveness: 2/1, 2/5, 3/4, 3/6, 3/8, 3/9, 3/21, 6/15, 7/18, 8/10, 9/10, 10/27, 11/6, 11/7, 11/17.

Freedom: 1/7, 2/20, 2/27, 4/10, 4/30, 5/5, 5/6, 5/21, 6/14, 7/2, 7/4, 8/5, 9/11, 11/3, 11/17, 11/26, 12/30.

Giving: 1/16, 1/23, 4/5, 4/10, 4/15, 7/13, 7/29, 9/26, 10/17, 11/22, 12/23.

Grace: 1/2, 1/12, 2/3, 2/21, 2/22, 2/27, 3/5, 3/6, 3/7, 3/19, 3/26, 3/28, 3/30, 4/5, 4/8, 4/25, 4/26, 4/28, 4/29, 5/11, 5/22, 5/27, 5/30, 6/2, 6/3, 6/10, 7/7, 7/9, 7/11, 7/29, 8/3, 8/7, 8/10, 9/3, 9/5, 9/13, 9/20, 10/2, 10/9, 10/23, 10/25, 10/27, 11/8, 11/12, 11/17, 11/19, 11/22, 11/25, 11/27, 12/20, 12/29, 12/31.

Grandparents: 1/8, 1/21, 1/29, 3/18, 4/17, 5/15, 7/14, 9/9, 9/28, 10/1, 10/22, 11/17.

Growth: 1/2, 1/10, 1/22, 1/24, 3/2, 4/18, 4/22, 5/1, 5/10, 5/25, 5/27, 6/9, 6/16, 6/21, 6/22, 6/23, 7/6, 7/31, 8/3, 8/26, 9/1, 9/16, 11/15, 11/25.

Heaven: 1/10, 1/18, 1/25, 2/11, 2/29, 3/22, 3/30, 4/26, 4/28, 5/11, 5/14, 5/25, 6/14, 8/29, 10/8, 10/17, 10/21, 10/22, 11/9, 11/22.

Hell: 1/17, 3/9, 3/14, 3/16, 3/23, 3/24, 4/9, 4/13, 4/14, 4/25, 4/30, 4/23, 6/3, 7/13, 9/10, 10/2, 10/31, 12/4.

Holidays: (in the order of the calendar)

- New Year: 1/1, 1/2, 1/3, 12/30, 12/31.
- Sanctity of Life Day: 1/21, 1/22, 1/23, 4/29, 9/16, 11/4.
- President's Day: 1/20, 2/12, 2/21, 6/14, 8/17.
- Valentine's Day: 1/10, 2/14, 6/11, 6/24, 11/27.
- St. Patrick's Day: 3/17.
- Palm Sunday: 3/20, 3/21, 4/9.
- Easter Week: 3/4, 3/6, 3/16, 3/21, 3/22, 3/23. 3/24, 3/25, 3/26, 3/27, 3/28, 4/11, 4/12, 4/14, 4/16, 4/17, 4/20, 4/27.
- Mother's Day: 3/26, 5/7, 5/8.
- Memorial Day: 5/28, 5/29, 5/30.
- Flag Day/Patriotism: 2/21, 2/23, 2/27, 5/14, 5,21, 6/14, 7/2, 7/20.
- Father's Day: 1/9, 1/23, 2/20, 3/12, 3/18, 6/17, 6/18, 6/19, 8/23, 10/26.
- Independence Day/Freedom: 1/7, 1/8, 4/10, 5/21, 7/2, 7/4, 7/5, 9/11, 11/3, 11/26.
- Labor Day: 9/4, 9/5, 9/6, 9/7, 9/8.
- Yom Kippur, Day of Atonement – 9/10, 9/30.
- Veteran's Day: 1/8, 11/10, 11/11.
- Thanksgiving: 11/16, 11/17, 11/18, 11/19, 11/20, 11/21, 11/22, 11/23, 11/24, 11/25.
- Christmas/Advent: 3/25,11/28, 11/29, 12/1 through 12/26.

Holiness: 1/1, 2/2, 3/3, 3/16, 5/15, 5/25, 6/28, 7/11, 8/20, 9/8, 9/25, 10/25, 11/27, 12/25.

Holy Spirit: 2/13, 2/16, 4/13, 4/16, 4/17, 4/25, 5/3, 5/13, 5/16, 5/18, 5/19, 5/23, 5/30, 6/7, 6/9, 6/16, 6/19, 6/27, 7/3, 7/5, 7/17, 7/18, 7/28, 7/30, 8/14, 8/15, 8/17, 8/20, 8/25, 8/28, 8/30, 9/8, 9/15, 9/22, 9/23, 9/24, 9/29, 10/17, 10/18, 11/8, 11/14, 11/19, 12/12, 12/19.

Humor: 3/2, 5/13, 7/17, 7/29, 8/4, 8/19, 11/25, 12/5, 12/14, 12/15, 12/17, 12/22.

Jesus Christ: – He's in every day of the year; He is God in flesh, He is Lord.

Jewish: 1/4, 1/7, 3/20, 3/28, 4/1, 4/7, 4/13, 4/20, 6/9, 6/15, 7/3, 8/13, 9/10, 9/11, 9/30, 10/16, 12/7,12/23.

Joy: 1/2, 1/8, 1/28, 1/31, 2/2, 2/15, 2/22, 2/25, 2/29, 3/19, 3/22, 3/28, 4/7, 4/20, 5/24, 6/5, 6/7, 6/27, 7/7, 7/13, 7/22, 7/24, 8/4, 8/8, 8/19, 10/21, 10/30, 11/17, 11/19, 12/2, 12/3, 12/4, 12/5, 12/6, 12/7, 12/8, 12/11, 12/14, 12/15, 12/17, 12/21, 12/22, 12/25.

Judgment: 1/17, 3/6, 3/19, 3/23, 3/24, 4/5, 6/5, 7/19, 8/17, 9/15, 11/7.

Law: 1/4, 2/2, 2/6, 2/21, 3/4, 3/31, 4/15, 4/28, 5/14, 6/7, 6/8, 6/11, 6/28, 7/6, 7/8, 8/10, 12/2.

Light/Darkness: 2/1, 2/2, 2/17, 2/25, 3/4, 3/10, 3/11, 3/15, 3/27, 5/19, 5/29, 6/3, 6/7, 7/7, 7/21, 8/5, 8/16, 8/30, 9/2, 9/14, 9/14, 9/27, 10/27, 10/29, 10/31, 11/2, 12/4, 12/9, 12/11, 12/17.

Lost: 1/17, 1/30, 2/20, 3/17, 3/19, 4/14, 4/28, 5/28, 7/1, 7/13, 9/6, 10/19, 11/5, 12/24.

Love/Marriage: 1/10, 1/11, 1/31, 2/3, 2/20, 2/27, 3/6, 3/20, 3/25, 3/26, 4/5, 5/22, 6/1, 6/44, 6/6, 6/7, 6/11, 6/13, 6/24, 6/30, 7/15, 7/20, 7/30, 8/5, 8/6, 8/8, 8/16, 8/19, 9/6, 9/14, 9/16, 9/21, 10/6, 10/11, 10/18, 10/25, 10/26, 10/27, 10/30, 11/2, 11/8, 11/22, 11/27, 11/30, 12/14, 12/25, 12/31.

Men/Male: 1/16, 1/23, 1/26, 2/2, 2/14, 2/21, 2/23. 2/24, 2/29, 3/17, 4/18, 4/20, 4/28, 5/1, 5/5, 5/7, 5/21, 5/26, 5/27, 6/17, 6/25, 7/2, 7/4, 7/6, 7/21, 7/30, 8/5, 8.13, 8/14, 9/14, 9/15, 9/18, 9/23, 9/25, 10/1, 10/14, 10/15, 10/26, 10/28, 11/2, 11/7, 11/10, 11/11, 11/15, 11/17, 11/18, 12/5, 12/7, 12/12, 12/14, 12/17, 12/18, 12/22, 12/23, 12/25, 12/16, 12/27, 12/31.

Mission: 1/17, 4/14, 4/16, 5/28, 6/3, 7/13, 8/13, 9/1, 9/29, 10/8, 10/16, 11/30, 12/12.

Money: 1/10, 3/1, 4/4, 4/5, 4/7, 4/10, 4/13, 4/23, 5/2, 6/7, 6/28, 7/9, 9/26, 10/17, 12/11.

Nature/Creation: 1/22, 1/30, 2/4, 2/21, 3/28, 4/24, 5/14, 6/2, 6/10, 6/20, 6/21, 6/23, 7/24, 8/7, 9/3, 9/5, 9/21, 12/1, 12/23.

Obedience: 2/17, 4/7, 6/18, 6/27, 7/15, 7/16, 9/7, 9/26, 11/9.

Peace: 1/4, 1/7, 1/13, 1/20, 1/31, 2/3, 2/15, 2,18, 2/22, 3/6, 3/8, 3/20, 3/21, 4/14, 4/20, 4/25, 4/29, 5/4, 5/18, 5/19, 5/24, 6/1, 6/7, 6/15, 6/20, 6/27, 7/2, 7/13, 7/22, 7/31, 8/9, 8/19, 9/24, 9/25, 10/4, 11/3, 11/11, 12/7, 12/8, 12/14, 12/15, 12/18.

Power: 1/3, 1/12, 1/13, 1/23, 2/2, 2/5, 2/13, 2/14, 2/15, 2/26, 3/1, 3/2, 3/3, 3/4, 3/6, 4/3, 4/5, 4/24, 4/28, 5/1, 5/12, 5/13, 5/17, 5/20, 5/22, 5/23, 5/24, 5/27, 5/30, 6/3, 6/7, 6/9, 6/14, 6/18, 6/20, 6/27, 7/5, 7/10, 7/23, 7/28, 8/3, 8/10, 8/13, 8/17, 8/29, 9/6, 9/14, 9/17, 9/20, 9/27, 9/29, 10/2, 10/6, 10/8, 10/10, 10/12, 10/17, 10/23, 11/2, 11/8, 11/20, 11/30, 12/4, 12/9, 12/30.

Prayer: 1/3, 1/8, 1/18, 1/20, 1/22, 1/30, 1/31, 2/3, 2/4, 2/25, 2/21, 2/26, 2/27, 3/2, 3/16, 3/20, 3/22, 3/23, 3/31, 4/26, 5/1, 5/4, 5/10, 5/20, 5/26, 6/3, 6/7, 6/12, 6/16, 6/18, 7/1, 7/2, 7/3, 7/6, 7/10, 7/14, 7/28, 7/31, 8/5.

Resurrection: 1/4, 2/7, 3/16, 3/20, 3/22, 3/23, 3/24, 3/25, 3.27, 3/28, 3/30, 4/10, 4/16, 4/17, 4/23, 4/30, 5/23, 6/1, 6/15, 6/16, 7/3, 9/19, 9/22, 10/10, 10/29, 10/31, 12/4, 12/20.

Revival/Renewal: 2/1, 2/20, 2/23, 2/26, 4/16, 4/21, 7/10, 7/26, 9/4, 9/16, 9/22, 11/20.

Second Coming: 7/12, 9/12, 9/13, 9/30, 10/27, 11/6, 12/4, 12/20, 12/21, 12/25.

Self/Pride: 1/2, 1/5, 2/16, 2/17, 3/16, 3/23, 4/5, 4/8, 4/19, 4/26, 4/29, 6/28, 7/7, 7/18, 7/20, 7/30, 8/10, 8/14, 8/30, 10/18, 10/22, 11/15, 11/20, 11/29, 12/4, 12/7.

Service: 1/20, 1/24, 2/3, 2/16, 3/5, 3/13, 8/2, 8/26, 10/15, 11/10.

Sex: 1/17, 2/1, 2/11, 2/20, 4/3, 4/21, 5/16, 6/4, 6/25, 6/28, 7/8, 8/24, 10/13, 11/7, 12/27.

Sin: 1/2, 1/13, 1/17, 1/24, 2/2, 2/3, 2/5, 2/6, 2/17, 2/20, 2/26, 3/3, 3/4, 3/6, 3/8, 3/9, 3/14, 3/16, 3/21, 3/23, 4/8, 4/10, 4/13, 4/21, 4/25, 4/26, 4/27, 4/28, 5/16, 5/17, 5/24, 6/3, 6/10, 6/14, 6/15, 7/2, 7/4, 7/8, 7/15, 7/18, 7/30, 8/3, 8/10, 8/15, 8/24, 8/28, 9/1, 9/10, 9/16, 9/27, 10/23, 10/25, 10/27, 11/6, 11/7, 11/11, 11/17, 11/19, 11/26, 12/7, 12/10, 12/11, 12/18, 12/27.

Spirituality: 1/2, 1/16, 1/24, 1/25, 1/26, 1/27, 1/28, 2/8, 2/16, 2/19, 2/27, 2/29, 3/2, 3/3, 3/10, 3/11, 3/23, 3/31, 4/2, 4/22, 4/25, 4/27, 5/3, 5/4, 5/11, 5/12, 6/3, 6/9, 6/20, 6/22, 6/23, 7/2, 7/3, 7/6, 7/13, 7/20, 7/22, 7/28, 8/1, 8/27, 8/31, 9/2, 9/4, 9/7, 9/22, 10/9, 10/26, 10/27, 10/30, 10/31, 11/2, 11/4, 11/5, 11/20, 11/28, 12/31.

Temptation: 1/6, 1/11, 2/19, 3/24, 4/16, 5/16, 6/25, 7/9, 8/13, 8/23, 10/25, 10/27.

Thought/Mind: 1/6, 1/9, 1/17, 2/4, 2/10, 2/17, 2/23, 3/9, 3/16, 3/25, 3/26, 4/2, 4/4, 4/13, 4/26, 5/16, 5/27, 6/10, 6/18, 6/30, 7/18, 8/10, 8/16, 8/17, 9/14, 9/24, 10/11, 10/14, 11/8, 11/15, 11/17, 11/22, 11/26, 11/29, 11/30, 12/3, 12/18, 12/26, 12/31.

Time: 1/2, 1/3, 1/15, 2/5, 2/26, 2/29, 3/3, 3/28, 3/31, 4/18, 4/24, 4/30, 6/2, 6/3, 6/4, 6/9, 6/10, 6/11, 6/17, 6/20, 6/21, 6/22, 6/23, 7/7, 7/12, 8/1, 8/19, 9/7, 9/12, 9/16, 9/22, 10/3, 10/12, 10/20, 10/21, 11/1, 11/16, 11/23, 12/3, 12/7, 12/11, 12/14, 12/19, 12/21, 12/23, 12/31.

Tongue/Mouth: 1/17, 2/16, 2/22, 3/18, 4/25, 5/4, 7/1, 8/3, 8/7, 8/19, 9/17, 10/14, 11/15, 12/21.

Truth/Lies: 1/4, 1/12, 1/24, 2/10, 2/11, 2/16, 2/17, 2/18, 2/22, 4/4, 4/24, 5/19, 5/23, 5/27, 7/6, 7/17, 8/24, 8/30, 9/17, 9/24, 9/28, 10/14, 10/21, 10/22, 10/23, 11/1, 11/4, 11/7, 11/19, 11/29, 12/19, 12/23, 12/26.

Victory: 1/8, 2/9, 3/16, 3/24, 4/9, 4/29, 5/5, 5/7, 8/11, 9/23, 10/10, 12/30.

Vision: 3/17, 5/1, 5/29, 10/19, 10/29.

War: 1/8, 1/22, 1/29, 2/12, 2/19, 3/6, 4/9, 4/10, 4/21, 5/5, 5/6, 5/21, 5/27, 5/29, 6/14, 6/16, 6/25, 7/2, 7/26, 8/23, 9/15, 9/16, 9/18, 9/27, 11/2, 11/11, 11/19, 12/4, 12/7, 12/18.

Witness: 1/4, 3/24, 4/16, 5/9, 5/22, 5/28, 9/5, 9/12, 9/29.

Women: 1/7, 1/16, 1/23, 2/3, 2/5, 2/21, 4/5, 4/28, 4/29, 5/1, 5/6, 5/7, 5/8, 5/10, 5/15, 5/26, 6/25, 6/28, 7/6, 7/8, 7/11, 7/14, 7/30, 8/30, 9/23, 9/28, 10/1, 11/10, 11/17, 11/22, 11/26, 12/5, 12/9, 12/14, 12/25.

Work: 1/14, 1/18, 1/24, 1/31, 2/12, 2/24, 2/26, 3/5, 4/18, 4/19, 5/2, 5/10, 5/24, 6/8, 7/1, 7/5, 7/21, 8/2, 8/5, 8/6, 8/11, 8/15, 9/4, 9/5, 9/6, 9/7, 9/8, 9/25, 10/25, 10/18, 12/6.

Worship: 1/16, 1/24, 1/25, 1/27, 1/28, 2/2, 3/11, 3/26, 4/22, 5/8, 5/11, 6/29, 7/18, 7/24, 7/29, 9/3, 9/8, 9/17, 9/22, 10/4, 10/25, 11/4, 11/28, 12/10, 12/24, 12/27, 12/28, 12/29.

Youth/Teens: 1/10, 1/17, 1/30, 2/3, 2/20, 3/17, 4/18, 4/19, 5/28, 7/11, 8/27, 10/2, 12/30.

9 781594 679391

CPSIA information can be obtained at www.ICGtesting.com
Printed in the USA
BVOW05s0811130515

400203BV00001B/7/P

9 781594 679391